W9-CPF-849

NEW INTERNATIONAL
BIBLICAL COMMENTARY

New Testament Editor,
W. Ward Gasque

LUKE

New Testament Series

NEW INTERNATIONAL BIBLICAL COMMENTARY

LUKE

CRAIG A. EVANS

Based on the New International Version

paternoster press

For my Father
RICHARD J. EVANS

© 1990 by Craig A. Evans
Hendrickson Publishers, LLC
P. O. Box 3473
Peabody, Massachusetts 01961-3473
U.S.A.

First published jointly, 1995, in the United States by Hendrickson Publishers and
in the United Kingdom by the Paternoster Press,
P. O. Box 300, Carlisle, Cumbria CA3 0QS.
All rights reserved.

Printed in the United States of America

Sixth printing — January 2005

Library of Congress Cataloging-in-Publication Data

Evans, Craig A.
    Luke / Craig A. Evans: New Testament editor, W. Ward Gasque.
    (New International biblical commentary; 3)
    Includes bibliographical references and indexes.
    1. Bible. N.T. Luke—Commentaries. I. Gasque, W. Ward.
  II. Title. III. Series.
  BS2595.3.E83 1990
  226.4′077—dc20   90–37287
                                      CIP

ISBN 0–943575–31–1 (U.S. softcover)
ISBN 1–56563–122–6 (U.S. hardcover)

British Library Cataloguing in Publication Data

Evans, Craig A.
    Luke. — (New International Biblical Commentary Series; Vol. 3)
    I. Title. II. Series.
    226.407

ISBN 0–85364–657–0 (U.K. softcover)

Table of Contents

Foreword
New International Biblical Commentary

Although it does not appear on the standard best-seller lists, the Bible continues to outsell all other books. And in spite of growing secularism in the West, there are no signs that interest in its message is abating. Quite to the contrary, more and more men and women are turning to its pages for insight and guidance in the midst of the ever-increasing complexity of modern life.

This renewed interest in Scripture is found both outside and inside the church. It is found among people in Asia and Africa as well as in Europe and North America; indeed, as one moves outside of the traditionally Christian countries, interest in the Bible seems to quicken. Believers associated with the traditional Catholic and Protestant churches manifest the same eagerness for the Word that is found in the newer evangelical churches and fellowships.

We wish to encourage and, indeed, strengthen this world-wide movement of lay Bible study by offering this new commentary series. Although we hope that pastors and teachers will find these volumes helpful in both understanding and communicating the Word of God, we do not write primarily for them. Our aim is to provide for the benefit of every Bible reader reliable guides to the books of the Bible—representing the best of contemporary scholarship presented in a form that does not require formal theological education to understand.

The conviction of editor and authors alike is that the Bible belongs to the people and not merely to the academy. The message of the Bible is too important to be locked up in erudite and esoteric essays and monographs written only for the eyes of theological specialists. Although exact scholarship has its place in the service of Christ, those who share in the teaching office of the church have a responsibility to make the results of their research accessible to the Christian community at large. Thus, the Bible scholars who join in the presentation of this series write with these broader concerns in view.

A wide range of modern translations is available to the contemporary Bible student. Most of them are very good and much to be preferred—for understanding, if not always for beauty—to the older King James Version (the so-called Authorized Version of the Bible). The Revised Standard Version has become the standard English translation in many seminaries and colleges and represents the best of modern Protestant scholarship. It is also available in a slightly altered "common Bible" edition with the Catholic imprimatur, and a third revised edition is due out shortly. In addition, the New American Bible is a fresh translation that represents the best of post–Vatican II Roman Catholic biblical scholarship and is in a more contemporary idiom than that of the RSV.

The New Jerusalem Bible, based on the work of French Catholic scholars but vividly rendered into English by a team of British translators, is perhaps the most literary of the recent translations, while the New English Bible is a monument to modern British Protestant research. The Good News Bible is probably the most accessible translation for the person who has little exposure to the Christian tradition or who speaks and reads English as a second language. Each of these is, in its own way, excellent and will be consulted with profit by the serious student of Scripture. Perhaps most will wish to have several versions to read, both for variety and for clarity of understanding—though it should be pointed out that no one of them is by any means flawless or to be received as the last word on any given point. Otherwise, there would be no need for a commentary series like this one!

We have chosen to use the New International Version as the basis for this series, not because it is necessarily the best translation available but because it is becoming increasingly used by lay Bible students and pastors. It is the product of an international team of "evangelical" Bible scholars who have sought to translate the Hebrew and Greek documents of the original into "clear and natural English . . . idiomatic [and] . . . contemporary but not dated," suitable for "young and old, highly educated and less well educated, ministers and laymen [*sic*]." As the translators themselves confess in their preface, this version is not perfect. However, it is as good as any of the others mentioned above and more popular than most of them.

Each volume will contain an introductory chapter detailing the background of the book and its author, important themes, and other helpful information. Then, each section of the book will be expounded as a whole, accompanied by a series of notes on items in the text that need further clarification or more detailed explanation. Appended to the end of each volume will be a bibliographical guide for further study.

Our new series is offered with the prayer that it may be an instrument of authentic renewal and advancement in the worldwide Christian community and a means of commending the faith of the people who lived in biblical times and of those who seek to live by the Bible today.

W. WARD GASQUE

Preface

My interest in the writings of the evangelist Luke began when I was a doctoral student at Claremont Graduate School. There I had the privilege of learning from James A. Sanders, whose interest in this New Testament writer is well known. Compounding my good fortune was the visit of David L. Tiede as a Visiting Scholar during the 1978–79 academic year. David's Luke–Acts Seminar was the highlight of the year. Out of this visit he produced *Prophecy and History in Luke–Acts* (Philadelphia: Fortress, 1980), a book from which I have learned much. My interest in Luke continued, and so it was with much enthusiasm that I accepted W. Ward Gasque's kind invitation to write the commentary on Luke for the New International Biblical Commentary. A major challenge in writing a commentary of this type is, on the one hand, to take into account the best of critical scholarship and, on the other, to keep the commentary intelligible and relevant for the non-expert. I have, therefore, resisted the temptation to plunge deeply into many critical issues and technical features that attend the study of the Gospels in general and the Gospel of Luke in particular. Nevertheless, I think that the critical scholar will find in this commentary many items of interest. It would be hoped, of course, that those readers for whom this commentary series is primarily intended will also find the commentary readable and stimulating. All quotations, including those in bold, are from the NIV, unless otherwise noted.

Richard A. Wiebe, Reference Librarian for Trinity Western University, is to be thanked for preparing the indexes.

Trinity Western University
Langley, British Columbia
January, 1990

Abbreviations

Frequently Cited Works

Brodie

Thomas L. Brodie, *Luke the Literary Interpreter: Luke–Acts as a Systematic Rewriting and Updating of the Elijah–Elisha Narrative in 1 and 2 Kings*. Rome: Angelicum, 1981.

Ellis

E. Earle Ellis, *The Gospel of Luke*, rev. ed.; NCB. London: Oliphants, 1974.

Evans

C. F. Evans, "The Central Section of St. Luke's Gospel," in D. E. Nineham, ed., *Studies in the Gospels: Essays in Memory of R. H. Lightfoot*. Oxford: Basil Blackwell, 1955, pages 37–53.

Fitzmyer

Joseph A. Fitzmyer, *The Gospel According to Luke*, 2 vols., AB 28 and 28a. Garden City: Doubleday, 1981–85.

Gundry

Robert H. Gundry, *Matthew: A Commentary on his Literary and Theological Art.* Grand Rapids: Eerdmans, 1982.

HBD

Paul J. Achtemeier, ed., *Harper's Bible Dictionary*. San Francisco: Harper & Row, 1985.

Lachs

Samuel Tobias Lachs, *A Rabbinic Commentary on the New Testament: The Gospels of Matthew, Mark, and Luke*. New York: Ktav, 1987.

LCL

Loeb Classical Library. Cambridge, Mass.: Harvard University Press.

Leaney

A. R. C. Leaney, *A Commentary on the Gospel according to St. Luke,* Harper's New Testament Commentary. New York: Harper & Row, 1958; reprinted, Peabody, Mass.: Hendrickson, 1988.

Marshall	I. Howard Marshall, *Commentary on Luke*, NIGTC. Grand Rapids: Eerdmans, 1978.
J. T. Sanders	Jack T. Sanders, *The Jews in Luke–Acts*. Philadelphia: Fortress, 1987.
Schweizer	Eduard Schweizer, *The Good News according to Luke*. Atlanta: John Knox, 1984.
Talbert	Charles H. Talbert, *Reading Luke: A Literary and Theological Commentary on the Third Gospel*. New York: Crossroad, 1982.
Tannehill	Robert C. Tannehill, *The Narrative Unity of Luke–Acts: A Literary Interpretation: Volume One: The Gospel According to Luke*, Foundations and Facets. Philadelphia: Fortress, 1986.
Tiede	David L. Tiede, *Luke*, ACNT. Minneapolis: Augsburg, 1988.

Other Abbreviations

AB	Anchor Bible
ACNT	Augsburg Commentary on the New Testament
ATLA	American Theological Library Association
BZ	*Biblische Zeitschrift*
BZNW	*Beihefte zur Zeitschrift für die neutestamentliche Wissenschaft*
CBQ	*Catholic Biblical Quarterly*
EvQ	*Evangelical Quarterly*
ExpTim	*Expository Times*
HNTC	Harper's [=Black's] New Testament Commentaries
JBL	*Journal of Biblical Literature*
JSNT	*Journal for the Study of the New Testament*
JSNTSup	*Journal for the Study of the New Testament, Supplements*
JTS	*Journal of Theological Studies*
KJV	King James Version (Authorized Version)
LXX	Septuagint
NASB	New American Standard Bible

NCB	New Century Bible Commentary
NIGTC	New International Greek Testament Commentary
NovT	*Novum Testamentum*
NT	New Testament
NTS	*New Testament Studies*
OT	Old Testament
RB	*Revue Biblique*
RSV	Revised Standard Version
SBL	Society of Biblical Literature
SBLDS	Society of Biblical Literature Dissertation Series
SBLMS	Society of Biblical Literature Monograph Series
TS	*Theological Studies*
WUNT	Wissenschaftliche Untersuchungen zum Neuen Testament
ZNW	*Zeitschrift für die neutestamentliche Wissenschaft*

Introduction

If asked who the major theologians of the New Testament are, most Christians would probably mention Jesus, John, and Paul. Few would think of Luke; and yet his two-volume work, Luke–Acts, amounts to approximately one fourth of the entire New Testament! No other contributor to the New Testament wrote as much. No doubt because they primarily view Luke as a historian, readers of the New Testament are not inclined to view Luke as a significant theologian. Nevertheless, the last few decades have seen a marked increase in scholarly interest in Luke–Acts, and although interest in Luke's trustworthiness as a historian continues to be a topic of debate (note the recent work of Martin Hengel), more and more emphasis has been placed on the evangelist's theology. The recent commentaries of I. Howard Marshall, Joseph Fitzmyer, and David Tiede provide ample evidence of this trend. This new commentary intends to take into account some of this recent discussion and to present it in a way that is both understandable and exciting to the student of Scripture.

1. Authorship, Occasion for Writing, and Recipients

Tradition holds that the author of the anonymous two-volume work, Luke–Acts, was the physician Luke, traveling companion of the Apostle Paul. This position receives support from a few references in the New Testament (see Philem. 24; Col. 4:14; 2 Tim. 4:11; and the so-called we sections of Acts 16:10–17; 20:5–15; 21:1–18; 27:1–28:16) and from a fairly early and unanimous tradition among the church fathers. The ancient title, the "Gospel according to Luke," appears at the end of the Gospel in the oldest surviving Greek manuscript (P^{75}), which is dated ca. A.D. 175–225. Although this tradition is not certain (nor is it vital to our understanding of the Gospel of Luke) and has been challenged by several scholars in modern times, it will serve the purposes of this commentary to give it provisional acceptance. Of even less certainty is the tradition that the evangelist Luke was a native of Syrian Antioch, although it remains a possibility. From a careful study of Luke–Acts certain other details may be deduced, some of which are corroborated by early church traditions. Luke was almost certainly a Gentile, though not necessarily a Greek. That he had a keen interest in, and probably was a former member of, the Jewish synagogue is apparent; and that he was quite at home with the Greek Bible (i.e., the Greek translation of the Hebrew Scriptures called the Septuagint and abbreviated LXX) can be seen by his numerous quotations from and allusions to it. Luke's biblical interests, however, appear more concerned with the historical and prophetic elements than with the legal. Therefore, unlike Matthew, Luke does not often address Pharisaic issues. (For more on Luke's biblical views see section 5 below.)

Luke's occasion for writing his two-volume work was probably the aftermath of the destruction of Jerusalem and the temple. This catastrophe was naturally of immense significance for Jews (both in Palestine and abroad), but it was of great import for Christians as well. Such a destruction would readily lead to questions asking why it had happened; and the Christians as much as the Jews were interested in finding an answer. A major reason for writing, it is contended, was to answer this question. For most of the faithful (whether Jewish or Christian) the answer was to be found in the ancient Scriptures. Luke saw a correlation between the first destruction of Jerusalem and the temple (586 B.C.) and the second destruction (A.D. 70). It is no coincidence that in the two passages of his Gospel in which he gives his readers Jesus' words on the subject, the language and vocabulary are drawn heavily from the LXX's account of the first destruction of Jerusalem at the hands of Nebuchadrezzar (see Luke 19:41–44; 21:20–24; and Jer. 6:6; Ezek. 4:4; 26:8). For Luke, Jerusalem was destroyed a second time because of its failure, like the first time, to heed the prophetic voice and to recognize the presence of God's salvation, or, in biblical parlance, God's "visitation." This idea is unmistakably expressed in Luke 19:41–45, parts of which read: "And when He [Jesus] approached, He saw the city and wept over it, saying, 'If you had known in this day, even you, the things which make for peace! But now they have been hidden from your eyes. For the days shall come upon you when your enemies . . . will level you to the ground and your children within you. . . . because you did not recognize the time of your visitation' " (NASB). It is important to observe that this lamentation immediately follows the account of the Triumphal Entry where Jesus had been greeted as "king" (19:29–40). As king (see v. 38) Jesus presents himself to Jerusalem; but knowing that he would not be received, he weeps for the doomed city. The Prince of Peace had been turned away, and in his place a few years later a militant messianic pretender would lead Israel in a disastrous war with Rome.[1]

In all likelihood, Luke's readers were Gentile Christians. This is seen principally in Luke's omission of items that would be chiefly of interest to Jews and in his avoidance of terminology that presupposes knowledge of Hebrew and/or Aramaic. (That is not to say, however, that Luke's writing style betrays no Semitic influence; see section 4 below.) That he intended his two-volume work for such an audience also seems apparent because of his basic theological concern to show how Gentiles figure in God's plan of salvation, as revealed in the Scriptures and as seen in the missionary outreach of the apostles. To this latter aspect the second volume, the Book of Acts, addresses itself quite specifically. (For more on Luke's views of the Gentiles see section 5 below.)

2. Luke and the Other Gospels

There are four Gospels among the 27 writings of the New Testament. Three of them (Matthew, Mark, and Luke) are called the "Synoptic" Gospels because they parallel each other so closely they can be "seen together" (*syn* means "together"; *optic* means "see"). Books that put these three Gospels in parallel columns are called harmonies or synopses. The Fourth Gospel, John, although bearing a few similarities to the Synoptics, is quite distinct.

No one who has carefully read the three Synoptic Gospels can fail to recognize the numerous parallels. One episode after another appears in all three Gospels. The "Synoptic Problem" is the attempt to explain the relationship between these parallels (which in the Greek text are often verbatim). Most scholars today believe that Mark was the earliest Gospel written (ca. A.D. 70), while Matthew and Luke, independently utilizing copies of Mark and another source that consists primarily of Jesus' sayings, were written some years later (ca. A.D. 75–85). Other scholars, however, have argued that Matthew, and not Mark, was the first written Gospel. This debate continues in full force.

This commentary assumes that Mark is indeed prior. This assumption is held for two primary reasons. First, the differences almost always are best explained in terms of Matthean and/or Lucan redaction (or editing) of Mark, and not vice versa. Second, where Mark offers no narrative (such as no nativity or resurrection appearances), and hence cannot be followed, Matthean and Lucan divergence is its greatest. If Mark had followed Matthew and/or Luke, one must wonder why the evangelist chose to omit these narratives (and other materials, such as the Sermon on the Mount). For these reasons, and for others, Marcan priority is accepted. If this conclusion is correct, then the study of the Gospels of Matthew and Luke is greatly facilitated by a comparison with Mark, since such a comparison reveals more vividly the distinct emphases and concerns of the later Gospel writers (or "evangelists"). Whereas Mark may only allude to an Old Testament verse, Matthew, who is apparently quite concerned to show how Jesus as Messiah has fulfilled Old Testament messianic prophecy, will often provide a formal quotation (cf. Mark 4:12 with Matt. 13:13–15). In the commentary that follows there will be frequent mention of how a comparison with Mark reveals how the evangelist Luke has attempted to tell the story of Jesus in his own unique way.

Besides Mark, there is another source common to Matthew and Luke, which originally was a collection of Jesus' sayings. This sayings source (called "Q," from the German word *Quelle*, "source") provides yet another opportunity for comparison. Whereas Matthew may wish to convey a certain idea with a saying from Q, Luke is able to convey quite another thought with the same saying. When this editorial tendency is compared with the respective ways in which Mark has been edited, the interpreter is able to perceive the overall emphases of these two evangelists. Matthew and Luke utilized most of Mark (between them approximately 95% of Mark's contents), which provided them with a basic narrative framework, and supplemented this framework with the contents of Q, which apparently contained no narrative. Although some scholars have maintained that Q was a written document, much like Mark, others suspect that the material common to Matthew and Luke may derive from a variety of written and oral sources, and not necessarily from a single document. This commentary assumes the latter view.[2]

Outside of the canonical Gospels there is a host of apocryphal Gospels that are, for the most part, of little historical value.

Often these Gospels appear to be motivated by a desire to fill in the gaps of Jesus and his parents' lives left by the canonical Gospels. They purport, for example, to give us information about Mary's own supposed miraculous birth and childhood before her betrothal to Joseph. Other accounts tell us of amazing experiences in Egypt while hiding from the wrath of Herod, of Jesus' boyhood in Nazareth, and of his and Joseph's skills as carpenters. Although quite often particular views and beliefs are championed by these fanciful events, underlying all of them is a desire to know more about Jesus.[3]

3. Luke and the Old Testament

For the evangelist Luke the Old Testament (i.e., the LXX) was as much a vital source as Mark and Q. This is true not simply because it is often quoted, for the other three evangelists frequently quote or allude to the Old Testament; but it would appear that it provided Luke with information as to what happened in the life of Jesus, what it means, and how it should be told. Two major portions of the Old Testament have played central roles in the composition of the Gospel. Large sections of Luke (chaps. 7–10, 22–24) and Acts (chaps. 1–9) draw in various ways upon the Elijah/Elisha narratives of 1 Kings (chaps. 17–21) and 2 Kings (chaps. 1–8).[4] Another large section of Luke, which is sometimes called the "Central Section" (9:51–18:14), parallels Deuteronomy (chaps. 1–26).[5] Why the evangelist has done this will be addressed throughout the commentary, but in section 5 below a general explanation will be offered. Suffice it to say that in reality Luke has made use of at least three major literary works in composing his Gospel: Mark, Q, and the Septuagint.

4. Luke's Literary Style

Of all the Gospels, Luke's literary style comes closest to the style of the ancient Greek classical writers. The most obvious example of this style occurs in the opening four verses of his Gospel, known as the Prologue (or Preface, see commentary on 1:1–4 below). However, another important feature in Luke's writing style is his frequent use of the vocabulary of the LXX. Semitic features often appear because Luke found them in his sources; but many times Luke consciously and deliberately utilizes the language and vocabulary of the LXX in order to present his account in what may be called "biblical Greek." For example, Luke describes Jesus in 9:51 as having "set his face to go to Jerusalem," an expression which is probably meant to recall the prophet Ezekiel whom God commanded: "Son of man, set your face toward Jerusalem and preach against the sanctuaries; prophesy against the land of Israel" (Ezek. 21:2, RSV).[6]

There are also traces of a very subtle sense of humor, seen especially in the Book of Acts. One is reminded of Rhoda the agitated servant-girl who left Peter locked outside in the street (Acts 12:13-16). Luke is also fond of understatement, as can be seen in the reference to the Ephesian riot as "no small disturbance" (Acts 19:23; see also Acts 12:18; 26:26). Luke is a powerful writer who is able to blend sobering theological truths with a dramatic and exciting story. Anyone reading his Gospel can scarcely fail to enjoy this writer who is both, as Howard Marshall has put it, historian and theologian.[7]

5. Major Themes and Emphases in Luke

In the aftermath of the destruction of Jerusalem and the second temple (A.D. 70) Luke and his community had begun to sense some of the questions and problems that were being raised by Jewish and Gentile Christians and non-Christian Jews. No doubt the burning question concerned the destruction. Why had the revolt of the militant messianic figure Simon bar Giora met with total defeat? Did this disaster indicate that the promises of Scripture were not to be fulfilled? Or, was the disaster a judgment upon Jerusalem for some particular sin? As discussed in section 1 above, Luke, and probably most Christians of his time, saw in the destruction of Jerusalem a fulfillment of Jesus' prophecy. Moreover, they surely believed that it was a consequence of Jesus' having been rejected (see Luke 19:41-45; 21:20-25; 23:27-31). But there were other, and often related, questions that were being raised as well. Why had Jesus not yet returned as promised? What was the church's task while it waited for the Lord? Why were the Jews continuing to reject the gospel? How do the Gentiles relate to Israel and its promises? Luke attempts to answer these questions in his two-volume work.

The reader should quickly recognize that Luke has placed his account squarely into the framework of history, both secular and sacred. The speeches found in the first two chapters of the Gospel attest that in the births of John the Baptist and Jesus, God has begun a work that continues the dramatic story of Israel's sacred history. In various ways these speeches express the confidence that in the birth of Jesus and his forerunner God has set the stage for the era of salvation.

But Luke's account is not detached from secular history, as can be seen by its numerous references to various leaders and events, many of which can be dated with precision. Luke notes that John the Baptist was conceived in the days of Herod, king of Judea (Luke 1:5), with Jesus' own conception six months later (Luke 1:26–31). The evangelist tells us of a census decreed by Caesar Augustus (Luke 2:1), when Quirinius was governor of Syria (Luke 2:2). We are told that John's preaching began in the fifteenth year of the reign of Tiberius Caesar (A.D. 28), when Pontius Pilate was governor of Judea (A.D. 26–36), and when Herod, Philip, and Lysanius were tetrarchs of surrounding regions (Luke 3:1). This was the time of the high priests Annas and Caiaphas (Luke 3:2). Eventually Jesus himself would encounter most of these people, following his arrest (Luke 22–23). In his second volume Luke tells us of the failure of three previous messianic claimants, Theudas, Judas the Galilean (Acts 5:36–37), and the Egyptian (Acts 21:38). The evangelist mentions the famine in the days of Emperor Claudius (Acts 11:28), as well as the emperor's decree that all Jews leave the city of Rome (A.D. 49; Acts 18:2). Luke also refers to the Proconsul Gallio (A.D. 52; Acts 18:12) and to Paul's later appearances before Felix, Festus, and Agrippa (A.D. 60; Acts 24–26).

The Third Evangelist seems to have at least two reasons for emphasizing the historical context of his accounts of Jesus and the early church. First, Luke is trying to show that the story of Jesus, for all its freshness and newness, is in reality in continuity with the long history of God's dealings with his covenant people Israel. Luke wants the reader to realize that the life of Jesus represents a major event in what scholars sometimes call Israel's "salvation history." Second, Luke's historical references include secular persons and events in order to underscore the relevance of Jesus for the world at large. Jesus is not merely one more prophet sent to Israel for Israel's sake. Rather, Jesus is God's Son (see Luke's genealogy of Jesus and compare it with that found in Matthew) sent to the world. Jesus is portrayed, as one commentator has put it, as Benefactor of humankind.[8] Thus, through his historical references and orientation Luke is able to bind together the sacred history of Israel with secular world history. He is able to make the particular, exclusive religion of Israel available and applicable to humankind in general. This movement away from the narrower context of Palestine and Judaism to the world and to all races and tribes of humankind is worked out in the Book of Acts.

Luke's historical emphasis has led scholars to conclude that he views history as consisting of three major epochs. According to Joseph Fitzmyer,[9] the first epoch may be described as the "Period of Israel," which begins with Genesis and concludes with the appearance of John the Baptist (Luke 1:5–3:1). Luke designates this period as the time of "the law and the prophets" (Luke 16:16a). The second epoch is the "Period of Jesus," which begins with his baptism and concludes with his ascension (Luke 3:2–24:51). This is the period of Jesus' ministry, death, and resurrection, during which time "the kingdom of God is preached" (Luke 16:16b). The third epoch is the "Period of the Church," which begins with Jesus' ascension and will conclude with his return (Luke 24:52–Acts 1:3–28:31). During this period of time it is the duty of the church to proclaim the Word of God throughout the world (see Acts 1:8).

As the gospel spreads, the question of how the Gentiles fit into God's plan of redemption becomes acute. Because many Gentiles did indeed believe and joined the rapidly growing church, the question naturally arose: What did a predominantly Gentile movement have to do with Israel and the promises of the Jewish Scriptures? For Luke the answer had positive and negative aspects. Positively, the gospel of the kingdom was to be offered to everyone. The Book of Acts chronicles the spread of the gospel first to the Jews (Acts 2:5–7:60), then to the Samaritans, who were "half" Jewish (Acts 8:2–24), next to "God-fearing" Gentiles who had received prior instruction in the Jewish faith (Acts 10:1–11:18), and finally to Gentiles who had never had any contact with Judaism (Acts 13:2–28:31). Paul's habit during his missionary journeys of first entering the synagogue in order to preach to his fellow Jews (see Acts 13:16–41; 14:1–3; 17:1–3, 10–12; 18:2–

4) reflects this pattern and is expressed by his well-known philosophy of evangelism: "to the Jew first and also to the Greek" (Rom. 1:16; 2:10). Another positive evidence of the legitimacy of Gentile membership and participation in this Jewish messianic movement was the Gentile reception of the Holy Spirit. Like the Jewish apostles (Acts 2:2–4), the Samaritans and Gentiles also received the Holy Spirit (Acts 8:14–17; 10:44–47; 11:15–18). The first Christians, regardless of ethnic identity, were, in the words of Paul, "baptized into one body . . . and we were all given the one Spirit to drink" (1 Cor. 12:13).

Luke also offers a negative answer to the Gentile question. An explicit reason for the missionaries' turning to the Gentiles was Jewish unbelief and rejection of the gospel. That the Jewish religious leadership was opposed to the apostolic preaching is evident early in the Acts account (Acts 4:1–22; 5:17–42). Such opposition represents only a continuation of the unbelief that Jesus had encountered earlier (Luke 19:47–48; 20:1–8, 19–20; 22:47–23:25) and that was characteristic of stubborn Israel (Luke 13:34). Indeed, Luke traces the unbelief of the Pharisees directly to the ministry of John the Baptist: "But the Pharisees and experts in the law rejected God's purpose for themselves, because they had not been baptized by John" (Luke 7:30). The formal shift from evangelism directed primarily toward Jews to evangelism directed toward Gentiles, however, is seen in Paul's thematic sermon in Acts 13:16–47. Paul warns his fellow Jews not to be hard-hearted in response to the gospel and cites the ominous prophecy of Habakkuk: "Look, you scoffers, wonder and perish, for I am going to do something in your days that you would never believe, even if someone told you" (Hab. 1:5, cited in Acts 13:41). As Paul had feared, the Jews began "contradicting the things spoken . . . and were blaspheming" (Acts 13:45, NASB). Thus Paul declares: "We had to speak the word of God to you first. Since you reject it and do not consider yourselves worthy of eternal life, we now turn to the Gentiles" (Acts 13:46). For justification of this new strategy Paul cites Isa. 49:6, a portion of which had been cited by Simeon (Luke 2:32), who upon seeing the infant Jesus recognizes the significance of Jesus for the world: "I have made you a light for the Gentiles, that you may bring salvation to the ends of the earth" (Acts 13:47). Unlike the unbelieving and rebellious Jews, the Gentiles rejoice and respond in faith (Acts 13:42–43, 48).

This shift from Jews to Gentiles can be traced back to the very heart of Jesus' teaching concerning membership in the kingdom of God and really does not represent an ad hoc solution to an unexpected development. In numerous passages, some of which are found only in Luke's Gospel, Jesus declares, on the one hand, that those who by outward appearances and according to human standards are judged most likely to enjoy God's favor are not always receptive to God's presence. Many who are "confident" of their salvation and reward will some day find themselves judged. On the other hand, many of those who appear to be less religious or who have apparently received few of life's blessings will some day be rewarded and blessed. The classic example of this idea is to be seen in the Parable of the Rich Man and Lazarus (Luke 16:19–31). The rich man had every good thing that life could offer. He was well dressed and well fed and lived in a mansion. Outside his gate, however, was poor Lazarus, who was ill-clad, undernourished, sick, and without shelter. Contrary to views popular in first-century Palestine, Lazarus went to heaven and the rich man went to hell. Why was there such an outcome and why was this outcome contrary to popular expectation? We are not told that Lazarus was virtuous; neither are we told that the rich man was particularly evil (though by inference he seems to be quite insensitive to the needs of his poor neighbor). The rich man goes to hell but not because he was rich or because he ignored Lazarus; likewise, Lazarus goes to heaven but not because he was poor and sick. The point that the Lucan Jesus makes with this parable is that outward appearances, social standings, and standards of living provide no certain indication of one's standing before God.

Such a parable would surprise, if not shock, some first-century Palestinian Jews who assumed that health and wealth were sure signs of God's blessing, while illness and poverty were certain signs of God's wrath. Such a theology, it has been argued by at least one scholar, is derived from the Old Testament promise (and warning), especially as it can be seen in Deuteronomy, that if Israel were obedient to the covenant it would be blessed, but if disobedient it would be cursed.[10] Blessings and cursings were thought of primarily in terms of material items. "Blessings" manifest themselves as good crops, large herds of cattle and sheep, gold and silver, and peace, while "cursings" could include drought, famine, pestilence, and war. In Jesus' day this idea was inverted (i.e., reverse sequence of logic) and applied to the individual: If you are blessed (i.e., healthy and wealthy), then you must have been obedient and righteous (like Pharisees, Sadducees, and priests), but if you are cursed (i.e., sick and poor), then you must be disobedient and wicked (like harlots, tax collectors, and other "sinners"). Jesus challenges these unfounded assumptions and teaches that, on the contrary, it is the poor, the sick, and the needy who are often most aware of their spiritual needs and are therefore more receptive to God's word of mercy and forgiveness. (Indeed, has it not often been the case, according to biblical history, that when Israel is poor and humble before the nations that God delivers in mighty ways?) This misunderstanding of the teaching of Deuteronomy concerning God's standards of evaluation has led Luke to order his Central Section (10:1–18:14) to correspond with Deuteronomy 1–26. The parable of the self-righteous Pharisee and the contrite tax-collector (Luke 18:9–14) exemplifies the need to reassess one's assumptions about God's standards of evaluation. Whereas the "certain ruler" (Luke 18:18–30) cannot do God's will and follow Jesus because of his wealth, in stark contrast Zacchaeus the tax-collector is willing to repay those whom he has cheated and to give to the poor (Luke 19:1–9). Perhaps the most poignant illustration takes place in the house of Simon the Pharisee (Luke 7:36–50), where the harlot washes and dries the feet of Jesus with her tears and hair. Jesus declares that it is the one who owes much and is forgiven who loves the most (see v. 47). The self-righteous person is incapable of recognizing his or her need and hence has little gratitude for God's loving mercy.

For Luke the community of believers is composed of Jews, Samaritans, and Gentiles—all who hear and obey the gospel, the Word of God. Because of the presence of non-Jews in this community the question naturally arises as to the church's relationship to historic, biblical Israel. It is incorrect to think that Luke sees Israel as no longer part of God's plan. This is certainly not the sentiment throughout his Gospel (see especially the speeches of Luke 1–2). When Zacchaeus declared his generosity, Jesus said: "Today salvation has come to this house, because this man, too, is a son of Abraham" (Luke 19:9). The idea of referring to a repentant, righteous one as a true son of Abraham is quite similar to Paul's argument that God regards everyone as righteous who responds to the promise of the gospel in faith, as Abraham, father of Israel, had responded to God's promise in Gen. 15:6 (see Rom. 4:1–25). But Luke is not saying, though, that the people of God, the church, make up a new or "spiritual" Israel. What I think Luke is trying to show, and here I follow the insights of Jacob Jervell, is that there has been always only one people of God.[11] Before the time of Jesus, this people of God was identified exclusively with Israel. But with the advent of Jesus and the ingathering of Gentiles from all nations, by which the promises given to Abraham concerning the blessing of the Gentiles (Gen. 12:3; 17:4; 22:18) are now fulfilled (see Acts 3:25 where Gen. 22:18 is quoted), the people of God consist of ethnic Israel and Gentiles. The people of God, however, are only those who have believed in the gospel of Jesus Christ. Not all have believed. This unbelief has led, as Jervell has concluded, to ethnic Israel's division. Some of ethnic Israel believe in Jesus (indeed, thousands believe according to Acts 2–3) and so are part of the people of God, but others reject Jesus and so are considered in a state of disobedience and blindness. This disobedience may be traced from Jesus' first recorded sermon (Luke 4:16–30) to the last recorded exchange between Paul and unbelieving Jews (Acts 28:13–29). It is, of course, Paul's conviction that "Israel has experienced a hardening in part until the full number of the Gentiles has come in. And so all Israel will be saved . . ." (Rom. 11:25–26). I believe that the evangelist Luke also shared in this hope (see section 6 below).

Finally, Luke's Gospel is in a very real sense the Gospel of the Good News to the poor.[12] Throughout this Gospel we are provided many examples of Jesus' compassion for the poor and the powerless, for the downcast and the disenfranchised. The reader will be moved by the tender scenes in which Jesus extends God's love and forgiveness to those for whom, it would seem, all hope had been lost. But then that is what Jesus' mission is all about, "for the Son of Man came to seek and to save what was lost" (Luke 19:10; cf. also Luke 15:1–32).

6. *Was the Evangelist Luke Anti-Semitic?*

Recently one scholar has argued at length that Luke was thoroughly anti-Semitic. The evangelist, Jack T. Sanders believes, does not merely polemicize against Judaism that rejects Christianity, but hates all Jews, whether they have become Christians or not.[13] Is this assessment of Luke accurate? I do not think so. This assessment is completely erroneous for the following four reasons.

First, J. T. Sanders misinterprets several passages in Luke–Acts. For example, he thinks that Jesus' Nazareth sermon in Luke 4:16–30 foreshadows the rejection of the Jews. The episode seems, rather, to foreshadow Jesus' rejection. Jesus is rejected because his ministry will open the kingdom to Gentiles and others whom many religious Jews felt were unworthy. Another example is Sanders's interpretation of the Parable of the Good Samaritan (Luke 10:30–35). He concludes that this parable teaches that salvation can be obtained only by behaving in a non-Jewish manner. Again, this misses the point. The parable actually teaches that anyone, even a Samaritan, can fulfill the highest ethical demands of the law. Throughout this commentary other examples will be discussed.

Second, J. T. Sanders tends to ignore or minimize the significance of passages in Luke that reflect a favorable attitude toward Jews and Judaism. In his infancy narrative Luke offers speech after speech that proclaims God's fulfillment of Israel's deepest hopes and aspirations. For example, the angel tells Mary that her expected son "will reign over the house of Jacob [i.e., Israel] forever" (Luke 1:33a). Likewise, in the Magnificat, Mary praises God for having "helped his servant Israel, remembering to be merciful to Abraham and his descendants forever" (1:54–55a). Similarly in the Benedictus, Zechariah blesses the "God of Israel" for having "come [lit. "visited"] and redeemed his people" (1:68). Finally, we are told of righteous Simeon, who looked for the "consolation of Israel" (2:25) and who in the Nunc Dimittis blesses God for preparing a salvation that is "a light for revelation to the Gentiles," a salvation that will redound "for glory to [God's] people Israel" (2:30–32). It is difficult to imagine that these words were penned by one who hated the Jews and longed for their destruction. If these words are taken at face value, it seems clear that the evangelist understands the Christian gospel to be of benefit to the Jews.

Third, J. T. Sanders fails to compare Luke's polemical statements against explicit expressions of religiously inspired hatred (whether racial or not) that derive from the first century or thereabouts. Pharisees hate Sadducees and the common "people of the land." Sadducees hate the Pharisees. Qumranian Jews hate all other Jews, especially those who oppose them. And, of course, there are numerous expressions of hatred directed against Samaritans and Gentiles. These polemical statements typically assert that such-and-such a group is ignorant, immoral, and damned. But some of these groups even go so far as to pray that their enemies not be saved from the error of their way. Luke's polemic bears no resemblance to these expressions. His polemic is closer to what is found in the Jewish Scriptures (i.e., the Old Testament). The Old Testament contains numerous passages that condemn Israel for its sin. Israel is described as persistently turning its back on God (1 Sam. 8:7–8; 2 Kings 17:7–23; 2 Chron. 36:11–16; cf. Luke 13:33–35; Acts 7:51–53). The prophet Isaiah is so incensed at his own countrymen that he asks God not to forgive them (2:6, 9). In stark contrast to this prophetic petition, Jesus and the martyred Stephen pray that their persecutors be forgiven (Luke 23:34; Acts 7:60).

This leads to the fourth and final error in J. T. Sanders's assessment of Luke. Sanders holds that Luke is an "outsider" who views the entire Jewish people as completely separate from the Lucan community. Because of this perspective, Sanders takes Luke's critical statements as sweeping condemnations of the Jewish people. I think, however, that this approach is wrong. Luke does not regard himself as an outsider. He views himself as part of Israel (though not necessarily a Jewish-born person), that part of Israel that has come to have faith in Jesus as Messiah. Therefore, Luke's critical statements should be seen as prophetic in-house criticism. As an "insider" Luke is enjoining Israel to change its attitude toward Jesus and the "Way." Seen in this light, Luke's criticisms of non-Christian Israel are hardly more severe than what recurs throughout the writings of Israel's prophets.[14]

It is simplistic and misleading to label Luke's criticism of Jewish religious leaders and various Jewish beliefs and practices as "anti-Semitic." Anything critical of something Jewish should not automatically be construed as anti-Semitism. The logic of this kind of uncritical analysis would result in finding anti-Semitism in Jesus, Paul, Jewish sects, and most of the Old Testament. Luke emphasizes Jewish responsibility for Jesus' death, not because of anti-Semitic hatred, but because of his desire to place the Messiah's death firmly within the framework of biblical (i.e., Israelite) history. Jesus' rejection and death are prophesied in the Scriptures and are in keeping with Israel's "historic" (biblical) habit of persecuting the prophets. Jesus' rejection and death at the hands of Israel's religious leaders gives Jesus' death its meaning. For this reason, too, Luke portrays Jews as the leading antagonists of the apostles in Acts. The struggling emergence of the Christian faith, which finds its way to the capital of the Roman Empire, is ultimately a Jewish affair.[15]

7. Basic Outline of the Gospel of Luke

Preface	1:1–4
The Births of John the Baptist and Jesus	1:5–2:52
Jesus' Preparation for Ministry	3:1–4:13
The Galilean Ministry	4:14–9:50
The Journey to Jerusalem	9:51–19:27
The Jerusalem Ministry	19:28–21:38
The Passion of Jesus	22:1–23:56
The Exaltation of Jesus	24:1–53

Notes

1. Many of my ideas have been shaped by David L. Tiede, *Prophecy and History in Luke–Acts* (Philadelphia: Fortress, 1980).

2. For a recent scholarly assessment of Q, see John S. Kloppenborg, *The Formation of Q: Trajectories in Ancient Wisdom Collections,* Studies in Antiquity & Christianity (Philadelphia: Fortress, 1987).

3. The standard English translation of many of these apocryphal gospels is found in E. Hennecke and W. Schneemelcher, *New Testament Apocrypha,* 2 vols., trans. R. McL. Wilson (Philadelphia: Westminster, 1963). For additional bibliography see J. H. Charlesworth, *The New Testament Apocrypha and Pseudepigrapha: A Guide to Publications, with Excurses on Apocalypses,* with J. R. Mueller; ATLA 17 (Metuchen, N. J. and London: American Theological Library Association, 1987). Some one hundred of these writings are noted. For most of the gnostic apocryphal gospels and writings see J. M. Robinson, ed., *The Nag Hammadi Library,* 2nd. ed. (San Francisco: Harper & Row, 1989).

4. For this insight I am indebted to T. L. Brodie, *Luke the Literary Interpreter: Luke–Acts as a Systematic Rewriting and Updating of the Elijah–Elisha Narrative in 1 and 2 Kings* (Rome: Angelicum University, 1987).

5. These parallels were first pointed out by C. F. Evans, "The Central Section of St. Luke's Gospel," in D. E. Nineham, ed., *Studies in the Gospels: Essays in Memory of R. H. Lightfoot* (Oxford: Basil Blackwell, 1955), pp. 37–53.

6. For more discussion see J. A. Fitzmyer, *The Gospel According to Luke I–IX*, AB 28 (Garden City: Doubleday, 1981), pp. 113–25.

7. I. H. Marshall, *Luke: Historian and Theologian* (Exeter: Paternoster, 1970).

8. The idea comes from F. W. Danker, *Luke* (Philadelphia: Fortress, 1976).

9. Fitzmyer, *Luke I–IX*, p. 185, modifying H. Conzelmann, *Theology of St. Luke* (New York: Harper & Row, 1961).

10. J. A. Sanders, "The Ethic of Election in Luke's Great Banquet Parable," in J. L. Crenshaw and J. T. Willis, eds., *Old Testament Ethics* (New York: Ktav, 1974), pp. 247–71.

11. J. Jervell, *Luke and the People of God: A New Look at Luke–Acts* (Minneapolis: Augsburg, 1972), pp. 41–74.

12. On Luke's view of wealth see L. T. Johnson, *The Literary Function of Possessions in Luke–Acts*, SBLDS 39 (Missoula: Scholars, 1977).

13. J. T. Sanders, "The Parable of the Pounds and Lucan Anti-Semitism," *TS* 42 (1981), pp. 660–68; idem, "The Prophetic Use of the Scriptures in Luke–Acts," in C. A. Evans and W. F. Stinespring, eds., *Early Jewish and Christian Exegesis*, W. H. Brownlee Festschrift; Homage 10 (Atlanta: Scholars, 1987), pp. 191–98; idem, *The Jews in Luke–Acts* (Philadelphia: Fortress, 1987). Note: Throughout the commentary there are references to J. T. Sanders. He is not to be confused with J. A. Sanders.

14. For a very helpful essay on this aspect of the problem see M. Salmon, "Insider or Outsider? Luke's Relationship with Judaism," in J. B. Tyson, ed., *Luke–Acts and the Jewish People* (Minneapolis: Augsburg, 1988), pp. 76–82, 149–50.

15. For a better assessment of Luke's attitude toward the Jews see Robert L. Brawley, *Luke–Acts and the Jews: Conflict, Apology, and Conciliation*, SBLMS 33 (Atlanta: Scholars, 1987).

§1 Luke's Preface (Luke 1:1-4)

The first four verses of Luke's Gospel make up what is sometimes called a "prologue" or "preface." Since these verses, which are only one sentence in the Greek, actually function as a literary preface, it is probably best to regard them as Luke's preface introducing his Gospel. Since Luke 3:1-2, however, also functions as an introduction to the Gospel and since some of the components found in the infancy narratives of chaps. 1-2 appear to be loosely connected, it has been suggested that Luke added chaps. 1-2 after having earlier written chaps. 3-24. This could very well have been the case. As it now stands the preface introduces the entire two-volume work (which Luke himself calls a "narrative" [*diēgēsis*]), although it chiefly has in view the first volume, the Gospel. The briefer preface of Acts 1:1-2 ("In my former book [i.e., the Gospel], Theophilus, I wrote about all that Jesus began to do and to teach . . . ") harks back to the Gospel preface and thus provides an important link between the Gospel of Luke and the Book of Acts.

Luke's preface is unique among the canonical Gospels. Mark's Gospel begins abruptly, "The beginning of the gospel [or Good News] about Jesus Christ, the Son of God" (Mark 1:1), cites portions of Mal. 3:1 and Isa. 40:3 (1:2-3), and then immediately moves into a description of the appearance and preaching of John the Baptist (1:4-8). We derive the literary designation "Gospel" from this first verse of Mark. Matthew calls his Gospel a "record [lit. "book"] of the genealogy of Jesus Christ" (Matt. 1:1) and then lists a genealogy from Abraham to Joseph (1:2-18). John's Gospel begins with a poetic, hymnic prologue (1:1-18) that is, like Luke's preface, somewhat detached from the narrative that follows.

Luke's preface is also unique among the Gospels (indeed, among all of the writings of the NT) in that it is written in a very sophisticated literary style that is reminiscent of the prefaces of some of the classical historians of antiquity, such as Herodotus, Thucydides, and Polybius (see Talbert, pp. 7-11). The most instructive parallel, however, may be the prefaces with which the first-century Jewish historian Josephus introduces his two-volume work, *Against Apion*. Portions of the preface to the first volume read: "In my history of our Antiquities, most excellent Epaphroditus, I have, I think, made sufficiently clear . . . the extreme antiquity of our Jewish race. . . . Since, however, I observe that a considerable number of persons . . . discredit the statements in my history . . . I consider it my duty to devote a brief treatise to all these points . . . to instruct all who desire to know the truth concerning the antiquity of our race. As witnesses to my statements I propose to call the writers who, in the estimation of the Greeks, are the most trustworthy authorities on antiquity as a whole" (1.1-4, from Marshall, p. 39, citing LCL). Portions of the preface to his second volume read: "In the first volume of this work, my esteemed Epaphroditus, I demonstrated the antiquity of our race . . . I shall now proceed to refute the rest of the authors who have attacked us" (1.1-2, from Marshall, p. 39, citing LCL). The parallels between the prefaces of Josephus and those of Luke are significant and instructive. Many of the words and phrases that are commented on in the notes parallel various items in Josephus. That Luke's prefaces really do point to a single author of Luke-Acts receives support from the prefaces found in *Against Apion*.

Luke states in v. 1 that **many have undertaken to draw up an account**. How many people Luke has in mind is uncertain. Probably he is referring to Mark and Q and perhaps to another source or two from which he may have obtained some of the material that is special to his Gospel (sometimes called the "L" source). The reference to **the things that have been fulfilled among us** anticipates the accomplishments mostly recorded in the second volume, the Book of Acts. **Among us**, by which phrase Luke includes himself as a participant, also anticipates Acts, particularly the "we sections" (Acts 16:10-17; 20:5-15; 21:1-18; 27:1-28:16), where Luke is himself an eyewitness.

In v. 2 Luke tells us that his information comes from what has been handed down from **eyewitnesses and servants of the word** (of God), which probably refers to the particulars of the Gospel story. Luke assures us that he has **carefully investigated** the information that he has obtained from eyewitnesses and various other sources, and now feels that he is in a position **to write an orderly account for** his friend **Theophilus** (v. 3). His purpose in writing is so that his friend **may know the certainty of the things** that he has been **taught** (v. 4). It is possible that Theophilus, who was probably a new Christian, had become unsettled by some teaching that was not in keeping with apostolic tradition. In any case, Luke intends for his reader(s) to receive an accurate account of **everything**, that is, of every essential aspect of the life and ministry of Jesus and the founding and growth of the church.

Additional Notes §1

Hans Conzelmann's argument (*The Theology of St. Luke* [San Francisco: Harper & Row, 1961], pp. 16 n. 3, 172) that Luke was not the author of chaps. 1–2 is unconvincing when it is realized that important theological themes found in these chapters receive further and fuller treatment later in the Gospel and in Acts. For a better assessment see Tiede, pp. 38–40.

1:1–4 / The preface to the *Letter of Aristeas to Philocrates* (1:1–12) also parallels Luke's preface: "Inasmuch as the account of our deputation to Eleazar, the High Priest of the Jews, is worth narrating, Philocrates, and because you set a high value, as you constantly remind me, on hearing the motives and purposes of our mission, I have endeavored to set the matter forth clearly. I appreciate your characteristic love of learning, for it is indeed men's highest function 'ever to add knowledge, ever to acquire it,' either through researches or by actual experience of affairs" (from M. Hadas, ed., *Aristeas to Philocrates* [New York: Harper & Row, 1951], p. 57).

The historical emphasis of Luke's preface may have been designed as polemic against an incipient gnosticizing tendency to minimize the importance of Jesus' real, historical, earthly life. For more on this general theme see Charles H. Talbert, *Luke and the Gnostics: An Examination of the Lucan Purpose* (Nashville: Abingdon, 1966).

1:1 / **Account** literally may be translated, "narrative," a word possibly suggested to Luke by its verbal form in LXX Hab. 1:5, which the evangelist will later record Paul quoting in Acts 13:41 as an OT text that is vital to the Christian explanation of Jewish unbelief (see Introduction above). LXX Hab. 1:5, as quoted in Acts, reads in part: "I am going to do something in your days [cf. Acts 2:17] . . . that you would never believe, even if someone [like Luke] told [or narrated it to] you."

1:2 / The expression, **they were handed down**, comes from the same word from which we derive our word "tradition" (i.e., "that which is handed down"). See Paul's references to the tradition which he has received in 1 Cor. 11:2 (order in the family), 1 Cor. 11:23 (Lord's Supper), and 1 Cor. 15:3 (death, burial, and resurrection of Jesus). What Luke is saying is that the eyewitnesses of Jesus' life and ministry have "handed down" the apostolic gospel tradition from which he will attempt to compose his own account.

Those who from the first were eyewitnesses refers to the original disciples who became Jesus' apostles and were eyewitnesses of his life and ministry. This is illustrated in Acts 1:21–22, where Judas' replacement must have been an eyewitness from the beginning of Jesus' ministry, commencing with the baptism of John. Luke, however, may also intend to refer to the eyewitnesses of the various episodes involved in the infancy narratives of chaps. 1–2.

1:3 / **I myself have carefully investigated everything**: Luke claims to have done his homework and so now is in a position to write a reliable account.

Whereas **from the first** in v. 2 referred to the beginning of Jesus' ministry (and possibly to his and John's birth narratives), the similar phrase, **from the beginning**, in v. 3 translates a different word and refers to the proper starting place for the account (i.e., "from the top").

Theophilus: Because of his Gentile name and because he is addressed **most excellent**, some commentators have suggested that Theophilus was a Roman official to whom Luke addressed his Gospel in an effort to defend Christianity against misinformation and slander. Although it is true that Luke takes pains to show, especially in Acts, that the first Christians were law-abiding citizens, it is much more likely that Theophilus was a new convert, and perhaps an influential one, too, who was in need, as v. 4 suggests, of an exact and authoritative account (see Schweizer, pp. 13–14). Another suggestion has been made that since the name Theophilus means "friend of God," the name is meant to refer symbolically to anyone who is open to God's truth. This idea is unlikely, however, when it is recognized that Theophilus was a name common to Jews, Greeks, and Romans in the first century. Moreover, had Luke meant to address his Gospel to "friends of God" and not to a person named Theophilus, he could (and I think would) have done so in plain speech.

§2 *The Births of John the Baptist and Jesus Foretold (Luke 1:5–56)*

One of the problems in comparing the Synoptic Gospels is accounting for the distinctive features of the birth narratives in Matthew and Luke. On the one hand, Matthew mentions an angelic announcement to Joseph (1:20), the Magi (2:1), a star (2:2), the flight to Egypt (2:13–14), and the slaughter of the infants (2:16). Luke's account contains none of these items. Moreover, only Matthew cites Isa. 7:14 (see 1:23), Mic. 5:2 (see 2:6), Hos. 11:1 (see 2:15), and Jer. 31:15 (see 2:18) as fulfilled in Jesus' birth. On the other hand, only Luke mentions the announcement and birth of John the Baptist (1:13, 57), an angelic announcement to Mary (1:26–33), a meeting between Mary and Elizabeth (1:39–40), a census of Caesar Augustus requiring every male to return to his own home city (2:1–4), the birth in the manger (2:6–7), and the visit of the shepherds (2:8–20). Moreover, only Luke provides us with the eloquent canticles and speeches uttered by some of the major figures in his infancy narrative (the Magnificat, 1:46–55; the Benedictus, 1:68–79; the Angelic Anthem, 2:13–14; and the Nunc Dimittis, 2:28–32).

Nevertheless, there are numerous significant points of contact between the Matthean and Lucan accounts. Jesus' birth is during the reign of Herod the Great (Luke 1:5; Matt. 2:1); Mary is only engaged to Joseph (Luke 1:27, 34; 2:5; Matt. 1:18); Joseph is a descendant of David (Luke 1:27; 2:4; Matt. 1:16, 20); an angel announces Jesus' coming birth (Luke 1:28–31; Matt. 1:20–21); the conception of Jesus is through the Holy Spirit (Luke 1:35; Matt. 1:18, 20); the name "Jesus" is assigned by heaven (Luke 1:31; Matt. 1:21); Jesus is to be the "Savior" (Luke 2:11; Matt. 1:21); Jesus is born at Bethlehem (Luke 2:4–7; Matt. 2:1); and Jesus and family settle in Nazareth of Galilee (Luke 2:39, 51; Matt. 2:22–23). (For further discussion see Fitzmyer, pp. 304–21.)

One wonders how to account for all of the similarities and differences in the Lucan and Matthean infancy narratives. The numerous parallels make it unlikely that the Matthean and Lucan traditions originated separately, while in light of the many differences it is hard to see how they derive from a common literary source. Furthermore, the traditional explanation that the Matthean account goes back to Joseph, while the Lucan account goes back to Mary, is not very realistic (see Tiede, p. 47). After all, surely Joseph and Mary related to one another their experiences and so, years later, their accounts would probably be quite similar. The explanation, therefore, must lie elsewhere. I offer the following tentative suggestion: Eventually the church took an active interest in the details of Jesus' birth and early life. Prompted by a conviction that surely a life as important as this one would have had an unusual or at least a theologically significant beginning, early Christians became more interested in learning about Jesus' birth and early life. What details were known, or could be remembered, came to be related to various OT passages which the early church understood in a messianic sense. Although the distinct traditions that eventually would be written down in the Gospels of Matthew and Luke held many things in common (as listed above), there were several distinctive features. To these features early Christian interpretations (based on the OT, but anecdotal in nature) attached themselves. For Matthew, certain items were selected and related to particular OT passages (as mentioned above). For Luke, however, this OT/Christian interpretation took shape primarily in terms of the various canticles found in chaps. 1–2. All of this is not to say, however, that Luke (or Matthew, for that matter) fabricated his infancy stories. That he took an active editorial hand in their presentation is beyond all reasonable doubt. But it is also very likely that these stories were part of the tradition that had been "handed down . . . by those who from the first were eyewitnesses" (Luke 1:2).

Another distinctive feature of Luke's account is the parallelism between the births of John and Jesus. For both sets of parents the conception of a child was unexpected: Elizabeth was old and barren (1:7), and Joseph and Mary were not yet married (1:26–27). The angel Gabriel appears to one parent of each child (to Zechariah, 1:11–19; to Mary, 1:26–38). Both future parents are "troubled" (Zechariah, 1:12; Mary, 1:29). Both are told not to fear

(Zechariah, 1:13; Mary, 1:30). Both are promised a son (Zechariah, 1:13; Mary, 1:31). Both are given the names for their unborn sons (Zechariah, 1:13; Mary, 1:31). Both sons will be "great" (Zechariah, 1:15; Mary, 1:32). Both parents ask, "How?" (Zechariah, 1:18; Mary, 1:34). Both are given signs (Zechariah, 1:20; Mary, 1:36). There is joy over the birth of each son (John, 1:58; Jesus, 2:15–18). Following John's circumcision, neighbors react in fear, sensing God at work (1:59–66). Following Jesus' circumcision, the righteous Simeon and Anna recognize that in Jesus God was at work (2:21–38). On both occasions canticles are sung (because of John, the Benedictus, 1:68–79; because of Jesus, the Nunc Dimittis, 2:29–32). Finally, Luke tells us of both young sons: "The child grew and became strong . . . " (of John, 1:80; of Jesus, 2:40).

These parallels suggest that Luke wishes the reader to recognize at least three things: First, John and Jesus are "twin agents of God's salvation" (Fitzmyer, p. 315). Although other characters play a role in God's plan of redemption, John and Jesus are unquestionably the major figures. Second, in every respect of his life, as well as his later ministry, John is Jesus' forerunner, even in his conception and birth. Third, in every respect Jesus is superior to John. John's birth is certainly unusual, but Jesus' birth is without equal. John will be great *before* the Lord (1:15), but Jesus will himself be *called* Lord (2:11). Whereas Zechariah's question to Gabriel brings muteness (a punitive sign), when Mary asks Gabriel how these things could be, no punitive action is taken—indeed, instead of a mute testimony, she breaks forth in song (the Magnificat, 1:46–55).

1:5–25 / In the opening paragraph of his account of the birth of John the Baptist (1:5–7) Luke tells his readers three things about the parents of John. First, he emphasizes that both parents were of priestly descent. **Zechariah** his father was a priest of the **division of Abijah** (see note below), while his mother Elizabeth was from the family of **Aaron**, the brother of Moses and Israel's first priest. This priestly heritage is significant since it relates John to the religious history of Israel, a history which reaches its climax in the appearance of Jesus. Furthermore, just as a priest functions as an intermediary between God and Israel, so John the Baptist will call Israel back to God in preparation for Messiah (see commentary on 2:11). Second, Luke tells us that John's parents **were upright in the sight of God, observing all the Lord's commandments and regulations blamelessly** (v. 6). Not only do their faithful and righteous lives qualify them for their role, but it removes any question of sin or guilt that Elizabeth's barrenness might have implied. Third, Luke reports that **they had no children** and now both parents were very old (v. 7). Childlessness was considered a terrible misfortune and was often considered a disgrace and perhaps even a judgment of God. Elizabeth's predicament is no doubt meant to recall the similar problem of some of the famous women in the OT, such as Sarah (Gen. 16:1), Rebekah (Gen. 25:21), Rachel (Gen. 30:1), the mother of Samson (Judges 13:2), and Hannah (1 Samuel 1-2). Also, like Sarah, Elizabeth was beyond childbearing age.

In the next paragraphs (vv. 8-17) Luke reports the announcement of the angel Gabriel to Zechariah that his wife **Elizabeth will bear . . . a son** who is to be named **John** (v. 13). The angel further tells Zechariah that his son will be a cause of great rejoicing (v. 14), since he signals the beginning of God's redemptive work. He then summarizes the key features of his future character and ministry. As a Nazirite (see note below) he will not **take wine or other fermented drink** but **will be filled with the Holy Spirit** (v. 15). Like Elijah (see Mal. 4:5-6), **many of the people of Israel he will bring back to the Lord** (v. 16). . . . **And he will go on before the Lord** (see Mal. 2:6; Sir. 48:10) . . . **to make ready a people prepared for the Lord** (v. 17).

Like other skeptical husbands (such as Abraham, Gen. 15:8), Zechariah wants a sign as proof for this startling announcement (see also Judges 6:37-40 where Gideon requests a sign), as if the appearance of the angel were insufficient. Because Zechariah **did not believe** the **words** of the angel he remains mute until the promise is fulfilled (v. 20). Zechariah had asked for a sign, and for his sign he became mute and, in light of v. 62, apparently deaf as well. Because of his delay in coming out of the temple (v. 21) and because of his muteness (and possibly because of the look on his face), the people outside the temple awaiting his blessing (see Num. 6:24-26) conclude that **he had seen a vision in the temple** (v. 22). Such a conclusion is not surprising when one remembers that the best known account of a prophetic vision taking place in the temple was that of Isaiah (Isa. 6:1-5; see also Ezek. 10:3-19).

As the angel had announced, **Elizabeth became pregnant** (v. 24). Luke's reference to her remaining secluded **for five months** (v. 24) anticipates Mary's visit when Elizabeth was in her sixth month of pregnancy (vv. 36–40). Elizabeth's gratitude, expressed in v. 25, **The Lord has done this for me. . . . He has shown his favor and taken away my disgrace**, echoes the statement of Rachel, following the birth of Joseph: "God has taken away my reproach" (Gen. 30:23, NASB; see also Gen. 21:6; Isa. 4:1). Although the conception and birth of John the Baptist were indeed amazing, if not miraculous, they will be overshadowed by the announcement to Mary that follows.

1:26–38 / **In the sixth month, God sent the angel Gabriel to Nazareth, a town in Galilee** (v. 26). With the second sending of Gabriel a similar sequence of events begins to unfold. Only this time, it is the announcement of the birth of the Savior himself, the one before whom John is to go. (On the parallels between the announcements of the births of John and Jesus see Tiede, pp. 45–46.) It is significant that **Joseph** is a **descendant of David** (v. 27), for that ancestry qualifies Jesus for his messianic role and makes what Gabriel says in vv. 32–33 possible. Mary is told that she will have a **son** and that she is **to give him the name Jesus** (v. 31, a name which originally meant, "Lord, help!" but had come to be understood as meaning "salvation"; see Matt. 1:21). What Gabriel says in the next two verses echoes the great Davidic covenant of 2 Samuel 7 in which King David is promised that his throne and kingdom would be established forever. Fitzmyer (p. 338) has listed the following parallels:

	2 Sam.		Luke
7:9	"a great name"	1:32	"he will be great"
7:13	"the throne of his kingdom"	1:32	"throne of his father David"
7:14	"he will be my son"	1:32	"son of the Most High"
7:16	"your house and your kingdom"	1:33	"king over the house of Jacob forever"

These parallels indicate that Luke sees in the birth of Jesus the fulfillment of the hope that a descendant of David would some day arise, as promised in Gen. 49:10; 2 Sam. 7:9–16; Isa. 9:1–7; 11:1–3. Although there was no uniform concept of the Messiah,

or Christ (see commentary on 2:11), with some believing that he
would be a priest and therefore would be from the tribe of Levi,
the most popular view was that the Messiah would be a "son of
David" who would liberate Israel (e.g., Pss. Sol. 17:23–51).

Unlike the question of Zechariah (v. 18) Mary's question,
How can this be? (v. 34) carries no connotation of unbelief. Since
Mary is only engaged to Joseph and is therefore still a **virgin** (see
v. 27; 2:5) her question is a natural one. The angel explains that
her pregnancy will result from the **Holy Spirit**, and for this reason
her child **will be called the Son of God** (v. 35). As evidence for
the possibility of this extraordinary promise, Gabriel tells Mary
about Elizabeth's pregnancy. Mary gives her classic response: **I
am the Lord's servant . . . may it be to me as you have said** (v. 38).

1:39–56 / The meeting between Mary and Elizabeth
where Elizabeth acknowledges Mary's superior role (see especially
v. 43) anticipates and parallels the meeting of John and Jesus, at
which time the Baptist will acknowledge that Jesus is greater
(3:15–17, 21–22). Even while yet in the womb John leaps for joy
at the presence of Mary (v. 41). Elizabeth's filling **with the Holy
Spirit** (v. 41) is the first of many other fillings which Luke will
record (especially in the Book of Acts; see Luke 1:67; 2:25; Acts
2:4; 4:8; 13:9). Usually in Luke's writings, before one opens his
or her mouth to praise God and recite the gospel, he or she is
"filled with the Holy Spirit."

After Elizabeth's greeting and blessing, Mary breaks forth
with a song of exaltation, known as the Magnificat (vv. 46–55;
the name is from the opening word in the Latin version). Although there are a few quotes from and allusions to the Psalms,
the Magnificat's closest parallel is Hannah's song of thanksgiving
(for the birth of Samuel) in 1 Sam. 2:1–10, which begins like the
Magnificat: "My heart exults in the LORD" (NASB). That the Magnificat would parallel Hannah's song is appropriate for two major
reasons: First, like Hannah's song of thanksgiving, the Magnificat expresses gratitude for a pregnancy (in Hannah's case, a much-
wanted pregnancy; in Mary's case, quite unexpected). Second,
as in Hannah's case, the child is to become great in God's service
and is to have a vital ministry to Israel. Moreover, many elements
in Hannah's song could be readily understood as having messianic significance. There is reference to "deliverance" (v. 1), reference to the Lord's "king" in v. 10, and, also in v. 10, a reference

to the Lord's "anointed" or "messiah." Both songs also express the idea of reversal (e.g., exalting the humble, humbling the exalted, etc.; see 1 Sam. 2:4–8; Luke 1:51–53), which, as will be seen throughout this Gospel, is an important theme. However, possibly the single most important part of the Magnificat occurs in the last two verses: **He has helped his servant Israel, remembering to be merciful to Abraham and his descendants forever, even as he said to our fathers** (vv. 54–55). These **descendants** include *Gentiles* as well as the Jewish race, as can be seen in God's promises to Abraham (see Gen. 12:3; 17:4–5; 22:18). Reference to God's promises to Abraham is also made by Zechariah following the birth of John (see v. 73).

Additional Notes §2

1:5 / **Herod** refers to Herod the Great, who was granted the title "king" by the Roman Senate in 40 B.C. He did not gain control over Palestine (which is what Luke means when he says **Judea**) until 37 B.C., which he ruled until his death in 4 B.C. Luke's chronology is vague at this point, but according to Matt. 2:1, 15, 19–20, John and Jesus must have been born shortly before Herod's death.

Zechariah is the name of other OT priests (1 Chron. 15:24; 2 Chron. 35:8; Neh. 11:12). The name, which means "the Lord has remembered," may be noteworthy in view of John's unusual conception and calling. According to later Christian legend, Zechariah was a high priest (see *Protevangelium of James* 8:1–3); but this, of course, is incorrect.

priestly division of Abijah: There were 24 orders or divisions of priests (see 1 Chron. 23:6; 24:7–18; Neh. 12:1–7). Each priestly division "served twice a year in the Jerusalem Temple, for a week at a time" (Fitzmyer, p. 322; see also Lachs, pp. 16–17). It was during one of his weeks of priestly service that Zechariah was visited by the angel.

1:10 / Lachs (p. 17) notes that people praying outside the temple was not normal practice.

1:11 / **an angel of the Lord appeared**: An "angel of the LORD" appeared to Samson's mother in Judges 13:3. In Luke 1:19 the angel identifies himself as Gabriel (see Dan. 9:21, where Gabriel appears at the ninth hour [i.e., 3 p.m.], the hour of prayer and evening sacrifice). Elsewhere the "angel of the Lord" appears in Luke 2:9; Acts 5:19; 8:26; 12:7, 23.

1:13 / **your prayer has been heard**: We are not told what Zechariah's prayer was. In his temple duties he naturally would pray for Israel's redemption, although he and his wife no doubt had often prayed for a son. Thus, both prayers were answered in the conception of John, for he would be their long-awaited son and the forerunner of the Messiah.

John means "the Lord has shown favor." Heavenly imposed names usually related to one's destiny. Elsewhere in biblical literature names are imposed (see Gen. 32:28; Isa. 9:6; Matt. 1:21; Luke 1:31).

1:14–18 / The angel's announcement of the birth of John echoes Scripture at many points: Num. 6:3; Judg. 13:4 (v. 15); Mal. 2:6 (v. 16); Mal. 3:1; 4:5–6; Sir. 48:10; 2 Sam. 7:14 (v. 17); and Gen. 15:8 (v. 18). Comparing the Baptist to the anticipated return of Elijah in the eschatological age is not distinctly Christian (cf. Mark 1:2; 9:11–12) but finds expression in rabbinic writings as well: m. *'Eduyyot* 8.7; *Pesiqta Rabbati* 4.2; 33.8; *Seder Eliyyahu Zuta* 1 (169); *Sipre Deut.* 342 (on 33:2); *Midrash Psalms* 3.7 (on 3:6).

Talbert (pp. 27–30) suggests that Luke presents the Baptist as a "prototype of the Christian evangelist." He cites Luke 1:14–17, 57–80; 3:1–20; 7:24–35.

1:15 / **He is never to take wine or other fermented drink**: Abstinence from alcoholic beverages is the main requirement of the Nazirite vow (see Num. 6:3; Judg. 13:7; LXX 1 Sam. 1:11). The **fermented drink** is a beverage made from grain (perhaps something like beer). Instead of being empowered by alcohol (for in antiquity there was the belief that intoxication could lead to divine possession and powers), John would be empowered by the **Holy Spirit even from birth**. (On the connection between wine and the Spirit see Eph. 5:18.) The scriptural allusions might be "Luke's way of indicating that John is to be a Nazarite prophet" (Lachs, p. 18).

1:17 / The idea of the return of **Elijah** as the forerunner of the Messiah does not occur in Judaism outside of the NT. But because both Elijah and Messiah were related to the end times their association is understandable. John's mission is to "turn the hearts of fathers to their children" (from Mal. 4:6, RSV). One of the themes in Jewish messianic expectation concerned family strife. In the Mishnah (*Sotah* 9.15), Mic. 7:6 is cited (" . . . daughter rise up against her mother . . . ") and applied to the times of the Messiah. Remarkably, Mic. 7:6 also appears in the Synoptic tradition in the same context (see Matt. 10:21, 35–36; Mark 13:12; Luke 12:53). See *HBD*, pp. 256–58.

1:19 / **Gabriel**: Few angels are mentioned by name in biblical and related literature: Gabriel (Dan. 8:16; 9:21); Michael (Dan. 10:13; 12:1); Raphael (Tob. 3:17; 1 Enoch 9:1; 20:7); Uriel (1 Enoch 9:1; 19:1); Phanuel (1 Enoch 40:9). The name "Gabriel" apparently means "God is my hero/warrior" (Fitzmyer, p. 328).

1:26–38 / For a discussion of divine/angelic annunciations and their OT antecedents see Talbert, pp. 18–21.

1:27 / Luke uses the form *Mariam* (or *Miriam*) for the name **Mary**, probably to recall the famous sister of Moses and Aaron, and so strengthens the link between Elizabeth (a descendant of Aaron, 1:5) and Mary. The other Gospels use the form *Marias*.

1:32 / He will be great and will be called the Son of the Most High: An Aramaic fragment found at Qumran (Cave 4) reads: "(he) shall be great upon the earth, [O King!] . . . he shall be called [son of] the [g]reat [God], and by his name shall he be named. He shall be hailed (as) the Son of God, and they shall call him Son of the Most High" (Fitzmyer, p. 347). To whom reference is made, however, is not clear due to the fragmentary condition of the text. The angelic annunciation, of course, in 1:32b alludes to the Davidic covenant of 2 Samuel 7 and applies it to Jesus. Elsewhere in the infancy narrative Jesus' Davidic descent is emphasized (Luke 1:69; 2:4, 11). On the expression, "Most High," see *Jub.* 16:18; *1 Enoch* 9:3; 1QapGen 12.17; as well as Luke 1:76.

1:33 / he will reign over the house of Jacob forever; his kingdom will never end: This statement is a succinct summary of Israel's messianic hopes (see Mic. 4:7; Dan. 2:44; 7:14). "The patriotic strain is once more apparent" (Leaney, p. 83).

1:46 / Mary said: Some commentators have maintained that Luke originally composed the Magnificat for Elizabeth, as a parallel to Zechariah's Benedictus (vv. 68–79), especially since it is Elizabeth, not Mary, who was "filled with the Holy Spirit" (v. 41). Schweizer (p. 15) appears to lean this way. Since no Greek manuscript, however, reads "Elizabeth said," such a proposal remains no more than sheer speculation. It has also been observed that some of the contents of the Magnificat scarcely seem appropriate to the occasion. The Magnificat reads more like a warrior's song of victory than that of a young maiden praising God for the gift of a child. Accordingly, it has been suggested that underlying the Magnificat is an early Christian hymn praising God for vindicating Jesus through his resurrection. This is possible, but again it is quite speculative, for there is no mention of Jesus or the resurrection. More probably the Magnificat represents an early Christian hymn, thought to derive from Mary, that has been enriched by components reflecting Israel's psalms of military celebration. Consider the following scriptural allusions:
My soul glorifies [or magnifies] **the Lord**: 1 Sam. 2:1; Ps. 69:30; 34:3; 35:9; Sir. 43:31.

1:47 / my spirit rejoices in God my Savior: Hab. 3:18; LXX Ps. 25:5.

1:48 / for he has been mindful of the humble state of his servant: 1 Sam. 1:11; 9:16; cf. Gen. 16:11; 29:32; Ps. 113:5–6.
From now on all generations will call me blessed: Gen. 30:13.

1:49 / for the Mighty One: LXX Ps. 89:9; LXX Zeph. 3:17.
has done great things for me: Deut. 10:21.
holy is his name: Ps. 111:9.

1:50 / **His mercy extends to those who fear him**: Ps. 103:13, 17. **from generation to generation**: Ps. 89:2.

1:51 / **He has performed mighty deeds**: Lit. "He has acted mightily with his arm." Ps. 89:10.

1:52 / **He has brought down rulers from their thrones but has lifted up the humble**: 1 Sam. 2:4, 7; Job 12:19; Ezek. 21:31; Sir. 10:14.

1:53 / **He has filled the hungry with good things**: 1 Sam. 2:5; Ps. 107:9.
but has sent the rich away empty: Job 22:9.

1:54 / **He has helped his servant Israel**: Isa. 41:8–9. **remembering to be merciful**: Ps. 98:3.

1:55 / **and his descendants forever**: 2 Sam. 22:51. **our fathers**: Mic. 7:20.

It is worth noting that in the Targum's version of 1 Sam. 2:1–10, Hannah's song of thanksgiving is transformed into an apocalypse foretelling the eventual triumph of Israel's Messiah. One wonders if a messianic understanding of this passage was in circulation as early as the first century, perhaps in part accounting for the Magnificat's relationship to Hannah's song. For more on Luke's allusions to the OT and its language see Tannehill, pp. 18–19.

1:57–66 / The accounts of the birth and naming of John the Baptist contain a few interesting features. Apparently Elizabeth's neighbors and relatives were not aware of her pregnancy (v. 58; according to v. 24 she had been in seclusion), for when they hear of the birth of her son (v. 57), they then realize that **the Lord had shown her great mercy, and they shared her joy** (v. 58). This rejoicing fulfills the prophecy of v. 14. Because of her advanced age and history of infertility, her bearing a child would no doubt have amazed everyone who heard of it. Although it is not a Jewish custom to name a child at the time of his circumcision, a formal announcement of the child's name at that time was not unusual. It appears that in the week following John's birth, the neighbors and relatives of Elizabeth and Zechariah had assumed that the child would be named after his father. In fact, v. 59 might be literally translated, "they were calling it [the child] Zechariah." Elizabeth tells them that the boy is to be named John (v. 60). This seemed to be a strange choice, since the parents had no ancestors named John (v. 61), so they asked Zechariah (by sign language) what he should be named (v. 62). To everyone's astonishment, Zechariah agreed with Elizabeth (v. 63) and, as a divine sign that "John" was indeed the correct name, he was suddenly able to speak (v. 64). The last word that Zechariah had spoken before losing his speech had been an expression of doubt (v. 18), but on this, the first occasion that he could speak again, he praised God. It is quite possible that this praise is the Benedictus itself (vv. 68–79), which Luke reserves telling until he recounts the fear and amazement of the **neighbors** (vv. 65–66). The question that they raise, **"What then is this child going to be?"** (v. 66) adds drama to the story and only makes the reader more eager with anticipation. This is another example of Luke's skill as a narrator.

1:67–79 / In singing the Benedictus (vv. 68–79) Zechariah utters at last a blessing which he had been expected to pronounce some nine months earlier (see commentary on vv. 21–22). Virtually every line of this song is derived from the OT (see notes below). The main thrust of the song is summarized in v. 68: "Blessed be the Lord God of Israel, for he has visited and redeemed his people" (RSV). The key word in this verse is the verb "to visit" (NIV: **has come**). In the LXX this word often occurs in reference to "God's gracious visitation of his people" (Fitzmyer, p. 383). The following examples should make this idea clear: With reference to God's intention to deliver Israel from Egypt, Exod. 4:31 states in part: "they heard that the LORD had visited the people of Israel and that he had seen their affliction" (RSV). In Ruth 1:6 the discouraged Naomi decides to return to Bethlehem, "for she had heard . . . that the LORD had visited his people and given them food" (RSV). (See also the petitions found in Pss. 80:14; 106:4.)

Zechariah specifies in v. 69 why he believes that redemption has come: It has come because God has **raised up a horn of salvation for us in the house of his servant David**. It should be noted that although there are promises of deliverance **from our enemies** (vv. 71, 74), this song contains no overt elements of the militant messianism that was part of the popular view. Rather, the emphasis is on personal piety (v. 75), forgiveness of sins (v. 77), illumination (vv. 78–79), and peace (v. 79). The reference to **the oath he swore to Abraham** (v. 73) complements the earlier reference to this patriarch in the Magnificat (v. 55). The promise that God made to Abraham, that in him Israel and all nations would be blessed, is now coming to fulfillment in the birth and preparation of John the Baptist. The Benedictus concludes with a phrase taken from Isa. 9:1–2. This is a crucial point since this Davidic messianic passage contains the expression, "Galilee of the Gentiles" (NASB), which could provide a link between the Davidic messianic traditions and the blessing of the Gentiles through Abraham.

1:80 / With this brief, summarizing verse, which is probably meant to correspond to the similar ones referring to Jesus (2:40, 52), John the Baptist fades from the scene to reappear later in his ministry of repentance and baptism. Concerning why he retreated to the **desert** and what he did there while growing up, Luke tells us nothing (see note below).

Additional Notes §3

1:59 / With regard to the circumcision of John, Ellis (p. 78) makes the following interesting comment: "According to an ancient Jewish custom the child was circumcised upon a chair called the 'throne of Elijah' with the hope that he might be the long-awaited prophet." If this custom were known in the days of Zechariah, then the background against which we must view John's circumcision takes on an additional element of drama.

1:65–66 / The numerous witnesses of the extraordinary happenings surrounding the circumcision and naming of John may help explain, at least in Luke's mind, why the Baptist's ministry was met with widespread acclaim ("multitudes" came to his wilderness baptism, 3:10).

Although Luke records no one asking the question of Jesus, **"What then is this child going to be?"** the reader is left asking the question implicitly.

1:68–79 / Like the Magnificat (1:46–55), the Benedictus is replete with scriptural allusions and language:

1:68 / **Praise be to the Lord, the God of Israel**: 1 Kings 1:48; 1 Chron. 16:36; Pss. 41:13; 72:18; 106:48.

he has come: Lit. "he has visited." Exod. 4:31; Ruth 1:6; Pss. 80:14; 106:4.

and has redeemed his people: Ps. 111:9.

1:69 / **He has raised up a horn of salvation**: 2 Sam. 22:3; Pss. 18:2; 89:24; 132:17; Ezek. 29:21; cf. 1 Sam. 2:10. Ellis (p. 78) states: "As an animal's strength is in its horn so God is a horn in effecting his mighty act of salvation" (see Deut. 33:17).

the house of his servant David: Cf. 2 Sam. 7:11–13.

1:70 / **(as he said through his holy prophets of long ago)**: Fitzmyer (p. 384) notes that this expression is paralleled to some extent at Qumran: 1QS 1.3; 4QpHos 2.5. He suspects that it is a Lucanism. He may be right, for not only does it intrude in the canticle, it also reflects the evangelist's interest in the general witness of the prophetic scriptures (cf. Luke 24:25, 44).

1:71 / **salvation from our enemies and from the hand of all who hate us**: 2 Sam. 22:18; Pss. 18:17; 106:10.

1:72 / **to show mercy**: LXX Gen. 24:12; cf. Judg. 1:24; 8:35; Ruth 1:8.

to our fathers: Mic. 7:20.

to remember his holy covenant: Exod. 2:24; Lev. 26:42; Pss. 105:8; 106:45.

1:73 / **the oath he swore to our father Abraham**: Gen. 26:3; Jer. 11:5; Mic. 7:20; cf. Gen. 22:16–17.

1:74 / **to rescue us from the hand of our enemies**: Cf. Ps. 97:10. The "enemies" may either be the Romans or any who oppose the Christian faith; see Leaney, pp. 89–90.
to serve [or worship] **him without fear**: Josh. 24:14.

1:75 / **in holiness and righteousness before him all our days**: Isa. 38:20.

1:76 / **a prophet of the Most High**: The expression parallels the designation of Jesus as "Son of the Most High" (see Luke 1:32 and note above for references). "Prophet" probably alludes to Mal. 4:5.
you will go on before the Lord to prepare the way for him: Mal. 3:1; Isa. 40:3.

1:77 / **through the forgiveness of their sins**: Jer. 31:34; Mark 1:4.

1:78 / **the rising sun will come to us**: Mal. 4:2 (LXX 3:20). Schweizer (p. 43) thinks that the "rising" may also refer to the appearance of the Davidic "Branch," and so he cites LXX Jer. 23:5; Zech. 3:8; 6:12; 4QFlor 1.11; 4QPatr 3. On p. 40 he cites Isa. 60:1–2 as well. Lachs (p. 27) also suggests Isa. 11:1; see also Leaney, pp. 90–91.

1:79 / **to shine on those living in darkness and in the shadow of death**: Ps. 107:10; Isa. 9:2; 42:7.
to guide our feet into the path of peace: Isa. 59:8.
Like the Magnificat, the Benedictus embodies Israel's nationalistic hopes and aspirations. Tiede (p. 60) is correct when he says that "according to Luke, Zechariah's words are the Holy Spirit's testimony to God's saving purpose and plan. None of it will fail to be fulfilled."

1:80 / **desert**: Not long after the discovery of the scrolls and ruins in the Dead Sea area some scholars began to wonder if the reference to John's upbringing in the wilderness might suggest that he had actually been a former member of the Qumran (or Essene) community, or at least associated with it at some time in his life. The suggestion is fascinating, though not easily proven. Fitzmyer (p. 389) thinks that the suggestion is "plausible."

§4 The Birth of Jesus (Luke 2:1–52)

2:1–7 / The primary purpose of this first paragraph is to set the stage for the angelic anthem (vv. 13–14) and the visit of the shepherds (vv. 15–20). Another purpose, however, is to place the birth of Jesus in the context of Rome's greatest emperor, Caesar Augustus (see note below). Just as the edict of the Persian king Cyrus to rebuild Jerusalem and the temple accomplished God's plans (see 2 Chron. 36:22–23; Ezra 1:1–4; Isa. 44:28–45:1), so Augustus' order that a **census should be taken** played an important part in God's redemptive plan. The census was to ascertain the income, property, and wealth of the inhabitants for purposes of taxation. Since **everyone** was to **register** in **his own town** (v. 3), **Joseph** went to **Bethlehem** (v. 4). For Luke, the significance of the trip to Bethlehem (see Mic. 5:2), and the visit of the shepherds as well (Ezek. 34:23; 37:24), is to be found in its Davidic background. Luke has framed his account in such a way that during the reign of the earth's greatest king, Caesar Augustus, the son of **Joseph**—a man from the **line of David** (v. 4), Israel's greatest king and father of the Messiah—was born. Bethlehem was the **town of David** (v. 4), so it was only appropriate that David's messianic descendant also be born there. Why **Mary** would have accompanied Joseph (v. 5) has puzzled some commentators, since her presence for the registration was not necessary. In view of her pregnancy's full term, however, and in view of the criticism which might have been directed against her for being pregnant before her marriage, it is not surprising that she accompanied Joseph (see note below). Of course, for the purposes of Luke's narrative the two must be kept together, for although only Joseph himself really has to go to Bethlehem, it is the birth of Jesus that must take place in the city of David and occasion the angelic anthem and the visit of the shepherds. That Jesus was born in a stable (or cave) and laid **in a manger** (i.e., a feeding trough, v. 7) reflects Luke's concern for the poor and the humble, but it also paves the way for the shepherds' visit.

2:8–20 / The story of the shepherds supplies the occasion for yet another heavenly witness (i.e., the angelic anthem, vv. 13–14) and strengthens the connection between Jesus and King David. David, it is to be remembered, was himself a shepherd (1 Sam. 16:11), and in some of the psalms, many of which are attributed to him, he refers to God as a shepherd and to God's people as sheep (Ps. 23:1; 28:9; 100:3). Moreover, the prophets promised that God would someday raise a new David to act as Israel's shepherd (Ezek. 34:23). In first-century Palestine shepherds did not have the reputation for being overly circumspect with regard to the property of others. They were often held in contempt and considered as nothing more than roving vagabonds and thieves. Whether Luke had this idea in mind is not certain, but if he did, then the lowly shepherds anticipate the blessings many other such persons of low estate will receive from Jesus during his ministry (see Talbert, pp. 33–34). (If Luke viewed the shepherds as thieves, then ironically we have both Jesus' birth and death in the company of criminals [see Luke 23:32–43].) One **night** while the **shepherds** were tending **their flocks** (v. 8) an **angel of the Lord appeared to them** (v. 9). This angel is probably Gabriel (see 1:19, 26; see note on 1:11 above), who has on other occasions appeared to make important announcements. The angel's appearance is not a cause for alarm (vv. 9–10), for he has not come in judgment, as is sometimes the case (e.g., 2 Kings 19:35). But he has come bringing a message of **good news of great joy that will be for all the people** (v. 10). The good news is stated simply in v. 11: **Today in the town of David a Savior has been born to you; he is Christ the Lord**. Often Luke uses the word "today" in the sense of the arrival of the day of salvation (see note below). **Town of David** refers, of course, to Bethlehem; appropriately, the first time Luke uses the word "today" it is in connection with the birth of the messianic son of David. The angel calls the newborn infant "Savior," "Christ," and "Lord." These titles call for some discussion.

Savior: Although John's Gospel refers to Jesus as "Savior" (4:42), among the Synoptics only Luke calls Jesus Savior. Mary calls God "my Savior" in the Magnificat (1:47), while here in 2:11 the title is applied to Jesus. The only other Lucan references to Jesus as Savior are in Acts (5:31; 13:23). This title would have been meaningful to both Jews and Gentiles. The word "savior" occurs in the OT in reference to various individuals (Judg. 3:9, 15) and to God himself (1 Sam. 10:19; Isa. 45:15, 21). All of these verses in the LXX use the word "savior" that Luke uses in 2:11. In the Greek and Roman worlds the word "savior" (*sōtēr*) was often applied to the gods (such as Zeus) and to great military and political figures. One ancient inscription calls Julius Caesar "god manifest and common savior of human life" (Fitzmyer, p. 204). Thus, the reference to Jesus as "Savior" would be a title readily understood and appreciated among Jews and Gentiles.

Christ: The angel also attributes to Jesus the popular title of Christ (*christos*). The word "Christ" is the Greek translation of the Hebrew word "messiah." Both words mean "anointed." To be anointed means to be recognized and consecrated in some special capacity, usually as king, and usually as God's agent. This word, of course, was the common title applied to the person whom God would someday raise up as Israel's deliverer. Therefore, to announce that the Messiah was born would be to announce the arrival of the day of Israel's deliverance. Such "deliverance" was normally understood in a military sense. Usually the Messiah was viewed as conquering Israel's enemies and exalting Israel (as is reflected to a certain extent in the Magnificat, see especially 1:51-52). Although there is no controversy in 2:11 over this type of messianic expectation, the next time that the word "today" appears announcing the arrival of the messianic era (4:21), such controversy will be at issue (see commentary on 4:14-30). But for now, Luke's readers must wait in suspense, wondering (as does Mary in 2:19) what all these things mean.

Lord: Finally, the angel also calls Jesus the "Lord" (*kyrios*, see note below). This title is by far the most common title for Jesus in the Lucan writings. The word is used of both God himself and of Jesus. "Lord" sometimes translates the divine name Yahweh ("The One Who Is"; see Exod. 3:14) and probably is to be understood in 2:11 in terms of the incarnation; that is to say, the Lord is present in Jesus. This idea is found in early Christianity as is evidenced by the confession "Jesus is Lord" (1 Cor. 12:3; Rom. 10:9; see Fitzmyer, pp. 200-204).

As in the case of Zechariah (1:18-20) and Mary (1:36), the shepherds, too, are given a sign (i.e., corroborating evidence) confirming the angelic announcement: They will **find a baby wrapped in cloth and lying in a manger** (v. 12). This final state-

ment brings the narrative to its climax when **a great company
of the heavenly host . . . praising God** appears (v. 13). The
phrases used by Luke in this verse are derived from his Greek
Old Testament (see 1 Kings 22:19; Ps. 148:2). The angelic anthem
consists of two parts: [May there be] **glory to God in the highest**, and [may there be] **on earth peace to men on whom his favor rests** (v. 14; see note below). The second part of the anthem
probably reflects the idea of election, which appears often in the
Lucan writings (in addition to those Gospel passages that will
be discussed, see Acts 13:48). The anthem calls for "peace" (i.e.,
šālôm, or well-being) upon earth (i.e., upon the inhabitants of
earth), for those whom God will show favor. Luke probably
understands this favor in terms of the gospel of salvation which
is made possible by the birth of the Messiah. Luke may see the
reference to peace in contrast to the celebrated "peace of Augustus" (*Pax Romana*). The peace that the Messiah brings is the
reconciling peace between humankind and God (see Isa. 9:6;
Ellis, p. 82).

As abruptly as they appeared, the angels returned to heaven
(v. 15), leaving the shepherds to hurry off to see **Mary and Joseph,
and the baby, who was lying in the manger** (v. 16). **When they
had seen** Jesus, **they spread the word concerning what had been
told them about this child** (v. 17). To whom the **all** of v. 18 refers
is not clear. Possibly Luke has in mind the guests of the inn; in
any case, the people **who heard it were amazed**. The independent witness of the shepherds satisfies Luke's concern that there
be *two* witnesses to heavenly events, in keeping with the requirements of the law concerning the giving of testimony (Deut. 19:15;
see Luke 24 where there are two on the road to Emmaus, as well
as two separate resurrection appearances and two separate references to the witness and fulfillment of the Scriptures). Not only
has the angel of the Lord appeared to Mary and Joseph announcing the birth of the Messiah, but he has also appeared to the shepherds. While the shepherds return, **glorifying and praising God**
(v. 20), **Mary treasured up all these things and pondered them
in her heart** (v. 19). Luke could be hinting that his source of information goes back to Mary herself (see also v. 51).

2:21–40 / The next major section of the narrative concerns
Jesus' circumcision and presentation at the temple. As in the case

of John (1:59-60), at the time of his circumcision Jesus is given the name that the angel told to his parents (v. 21). Also, just as the naming of John led to his presentation and to a prophetic utterance (1:64-79), the naming of Jesus is followed by his presentation and a prophetic utterance (2:22-32). The rituals performed by Joseph and Mary in vv. 22-24 show that the parents of Jesus are pious Jews who faithfully observe the requirements of the **Law of the Lord** (see Exod. 13:1-2; Lev. 12:4). Their offering of **a pair of doves** indicates that Joseph and Mary were people of humble means (see Lev. 12:8). The introduction of **Simeon** (v. 25) allows Luke to confirm further the previous announcement of Jesus' messianic identity and destiny. This is seen in the description of Simeon as **righteous and devout**, a man **waiting for the consolation of Israel** (v. 25, see 2:38), and in what he says in vv. 29-32. Obviously, in beholding Jesus, Simeon recognizes that Israel's consolation at long last is at hand. The reference to the Holy Spirit (vv. 25, 27) prepares for the proclamation of praise and thanksgiving (i.e., the Nunc Dimittis, vv. 29-32). As a watchman who now feels that his duty has been done (see Fitzmyer, p. 428), Simeon requests that the Lord let his **servant** go **in peace** (v. 29). In seeing Jesus he has beheld the **salvation** (v. 30) that God has **prepared in the sight of all people** (v. 31; see Isa. 52:10). The reference to the light for revelation to the Gentiles (v. 32; see Isa. 42:6; 49:6) further clarifies this idea and anticipates the universality of the gospel, a theme that finds its roots in the promises given to Abraham (see commentary on 1:55, 73). The second half of v. 32, however, must not be overlooked. This salvation of God will bring **glory to** God's **people Israel** (see Isa. 46:13). Even though God's mighty act of salvation will extend to all of the nations, Israel's place of preeminence will not be lost. It is important to stress this point, for often in appreciating Luke's emphasis that God's salvation has been extended to the Gentiles it is assumed that Israel no longer has a role to play or no longer enjoys God's favor. Israel will indeed reject Messiah and for this grievous error will suffer a catastrophe (see Luke 19:41-44); but if Gabriel's words to Mary (1:30-33) mean anything, Israel is not set aside. Although it cannot be argued here (see the discussion in the Introduction), Luke sees much, if not most, of ethnic Israel in a state of obdurate disobedience, a condition that is neither permanent nor out of keeping with the prophetic Scriptures (see Luke 21:22;

24:25–27; Acts 13:40–41; 28:23–28; Rom. 11:25–32). This idea of
a split in Israel is made explicit in vv. 34–35: **This child is destined to cause the falling and rising of many in Israel, and to
be a sign that will be spoken against, so that the thoughts of
many hearts will be revealed. And a sword will pierce your own
soul too.** The last part of v. 34 and the first part of v. 35 anticipate
Jesus' personal rejection (see Luke 22:66–23:5) and Jewish rejection of the apostolic preaching (see Acts 4:18; 5:17–18; 6:13–14;
8:1; 13:45; 14:2, 19; 17:5–6, 13; 21:27–28; 24:2–9; 25:2–3; 28:23–
28). The last part of v. 35 refers to the sharp **sword** that **will pierce**
Mary's own **soul**. Down through the centuries numerous explanations have been offered for this statement. Perhaps the most
popular interpretation is that Jesus' rejection and death will cause
terrible sorrow for Mary, as possibly depicted in John 19:25–27
(so Marshall, pp. 122–23). The problem with this interpretation
is that it relies on John's Gospel. Luke, however, does not depict
Mary grieving at the foot of the cross. Another interpretation that
has the advantage of being based upon Luke alone is that the
sword refers to the division that Jesus will cause in Israel, of which
Mary is a part (so Fitzmyer, pp. 429–30; see also Schweizer, p.
57). In Luke 12:51–53 Jesus warns that on account of him families
will be divided. Understood this way, Simeon's statement to Mary
parallels the rest of the oracle. Just as Jesus will cause division
in Israel in general, so his own mother in particular will experience anguish over her son's message and ministry.

Possibly in keeping with his desire to present two witnesses,
Luke next depicts the response of the **prophetess, Anna** (v. 36).
"Anna" is the same as the OT name Hannah and might be in-
tended to recall Samuel's mother (1 Sam. 1–2), especially in light
of the similarity between the temple presentations of the infants
Samuel (1 Sam. 1:22–24) and Jesus (Luke 2:22). There are other
Samuel/Jesus parallels as well, the basic points of which have been
laid out as follows:

	Samuel		*Jesus*
1 Sam.		Luke	
1:22	presentation of child to the Lord	2:22	presentation of child to the Lord
2:1–10	Hannah sings praises of thanksgiving	2:36–38	Anna praises God and gives thanks
2:20	Eli blesses Samuel's parents	2:34	Simeon blesses Jesus' parents

2:26	Refrain A: "Now the boy Samuel continued to grow both in stature and in favor with the LORD and with men" (RSV; see also 2:21).	2:40	Refrain A': "And the child grew and became strong; he was filled with wisdom, and the grace of God was upon him" (see also Luke 1:80).
3:1–18	ministry in the temple (without parents) and a message to Eli the priest	2:41–51	visit to the temple (without parents) and discussion with religious teachers
3:19	Refrain B: "And Samuel grew, and the LORD was with him and let none of his words fall to the ground" (RSV).	2:52	Refrain B': "And Jesus increased in wisdom and in stature, and in favor with God and man" (RSV).

In some ways Anna parallels the boy Samuel. Just as Samuel does not actually enter the temple (i.e., the tabernacle) permanently until he is weaned (1 Sam. 1:22–24), so Anna does not, apparently, attach herself to the temple continually until her widowhood (Luke 2:36–37). As Samuel remained in the temple communing with God, so Anna for many years **worshiped** God **night and day, fasting and praying** (v. 37). Although Luke does not record a single word of what Anna spoke, he does tell us that **she gave thanks to God and spoke about the child to all who were looking forward to the redemption of Jerusalem** (v. 38). Even this aspect of Anna's activity recalls Samuel's ministry in bringing Israel relief from oppression by the Philistines (see 1 Sam. 7:3–13).

Verses 39–40 bring the presentation narrative to a close. **When Joseph and Mary had done everything required by the Law of the Lord, they returned to Galilee to their own town of Nazareth** (v. 39). Just as John "grew and became strong in spirit" (1:80), so in a similar way Luke describes Jesus (see the Samuel parallels above).

2:41–52 / Although this is not exactly an infancy story, it is apparent that Luke intends this episode of the finding of Jesus in the temple to be part of his larger narrative. This episode concludes with a refrain (v. 52) similar to those closing other episodes within the infancy narratives (1:80; 2:40). This incident serves as a transition from the infancy to the adulthood of Jesus.

It also illustrates Jesus' growth and wisdom (2:40). The opening verse not only sets the stage for the episode itself, but once again underscores the faithfulness and piety of Joseph and Mary. Seen against the Passover celebration, Jesus' teaching in the temple may very well anticipate his final teaching in the temple at Passover time during Passion Week (see Luke 21:37).

The whole incident raises a number of difficult questions if scrutinized primarily from a historical and psychological perspective. For example, how could the boy Jesus be overlooked for an entire day (v. 44); and where did Jesus sleep for the three nights that he was alone (v. 46)? Furthermore, with his great wisdom, why did he not have more consideration for his parents? But Luke has no interest in answering these questions, since they have nothing to do with the point of this narrative. The point of the narrative has to do with Jesus' sense of mission and his preparation for it. This is most evident in the questions he asks his relieved (and possibly perturbed) parents: **"Why were you searching for me? . . . Didn't you know I had to be in my Father's house?"** (v. 49). This incident, like the visit of the shepherds (vv. 16–20), was **treasured** by Mary **in her heart** (v. 51). With the refrain of v. 52 (see the Samuel parallels above) the narrative of Jesus' infancy, as did that of John's (1:80), draws to a close. When Jesus next appears on the scene it will be as an adult ready to begin his public ministry.

Additional Notes §4

2:1 / **Caesar Augustus**: Caesar Augustus brought an end to the bitter Roman civil wars, and his long reign (27 B.C. to A.D. 14) brought peace and prosperity throughout the empire (see Fitzmyer, pp. 399–400).

2:1–2 / **census**: Numerous difficulties attend Luke's reference to the **first census** (v. 2) ordered by **Caesar Augustus** (v. 1) when **Quirinius was governor of Syria** (v. 2). The difficulties may be summarized as follows (for a fuller discussion see Marshall, pp. 100–104; Fitzmyer, pp. 401–5): (1) According to Matt. 2:1 Jesus was born in the days of Herod. Since it is an established fact that Herod died in 4 B.C., Jesus' birth must have been prior to Herod's death (but not much before according to Jesus' age in Luke 3:1, 23 and according to Matt. 2:15, which says that Herod died while Jesus was still quite young). The problem is that there is no record of a census ordered by Augustus during this time. It is hard to imagine that in all of the ancient histories there would not be a single reference to an empirewide census. (2) There is, however, a record of a census ordered during the time when Quirinius was governor of Syria, but this was in A.D. 6–7, after the exile of the tetrarch Archelaus. It has been suggested that perhaps Quirinius was governor of Syria on another earlier occasion, but this provides no real solution since Quintilius Varus was governor the last two years of Herod's life (6–4 B.C.) and Sentius Saturninus the three years before that (9–16 B.C.). We do not know who was governor during 3–2 B.C., but since that would be after Herod's death, this period offers no solution. An inscription fragment has often been cited to show that Quirinius was governor of Syria on an earlier occasion (see Marshall, p. 103), but this fragment does not actually cite Quirinius by name, nor does it necessarily point to a second governorship of Syria. Furthermore, the suggestion that Quirinius was a sort of military governor of Syria alongside the (civil) governor Saturninus is sheer guesswork, and its date is really too early to be of much help. (3) In Acts 5:36–37 Luke mentions two messianic claimants. Judas the Galilean, we are told, arose in the days of the census. This is surely a reference to the census of Luke 2:1–2.

Josephus (*War* 7.253) tells of an uprising against the census and the taxation resulting from it, led by this Judas of Galilee during the rule of Quirinius. The Acts passage tends to confirm the suspicion that Luke 2:2 does indeed refer to the census that was taken during the rule of Quirinius in A.D. 6–7, about ten years or so after the birth of Jesus. However, the major problem in Acts 5:36–37 is the reference to Theudas (v. 36) and the statement in v. 37 that *after* him Judas arose. According to Josephus (*Antiquities* 20.97), Theudas led a revolt when Fadus was governor (A.D. 44). If Josephus is correct (and he is not always reliable) and if he is referring to the same Theudas mentioned in Acts 5:36 (in which case Josephus and Luke are clearly at odds), then it may be that Luke is confused (or better, that his sources were unclear and/or incomplete). However, since in many other cases Luke proves to be much more reliable than Josephus, it may be wise in this case to suspend judgment.

There is some evidence (Marshall, p. 104) that because of strained relations between Augustus and Herod in the latter's later years, the Roman emperor demanded that Herod's subjects swear an oath of allegiance. After Herod's death, and after the relatively brief and incompetent rule of his son Archelaus as tetrarch of Judea, a census was ordered. Luke could have viewed the entire sequence as a single episode, or at least as culminating in the census that was ordered in the days when Quirinius was governor. Furthermore, Luke's peculiar usage of the word "first" (*prōtos*) may support this line of reasoning. As is noted by most commentators, Luke's use of the word "first" is grammatically awkward. Marshall has suggested (p. 104) that perhaps Luke means "before" (a legitimate meaning for *prōtos*) in the sense of "this was the census before [the one issued when] Quirinius was governor of Syria" in an effort to differentiate between the census to which he refers in 2:1–2 and the better known census taken A.D. 6–7. This solution, however, is troubled by the reference to the census in Acts 5:37 (where Luke implies no such differentiation) and by the proposed translation of 2:2, which admittedly renders *prōtos* in an unusual way. Perhaps Marshall's conclusion is the most judicious: "No solution is free from difficulty, and the problem can hardly be solved without the discovery of fresh evidence" (p. 104).

2:5 / **pledged to be married**: This word may be translated literally as "engaged" (NASB), "betrothed" (RSV), or even as "married." In fact, some manuscripts state that Mary was "his wife" (KJV reads "his espoused wife"). Even if Luke meant that Mary was now married to Joseph, the advancement of her pregnancy far beyond the time that had elapsed since their marriage would have been obvious to all in Nazareth and possibly, if not probably, would have led to harsh criticisms and insults. (That such may have been the case in the years following his birth may be in view in the critical remarks found in John 8:41.) Whether Mary was married or still engaged, it is not difficult to understand why she, despite being near to giving birth, would have preferred to accompany Joseph.

2:7 / **She wrapped him in cloths**: Compare Wisd. 7:4: "I was nursed with care in swaddling cloths" (RSV); see also Ezek. 16:4.

2:9 / **the glory of the Lord**: A common OT expression; see Exod. 16:7.
shone: The appearance of God is often associated with light; see Exod. 24:17.

2:11 / **Today**: See Luke 4:21; 5:26; 12:28; 13:32, 33; 19:5, 9; 22:34, 61; 23:43.
Christ the Lord: Some manuscripts read "the Lord's Christ," as in Luke 2:26. But it is likely that the reading read by the majority of manuscripts, the reading which underlies the NIV, is the original one; for further discussion see Leaney, pp. 95–96. "Lord" does not always imply deity, for at times it denotes nothing more than "sir." But when used in the absolute sense, the sense it appears to have in Luke 2:11, it refers to deity.

2:12 / **This will be a sign to you**: Compare Exod. 3:12; 2 Kings 19:29.

2:13 / **a great company of the heavenly host**: Compare 1 Kings 22:19.

2:14 / **Glory to God in the highest**: Although an exact equivalent of this phrase does not occur in the OT, there are parallels in the Apocrypha: 1 Esdras 9:8 ("give glory to the Lord"); Bar. 2:18 ("will ascribe to thee glory . . . O Lord").
peace: The Messiah was to bring peace; Isa. 52:7; 57:19; Leaney, p. 96.
The translation, **to men on whom his favor rests**, is to be preferred to the well-known translation found in the KJV, which is based on a

faulty reading in some late manuscripts: "good will toward men." There are parallels to this expression in the Dead Sea Scrolls (see Fitzmyer, pp. 411–12).

2:22 / **When the time of their purification according to the Law of Moses had been completed**: Luke's "their" is somewhat misleading, for, strictly speaking, this would be a time of purification for the mother *only* (and not also for the father or for the infant). For seven days the woman is unclean and for 33 days more she remains confined (Lev. 12:2–8; see Lachs, p. 31).

Jerusalem: The name of this historic city occurs in the Lucan writings more frequently than in any other book in the NT. Tradition has identified the city with Salem; see Gen. 14:18; *HBD*, pp. 463–73.

2:23 / **Every firstborn male**: Lit. "every male opening the womb." This verse is a paraphrase of Exod. 13:2. Luke would have the reader understand, of course, that Jesus' dedication transcends the routine dedications of all other Jewish firstborn sons.

2:25 / **consolation of Israel**: Simeon's hope is grounded in the scriptural promises of the "restoration of the kingdom to Israel" (Tiede, p. 75; see Isa. 40:1; 49:6; 61:2).

2:29–32 / The Nunc Dimittis, like the Magnificat (1:46–55) and the Benedictus (1:68–79), also echoes various scriptures:

2:29 / **dismiss your servant in peace**: LXX Gen. 15:15; cf. Acts 15:33.

2:30–31 / **For my eyes have seen your salvation, which you have prepared in the sight of all people**: Isa. 40:5 (see Luke 3:6); 52:10. Luke's word for "salvation" (*sōtērion*) is relatively rare in the NT, with three of its four occurrences in Luke–Acts. Tannehill (pp. 40–42) notes that Luke borrowed it from the LXX (as seen in the evangelist's citation of Isa. 40:5) and probably wanted the reader to understand that Simeon was one of the first to see God's salvation, a salvation which, thanks to the apostolic mission, the whole Roman Empire would eventually see.

2:32 / **a light for revelation to the Gentiles**: Isa. 42:6; 49:6; 60:1. Isa. 49:6 will be quoted later in Acts 13:47; 26:23.

and for glory to your people Israel: LXX Isa. 46:13.

2:34 / **the falling and rising of many in Israel**: J. T. Sanders (p. 161) correctly believes that the reference here is to the whole story of Luke–Acts. But he is incorrect when he suggests that Acts 1–5 reflects Israel's "rise," while Acts 6–28 reflects Israel's "fall." Not only has he unjustifiably reversed the sequence of falling and rising, it is unlikely in the first place that Luke attaches any temporal sense whatsoever to these words. It is more likely that he simply means that some will fall and some will rise (see Schweizer, p. 57), perhaps in the sense of reversal (see Tannehill, p. 29; and on p. 29, n. 37 Tannehill, in reference to Luke 2:34, refers to "upheaval *within* Israel"). By implication Israel will be divided in its response to Jesus (see Acts 28:24–25).

2:36 / **a prophetess, Anna**: "Anna" is the Greek form of the Hebrew name Hannah. It has already been noted that the story of Hannah's giving birth to and raising Samuel in 1 Samuel 1–2 contributed to Luke's infancy narrative (see commentary and notes on 1:46–55 above). It is interesting to note that according to Jewish tradition, Hannah, Samuel's mother, was a prophetess (b. *Megilla* 14a; as noted by Lachs, pp. 32–33).

2:42 / **Twelve**: There was no requirement to participate in religious activities as an adult until the age of thirteen. By showing Jesus' participation in religious activities before that age, Luke again underscores the piety and righteousness of the holy family. But there may be more to it. Lachs (p. 34) plausibly suggests that Luke may have been influenced by the tradition that Samuel began his prophetic activity at the age of twelve (see Josephus, *Antiquities* 5.348). This could very well be the case in light of the deliberate and frequent allusions to the story of Samuel's birth and upbringing (v. 40 above echoes parts of 1 Sam. 2:21, 26, while the Magnificat [Luke 1:46–55] is modeled after Hannah's song of thanksgiving in 1 Sam. 2:1–10). For a list of other twelve-year-old prodigies see Schweizer, p. 63.

2:46 / **sitting among the teachers**: Late apocryphal legends (e.g., *The Infancy Gospel of Thomas* 19:2) tell of Jesus in the temple or in the synagogue overwhelming the teachers of the law with his profound knowledge and wisdom.

§5 The Preaching of John the Baptist (Luke 3:1–20)

3:1–6 / Luke relates the appearance of John the Baptist to the political and religious authorities of the time, just as he did in the infancy narratives of John (1:5) and Jesus (2:1–2). (For details regarding these authorities see notes below.) The second half of v. 2 brings John back into the story: **The word of God came to John son of Zechariah in the desert** (see 1:80). The expression is reminiscent of the calls that God extended to the OT prophets (Isa. 38:4; Jer. 13:3) and is actually borrowed from the LXX version of Jer. 1:1–2 ("the word of God came to Jeremiah son of Hilkiah"). From this we may infer that Luke views John on the same level as the OT prophets (which is in keeping with John's inclusion with the prophets in Luke 16:16). Now John is able to begin his ministry of preparing Israel for the appearance of the Messiah (as foretold in 1:15–17).

In Luke 3:3 John's preaching begins on a note significantly different from Matthew's account. Unlike Matt. 3:2, where reference to repentance and the nearness of the kingdom is the first thing uttered by John, in Luke the reference is to **repentance** and **forgiveness of sins**, with no mention of the kingdom. (Even though in Mark's account neither does John make reference to the kingdom, Jesus does so right at the beginning of his ministry in 1:15.) By way of contrast, in Luke's account the emphasis of John's preaching falls more heavily on the ethical requirements, though there are eschatological and messianic elements (see 3:8–14). Another unique feature in Luke's account is the longer quotation from Isaiah. Whereas Matthew (3:3) and Mark (1:2–3) quote only Isa. 40:3 (Mark also includes a portion of Mal. 3:1), Luke (3:4–6) extends the quotation to include Isa. 40:4–5 (see note below). The reason for this longer quotation is found in the last verse of the Isaiah passage: **And all mankind shall see God's salvation!** (Luke 3:6). The call to repentance, seen more clearly in the first part of the Isaiah quotation (**Prepare the way for the**

Lord . . .), now has a universal application ("all mankind"), a major theme in Lucan theology (see Introduction). By extending this quotation Luke verifies that at the very inauguration of the messianic era the call for repentance and preparation for the Messiah is not extended to the Jews only.

3:7–17 / Because of his interest in matters pertaining to the law of Moses and the oral traditions of the Jewish teachers, Matthew (3:7a) states that "many of the Pharisees and Sadducees" came to John's baptism. By introducing John's speech this way (which begins at 3:7b), the sharp words of condemnation (**"You brood of vipers!"**) are directed against Israel's religious leadership. Luke, however, refers to **the crowds** (3:7a) and thereby makes John's call for repentance more general in application. John wants the people to **produce fruit in keeping with repentance** (v. 8a). He is not interested in a change in theology or in religious rituals but in a changed way of living. His statement in v. 8 warns the people that physical descent from **Abraham** is no substitute for genuine repentance and a changed life. The implication (seen in v. 9) is that failure to make a sincere change will result in judgment. John reminds them that **out of these stones God can raise up children for Abraham** (v. 8b). If God can create the world out of nothing, if he can create a nation out of two aged and infertile people (Sarah and Abraham), then God can create for himself a people who will love and obey him. John's words strike at the very heart of the presumption held by many of the religious of Israel, and because of this they provide a fitting introduction for Jesus, whose teachings will likewise explode cherished but erroneous views.

John's statement that the ax is already at the root of the trees (v. 9a) not only points to the urgency of the moment, but recalls popular prophetic imagery in which judgment is also in view (see Isa. 6:13; 10:33–34; Jer. 6:6); furthermore, it anticipates similar aspects of Jesus' teaching (Luke 13:6–9). The warning that the **tree that does not produce good fruit will be cut down and thrown into the fire** (v. 9b) is the same warning as in v. 17 in which the Messiah (see v. 15) **will burn up the chaff with unquenchable fire** (see also John 15:1–6). These grim warnings were readily understood, and so **the crowd** asked, **"What should we do then?"** (v. 10). John replies by giving two specific examples that illustrate the general principle of compassion and generosity: providing food and clothing to those without (v. 11).

This reply, as those in vv. 13–14, reflects Luke's concern with the use of wealth and possessions. The question of the **tax collectors** furthers the development of this theme (v. 12). Often dishonest and rich and viewed as a collaborator with Israel's Gentile oppressors, the tax collector was one of the most despised persons in Israel (see Luke 18:9–14; 19:1–10). Because they acquired much of their wealth by gouging their fellow citizens, John tells them to **collect** only what is **required** (v. 13; see note below). Others who were in position to take advantage of people were the **soldiers** (i.e., Jewish policemen), who could use their authority and power to their own advantage (v. 14). John tells them to **be content with** their **pay**. Interestingly, both groups (i.e., the tax collectors and the soldiers) have problems with greed and are in positions of authority that enable them to satisfy this greed. All of John's answers contribute significantly to Luke's views about possessions and wealth. According to Luke, the evidence of true repentance is chiefly seen in the ethics of contentment and generosity.

The theme shifts in vv. 15–17 from ethics to messianic expectation. **All** of the crowd were **wondering in their hearts if John might possibly be the Christ** (v. 15), which leads very naturally to the Baptist's explanation of his role as forerunner of the Messiah. Although his is a baptism of **water**, the baptism of the Messiah will be one of **Holy Spirit and fire** (v. 16). The mention of fire in v. 17 assures us that the fire of v. 16 has a sense of judgment (and not, e.g., like the reference to the "tongues of fire" of Pentecost in Acts 2:3; see note below). John is saying that those prepared and ready to receive the Messiah will experience a baptism of the Holy Spirit, but those who refuse him will undergo a baptism of fire.

Verse 18 is transitional; Luke summarizes the Baptist's ministry and sets the stage for his imprisonment. John's urging the people to repent leads to his conflict with Herod Antipas. Verse 19 explains why **Herod** found John's preaching offensive. In condemning Herod's marriage to his former sister-in-law, John no doubt invoked the command of Lev. 18:16: "You must have no intercourse with your brother's wife, since she belongs to your brother" (Fitzmyer's literal translation, pp. 477–78). Embarrassed and outraged, **Herod** had **John** put **in prison** (v. 20) and eventually had him executed (implied in Luke 9:7–9, but not actually reported anywhere in Luke). Josephus in his *Antiquities* (18.116–117) states that Herod had John the Baptist imprisoned and executed before his popular ministry could lead to an uprising. According to Josephus, Herod feared that the people would regard John as a messianic figure and revolt. The people's speculation about John's identity in v. 15 supports this suggestion. The reasons given by Josephus and Luke for Herod's actions are not necessarily contradictory but may in fact complement one another. The real reason Herod did away with John could be the reason cited by Luke, while the excuse cited by Josephus may represent the "official" justification (i.e., "national security" required the elimination of a potential trouble-maker).

Although John's ministry was apparently quite brief, it was a ministry of immense importance and one, too, that had a lasting impact, as can be seen by the numerous references to him and to this ministry throughout the Lucan writings (Luke 5:33; 7:19, 22, 24; 9:7, 9; 16:16; 20:6; Acts 1:5, 22; 11:16; 13:24–25; 19:3–4).

Additional Notes §5

3:1–2a / In the fifteenth year of the reign of Tiberius Caesar: **Tiberius** became co-regent (i.e., co-ruler) with Augustus his father A.D. 11 or 12. If Luke means the **fifteenth year** since the co-regency, then the year that John appeared would be A.D. 26/27, when Jesus was about thirty years old (Luke 3:23), since he was born around 4 B.C. (see note on 2:1–2 above). Another attractive aspect about this date is that in all probability A.D. 26/27 was a Jubilee year (i.e., every fiftieth year when debts were canceled; see Lev. 25:10). Some scholars suspect that Jesus' announcement of the "acceptable year of the Lord" (Luke 4:19) may have been intended to be an allusion to the year of Jubilee (see Marshall, p. 184, and commentary and notes on 4:14–30 below). If this is correct, then the A.D. 26/27 date receives added support. The chief difficulty with this date, however, is that normally the reigns of rulers are not dated back to co-regencies but to the year when the regent becomes sole ruler (see Fitzmyer, p. 455). Since Tiberius did not become sole ruler until A.D. 14, Luke's date may refer to A.D. 29 (or 28, if 14 is counted as the first year). For a fuller discussion of the problems of dating see Harold W. Hoehner, *Chronological Aspects of the Life of Christ* (Grand Rapids: Zondervan, 1977), pp. 29–44.

Pontius Pilate was governor of Judea: After the exile of Archelaus in A.D. 6, **Judea** became a Roman province under the authority of Roman governors (or "prefects"; "procurator" not being used until after the time of Pilate). **Pilate** served as **governor** from A.D. 26 to 36, during which time he frequently outraged his Jewish subjects by forcing Roman customs and religion upon them (see Josephus, *War* 2.169–177; *Antiquities* 18.55–59). See also Luke 13:1 where reference is made to "the Galileans whose blood Pilate had mixed with their sacrifices." It was by Pilate's authority, of course, that Jesus was crucified (see Luke 23:1–7, 13–25). Pilate's rule ended in A.D. 36 when Tiberius had him recalled. See *HBD*, pp. 796–98.

Herod tetrarch of Galilee: **Herod** refers to Herod Antipas, son of Herod the Great (see Luke 1:5). When his father died (4 B.C.) Herod Antipas became a tetrarch ("ruler of a fourth-part"). He ruled Galilee and Perea until deposed and exiled by Emperor Caligula in A.D. 39 for asserting his right to be called "king" (see Mark 6:14 where Herod Antipas is called "king"). This is the Herod before whom Jesus was accused and mocked (see Luke 23:8–12).

his brother Philip tetrarch of Iturea and Trachonitis: **Philip** also received a fourth of his father's kingdom and ruled from 4 B.C. to A.D. 34. After his death his realm became part of the Roman province of Syria. Luke's reference is vague since it was (and still is) unclear just exactly what territory made up Philip's realm. (Josephus refers to the districts of Philip twice, but his lists do not agree completely; see *Antiquities* 17.317–320 and 17.188–192.) According to Mark 6:17 and Matt. 14:3, Herodias was apparently the widow of Philip, but Luke says only "his brother's wife" (see Luke 3:19), possibly because he was aware that Josephus (*Antiquities* 18.109–115) states that Herodias had been married to another Herod and not to Philip (see Fitzmyer, p. 477). With reference to Philip, Marshall states (p. 134): "He was reckoned the best of the Herodian rulers."

Lysanius tetrarch of Abilene: Years ago some commentators felt that Luke had confused someone with a Lysanius who had ruled over parts of Syria decades earlier and who had been executed by Mark Antony in 36 B.C. Furthermore, it was argued that it was inappropriate of Luke to refer to rulers other than the four sons of Herod the Great as "tetrarch." It has since been learned, however, that "tetrarch" had come to mean "ruler" in a general sense and could be applied to persons other than the four original tetrarchs of the Herodian family. Moreover, Josephus makes a few vague references to a Lysanius to whom belonged a "tetrarchy" (*Antiquities* 20.137–140) and who ruled the city of "Abila," the capital city of Abilene (*Antiquities* 19.97–99; 20.137–140; see also *War* 2.214–217; 2.247–249). The question was finally settled decisively in favor of Luke's accuracy when an inscription from ancient Abilene dating from A.D. 15 to 30 was found containing a reference to "Lysanius the tetrarch" (Fitzmyer, pp. 457–58; Ellis, p. 88; Marshall, p. 134). Nevertheless, why Luke mentions this particular ruler, one who would play no role whatsoever in the history of Jesus and the early church, remains unclear.

the high priesthood of Annas and Caiaphas: Although during the ministry of John and of Jesus **Caiaphas** was actually the high priest (A.D. 18–36)—for there was only one high priest at a time—**Annas** had been a high priest previously (A.D. 6–15), was Caiaphas' father-in-law, and probably still exercised considerable influence (that Jesus was brought to him [John 18:13] is evidence of his influence). It may have been customary out of respect to refer to former high priests as "high priest" (as is Annas in John 18:13, 19; Acts 4:6; see Fitzmyer, p. 458). Luke mentions both probably because supreme religious authority was shared by both. See *HBD*, pp. 31, 149.

One final note regarding 3:1–2a is in order. Dating the year of John's call by reference to the rule of various authorities is based upon an OT pattern that further underscores John's place among the prophets (see Isa. 6:1; Jer. 1:1–2; Ezek. 1:1–3).

3:2b–6 / **John son of Zechariah in the desert**: There are several interesting points of comparison between **John** and the Essenes (i.e., members of the Dead Sea community located near Wadi Qumran): (1) Both the Essenes and John ministered **in the desert**; the Essenes near the Dead Sea, John near the Jordan River (see note on Luke 1:80 above). (2) Both the Essenes and John practiced baptism as a rite signifying cleansing from "sin" (so John) or "evildoing" (so the *Rule of the Community* [1QS] 5.13–14). John's call for baptism centered around the demand for repentance and, although not employing the exact terminology, the Essene practice probably carried similar meaning. Fitzmyer (pp. 459–60) notes that from 150 B.C. to A.D. 250 there were numerous Jewish and Christian baptismal groups in Palestine. (3) Both the Essenes and John eagerly looked forward to God's intervention in human affairs. In the Gospels and Acts John's hope revolves exclusively around the Messiah who is to follow; but among the Essenes there is no clear and uniform concept of messianic expectation beyond the general fact that they awaited vindication and redemption. (4) In introducing the quotation from Isa. 40:3–5 Luke adds (v. 4) the word **book** (not found in Mark 1:2 or Matt. 3:3). This same quotation formula is found verbatim in several Essene writings (for examples see Fitzmyer, p. 460). (5) Not only is the quotation of Isa. 40:3–5 (or 40:3 in Matthew and Mark) linked with John's ministry, but the Essenes themselves cite this OT passage as justification for their peculiar lifestyle. These parallels make it reasonable to suppose that John may have had some contact with the Essenes prior to his public ministry (Josephus himself in *Life* 2 claims to have spent some time with the Essenes). His call to preach a baptism of repentance to all of Israel would, however, signal a break with the Essenes who were reclusive and exclusivistic.

the way: Lit. "the way" or "the road" (from *hē hodos*). This part of the Isaiah quotation may have held special significance for Luke, who frequently refers to obedience to the gospel as following the "Way" (see Luke 20:21; Acts 9:2; 16:17; 18:26; 19:9, 23; 22:4; 24:14, 22).

all mankind: This does not imply the exclusion of the Jewish people. On the contrary, the expression is universal and inclusive. Jews and Gentiles alike will see God's salvation. On the meaning of Isa. 40:3–5 in Luke and the NT see Klyne R. Snodgrass, "Streams of Tradition Emerging from Isaiah 40.1-5 and their Adaptation in the New Testament," *JSNT* 8 (1980), pp. 24–45.

shall see God's salvation: Recall Simeon's praise: "my eyes have seen your salvation, which you have prepared in the sight of all people" (2:30–31). Simeon was among the first to see God's salvation. John now announces that eventually all people will see it.

3:7 / crowds: According to Josephus, who also uses the word "crowds" with reference to John (*Antiquities* 18.118), the Baptist was very popular with the people.

"You brood of vipers!": The viper was a deadly snake in Palestine. Astonishingly, despite calling people such names, John was popular. Of course, since he was regarded as a prophet, John's colorful language would have been expected (see Isa. 59:5; for examples of the names that Jesus sometimes called his enemies see Luke 13:32; especially Matt. 23:14–33).

3:8 / Produce fruit: Lit. "make fruits." The figurative expression is appropriate in light of v. 9. Luke has the plural "fruits" instead of "fruit" as in Matthew, probably because he is thinking of the various examples that will be given in 3:11–14.

3:11 / John's ethical commands in this verse are quite similar to those found in Isa. 58:7.

3:12–13 / The paying of taxes (or tolls) frequently led to violence (e.g., the revolt of Judas the Galilean mentioned in Acts 5:37). **Tax collectors** were especially loathed because they were notoriously dishonest and were viewed as traitors and lackeys working for either Rome (which ruled Judea directly) or Herod (who ruled Galilee directly; see Luke 5:30; 7:34; 15:1 where "tax collectors and sinners" are considered virtually synonymous). For further discussion see John R. Donahue, "Tax Collectors and Sinners: An Attempt at Identification," *CBQ* 33 (1971), pp. 39–61; *HBD*, p. 841.

3:14 / some soldiers: These were probably Jewish soldiers, in Herod's or Rome's hire, not Roman soldiers; Fitzmyer, p. 470; Tiede, p. 90.

Don't extort money . . . be content with your pay: Josephus gave similar advice to his men: "I thanked them and advised them neither to attack anyone nor to sully their hands with rapine, but to . . . be content with their rations" (*Life* 47.244; from Lachs, p. 44).

3:16 / the thongs of whose sandals I am not worthy to untie: Among Jews the sandal was often a symbol of contempt (see Luke 9:5; Acts 13:51) and the unfastening of **sandals** was the task of a slave. Thus, in strongest language John is claiming to be utterly unworthy of the one who is to follow him.

3:17 / **unquenchable fire**: This expression probably echoes Isa. 66:24, a verse that appears in Mark 9:48, and may allude to the fires of "Gehenna," the word used for hell (from the Valley of Hinnom where garbage was burned in Jesus' time and where human sacrifice had taken place many centuries before).

§6 The Baptism and Genealogy of Jesus (Luke 3:21-38)

Following John's witness to Jesus (3:1-20), Luke provides three additional witnesses to Jesus' messianic identity and mission: (1) the witness of Jesus' own baptism, at which time the heavenly voice speaks (3:21-22); (2) the witness of his genealogy, which traces Jesus back to Adam, the son of God (3:23-38); and (3) the witness of Jesus' temptation, in which the character and commitment of Jesus are tested (4:1-13). These components in the Lucan narrative testify to Jesus' qualifications as Messiah and to his readiness to begin his ministry. The first two witnesses are examined in this section.

3:21-22 / Luke's statement that **Jesus** was the last to be **baptized** (v. 21) is strategic. By mentioning John's imprisonment so early in the narrative, an event which Mark (6:17-18) and Matthew (14:3-4) report much later, and by leaving the impression that Jesus is the last to be baptized, Luke succeeds in making a clean break between the end of John's ministry and the beginning of Jesus' ministry. The time of the Law and the Prophets is over; now the kingdom of God (which in Luke's account John does not proclaim) can be preached (i.e., by Jesus, see Luke 16:16).

At the moment of Jesus' baptism **the Holy Spirit descended on him** (v. 22a). This is the "anointing" which makes Jesus Messiah (i.e., "anointed one"; see Acts 10:38 and commentary on Luke 4:14-30 below). Tiede (p. 95) notes the parallel with 1 Sam. 10:1-10: " 'Has not the LORD anointed you to be prince over his people Israel?' . . . and the spirit of God came mightily upon [Saul], and he prophesied among them" (RSV). With his anointing Jesus is prepared to face the hardships and challenges of his ministry (see Luke 4:1-13, 29-30 for examples of such challenges right at the outset of his ministry). Luke's reference to the descent of the Spirit **in bodily form like a dove** (only Luke has "bodily form," see Mark 1:10; Matt. 3:16) may emphasize that the descent of the Holy Spirit was *real*, not visionary. Although the words spoken by the **voice** from **heaven** (v. 22b) may allude to a royal enthronement psalm (i.e., Ps. 2:7; some mss. read "today I have begotten thee"), a feature which might signify the installation of the newly anointed Jesus as king (see Acts 13:33 where Ps. 2:7 is actually quoted in reference to Jesus), the words may also allude to Isa. 42:1, one of the Servant Song passages of Isaiah. (On the significance of the Servant Songs for Luke's understanding of Jesus see commentary and notes on Luke 4:14-30 below.) The voice provides heavenly confirmation of Jesus' appointment as Messiah (see note below). Fitzmyer (p. 483) suggests that just as the voice at the baptism precedes the Galilean ministry, so the voice (which utters the same words) at the transfiguration (see Luke 9:35) precedes the journey to Jerusalem: "In both scenes the heavenly identification stresses the relation of Jesus to his Father, as an important phase of his earthly career begins."

Before leaving this part of Luke's narrative we may inquire why Jesus was baptized at all, especially since John's was a baptism of repentance and forgiveness of sins (3:3). That Jesus' baptism came to be viewed with some uneasiness in the Gospel tradition is seen in the gradual distancing that takes place between John and Jesus. Whereas Mark simply states that Jesus was "baptized by John" (1:9), Matthew has the Baptist protest that he is unworthy to baptize Jesus (3:13-15). Luke omits explicit reference to baptism *by John* (3:21) and has John imprisoned at (or before?) the very beginning of Jesus' ministry (3:19-20). Finally, in the Gospel of John the baptism of Jesus is omitted altogether, though the Baptist does witness the descent of the Spirit (1:29-34).

Another awkward aspect of the Baptist tradition is that not all of his disciples followed Jesus, and there is evidence that there was some rivalry between early Christians and the followers of John. (Acts 19:1-7 may represent Luke's attempt at reconciling the Baptists and Christians.) However, because Jesus is anointed with the Spirit at the time of his baptism (and because of the close association of baptism with the Spirit in early Christianity, see 1 Cor. 12:13), the evangelists are reluctant to set it aside. It is probable that as part of his preparation for ministry, Jesus himself had been an actual follower of John. Prior to his anointing he was still in training (as he was as a young boy listening to and asking questions of the teachers in the temple, Luke 2:46-47). His baptism need not be interpreted as an acknowledgment of sin, but rather as a declaration of his commitment and readiness to begin his work. (The familiar explanations that Jesus' baptism reveals his humanity, in that he identifies himself with humankind, or that his baptism symbolizes his taking the sin of the world upon himself [a view which may have some merit in interpreting the account in the Gospel of John], are scarcely supported by the Synoptic Gospel accounts.)

3:23–38 / Before launching into his account of Jesus' temptation and ministry Luke inserts, almost like a footnote (see Marshall, p. 157), the genealogy of Jesus (see note below). Several difficulties attend Luke's genealogy of Jesus. (Matthew's genealogy offers its own problems.) It would be far beyond the scope and purpose of this commentary to analyze and solve these problems. For our purposes four major features are worth mentioning, primarily in comparison with the Matthean genealogy (see Matt. 1:2–16). (1) Whereas Matthew's list of names *descends* from Abraham to Jesus, Luke's list *ascends* from Jesus through Adam to God. (2) Because Luke's list includes names from the period before Abraham it is much longer than Matthew's list (77 names to 42). Even his list from Abraham to Jesus is longer than Matthew's (56 names to 42). This difference is in large part explained by Matthew's scheme of "fourteen generations" between major persons and events, a scheme which requires only a select list (see Matt. 1:17). (3) Even where overlap occurs (i.e., from Abraham to Jesus), only about half the names cited by Matthew and Luke are held in common. (4) Many of the Lucan names, especially in the period between Adam and Abraham, are not found in OT genealogies or in any known genealogical records. Where Luke, or the tradition before him, obtained these names is completely unknown.

The proposal made some 500 years ago (Annius of Viterbo, ca. 1490) that Matthew has given us Joseph's genealogy, while Luke has given Mary's, provides no real solutions to the problems enumerated above but only creates new ones. I would suggest that although we cannot completely explain (or harmonize) the Matthean and Lucan lists, at least not with the available sources, we should assume that both Matthew and Luke (or the tradition before them) made use of *real* records and registries. (For Mat-

thew, of course, the OT provided most of the names.) Invented
genealogies would serve no useful purpose and, being open to
critical scrutiny of contemporaries, could have become a cause
for embarrassment. Had Jesus' genealogical records been una-
vailable, then in all probability Matthew and Luke would have
been content without them (as were Mark and John).

But why does Luke provide us with a genealogy, and why
does he locate it at this point in his Gospel? The answer to both
parts of this question appears in the last (human) name on his
list: **Adam** (v. 38). Because of his universalistic emphasis, Luke
wishes to trace the lineage of Jesus back to the first human being,
the father of *all* nations. When Luke refers to the promises made
to Abraham he probably has in mind the blessings that will result for the Gentiles as well as for Israel (see Gen. 22:18 and commentary on 1:55, 73 above), but since the idea of Abraham as
father of the Jewish race was so entrenched (and so presumed
upon—remember the words of the Baptist in Luke 3:8), it would
not have been in the best interests of his theology to culminate
his genealogy of Jesus in Abraham. By going back to Adam, Luke
finds *biblical* support for his presentation of Jesus as Savior of all
humankind. Moreover, the title "son of man," so popular in Luke's
Gospel (Jesus is called "son of man" in Luke twice as often as
in the other Synoptic Gospels), may have suggested the propriety
of including Adam's name in the first place, since '*ādām* in Hebrew literally means "man." Therefore, Luke's genealogy concludes appropriately, **the son of Adam** (or "man").

This word-play explains why Luke places the genealogy
where he does and why he arranges it in ascending order. Almost
certainly he wishes to draw a contrasting parallel between Adam
and Jesus, particularly with regard to their respective temptations.
Whereas Adam, the first **son of God** (v. 38), fell into sin when
tempted by the devil (Gen. 3:1–7; the "serpent" was understood
by early Jews and Christians as the devil, see Rev 12:9; 20:2), Jesus
the "son of man/Adam" (and "Son of God"; see Luke 4:3, 9), did
not (see commentary on 4:1–13 below). Although it is not wise,
nor in this case really necessary, to read Paul's Adam/Christ typology into Luke (see Rom. 5:12–21), the ideas are quite similar
and probably do have common roots.

Luke sees in Jesus' baptism and anointing (3:21–22) and
in his genealogy (3:23–38, with the emphasis on v. 38) Jesus'

preparation and validation for ministry. Jesus has been prepared
(by the anointing of the Spirit) and validated (by the heavenly
voice and by his genealogy), but now he must prove that he is
truly qualified. The subsequent temptation narrative offers such
proof.

Additional Notes §6

3:21 / Both Mark (1:10) and Matthew (3:16) state that
"immediately" after Jesus emerges from the waters of baptism the "Spirit
descended," thus linking the baptism very closely to the descent of the
Spirit. Luke, however, breaks this link by inserting the phrase, **as he was
praying**. This is yet another indication that Luke, as are Matthew and
John in their own ways, is trying to play down Jesus' relation to or dependence upon the Baptist. Luke simply tells us that Jesus was baptized
(perhaps by John, perhaps not), and then (later), while he prayed, the
heavens opened and the Spirit descended. Luke possibly sees a parallel
here with the apostles who pray and shortly thereafter receive the Spirit
(see Acts 1:14; 2:1–4).

Jesus was baptized too: Some evidence suggests that early Christians found Jesus' baptism somewhat embarrassing, either because it implied that Jesus, like his fellow Israelites, needed to repent, or because
it implied that Jesus was in some sense subordinate to John. All four
of the NT Gospels give evidence of this sensitivity: In Mark 1:7–8 the
Baptist freely acknowledges his unworthiness in comparison to Jesus;
in Matt. 3:14–15 the Baptist expresses his wish to be baptized by Jesus;
in John 1:29–34 the Baptist hails Jesus as the "Lamb of God" upon whom
he saw the Spirit descend; and in Luke 3:21 the Baptist is dropped from
the scene altogether; we are not told that he baptized Jesus. Indeed, according to v. 20 John has already been imprisoned, and therefore probably did not baptize Jesus. This same concern over the implications of
Jesus' baptism shows up in later Christian gospels. For example, in the
Gospel according to the Hebrews, when invited by his family to join them
in John's baptism, Jesus asks: "What have I committed that I should be
baptized by him, unless it be that in saying this I am in ignorance?" (from
Jerome, *Against Pelagius* 3:2, cited by Leaney, p. 237).

3:22 / **like a dove**: Talbert (p. 40) notes that the dove was a symbol of God's love for Jesus.

a voice came from heaven: The OT has examples of God speaking
to Israel, the most dramatic example being the giving of the Ten Commandments (see Exod. 19:16–20:20; Deut. 4:12). Later there developed
in Judaism the belief that God would occasionally speak from heaven
(usually like a clap of thunder, see John 12:28) in order to confirm some

important statement. Lachs (p. 47) thinks that this Christian tradition is such an instance. He cites the Tosefta, tractate *Hagiga* 2.5, as an example.

When the heavenly voice claims Jesus as **my Son, whom I love,** his adoption is not in view. That is to say, when the Spirit descended and the voice spoke, Jesus did not at that moment *become* God's Son. For Luke, Jesus was God's Son from his very conception (see 1:35). At his baptism Jesus is anointed by the Spirit, an anointing which is both symbolic (like a coronation) and enabling; while the voice does not *adopt* Jesus as God's Son, it *identifies* Jesus as God's Son (thus confirming the promise of 1:35).

There is no solid evidence that Ps. 2:7 was understood in a messianic sense prior to Christianity (Fitzmyer, p. 485). Ellis (pp. 91–92) has argued that the references to "my son the Messiah" in 2 Esdras 7:28–29 provide some evidence. But is Psalm 2 in mind? 1QSa 2.11–12 may allude to Ps. 2:7 ("when [God] begets the Messiah among them"), but the text is uncertain; see Fitzmyer, p. 339. The rabbis, however, interpret Ps. 2:7 messianically (see b. *Sukkah* 52a; *Midrash Psalms* 2.9 [on 2:7]). This is evidence that Christian interpretation of Ps. 2:7 was not entirely novel, unless we assume that the rabbis either borrowed from Christian exegesis or independently arrived at the same interpretation. Either assumption is implausible.

3:23a / Luke notes that **Jesus himself was about thirty years old when he began his ministry,** not because of his customary interest in chronology (as seen in 1:5; 2:1–2; 3:1–2), but probably because Num. 4:3 states that men must be at least thirty years of age to "enter the service, to do the work in the tent of meeting" (RSV). Luke wishes the reader to know that Jesus was the right age to begin his "service" and "work."

3:23b–38 / There really is no rule concerning where a genealogy should appear within a narrative; some precede the narrative, as does Matthew's (see also e.g., Gen. 11:10–29, where Abraham's genealogy is listed before his story begins in 11:31; perhaps Matthew followed this specific example); some appear within the narrative (e.g., although the story of Moses begins with his birth in Exod. 2:1–2, it is not until Exod. 6:14–20 that we are provided his genealogy); and some appear at the end of the narrative (e.g., Ruth 4:18–22).

Because of his own humble ancestry, Herod the Great confiscated and destroyed most of the records of Davidic descent, fearing a claim to the throne more worthy than his own. This jealousy and fear for his throne is dramatically illustrated in Matt. 2:1–18.

3:23b / **of Joseph:** We are told that Joseph was of Davidic descent (1:27; 2:4; cf. Matt. 1:20). After the infancy narrative and the story of the boy Jesus in the temple (Luke 2:41–52), Joseph drops out of the picture (though Jesus is still identified as "Joseph's son"; see Luke 4:22). It is usually assumed that Joseph died before Jesus' public ministry commenced. Joseph figures prominently in later Christian apocryphal traditions; e.g., *The Infancy Gospel of Thomas, The History of Joseph the Carpenter*, etc.

Heli: According to Matt. 1:16 Joseph's father was Jacob.

3:24–26 / **Matthat . . . Joda**: Nothing is known about these persons. They are not to be confused with biblical characters of the same name (such as Levi, Amos, or Nahum). It is not likely that Matthat is to be identified with Matthan of Matt. 1:15.

3:27 / **Joanan, the son of Rhesa**: Leaney (p. 112) and others have suggested that Rhesa is meant to be the Aramaic word for "prince" and that the original read "Prince Joanan, son of Zerubbabel." If this were true, then Hananiah in 1 Chron. 3:19 may have been the intended person. (Luke actually follows the spelling for Zerubbabel's name that is found in 1 Chron. 3:19.) Fitzmyer (p. 500), however, rightly regards this proposal as speculative and problematic. Therefore, nothing is known about Joanan or Rhesa.

Zerubbabel: The name means "offspring of Babylon," referring to his birth in the land of the Jewish captivity (Ezra 2:2). He served as governor of Judea after Cyrus' decree permitted the Jews to return to their homeland (ca. 520 B.C.).

Shealtiel: The name means "I have asked God" (for this child). Luke says that he was the son of **Neri**; Matthew (1:12) and 1 Chronicles (LXX 3:17) have him as the son of Jeconiah. Luke's Neri is unknown. Matthew's Jeconiah is the son of Jehoiakim, among the last of the Davidic rulers.

3:28–31 / **Melchi . . . Mattatha**: Nothing is known of these persons; their names appear in no known genealogical lists.

3:31 / **Nathan**: David's third son (2 Sam. 5:14; 1 Chron. 3:5). Here lies a major discrepancy between the Matthean and Lucan genealogies. Matthew (1:6) traces Jesus' line through Solomon, not through Nathan. Fitzmyer (p. 501) suspects that Luke has avoided the royal line from Solomon from to Jeconiah either because of the criticisms of some of these kings or because of prophetic oracles (e.g., Jer. 22:28–30; 36:30–31) that foretell the demise of the Davidic line.

David: Matthew's genealogy centers on David (Matt. 1:1, 6, 17). Luke, however, attaches no special significance to the famous founder of a dynasty that survived some four centuries (despite the fact that there were important references to David and the Davidic covenant in the infancy narrative; 1:32–33, 69; 2:11.) For the story of David see 1 Samuel 16–1 Kings 2 (=1 Chron. 11–29). "David" eventually came to be understood as archetype of the Messiah; see Isa. 9:6–7; 11:1–2; Ezek. 34:23, 24; 37:24, 25.

3:32 / **Jesse**: What little is known of David's father comes from 1 Sam. 16:1–20; 17:12–18. Jesse's hometown was Bethlehem (1 Sam. 16:1).

Obed: Obed is the grandfather of David; see Ruth 4:17, 21–22. He was the son of Ruth and Boaz.

Boaz: Boaz was a wealthy man of Bethlehem who married the widow Ruth from Moab; see Ruth 2–4.

Salmon: 1 Chron. 2:11.

Nahshon: Nahshon, whose sister married Aaron, assisted Moses in taking the census in the wilderness; see Exod. 6:23; Num. 1:7.

3:33 / **Amminadab**: According to 1 Chron. 2:10 and Matt. 1:4 Amminadab (see Num. 1:7) was the son of Ram (or Aram), but according to Luke (at least according to some mss.) he was the son of Admin, son of Arni (see note in NIV). Here is yet another discrepancy that is not easily explained. The NIV harmonizes Luke's genealogy by reading "son of Ram." This reading, however, is itself likely an attempt on the part of early scribes to bring about such an agreement.

Ram: Other than the appearance of his name in the genealogies of Ruth (4:19) and 1 Chronicles (2:9–10) nothing is known of this person. The Lucan genealogy probably originally read "Admin, son of Arni" (see Fitzmyer, p. 502), persons of whom absolutely nothing is known. The ms. tradition is very confused at this point.

Hezron: Hezron was a leader of the tribe of Judah (Gen. 46:12; Num. 26:21). Fitzmyer (p. 502) suspects that his name may mean "the Lean One."

Perez: Perez ("A Breach") and Zerah were twins born to Judah and Tamar (Gen. 38:29). Tamar had been the wife of one of Judah's sons.

Judah: Fourth son of Jacob (Gen. 29:35) and the patriarch after whom the tribe of Judah derives its name, a name which apparently means "Praise the Lord." For the biblical story of his life see Genesis 37–38.

3:34 / **Jacob**: Jacob, the great patriarch whose name was changed to Israel (Gen. 32:28), was the son of Isaac and Rebekah and twin brother of Esau. According to Gen. 25:26 the name Jacob means either "He Who Takes by the Heel" or "the Supplanter." For the biblical story of his life see Genesis 25–35, 45–49.

Isaac: Isaac was the son of the aged Abraham and Sarah. For the biblical story of his life see Genesis 21–28. Perhaps the best known episode in his life was when he was nearly offered up as a sacrifice by his father Abraham (Gen. 22:1–19).

Abraham: Abraham was the father of the Hebrew race. Prior to the birth of Isaac, Abraham's name was Abram ("Great Father"), before Isaac's birth God appeared to the patriarch (Gen. 17:1–21) and changed his name to Abraham ("Father of a multitude"). Although important allusions to the Abrahamic covenant are found in the infancy narrative (1:55, 73), Luke attaches no more significance to the name of Abraham here in the genealogy than he does to the name of David. For the biblical story of Abraham's life see Genesis 12–25.

Terah: For the names from Terah to Arphaxad, Luke is apparently drawing upon Gen. 11:10–26 and 1 Chron. 1:24–27. According to Gen.

11:31–32 Terah took his family to Haran, the place from which God would later call Abraham.

Nahor: Beyond the appearance of this man's name in Abraham's genealogy (Gen. 11:22; 1 Chron. 1:26) nothing is known of him. Fitzmyer (p. 502) notes that Nahor is a Mesopotamian name.

3:35 / **Serug**: See Gen. 11:20; 1 Chron. 1:26.

Reu: See Gen. 11:18; 1 Chron. 1:25. Fitzmyer (p. 503) suggests that the name is a shortened form or Reuel or Reuyah, meaning "Friend of God" or "Friend of the Lord."

Peleg: See Gen. 11:16; 1 Chron. 1:25. The name meant "Division"; see Gen. 10:25.

Eber: See Gen. 10:25; 11:17; 1 Chron. 1:25. It is from his name that the name "Hebrew" is derived, which in turn means "region beyond" (Fitzmyer, p. 503).

Shelah: See Gen. 11:15; 1 Chron. 1:24.

3:36 / **Cainan**: This name is only found in LXX Gen. 10:24; 11:12. According to the Hebrew text, Shelah is the son of Arphaxad. The name does appear earlier at 1 Chron. 1:2 ("Kenan"). See v. 37 below.

Arphaxad: Third son of Shem; see Gen. 11:12; 1 Chron. 1:24 ("Arpachshad").

Shem: One of the three sons of Noah, from whom the Semitic peoples descended. See Gen. 11:10; 1 Chron. 1:4, 24.

Noah: See Gen. 5:29, 32; 10:1; 1 Chron. 1:4. Because of Noah's righteousness God spared Noah and his family; see Genesis 6–9. According to the early and fragmentary columns of the *Genesis Apocryphon* (1QapGen) Noah's birth was marvelous, portending things to come. He reportedly lived 950 years.

Lamech: See Gen. 5:25, 28; 1 Chron. 1:3. He reportedly lived 777 years.

3:37 / **Methuselah**: See Gen. 5:21; 1 Chron. 1:3. Methuselah reportedly lived 969 years, the longest life of all of those who lived before the Flood. His Akkadian name probably means "man of God" (Fitzmyer, p. 503).

Enoch: See Gen. 5:18; 1 Chron. 1:3. Enoch is the righteous man who apparently did not die but was taken up to heaven after living 365 years (Gen. 5:24; Sir. 49:14; Jude 14). Various pseudepigraphal works are named after this mysterious figure.

Jared: See Gen. 5:15; 1 Chron. 1:2. He reportedly lived 962 years.

Mahalalel: See Gen. 5:13; 1 Chron. 1:2. He reportedly lived 895 years.

Kenan: See Gen. 5:9; 1 Chron. 1:2. He reportedly lived 910 years.

3:38 / **Enosh**: See Gen. 5:6; 1 Chron. 1:1. He reportedly lived 905 years.

Seth: See Gen. 5:3; 1 Chron. 1:1. He reportedly lived 912 years.

Adam: See Gen. 1:26–27; 2:7; 5:1; 1 Chron. 1:1. Adam, the father of the human race, reportedly lived 930 years.

God: Luke has traced Jesus' genealogy back to the Creator himself; see Gen. 1:1, 26–27; 2:7.

For a thorough study of the infancy narratives, including the genealogies of Jesus, the reader is encouraged to see Raymond E. Brown, *The Birth of the Messiah: A Commentary on the Infancy Narratives in Matthew and Luke* (Garden City: Doubleday, 1977).

Although Mark 1:12–13 records that Jesus was tempted, only Matthew (4:1–11) and Luke (4:1–13) provide us with accounts of the three specific temptations (which would suggest that the three temptations were part of the sayings source used by Matthew and Luke). A comparison of these two Gospels reveals that the second and third temptations found in one are in reverse order in the other (i.e., bread, pinnacle, kingdoms in Matthew; bread, kingdoms, pinnacle in Luke). Fitzmyer (pp. 507–8) believes that Matthew has retained the original order, which is reflected in the logical progression of the temptations (from desert-floor, to pinnacle of temple, to a high mountain) and in the descending order of Jesus' quotations from Deuteronomy (i.e., Deut. 8:3 in Matt. 4:4; Deut. 6:16 in Matt. 4:7; Deut. 6:13 in Matt. 4:10). (For further reasons see Gundry, p. 56.) If the Matthean order is original, then we must inquire why Luke transposed the second and third temptation scenes. The most plausible answer is that Luke wanted the temptation to climax in Jerusalem. Whereas in the Matthean version of the pinnacle temptation (see Matt. 4:5) Jerusalem is referred to as the "holy city," Luke wants the reference to be more explicit and so calls the city by its name (4:9). Jerusalem plays a significant part in Luke's story of Jesus. Only in Luke's Gospel does Jesus "set his face toward Jerusalem" (9:51) and then take the next ten chapters or so to get there (i.e., 9:51–19:27). The importance of Jerusalem for Jesus is hinted at in Luke 13:33: "surely no prophet can die outside Jerusalem!" (see commentary on 13:31–35 below). For Luke, Jerusalem is the city of Jesus' destiny, and therefore it is appropriate that the temptation scenes reach their climax there.

The next question concerns the meaning of the temptation narrative. Here it is necessary to offer answers on two levels. First, the original meaning of this narrative must be determined. Second, Luke's understanding and usage of the narrative must be determined. Let us first consider the original meaning. The setting

in the desert (v. 1) and staying in it **for forty days** (v. 2), during which time Jesus **ate nothing** (v. 2), are probably an intentional allusion to Moses' fast in the wilderness for forty days, at the end of which time he received and proclaimed the word of God (see Exod. 34:28; Deut. 9:9–18; perhaps also Elijah, 1 Kings 19:8). That such an allusion was intentional receives additional support when it is noted that all of Jesus' replies to the **devil** are quotations from Deuteronomy. Moreover, it has been shown that each of the three temptations reflects temptations to which the Israelites succumbed during their "desert" wanderings for "forty" years (see Fitzmyer, pp. 510–12).

The first temptation (4:3–4) recalls Israel's own period of testing: "the LORD your God has led you these forty years in the wilderness . . . testing you to know what was in your heart, whether you would keep his commandments, or not" (Deut. 8:2, RSV). Part of this "testing" was letting the Israelites become hungry so that they would have to trust God for their bread (the manna) and learn that "man does not live by bread alone, but . . . by everything that proceeds out of the mouth of the LORD" (Deut. 8:3, RSV). Israel, however, found this lesson difficult to learn, for the people grumbled against Moses and Aaron and had to be humbled (see Exod. 16:1–21). By refusing the devil's temptation to satisfy his needs (i.e., by ordering **this stone to become bread**)—as if God could not or would not meet them—Jesus affirmed his faith and reliance in God's provision, the very thing that Israel had failed to do (see Deut. 8:1–6).

The second temptation (4:5–8) alludes to Israel's tendency to chase after other gods: "And when the LORD your God brings you into the land . . . then take heed lest you forget the LORD. . . . You shall not go after other gods, of the gods of the peoples who are round about you; for the LORD your God . . . is a jealous God . . . " (Deut. 6:10–15, RSV). The **devil** offers Jesus **all the kingdoms of the world** (v. 5) if he would only **worship** him (v. 7). Unlike the Israelites, who so often became ensnared in idolatry, Jesus steadfastly affirms his loyalty to God alone by refusing the devil's offer and by quoting Deut. 6:13.

The third temptation (4:9–12) recalls Israel's testing of God with its demands at Massah and Meribah that the Lord provide water (Deut. 6:16b, alluding to Exod. 17:1–7). Unlike the people of Israel, however, Jesus will **not put the Lord** his **God to the test**

(v. 12; from Deut. 6:16a). In light of these allusions it is clear that the temptation narrative was originally understood as a demonstration of Jesus' unfailing faithfulness to God and his commandments. Such faithfulness qualifies him for his messianic role.

All of the suggestions put to Jesus by the devil reflect popular ideas and beliefs about what the Messiah would do when he appeared. Just as God had during the wilderness wanderings, the Messiah was expected to bring bread down from heaven, to subject the other kingdoms to Israel, and to perform some dazzling sign that would convince religious leadership (see Luke 11:16).

But the question may now be raised, what new significance, if any, does Luke attach to the temptation narrative? Coming, as it does, right after the genealogy, which concludes with "the son of Adam, the son of God" (3:38), it is possible that Luke sees in the temptation of Jesus ("If you are the Son of God . . . "; see note below) a parallel to the temptation of Adam, the first "son of God" (see commentary on 3:38 above). Whereas the first son of God fell into sin because of his failure to obey the command of God, the second Son of God remained faithful to God's commands. The three temptations, however, are probably not meant to correspond to the temptations that were presented to Adam, as one interpreter (J. Neyrey) has recently suggested. Whereas the temptation to eat (fruit in the case of Adam; bread in the case of Jesus) corresponds, at least superficially, the other temptations do not. The temptations of the Gospel tradition reflect the ideas found in Deuteronomy 6 and 8, not those found in Genesis 3. The evangelist offers no more than a general comparison of Jesus and Adam, "sons of God" through whom the destiny of the human race is so drastically affected.

Luke saw in the temptation a foreshadowing of what lay ahead for Jesus in Jerusalem. This is obvious, as has already been pointed out, from the explicit reference to Jerusalem (v. 9) and from Luke's making the temptation at Jerusalem the final, climactic temptation. Moreover, when Luke says, **when the devil had finished all this tempting, he left him until an opportune time** (v. 13), he surely anticipates the devil's return on the scene near the time of Jesus' passion in Jerusalem (see Luke 22:3, 31–32). For Luke, Jesus is engaged in combat with the devil and has, for now at least, emerged unscathed.

Finally, we may inquire into the nature of Jesus' actual experience. Does the temptation story reflect a historical, observable event? Or, was it, as some scholars have maintained (Leaney, p. 115), a vision or a parabolic illustration of the devil-inspired opposition to Jesus' ministry? It is not easy to decide, for problems attend all of these interpretations. But the one that seems the most plausible is the view that Jesus' temptations were visionary. The context for the temptation would suggest this interpretation. Jesus has spent a lengthy time in prayer, solitude, and fasting. Prayer and fasting often preceded heavenly visions (see Dan. 9:3, 20–21; Acts 10:30 in KJV). During this period of time Jesus meditates on the direction that his ministry should take. While Jesus does this, diabolical temptations are put to him that would divert him from his divine mission. Being fully committed to the word of God and being "full of the Holy Spirit," however, Jesus thwarts the tempter. (Talbert [pp. 44–46] observes that Jesus defeated Satan through correct use of Scripture.) Having emerged from this ordeal victorious, Jesus is now ready to announce the Gospel.

Additional Notes §7

Concerning the order of the three temptations, Talbert (p. 47) notes that "Psalm 106 gives the temptation of Israel in the same order as in Luke's narrative (food, false worship, putting the Lord to the test), an order also found in 1 Cor. 10:6–9." This could suggest that Luke's order is traditional and that it was Matthew who altered the sequence.

4:1 / Mark 1:12 states, "At once the Spirit sent him out into the desert," while a little less graphically Matt. 4:1 reads, "Then Jesus was led by the Spirit into the desert." Luke, though, in keeping with his Spirit-filling theme, puts it this way: **Jesus, full of the Holy Spirit, returned from the Jordan and was led by the Spirit in the desert**. Not only had Jesus been conceived through the Holy Spirit (1:35), but the Spirit had descended upon him at his baptism (3:22) so that he might endure the temptations and begin his ministry (see 4:14, 18).

4:2 / **tempted by the devil**: Luke consistently uses the word **devil** (lit. "slanderer") in the temptation story, although he uses the "Satan" (lit. "adversary") elsewhere (see Luke 10:18; 11:18; 13:16; 22:3, 31). Satan was thought of as the ruler of the demons and powers of darkness.

His mission is to oppose God's will. The temptation story thus paints a classic picture of the clash between Good and Evil.

4:3 / If you are the Son of God (see also 4:9): In this type of sentence construction the word translated "if" actually has the meaning of "since." The **devil** has no doubts regarding Jesus' identity, for that was made plainly evident at the baptism (3:22). Rather, the devil is making suggestions aimed at misdirecting Jesus' mission.

4:9 / highest point of the temple: There is uncertainty today as to just exactly what part of the **temple** should be considered the **highest point**. Probably the most popular and reasonable suggestion is the southeast corner of the temple that overlooks the Kidron Valley below. From this valley the southeast corner appeared as the "pinnacle" of the temple (Fitzmyer, pp. 516–17; Lachs, p. 51). See note on 19:45, 47 below.

4:12 / Do not put the Lord your God to the test: Lachs (p. 51) cites the following interesting rabbinic parallel: "R. Yannai said: 'A man should never stand in place of danger [purposely] saying that God will perform a miracle for him, for perchance no miracle will be performed for him' " (b. *Shabbath* 32a).

§8 Jesus Preaches at Nazareth (Luke 4:14–30)

4:14–15 / This brief summarizing section, probably derived from Mark 1:14–15, represents the beginning of Jesus' Galilean ministry (so Fitzmyer, p. 521; Ellis [pp. 33, 98–99] and Schweizer [pp. 96–97], however, see the beginning at 4:31). Luke wishes to make it clear that Jesus' ministry begins **in the power of the Spirit** as **he taught in their synagogues** (see 1:35; 3:22; 4:1), which parallels the inauguration of the apostolic preaching and teaching in Acts 2. These verses establish the context for an expanded account of one such teaching episode in a synagogue (4:16–30).

4:16–30 / The sermon at the **synagogue** in **Nazareth** provides the reader with an example of the content of Jesus' proclamation. This passage illustrates vividly Jesus' theology in contrast to the popular assumptions held by many of his Jewish contemporaries. In a very real sense this passage may be described as programmatic of the evangelist's theological concerns. The themes that are here presupposed and debated will recur frequently throughout Luke's account. Of all the passages in this Gospel this one is of critical importance and must be understood well if we are to appreciate the evangelist's theological perspective and major purpose for writing.

On the Sabbath day he went into the synagogue recalls Jesus' habitual concern with the things of God, from his childhood (see 2:49) to the beginning of his ministry (4:15). **As was his custom**, out of deference to the sacred Scriptures, Jesus **stood up to read** and the synagogue attendant handed him the **scroll of the prophet Isaiah**. Since it was the **Sabbath** a selection from the prophets was to be read, following the reading of a selection from Torah (the law of Moses, Genesis–Deuteronomy). Jesus unrolled the scroll and read from Isa. 61:1–2. He had chosen a popular passage in Isaiah, one which was understood as describing the task of the Lord's Anointed One, the Messiah (see notes below). Jesus concludes his quotation with the phrase (lit.): "to proclaim the acceptable year of the Lord" (v. 19) and omits the next phrase of Isa. 61:2 (lit.): "and the day of vengeance of our God." Why Jesus has cited Isaiah in this way becomes evident in the balance of his sermon.

When Jesus finished reading and sat down, **the eyes of everyone in the synagogue were fastened on him,** that is, they were watching him with great interest and anticipation. His hearers were surely wondering why Jesus had quoted this particular messianic text of Scripture. Jesus then declares that **"Today this scripture is fulfilled in your hearing"** (v. 21). The congregation is amazed, sensing that there is something special in the words that he spoke. The question, **"Isn't this Joseph's son?"** (v. 22), suggests pleasant surprise at hearing such a remarkable statement from one who was well known in **Nazareth** and surrounding parts.

In v. 23 Jesus demonstrates that he understands what the people expect of him. The proverb **"Physician, heal yourself!"** means that the healer or benefactor (in this case Jesus) should take care of his own and does not imply that Jesus himself has some deficiency or fault that needs correcting. The people of Nazareth expect Jesus to do the same things for them that he has done for the people of **Capernaum.** If Jesus' pronouncement that the Isaiah passage was truly fulfilled, then all could expect Jesus to do wonderful things for them. In v. 24, however, Jesus disappoints this expectation by stating that **no prophet is accepted in his home town.** The irony is that the word "accepted" (or "acceptable") in this verse is the same word found in v. 19 above. The prophet who is to announce the "acceptable" year of the Lord is himself not "acceptable" to his own people (cf. John 1:10–11). Underlying this expression is the long tradition of the rejected, persecuted, and martyred prophets of Israel. Those prophets who spoke the word of God often found themselves out of favor or "unacceptable" to the ruling political and religious establishments of their times (see note below). Instead of proclaiming what the authorities wanted to hear, the prophets of old spoke what God wanted said. So it is in the case of Jesus in the Nazareth synagogue. The people hear that the messianic era is at hand, and in this they rejoice; but they hear that it will not entail what they expect, and with this they become angry.

In vv. 25–27 Jesus explains and justifies his startling pronouncement by citing two OT examples involving **Elijah** and his disciple and successor **Elisha**. That he singled out these two figures is particularly appropriate since Elijah was regarded as the prophet of the last days who would prepare the way for the Messiah (see Mal. 3:1; 4:5–6). If the last days are truly at hand, then the Elijah/Elisha tradition would surely bear some relevance. Jesus recounts in vv. 25–26 the incident in which Elijah provides an unending supply of food for a Gentile **widow** and her son (1 Kings 17:8–16) and yet makes no such provision for any Israelite. In v. 27 Jesus tells of the incident in which Elisha healed **Naaman the Syrian** army officer of the dread disease **leprosy** (2 Kings 5:1–14; see Luke 5:12–14). In the minds of his Jewish listeners it was offense enough to be reminded that Elijah ministered to a poor Gentile widow, but it was intolerable to be oppressed by Roman occupation and then be reminded that Elisha healed a soldier of Syria, a country which had oppressed Israel in an earlier time.

What makes all of this preaching so "unacceptable" is that the people of Jesus' time expected Messiah to come and destroy Israel's enemies, not minister to them. With respect to messianic expectation the Jewish people of the first century held, by and large, to two basic beliefs: (1) Every generation believed that the coming of Messiah was very near and that he would probably come in their own time; and (2) all believed that when Messiah would come he would vanquish the Gentiles (and perhaps the corrupt of Israel) and restore and bless Israel. Isaiah 61:1–2 was a passage that was felt to witness to this second belief. It was believed that the blessings described in this OT passage were reserved for Israel alone, while the "day of vengeance" (that part of the quotation omitted by Jesus) was reserved for Israel's enemies. When Jesus announced that Isa. 61:1–2 was fulfilled **today**, he fulfilled the expectations of the first commonly held belief. However, when he announced that **no prophet is accepted** and then cited the examples of **Elijah** and **Elisha**, he flatly contradicted the second belief. This contradiction led to their outrage and the attempt to kill Jesus by throwing **him down the cliff**. Nevertheless, Jesus **walked right through the crowd and went on his way**. Whether or not Luke intends this escape to be miraculous is uncertain, for the passion of the **crowd**, once outside, may have abated somewhat. But what is certain is that Jesus' ministry was far from over.

Additional Notes §8

4:14–15 / Luke makes no mention of **Jesus** proclaiming the kingdom of God at this point in his ministry (contrast Mark 1:14–15). Luke wishes to avoid this popular (and misunderstood) theme until he has clarified Jesus' own views of messiahship, as seen in the Nazareth sermon.

4:16–21 / Luke's account of this **synagogue** service is our oldest and most detailed description of what took place in the early synagogue. Since the return from the Babylonian exile (ca. 586–516 B.C.) the Jewish people spoke Aramaic. (See the account in Neh. 8:1–8 in which Ezra and his scribes read the law of Moses and explain it to the people.) In the synagogue service a portion of the Hebrew Bible was read and then an "explanation" (or Targum) was given in Aramaic. This need probably gave rise to the custom of preaching a sermon after a brief reading of Scripture (see Acts 2:16–36; 13:16–41). By the end of the first century A.D., synagogue services consisted of the recitation of the Shema (Deut. 6:4–9; 11:13–21; Num. 15:37–41), the Eighteen Benedictions, the daily psalm, the priestly blessing (Num. 6:24–26), prayers, readings from Torah and the Prophets, and a homily (Lachs, p. 56). See also *HBD*, pp. 1007–8.

J. T. Sanders (pp. 165–68) thinks that the final rejection of the Jews is foreshadowed by Luke 4:16–30. I think that this interpretation is completely incorrect. The point of the passage is not that messianic blessings are to be withheld from the Jews, but that the common assumption that these blessings are restricted to a certain righteous few is wrong. It is Jesus who is rejected, not the Jews. Jesus is rejected for declaring that the Good News of the kingdom is for everyone, even Gentiles. For Luke, Jesus' true family is made up, not of those who are physically related to him, such as Jewish kinsmen, but of those "who hear the word of God and do it," whether Jewish or not (see 8:19–21). For further discussion see James A. Sanders, "From Isaiah 61 to Luke 4," in J. Neusner, ed., *Christianity, Judaism and Other Greco-Roman Cults* (Morton Smith Festschrift; Leiden: Brill, 1975), pp. 75–106, esp. pp. 96–104.

4:18 / **The Spirit of the Lord is on me . . . he has anointed me**: Tannehill (pp. 58–59, 62–63) has argued that Jesus' anointing (which refers back to the baptism, 3:22) is royal, not simply prophetic (contra Fitzmyer, pp. 529–30). I agree. It is his anointing that makes Jesus "Messiah," and in being presented as Messiah, Jesus is presented as David's successor, Israel's long-awaited king.

4:18–19 / Luke's quotation is from the Greek translation (LXX) of the Hebrew OT and is actually a combination of various parts of Isa. 61:1–2 and 58:6 (61:1a,b,d; 58:6d; 61:2a; with 61:1c and 61:2b,c omitted). Isaiah 61 and 58 are linked by common words and ideas (*dektos* ["acceptable"] in Isa. 61:2 and 58:5, *aphesis* ["release"/"forgiveness"] in 61:1

and 58:6). With regard to *aphesis*, Luke may acknowledge both senses (see Talbert, p. 55; Tannehill, pp. 65–66). Another noteworthy detail is the replacement of the verb meaning "to call for" in 61:2a with a verb meaning "to proclaim," thus suggesting that the Anointed One does more than merely "call for" the acceptable day of the Lord, he actually "proclaims" its arrival. Of course, such a modification lends itself very well to the nature of Jesus' preaching. The reference in Acts 10:35 to the person (in this case a Gentile) who is "acceptable" to God may allude to Luke 4:19.

In at least one of the writings of Qumran (11QMelchizedek 9–16) Isa. 61:1–2 is linked with Isa. 52:7. Judging by the paragraph indentations of the Great Isaiah Scroll of Qumran (=1QIsaiah), Isaiah 52:7 was thought to be the opening verse of the Suffering Servant Song (52:7–53:12). In the Aramaic version of the OT, known as the Targum, this Servant Song is unmistakably depicted as messianic (see 52:13; 53:10). In 11QMelch 16 the reference to "peace" (*šālôm*) in Isa. 52:7 is re-vocalized to mean "retribution" (*šillûm*), thus underscoring the aspect of vengeance and retribution found in the Isa. 61:1–2 passage (for further discussion see M. P. Miller, "The Function of Isa. 61,1–2 in Melchizedek," *JBL* 88 [1969], pp. 467–69). According to the people of Qumran, the Messiah's appearance meant comfort for them and judgment for their enemies (see also 1QH 15.15; 18.14–15). This may very well have been a widely held view. Underlying these ideas of vengeance and retribution was the popular understanding of the militaristic Messiah. That Luke is familiar with such a concept is apparent from Acts 5:33–39, where Gamaliel reminds the Sanhedrin of the (apparently military) failure of two messianic claimants, Theudas (v. 36) and Judas the Galilean (v. 37). Josephus knows of this Theudas and two others. Theudas (ca. A.D. 45), he tells us, claimed that he was a prophet and could command the river to part (*Antiquities* 20.97–98). Here is likely an allusion either to Moses parting the Red Sea (Exod. 14:21–22) or to Joshua's crossing of the Jordan River (Josh. 3:14–17). Later we are told of a man from Egypt (ca. A.D. 54) who claimed to be a prophet at whose command the walls of Jerusalem would fall down (*Antiquities* 20.169–170). This sign was probably inspired by the story of Israel's conquest of Jericho (Josh. 6:20; cf. Acts 21:38). Finally, Josephus tells us of another "imposter" who promised salvation and rest, if the people would follow him into the wilderness (*Antiquities* 20.188). Years later, Israel would suffer terribly as a result of following the popular messianic/military figures of Menachem and Simon bar Giora (first war with Rome, A.D. 66–70) and Simon bar-Kochba (second war with Rome, A.D. 132–135).

Although the words spoken at Jesus' baptism (3:22) and transfiguration (9:35) are usually understood as alluding to Ps. 2:7 (Cf. Marshall [p. 155], who calls the word "reminiscent of Ps. 2:7," but rejects any dependence on either Isa. 42:1 or Ps. 2:7; idem, "Son of God or Servant of Yahweh?—A Reconsideration of Mark I. 11," *NTS* 15 [1968–69], pp. 326–36.), Fitzmyer (pp. 485–86) has concluded that they more likely allude to Isa. 42:1. That passage, one of the Servant Songs of Isaiah, was often interpreted by early Christians (and some Jews) as messianic (best known is the Suffering Servant Song of 52:13–53:12). Marshall's view receives support from the quotation of Isa. 61:1–2 in Luke 4:18–19. Elsewhere in Luke's writings Jesus is actually called the Lord's "Servant" (Acts 4:27). Moreover, Acts 10:38 declares that "God anointed Jesus of Nazareth with the Holy Spirit" (RSV), which surely should be understood as a reference to his baptism, at which time the Spirit descended upon him, and to which Jesus himself alludes in his sermon (4:18–19). In light of these various references it is probably correct to say that Luke understands Jesus to have been officially "anointed" as Messiah ("anointed one") at his baptism. This is further confirmed by the heavenly voice, which alludes to Isa. 42:1, another Servant Song, and which qualifies him to apply Isa. 61:1–2 to himself as God's herald of "Good News" for the "poor," "downtrodden," etc.

Some commentators (Fitzmyer, p. 532; Marshall, p. 184; Tiede, p. 107) suggest that Luke may have had in mind the year of the Jubilee (every 50th year), which is described in Lev. 25:10–13, and which was intended to be a year of "release" (or "forgiveness") for debtors. According to the Qumran text mentioned above (11QMelchizedek), Leviticus 25 is referred to in connection with Isa. 61:1 and would seem to indicate that one of the tasks of the Messiah was to announce a year of Jubilee. Since the year A.D. 26/27 was a Jubilee year, Luke could have understood this as the year that Jesus began his messianic ministry (it is rejected by Schweizer, p. 89; Marshall, p. 184).

4:23 / The proverb, **Physician, heal yourself!** resembles proverbs found in both Greek ("A physician for others, but himself teeming with sores," Euripides, *Fragments* 1086) and Jewish ("Physician, heal your own lameness," *Genesis Rabbah* 23.5) traditions (both examples are taken from Fitzmyer, p. 535). The saying in the *Gospel of Thomas* 31 probably represents a variant version of the Synoptic saying: "A physician does not heal those who know him."

4:24 / **I tell you the truth**: Lit. "Amen [truly] I say to you." This is the only Hebrew word that Luke retains from his sources. The word "amen" comes from a Hebrew verb that means "to be established," "sure," or "certain," and its use is characteristic of Jesus' style of teaching.

no prophet is accepted: Jesus' words here and in 13:34 reflect a Jewish tradition that Israel routinely rejected and persecuted the prophets (2 Chron. 36:15–16; Pss. 78, 105, 106; Lam. 4:13; Acts 7:51–53). According to the pseudepigraphal work, *The Lives of the Prophets* (1:1; 2:1; 3:1–2; 6:2; 7:2), Isaiah, Jeremiah, Ezekiel, Micah, and Amos suffered martyrdom. One later rabbinic tradition portrays Jeremiah's reluctance to enter the prophetic vocation: "O Lord, I cannot go as a prophet to Israel, for when lived there a prophet whom Israel did not desire to kill? Moses and Aaron they sought to stone with stones; Elijah the Tishbite they mocked . . . " (from L. Ginzberg, *The Legends of the Jews* [Philadelphia: Jewish Publication Society of America, 1913], vol. 4, p. 295).

4:29 / **out of the town**: According to Lev. 24:14 executions were supposed to take place outside the city (see Acts 7:58; 14:19). That Luke (or the mob) had this thought in mind is not certain. Ellis (p. 98) thinks that the episode foreshadows "the day of his execution" (Luke 23:26–33). Lachs (p. 56) suggests that Jesus' being put out of the city might be an example of excommunication. In light of the meaning of the pericope this could very well be the case.

Modern Nazareth is situated on a **hill**, but exactly what **cliff** is referred to in this episode cannot be ascertained. On Nazareth see *HBD*, p. 689. Tiede (p. 110) makes the plausible suggestion that the idea was to throw Jesus down a cliff and then bury him with stones, the fate of the false prophet.

§9 Jesus Casts Out Demons (Luke 4:31–44)

With the exorcism in 4:33–36 we have the first of some twenty-one miracles performed by Jesus in the Gospel of Luke. These miracles may be assigned to four basic categories: Exorcisms, healings, resuscitations, and nature miracles. (1) In addition to the exorcism of the demon-possessed man in the synagogue, Jesus exorcises two other demon-possessed persons (the Gerasene "demoniac" in 8:26–39 and the mute man in 11:14). Luke 4:41 refers to exorcisms in general, while elsewhere in Luke demon possession and Satan are discussed (see 10:18; 11:15–20, 24–26). (2) The most common miracle, however, is healing. In addition to the healings that will be discussed below there are the healings of the leper (5:12–16), the paralyzed man (5:17–26), the man with the withered hand (6:6–11), the centurion's slave (7:2–10), the woman with the hemorrhage (8:43–48), the epileptic boy (9:37–43), the crippled woman (13:10–17), the man with dropsy (14:1–6), the ten lepers (17:11–19), the blind man (18:35–43), and the ear of the high priest's slave (22:50–52). Furthermore, there are references to healings in general (4:40; 5:15; 6:18; 7:21–22). Often the distinction between healing miracles and exorcisms is not sharply drawn. There is a reason for this. It was commonly believed that demonic forces were lying behind most illnesses and diseases. Epileptic seizures were commonly viewed as demonic convulsions. Consequently, it is not always easy to distinguish between a healing miracle and an exorcism. (3) Related to healing is the miracle of resuscitation. Luke narrates only two actual stories of Jesus' raising someone from the dead: the raising of the Nain widow's son (7:11–17) and Jairus' daughter (8:40–42, 49–56). Jesus states in Luke 7:22 that "the dead are raised" without any apparent reference other than that of the Nain widow's son. The word "raised" is in the plural, so presumably other resuscitations are in mind. Outside of Luke (and the Synoptic tradition) there is the dramatic account of the raising of Lazarus in John 11:43–44. (Of course, Jesus' own resurrection from the dead is a related miracle, but it was not performed by him, nor was it part of his public ministry, so it is usually treated separately.) (4) Finally, there are miracles sometimes classified as "nature" miracles. Luke provides three examples of this kind: the catch of fish (5:1–11), the stilling of the storm (8:22–25), and the feeding of the 5,000 (9:12–17). Although Luke's omission of the feeding of the 4,000 (Matt. 15:32–38; Mark 8:1–9) is understandable in light of its redundancy, it is curious that he chose to omit the episode of Jesus walking on the sea (Matt. 14:25–33; Mark 6:45–52; cf. John 6:16–21). Also, Luke probably chose to omit the cursing of the fig tree (see Matt. 21:18–22; Mark 11:12–14) because he felt that it was too vindictive on Jesus' part. Probably the best known nature miracle is the turning of the water into wine, a miracle story found only in John (2:1–11).

Whereas the Gospels record that the reaction to Jesus' miracles was often one of amazement (see Luke 5:26), the NT primarily understands miracles as signs indicating that God is present and is at work (see especially the Gospel of John). In Luke 7:18–23 Jesus cites, for the benefit of the imprisoned John, the miracles as evidence that he is truly the "One who is coming" (7:20). The real reason for the frequency of miracle stories in the Gospels, however, is to show that Jesus has power and authority over the demonic forces felt responsible for disease and demon possession. Furthermore, since it was commonly believed that leprosy and crippling diseases were frequently the result of (and punishment for) sin (see John 9:1–3), it was necessary that such conditions be physically healed as evidence of the forgiveness of sins and spiritual restoration (see Luke 5:20; 7:9; 8:48).

Luke 4:31–44 consists of four parts: the exorcism of the man in the synagogue (vv. 31–37); the healing of Simon's mother-in-law (vv. 38–39); a summary of healing and exorcisms (vv. 40–41); and Jesus' preaching in the synagogues. The references to synagogue(s) in the first and fourth parts loosely tie together the section. The main teaching of the passage is that Jesus teaches with authority, an authority that is even recognized by the demons, the authorities of darkness.

4:31–37 / The exorcism of the demon-possessed man in the synagogue **on the sabbath** is probably meant to complement the preceding account of Jesus' sermon in the synagogue at Nazareth (4:16–30). At Nazareth Jesus' authority was not recognized, but here at **Capernaum**, where Jesus had been before his visit to Nazareth (as implied by Luke 4:23), Jesus' teaching apparently does not provoke anger and resentment. Rather, the people **were amazed at his teaching, because his message had authority.** In contrast to Jesus' style of teaching, the Jewish teachers (whose oral law and traditions eventually become Mishnah and Talmud) cited one rabbi and sage after another when discussing a point of interpretation. A typical discussion would run something like this: "Rabbi so-and-so says this, but Rabbi such-and-such says that; however, the sages used to say . . . " (for numerous examples see Herbert Danby, *The Mishnah* [Oxford: Oxford University Press, 1933]). Jesus' teaching, however, was direct and explicit. He did not speculate or offer alternative suggestions; he did not appeal to authorities greater than himself.

But the authority behind Jesus' teaching was not simply a matter of style (or even content); Jesus' authority could manifest itself in great power. This power is demonstrated by the demon's recognition of Jesus as the **Holy One of God** and by the exorcism itself (see note below). The rabbis believed that they, too, had the power to cast out demons (see Ellis, p. 99). They usually attempted to do this by invoking the name of an OT worthy (e.g., the name of Solomon was a favorite). Similarly the apostles performed exorcisms and healings in the name of Jesus (see Acts 3:6; 4:10; 9:34; 16:18; see 19:13–17, where non-Christians unsuccessfully attempt an exorcism by invoking the names of Paul and Jesus).

When the people ask, **"What is this teaching?"** (see note below), the reader knows, for the reader has been told of Jesus' conception through the Holy Spirit (1:35), his anointing with the Holy Spirit at his baptism (3:22), his filling with the Holy Spirit during his successful encounter with the devil (4:1), and his own announcement at Nazareth that the Holy Spirit was upon him (4:18). Whereas **the people were amazed**, Luke has given his readers enough insight so that they are hardly surprised: In view of Jesus' preparation why should such awesome power amaze anyone?

4:38–39 / Although not obvious at first glance, the healing of Simon Peter's mother-in-law may actually be a sort of exorcism as well. In v. 39 Jesus **rebuked the fever.** The word "rebuke" is the same word often used in casting out demons (as it is used in v. 35 above). Whether Jesus thought of the fever as brought on by demonic power or whether he merely personified the illness is not easily decided. (It is quite unlikely, however, that demonic forces were in view when in Luke 8:24 Jesus "rebuked" the storm.) Clearly, though, Jesus has demonstrated his power over those forces which afflict and oppress humankind.

4:40–41 / These verses summarize Jesus' ministry of healing and exorcism. Even though Luke can cite only a few specific examples, he wants the reader to realize that much of Jesus' ministry was given over to healing and exorcism. Also, this summary affords Luke another opportunity to have the demons cry out **"You are the Son of God!"** which reinforces the earlier confession of v. 34 and may be another instance of Luke's double-witness motif (see commentary on 2:22–38). This exclamation recalls the heavenly voice at the baptism (3:22).

4:42–44 / **Jesus** is so popular, his cures in such great demand, that he has to seek out a **solitary place**. Even so, he is pursued, and when he is discovered, the crowds **tried to keep him from leaving them**. This enthusiasm for Jesus is due primarily to his healings and aid. In keeping with popular views about the blessings associated with the coming of the Messiah, the people expected such benefits and eagerly sought them. However, as the Nazareth sermon so graphically illustrated (4:16–30), Jesus' idea of the **good news of the kingdom of God** is less eagerly received. Jesus states that he must preach in **other towns also**. The idea of Jesus traveling is an important theme in Luke's Gospel and has been variously interpreted, but these options will not be discussed at length here. Suffice it to say that the Third Evangelist sees in Jesus' constant traveling and preaching a foreshadowing of the later travels of the apostles and preachers of the gospel in the Book of Acts.

Additional Notes §9

4:31 / **Capernaum** (meaning "City of Nahum") was referred to in the Nazareth sermon (see 4:16–30) and is mentioned again in 7:1 and 10:15. It was a town in Galilee on the west side of Lake Gennesaret (or "Sea of Galilee"). See *HBD*, pp. 154–55.

4:33 / **evil spirit**: In Jesus' times various expressions were used to describe demons, e.g., "unclean spirit" (Luke 4:36; 6:18), "evil spirit" (Luke 7:21; 8:2; 1QapGen 20.16–17), "spirit of affliction" (1QapGen 20.16), and even "spirit of purulence" (1QapGen 20.26). (The references to the *Genesis Apocryphon* [1QapGen] are taken from Fitzmyer, p. 544.) Physical ailments were often symptoms of demon possession (see Luke 8:29; 9:39; 11:14; 13:11).

4:34 / When the demon asks **"Have you come to destroy us?"** he refers to himself and to the other demons (not to his human host). This NT reference (and its parallel in Mark 1:24) reflects the popular belief that the dawning of the era of salvation would bring destruction to the forces of evil (see also the references to 1QM [the *War Scroll* from Qumran, cave 1] 1.10–14; 4.9; 14.10–11 cited by Fitzmyer, pp. 545–46). The cry of the demon provides further confirmation that Jesus is truly God's Son, the long-awaited Deliverer.

the Holy One of God: Taken over from Mark 1:24, this is an apparent messianic designation found only in the NT.

4:36 / **"What is this teaching?"**: The NIV's translation misses the point (lit. "What word [or thing] is this?"). The question has nothing to do with Jesus' teaching but with what Jesus has just done. A more accurate rendering would be, "What kind of power is this?"

4:38 / To Mark's parallel account (1:30) Luke adds the word **high** (lit. "great") in describing the fever. He emphasizes that Jesus has cured a serious, perhaps even life-threatening illness, and not some headache.

4:40 / **laying his hands on each one, he healed them**: The "laying on of hands" for purposes of healing is not found in the OT, nor does it appear in the later writings of the rabbis (i.e., the Mishnah, Talmud, and the commentaries called Midrashim). Fitzmyer (p. 553), however, is able to cite at least one example from one of the writings found in Qumran near the Dead Sea: "The imposition of hands as a gesture of healing . . . has turned up in 1QapGen 20.28–29 where Abram prays, lays his hands on the head of the Pharaoh, and exorcizes the plague/'evil spirit' afflicting the Pharaoh (and his household) for having carried off Sarai" (see Gen. 12:10–20; 20:8–18). The laying on of hands, as a sort of ordination, appears in Num. 8:10, where hands are laid on the Levites as part of their preparation for ministry. But for our purposes the most significant OT example is Moses' laying his hands on Joshua ("Jesus" in the LXX). The Lord commands Moses in Num. 27:18–19: "Take Joshua the son of Nun, a man in whom is the Spirit, and lay your hand on him; and have him stand before Eleazar the priest and before all the congregation; and commission him in their sight" (NASB). This passage suggests that Joshua possessed the Spirit prior to the laying on of Moses' hands. But note the difference in Deut. 34:9: "Now Joshua the son of Nun was filled with spirit of wisdom, for Moses had laid his hands on him . . . " (NASB). It is not hard to see how the NT practice of laying on hands for Spirit-filling and ordination could ultimately be derived from this passage (see Acts 6:6; 8:18; 13:3–4; 19:6; 1 Tim. 4:14; 5:22; 2 Tim. 1:6). The laying on of hands for purposes of healing, however, is very likely a natural derivation from the idea of laying on hands and receiving the Spirit. In Acts 9:12 Ananias is instructed in a vision to go "and place his hands on him [Paul] to restore his sight." When he lays his hands on Paul, however, Ananias states: "Brother Saul, the Lord . . . has sent me so that you may see again and be filled with the Holy Spirit" (Acts 9:17).

As has already been pointed out in the commentary above, in the minds of many there was a close connection between demon possession and illness. The converse was probably true, i.e., there was a close connection between Spirit-filling and healing. The popularity of the laying on of hands among Christians may have discouraged the practice among Jews; hence no reference to it in rabbinic writings exists, even though the practice had emerged in early Judaism, as evidenced by the Dead Sea Scrolls and the NT. Luke's reference to Jesus' laying on his hands anticipates the apostolic practice in the Book of Acts (see Acts 6:6; 8:18).

4:41 / would not allow them to speak, because they knew he was the Christ: The prohibition not to make known Jesus' messianic identity is a theme that is taken over in part from Mark. In the Marcan context the idea is that Jesus' messianic identity is to be kept a secret until Easter, when it will be more correctly understood.

4:43 / the kingdom of God: This is the first occurrence of this expression in Luke (6:20; 7:28; 8:1, 10; 9:2, 11, 27, 60, 62; 10:9, 11; 11:20; 13:18, 20, 28, 29; 14:15; 16:16; 17:20, 21; 18:16, 17, 24, 25, 29; 19:11; 21:31, 32; 22:16, 18; 23:51). References to "the kingdom" should be understood as reference the "kingdom of God" as well (11:2; 12:31, 32; 22:29, 30; 23:42). The expression summarizes the hopes and dreams of Jesus' Jewish contemporaries who longed for the fulfillment of the OT prophecies which spoke of a return of a golden era to Israel. See commentary on 17:20–21 and note on 17:21 below.

§10 A Great Catch of Fish (Luke 5:1-11)

Luke's story of the great catch of fish parallels Mark 1:16-20, which Luke expands, partly by utilizing other Marcan details (see Mark 4:1-2, where it is necessary for Jesus to preach to the crowds from a boat) and by drawing upon his own special information. (Some scholars think that Luke's information regarding the great catch of fish is somehow related to the similar episode in John 21:1-11.) Mark's account of the calling of Simon (Peter), James, and John takes place shortly after the baptism of Jesus (Mark 1:16-20). Although Jesus had begun to proclaim the kingdom of God (Mark 1:15), no reason is given for why these Galilean fishermen would be inclined to follow Jesus. But Luke's arrangement does afford a logical context. Jesus has been preaching throughout Galilee (4:14-15, 31-32, 43), has performed numerous healings and exorcisms (4:33-37, 40-41), and has healed Peter's mother-in-law (4:38-39). The miraculous catch of fish provides a fitting climax, and it becomes easy for the reader to understand why Peter, James, and John would drop their nets and follow after Jesus (See Talbert, p. 59).

Luke's view of Peter calls for a brief discussion. In the Lucan Gospel, Peter (who is called "Simon" consistently until Jesus changes his name to "Peter" in 6:14) enjoys a position of prominence among the disciples and a position of closeness, almost endearment, approximating the relationship between Jesus and the "beloved disciple" in John's Gospel. When one realizes to what extent the evangelist Mark cast the disciples, particularly Peter, in a negative light and that Luke utilized this Gospel as one of his major sources, one can appreciate the special effort this evangelist has undertaken in rehabilitating Peter. Although probably not the only reason, it would seem likely that Luke desired to portray Peter as positively as possible in view of his future prominence in the early church, as can be seen in Acts 1-11.

Luke's special interest in Simon Peter is seen in the miraculous catch of fish. When Jesus desired to board **one of the boats** so that he could address the crowds, he chose the one that belonged to **Simon** (v. 3). After the miraculous catch of fish it is Peter who cries out to Jesus (v. 8; see note below). Moreover, when Jesus speaks to the disciples (see Mark 1:17) Luke has him address Peter (v. 10). Elsewhere in Luke, Peter is portrayed as spokesman for the disciples (9:20, 33; 18:28, all of which come from Mark, but see 12:41) or is named as one of the two disciples sent to fetch the donkey on which Jesus would ride into Jerusalem (22:8; see Mark 14:13 where Peter is not named). Although Peter's close association with Jesus (along with James and John) is not unique to Luke (see 8:51; 9:28), there are several noteworthy features involving Peter found in the Lucan passion and resurrection stories. Only Luke recounts Jesus' prayer in behalf of Peter, that his faith may not fail and that afterward, having recovered, he might strengthen his brothers (22:31–32). (In contrast, Mark's account leaves the reader very much in doubt with regard to Peter's condition.) This then leads into Peter's assertion, also unique to Luke: "Lord, I am ready to go with you to prison and to death" (22:33). Later, when Jesus is arrested and Peter joins those standing by the fire (22:54–55), unlike Mark who then takes the reader inside to Jesus and his accusers (Mark 14:55–65), Luke proceeds immediately with Peter's denials (22:56–60). There are several minor differences between the Marcan and Lucan accounts, but the most noteworthy is where Luke alone tells us that after the cock crowed, "The Lord turned and looked straight at Peter" (22:61). Furthermore, whereas Mark tells us that after the cock crowed, Peter went outside and "wept" (14:72), Luke says that Peter "wept bitterly" (22:62). Luke's editorial activity heightens the pathos of this scene, leaving the reader with a sense of empathy for the fallen Peter. Following Jesus' resurrection, Mark only mentions the angel (or "young man") at the tomb, who commands the frightened women to tell Peter and the disciples that Jesus will appear to them in Galilee (16:7), but no actual appearance is recorded (Mark 16:9–20 had not yet been attached to the ending of Mark's Gospel when Luke made use of this document). Luke, however, reports in 24:34 that the Risen Christ did indeed appear to Peter. Luke also manages to cast Peter in a better light by omitting two of Peter's more embarrassing moments: the rebuke he received for disapproving of Jesus' passion plans (see Mark 8:32–33) and his reproach by Jesus for sleeping, instead of watching and praying (see Mark 14:37).

The central concern of the episode of the great catch of fish is not the miracle itself, but Jesus' call to Peter to begin preparation for his ministry as an apostle. Jesus has been teaching throughout Galilee (4:43), has performed healings and exorcisms (4:33–35, 40–41), and now, through the catch of fish, has extended his first call of discipleship (5:11). The miracle itself aptly illustrates Jesus' words in v. 10: **from now on you will catch men**. Peter the fisherman, a man who had expended his energies trying to catch fish for a living, has now left his nets behind and has begun his life's training as one of Christ's apostles.

Additional Notes §10

5:1 / Luke 5:1 contains Luke's first instance of the expression, the **word of God**, an expression that occurs frequently in both of his writings (see Luke 8:11, 21; 11:28; Acts 4:31; 6:2, 7; 8:14; 11:1; 13:5, 7, 44, 46, 48; 16:32; 17:13; 18:11). When the expression occurs in the Book of Acts it refers to the gospel, the message of the church. In Luke, of course, Jesus uses it in reference to the kingdom of God. By employing the same expression in both the Gospel and Acts, Luke links Jesus' preaching and the later apostolic preaching.

Lake of Gennesaret is also commonly referred to as the "Sea of Galilee" (see Mark 1:16; Matt. 15:29) into which and from which the Jordan River flows. See *HBD*, p. 330.

5:2 / **fishermen, who were washing their nets**: See E. F. F. Bishop, "Jesus and the Lake," *CBQ* 13 (1951), pp. 398–414.

5:3 / **Then he sat down and taught the people from the boat**: Lachs (pp. 66–67) notes that although it was customary for a rabbi to teach in the synagogue or academy, there are many examples of rabbis teaching out in the open.

5:5 / In this verse Jesus is called **Master** for the first time in the Gospel of Luke. Whereas the other Synoptic Gospels refer to Jesus as "Teacher" or "Rabbi," only in Luke is he called "Master," and only by his followers (see Luke 8:24, 45; 9:33, 49; 17:13).

5:8 / **Go away from me, Lord; I am a sinful man!**: Fitzmyer (p. 567) has correctly noted that Peter is not asking Jesus to get out of the boat, but to "leave the vicinity," i.e., wherever Peter is. In more fully coming to recognize who Jesus is, Peter is overwhelmed by his own sense of sinfulness and unworthiness; see Tiede, p. 118.

5:10 / **you will catch men** may be translated literally: "You will be catching [or taking] human beings alive." Mark's version (1:17) reads literally: "I shall turn you into fishermen of men." It has been suggested that because catching fish brings harm to the fish (in that they die), Luke has rephrased the words of Jesus to avoid such an implication. (Lachs [p. 66] suggests that Luke has misunderstood a Semitic idiom.) The word that Luke uses (i.e., "catching [or taking] alive") is used in the LXX "for saving persons alive from danger" (Marshall, p. 205; for examples he cites Num. 31:15, 18; Deut. 20:16).

5:11 / **followed him**: This is the first time that the word "to follow" occurs in Luke's Gospel, "where it often will be used of Christian discipleship" (Fitzmyer, p. 569; he cites Luke 5:27–28; 9:23, 49, 57, 59, 61; 18:22, 28). Josephus (*Antiquities* 8.354) states that Elisha "followed" Elijah (LXX 1 Kings 19:21). Lachs (p. 66) notes that the expression "to follow after" means to be a disciple of a rabbi.

Both of the healing stories of Luke 5:12–26 have religious implications. The healing of the leper (vv. 12–16) involves the issue of religious purity and impurity (or "clean" vs. "unclean"). The healing of the paralyzed man (vv. 17–26) involves faith and the forgiveness of sins. This healing story is the first of a series of episodes where Jesus encounters religious criticism and opposition. In 6:1–5 Jesus is accused of working on the Sabbath when he and his disciples picked grain to eat, while similar charges are brought for healing the man with the withered hand (6:6–11). At this point the plot begins to thicken as the religious authorities begin considering what to do with Jesus. Thus, Luke is able to make a transition from celebrated healings in chap. 4 to healings in chap. 5 that raise religious questions, and finally to healings in chap. 6 that lead to serious opposition and eventually to a plot to have Jesus killed. Implicit in all of this is Luke's desire to explain how one who could and did amaze so many with his benevolent power could end up being rejected and put to death.

5:12–16 / Although Jesus heals sufferers of every kind, few deserve as much pity as those who were afflicted with **leprosy** (see note below). Those who contracted leprosy, thought of as a contagious and incurable disease, were quarantined from society as directed by the law of Moses (see Leviticus 13–14). For these poor unfortunates life was lived in hopelessness and despair. Not only were lepers socially ostracized, but they were forced to bear the awful religious stigma of being "unclean." Many would have reasoned the condition was because of some particular sin or moral deficiency. Indeed, according to some rabbis, lepers were regarded as dead (Lachs, p. 153). It is no wonder then that when this person hears of the arrival of Jesus, the one of whom so many things were being reported (as implied by Luke 4:37), **he fell with his face to the ground and begged him, "Lord, if you are willing, you can make me clean"** (v. 12). Note that the leper does not ask Jesus to beseech God in his behalf; rather, his question implies that it is within Jesus' power to heal him. One cannot help but be moved by pity in imagining the leper's mixed feelings of hope and desperation as he threw himself down and begged Jesus. Even to appear among healthy persons would have required special courage. Jesus' response is immediate and effective: **"Be clean!"** (v. 13). **And immediately**, Luke tells us, **the leprosy left him**. But the healed man could not simply move back in with society, for in a case where a person's skin disorder did clear up he was required by the law of Moses to **show** himself **to the priest** (the phrase derives from Lev. 13:49) for formal approval and readmission into society. In presenting himself to the priest, of course, the healed man will be a **testimony to them** (v. 14). There is some debate about what exactly is meant here. The leper's healing is not a testimony to the priest, but the priest's approval of the leper's recovery is testimony or "proof" to society that the man is truly whole. In other words, Jesus has performed no trick, one that might be easily swallowed by gullible and excited crowds. What Jesus has done is to be examined by the authorities and so be confirmed.

Despite (or because of) all the popularity and the **crowds of people** that **came to hear him and to be healed of their sicknesses** (v. 15), **Jesus often withdrew to lonely places and prayed** (v. 16; see also 4:42). Luke often likes to make this point. We have already seen that the Spirit descended upon Jesus (3:21–22) during prayer. Luke also seems to be emphasizing that Jesus did not seek publicity or fame, but wished to avoid those things. Jesus wanted to do the Father's will.

5:17–26 / In the episode in which the paralyzed man is cured, Jesus encounters criticism from the religious leaders of his day for the first time. Criticism comes not because of the miracle per se, but because Jesus declared that the man's **sins are forgiven** (v. 20). This episode is strategic since it shows the beginning of the opposition that will eventually lead to Jesus' arrest, trial, and execution.

Luke derives this scene from Mark 2:1–12, but his minor modifications bring out his key emphases. First, Luke describes Mark's "crowd" (2:1–2) as **Pharisees and teachers of the law** (v. 17; see notes below). In doing this Luke demonstrates that Jesus' min-

istry quickly encounters opposition from the religious establishment. Second, Luke broadens the scope of Jesus' audience by telling us that these religious authorities came **from every village
of Galilee** (here he is thinking of Mark's reference to Capernaum
in 2:1) **and from Judea and Jerusalem**. This notification only
strengthens the first point that was made. The religious authorities who dispute Jesus' teachings and claims are from Judea and
even from Jerusalem, where the controversies would reach their
climax in the crucifixion (see the commentary on 4:1–13).

When Luke tells us that the **power of the Lord was present
for him to heal the sick** (v. 17), the stage is set for the appearance of the **paralytic** (v. 18). This power will be seen, not only
in the physical healing of the paralytic, but in the pronouncement of forgiveness. Apparently what has impressed Jesus is all
of the effort and trouble to which this sufferer and his friends
have gone in order to see him. Such effort could only indicate
faith. Jesus does not, however, immediately heal him, but tells
him that his **sins are forgiven** (v. 20; see note below). This pronouncement provokes the questions and murmurings among the
Pharisees and the teachers of the law (see note below). In their
view, **God alone** forgives **sins**; Jesus, in assuming this authority,
has spoken **blasphemy** (v. 21). Aware of this sentiment, Jesus challenges them with the question found in vv. 22–23. The question
suggests that if he can cure the outward manifestation of sin, i.e.,
the paralysis (see note below), then he can cure, or forgive, the
sin itself. By asking his critics which is **easier**, he backs them into
a corner. Anyone can "say" that someone's sins are forgiven, but
to do something, such as curing a physical ailment possibly
brought on by sin, is an altogether different question. Jesus then
heals the **paralyzed man** as proof that he **has authority on earth
to forgive sins** (v. 24). Here we find the real reason for the telling
of this story. But Jesus does not merely pronounce the man well,
he commands him to **get up, take** his **mat, and go home**. The
instantaneous healing dramatically proves his authority to forgive sins. Luke notes that the people respond to this demonstration of the power of God by giving praise. Luke often notes that
people respond with praise after such manifestations (see 13:13;
17:15; 18:43).

Although it becomes explicit later in 6:11, already the rift
between those who respond to Jesus in faith and praise and those

who respond in unbelief and anger has begun to appear. Even at the very moment when God's power was so dramatically evident, the seeds of violent opposition are sown.

Additional Notes §11

5:12 / **covered with leprosy**: Lit. "full of leprosy." The biblical reference to "leprosy" is general, including the actual disease itself (i.e., Hansen's bacillus), as well as a number of other skin disorders, such as psoriasis. Since the ancients could not be certain whether the disorder was minor and curable or dangerous and incurable, strict precautions were imposed, including exile (see Lev. 13:13; Num. 5:2–3; 12:10–12; Deut. 24:8; 2 Kings 5:27; 7:3–9; 15:5). See *HBD*, pp. 555–56.

Lord: Lit. "lord," but probably meant no more than "sir" on the lips of the leper, although it is possible that in Luke's time a divine connotation may have been sensed.

5:13 / **touched the man**: On touching and healing see Luke 7:14; 8:46; 13:13; 18:15; 22:51; Acts 5:15. Ellis (p. 103) suggests that touching for purposes of healing "seems to have its origin in the Elijah/Elisha healings"; however, see note on 4:40 above. That Jesus **touched** the leper is remarkable in view of popular beliefs and practices. By doing so Jesus demonstrates power and compassion.

5:14 / **Don't tell anyone**: This phrase, taken from Mark 1:44, in the Marcan context has to do with a special theme in Mark usually referred to as the "Messianic Secret." This theme manifests itself in Mark in terms of Jesus' commands of silence given to demons and healed persons, and in terms of the disciples' inability to understand Jesus and his teaching. Luke, in contrast, has no interest in this theme, but he does preserve a few pieces of it as he incorporates Marcan material into his Gospel. For Luke the prohibition not to tell anyone was probably understood in terms of Jesus' lack of interest in publicity and his desire for solitude and prayer (see 4:42; 5:16).

go, show yourself to the priest: By requiring this of the healed man Jesus is thinking of the regulations of Leviticus 13–14, with part of his statement actually derived from Lev. 13:49. Similar instructions are given to the ten lepers in 17:14. The **priest** refers to the priest on duty when the leper arrives for examination and the offering of his sacrifice (Fitzmyer, p. 575).

as a testimony to them: Because of its association with supernatural occurrences (see Exod. 4:6; Num. 12:10–12) leprosy often was believed to be the result of divine judgment. In this connection O. C. Edwards (*Luke's Story of Jesus* [Philadelphia: Fortress, 1981], p. 39) aptly remarks: "[Jesus'] implied argument is that it takes a supernatural person to cure a supernatural disease."

5:16 / **But Jesus often . . . prayed**: This is one of seven unique Lucan reports of Jesus praying; see Luke 3:21; 6:12; 9:18, 28, 29; 11:1; 23:46.

5:17 / **Pharisees and teachers of the law** were the guardians of the "oral law" (or "oral traditions"). The word "Pharisee" means "separated one." The Pharisees were laymen, but men very interested in the interpretation of and obedience to Scripture. The Pharisaic tradition would be taken over by the "rabbis" and be expanded, edited, and codified as Mishnah and Talmud (and other rabbinic writings). Unlike the Sadducees, who were wealthy, aristocratic, and very conservative theologically and politically, the Pharisees were more numerous and much more popular with the people. The Pharisees traced their origins back to the glorious days of the Maccabean struggle for freedom (167–146 B.C.). They were zealous for the Jewish faith and were champions of the messianic hope. They believed that if all Jews would dedicate themselves to a faithful observance of all of the laws of the law of Moses (which included the observance of their oral traditions, designed as a "fence" to protect the law; see *Pirqe Aboth* 1.1) God would raise up his Messiah and deliver Israel. Remarkably, the appearance of Jesus aroused interest, some of it positive, among the Pharisees. Indeed, Jesus and the Pharisees held many things in common (such as belief in resurrection and angels) and not all Pharisees opposed him. Their main problem with Jesus was that they viewed Jesus' attitude toward the law as too liberal, too permissive. Jesus associated with prostitutes, tax collectors, and other "sinners" too freely; moreover, he did not enjoin his disciples to observe those oral traditions so cherished by the Pharisees. Of course, to the extent that Jesus assumed divine prerogatives (such as forgiving sin) he aroused their indignation. Finally, although Jesus frequently quarrels with the Pharisees, and at times calls them names (see esp. Matt. 23:13–36), these men were not any more sinful, blind, or hypocritical than anyone else. What the twentieth-century reader may not realize is that because Christianity in Luke's time was criticized and opposed primarily by Pharisees, the Pharisees are portrayed in the Gospels as Jesus' chief enemies.

the power of the Lord is probably equivalent to the Holy Spirit (see 3:22; 4:1).

5:18 / Paralysis was another physical condition often associated with sin and divine judgment. In all likelihood such a connection was assumed by Jesus' audience, though not necessarily by Jesus himself.

5:19 / In Mark's account (see 2:4) the men "dug through the roof," i.e., they dug a hole through the clay and straw that made up the roof. Luke, however, says that the men made an opening in the **tiles**. Luke puts it this way probably for the sake of his Greco-Roman readers who would have been more familiar with tile roofs. It is, of course, not impossible that the house in this episode may have actually had a tile roof, for Roman architecture and building materials were present in first-century Palestine.

5:20 / The **faith** that Jesus saw in the men probably was no more than a faith in Jesus' ability to cure the sick man, although a vague sense of Jesus' messiahship may have been present. Luke (and his readers), however, may have understood this faith more in terms of later Christian belief concerning Jesus.

5:21 / **teachers of the law**: Lit. "scribes," not the same word as in v. 17 above. The scribes were professional transcribers of Scripture. By virtue of their literacy and expertise they were also regarded as authorities in matters pertaining to the interpretation of Scripture. See note on v. 17.

Blasphemy meant anything uttered about God that was demeaning or insulting (see Lev. 24:10–11, 14–16, 23). In this case Jesus' claim to **forgive sins** provoked the charge of blasphemy, since it was thought to be something that only God could do. Since all human sin is against God, only God, it was reasoned, could forgive sin.

5:23 / Lachs (p. 166), noting that the rabbis made the connection between sin and sickness, cites this interesting parallel: "R. Hiyya stated: 'The patient is not healed of his sickness until his sins are forgiven' " (b. *Nedarim* 41a).

5:24 / This verse contains the first Lucan reference to Jesus as the Son of Man, a recurring title (6:5, 22; 7:34; 9:22, 26, 44, 58; 11:30; 12:8, 10, 40; 17:22, 24, 26, 30; 18:8, 31; 19:10; 21:27, 36; 22:22, 48, 69; 24:7). There has been much debate about the meaning of this title. The most common use of "son of man" in the OT means simply "human being" (see Num. 23:19; Job 25:6; 35:8; Pss. 80:17; 144:3 and many more). But in the apocalyptic vision of Daniel, "son of man" seems to mean something more. Daniel 7:13–14 reads: " . . . with the clouds of heaven there came one like a son of man" to whom the "Ancient of Days" (i.e., God) gave "dominion and glory and kingdom" (RSV). That Jesus alludes to this passage at his trial when asked if he was the Messiah (see Matt. 26:64; Mark 14:62; Luke 21:27; cf. Rev. 1:13) suggests that "son of man" carried with it a messianic connotation. Moreover, scholars have pointed to passages in the pseudepigraphal work *1 Enoch* (see 46:2–4; 48:2; 62:5–7, 13–14; 69:27–29) as examples of how the "son of man" of Daniel 7 came to designate the Messiah. See further Fitzmyer, pp. 208–10.

An interesting question concerning v. 24 is whether Jesus is actually the speaker in the first part of the verse (as it is understood in most versions) or whether Luke is making his own editorial comment (as in Mark 13:14b). The primary reason for suspecting that the latter may indeed be the case is the abrupt grammatical break between **to forgive sins** and **he said to the paralyzed man**. The way it reads in the NIV, Jesus' statement in the first half of v. 24 is left incomplete. However, I think that there is no abrupt grammatical break in the middle of the verse because Jesus is not the speaker in the first part of the verse. I would suggest that it would be better to translate vv. 23–24 as follows: "Which is easier, to say, 'Your sins are forgiven,' or to say, 'Arise and walk'?" But in order that you [i.e., the readers] may know that the Son of Man has authority on earth to forgive sins, he said to the paralyzed, "I say to you, 'Arise, take up your bed and go home.' "

§12 Jesus' Fellowship with Tax Collectors (Luke 5:27–39)

The unifying theme that runs throughout the story of Levi's call (vv. 27–31) and the discussion about eating and fasting (vv. 32–39) concerns fellowship and lifestyle. In the minds of the Pharisees, Jesus' chief critics thus far in Luke's Gospel, Jesus has chosen to have fellowship with the wrong kind of people. Since they were the party of "separatists" (see note on 5:17 above) who believed that redemption would come about by separating themselves from every impurity and impure person (inspired by the admonition of Lev. 10:10), they were offended by Jesus' frequent association with persons considered religiously impure and sinful. From their perspective Jesus could hardly make religious claims while keeping such questionable company. Another aspect of Jesus' ministry that offended the Pharisees and others (such as the Essenes) who fasted often (see 18:12) and strictly monitored what food and drink they consumed was that Jesus apparently did not fast often, nor was he overly concerned about the religious purity of the food that he ate. Thus, in the eyes of his critics, not only did Jesus fellowship with the wrong kind of people, he also had adopted wrong habits.

The major difference between the outlook of the Pharisees and the approach taken by Jesus was that whereas the former were separatistic and exclusivistic, Jesus called people of every sort to himself. Jesus was not interested in isolating himself from sinners, but was interested in bringing change to the lives of sinners. Thus, the difference in religious philosophy between Jesus and the Pharisees was fundamental, making conflict inevitable.

5:27–32 / Like the miraculous catch of fish (5:1–11), the story of the calling of **Levi** serves a double purpose. First, it narrates the call itself and, second, it provides a context for the conversation between **Jesus** and the **Pharisees** that follows (cf. Matt. 9:9–13; Mark 2:13–17).

Having called three Galilean fishermen to discipleship (certainly dubious selections in the eyes of the Pharisees), Jesus nows calls a **tax collector by the name of Levi sitting at his tax booth** (see note below) with his customary summons: "**Follow me**" (v. 27). To include a tax collector among his intimate associates would be, in the minds of the Pharisees, beyond belief. Tax collectors were among the most detestable of all the outcasts of proper religious society. By adding the phrase, **left everything**, Luke emphasizes Levi's total commitment to Jesus. Indeed, the **great banquet** that follows underscores further that in Levi's mind a complete break with the past has been made. He invites many of his friends; among them, of course, would be a **large crowd of tax collectors and others**. It is likely that he wishes to introduce Jesus to his guests and to make known to all his decision to follow the man from Nazareth.

The call of Levi and the giving of the banquet furnish the occasion for the critical question of the Pharisees and the teachers of the law (see note below). They want to know **why** Jesus eats **with tax collectors and "sinners"** (v. 30). To eat with someone, usually referred to as table-fellowship, was a sign of friendship and compatibility. By eating with these people Jesus was identifying with them. But, since Jesus' table companions were religiously impure people, the Pharisees believed that Jesus was compromising his position as a teacher (let alone as the Messiah). Surely God could not work through someone who enjoyed fellowship with the dregs of Jewish society!

Perhaps because of the popular association between physical sickness/unrighteousness and health/moral righteousness (see note on 5:12 above) Jesus likens himself to a **doctor**. A doctor, of course, is needed not by those who are **healthy** (i.e., the righteous), but only by those who are **sick** (i.e., the unrighteous; v. 31). In the next verse Jesus drops the metaphorical language and declares that he has **not come to call the righteous, but sinners to repentance** (v. 32). Luke adds "to repentance" (or "reform"), emphasizing Jesus' summons to a change of life. By associating with the unrighteous, Jesus is not advocating a lowering of proper biblical standards of righteousness. On the contrary, the purpose of his ministry is to make it possible for the fallen to be lifted up to God's standards of righteousness.

5:33–35 / Jesus' eating habits and the controversy that they raised provide the link to the next section concerned with the question about fasting. Fasting was required of all only on the Day of Atonement (see Lev. 16:29) and in commemoration of the destruction of Jerusalem (see Zech. 7:3, 5; 8:19). Fasting was done frequently by **John's disciples** (see Luke 7:33) and the **disciples of the Pharisees** (Mondays and Thursdays; see Luke 18:12). Although Jesus had fasted during his time of testing in the desert (see Luke 4:2), he apparently did not himself fast frequently (or at least so that it could be noticed; see Matt. 6:16–18). Since fasting was viewed as a sign of serious religious commitment and was regarded as essential in preparing for Israel's long-awaited deliverance, it seemed strange and inappropriate that Jesus' disciples ate and drank regularly, especially in light of Jesus' preaching that the "year of the Lord's favor" had dawned (Luke 4:18–19). Jesus' response proves that he has a completely different idea about the coming of Israel's deliverance and his own relationship to it. Jesus likens himself to a **bridegroom** and his disciples as the **guests** of a wedding party. As long as he is present there is celebration (i.e., eating, drinking, and fellowship), but **when the bridegroom will be taken from them; in those days they will fast** (v. 35). The saying anticipates Jesus' departure from the scene, leaving the church to carry out the task of evangelism (as seen in the Book of Acts). During Jesus' absence, while the church is preparing for the Lord's return, fasting will be appropriate (see Acts 13:2–3).

5:36–39 / Jesus illustrates this with two similitudes, both teaching the incompatibility of the new and the old. Just as a **patch** of **new** (i.e., not shrunk) cloth does not patch an **old** garment well nor can **new** (i.e., unfermented) **wine** be accommodated in **old wineskins**, so the new ideas of the gospel will not be accommodated by old patterns of thought. Jesus' instruction about the poor, the sinners, and the unacceptable will not fit into old assumptions about how God judges and evaluates people. That this will be difficult to accept is seen in Jesus' final comment: **"And no one after drinking old wine wants the new, for he says, 'The**

old is better' " (v. 39). Jesus recognizes that old habits and ways of thinking are not easily changed.

Additional Notes §12

5:27 / Although there is some uncertainty as to the identity of **Levi** the **tax collector**, comparison with the parallel passage in Matt. 9:9, where the man sitting in the tax office is called "Matthew," and with the passage in Matt. 10:3, where this Matthew is identified as the "tax collector," would suggest that the Levi of Luke 5:27 and Mark 2:14 is the one called "Matthew" in the Gospel named after him. Mark's reference to "Levi, the son of Alphaeus" (2:14) has led to some confusion since Alphaeus is the name of the father of the other James, mentioned in Mark 3:18. (In fact, some early Christian scribes either out of confusion or out of a desire to harmonize Mark 2:14 with 3:18 replaced "Levi" with "James.") Since it was not at all unusual for first-century Jews to have two names, often one Semitic and the other Greco-Roman (e.g., Simon Peter, Saul/Paul), it is quite possible that Levi's full name was Levi Matthew, or the like (see Fitzmyer, pp. 589–90).

5:30 / **the Pharisees and the teachers of the law who belonged to their sect**: Luke wishes to identify these **teachers of the law** (lit. "scribes") more closely with the **Pharisees** (see note on 5:17 above) and so adds **their** to his Marcan source. The implication is that for now at least it is the Pharisees who are Jesus' real enemies. Tiede (p. 127) makes the valid point that the Pharisees were not motivated out of mean-spirited legalism in their quarrel with Jesus. They were critical of Jesus' style of ministry because to them it did not seem to square with Scripture's call to holiness (Lev. 10:10; 19:2) and separation (Neh. 10:28).

his disciples: The hostile questioning addressed to Jesus' **disciples** (instead of being addressed to Jesus himself) mirrors the situation of the early church when Christians had to face hostile questions and accusations concerning their practices and beliefs.

5:30, 32 / **sinners**: This epithet refers to those who could not or would not observe the law of Moses, particularly the oral laws and traditions of the scribes and Pharisees. The Pharisees regarded these people as having no hope for participation in the kingdom of God or the resurrection of the righteous. Lachs (p. 168) cites several rabbinic sources that discuss the undesirability of mingling, especially eating, with those who did not observe the laws of purity.

5:34 / The metaphor of Jesus as **bridegroom** occurs elsewhere in the NT (see Matt. 25:1–10; John 3:29) and underlies the idea of the church as the "bride of Christ" (see Eph. 5:23; Rev. 18:23; 21:2, 9; 22:17). The bride/bridegroom imagery may have been derived from the OT (see Isa. 49:18; 61:10; 62:5).

5:36–38 / A **patch from a new garment**, since it has not yet shrunk through washing, does not make a suitable patch for an **old** garment that has shrunk. Similarly, since **new wine** expands while it is fermenting, it needs to be put into **new wineskins** that are still capable of stretching. For further discussion see A. Kee, "The Old Coat and the New Wine: A Parable of Repentance," *NovT* 12 (1970), pp. 13–21. Leaney (p. 128) thinks that Luke has misunderstood the Marcan form of this parable (Mark 2:21). On the contrary, Luke has not only understood it, but in revising it, the evangelist has brought home its point more clearly (see Fitzmyer, pp. 600–601).

5:36 / **parable**: The word parable(s) occurs several times in Luke (6:39; 8:4, 9, 10, 11; 12:16, 41; 13:6; 14:7; 15:3; 18:1, 9; 19:11; 20:9, 19; 21:29). The Greek NT word "parable" (as well as its Hebrew equivalent) has a variety of meanings and usages. It may refer to a simple illustration, a proverbial saying, or an enigmatic saying. The idea of parabolic obscurity can be seen in Luke 8:9–11 (cf. Mark 4:10–13). The basic meaning of "parable" is *comparison*. A parable usually illustrates an abstract idea (faithfulness, duty, fruitfulness, forgiveness, prayer, judgment) with common, everyday experiences and observations. Like many fables, the parable usually contains a lesson or moral. Normally a parable is intended to make one basic point (the lesson) and is not to be allegorized (where every detail of the parable is assigned a value; see note on 10:29–35 below). However, a few of the parables are allegorized in the Gospels themselves (see Mark 4:1–20; Matt. 13:24–30, 36–43). Oftentimes a parable appears to have had only one basic point (or lesson), but the interpreter may well suspect that the tradition and/or the evangelist may have understood the parable, or parts of the parable, allegorically. As the parables are encountered, the question of what the parable originally meant and what later interpretations may have been assigned to it will be taken into account. See also the note on 8:9–10 below.

§13 More Controversy with the Pharisees (Luke 6:1–11)

Jesus implied in the previous section (5:27–39) that his authority superseded the rules of ritual purity. Jesus demonstrates in this section that he has authority over the Sabbath. This is seen in the first episode where Jesus' disciples picked and ate grain on the Sabbath (6:1–2), an action that Jesus defended against the charge that such activity amounted to "work" on the Sabbath (6:3–5). It reappears in the second episode when Jesus heals the man wit the withered (or paralyzed) hand and is accused of breaking the Sabbath (6:6–11).

6:1–5 / When **one Sabbath Jesus** and **his disciples** walked **through the grainfields** and **began to pick some heads of grain**, rubbing **them in their hands** and eating the **kernels**, they were doing what was permitted in the law of Moses (see Deut. 23:25 and note below). The issue, however, was whether or not they were actually doing what could be called "working" (i.e., the rubbing of the heads of grain) on the Sabbath. If they were, then they were violating the commandment forbidding work on the Sabbath (see Exod. 20:8–11; 23:12; Deut. 5:12–15). The Pharisaic understanding of what constituted work, however, was quite narrow. Consequently, in their eyes Jesus and his disciples were doing **what is unlawful on the sabbath** (v. 2; see note below).

Jesus, however, does not dispute about whether or not the rubbing of the heads of grain should be considered work. Rather, he cites the example of **David** who had **entered the house of God** and had eaten the **consecrated bread**, bread which is **lawful only for priests to eat** (see note below). Jesus argues that if it was lawful for David and his men to eat consecrated bread (and the rabbis agreed that David's action was justified in this case), then why would it not be lawful for Jesus (the "Son of David"; see Luke 18:38, 39; 20:41, 44) and his disciples to glean from the fields for some food? Jesus is implying that just as David was going about the task of establishing a new reign in Israel, so now Jesus is going about a similar task. Just as David's special circumstances made it permissible to eat the consecrated bread, so the present circumstances made it permissible for Jesus and his disciples to "harvest" some food for themselves. Jesus' authority, however, is even greater than was David's, for as the **Son of Man** he is **Lord of the Sabbath** (v. 5). Nevertheless, the next scene shows that the Lordship of Jesus will not be accepted by the Pharisees and their allies.

    6:6–11 / In the episode of the healing of the **man** whose **right hand was shriveled** (lit. "withered" or "dried up") conflict over the question of the **Sabbath** seemed planned on both sides. Since it was the Sabbath the **Pharisees and the teachers of the law** were watching **Jesus** closely **to see if he would heal on the Sabbath** (v. 7). If he did, they would then have grounds for accusing him. Jesus knew that he was being watched. He was in a **synagogue**, after all, and it was the Sabbath. Jesus just as easily could have made an appointment with the man for Sunday or Monday. But Jesus wanted to take the opportunity to make a point. His question cuts to the very heart of the issue: **"I ask you, which is lawful on the Sabbath: to do good or to do evil, to save life or to destroy it?"** (v. 9). Since the Pharisaic tradition allowed for deeds of mercy to be performed on the Sabbath (e.g., see m. *Yoma* 8.6 and b. *Shabbath* 132a), especially in life and death matters, Jesus' questions have backed his opponents into a corner. Later in Luke's Gospel, Jesus will accuse the Pharisees of being hypocrites for showing more concern for the well-being of an ox than a person on the Sabbath (see Luke 13:15; 14:5). Jesus then heals the man; but instead of praising God, as others had when Jesus had performed a healing or exorcism (see 5:26), the Pharisees **were furious and began to discuss with one another what they might do with Jesus** (see note below). The murmurs of "Blasphemy!" (5:21) and the questions about the company he kept had now given way to the beginning of a conspiracy to do away with Jesus (see note below).

Additional Notes   §13

6:1 / According to Deut. 23:25 grain could be picked from a neighbor's field, but a sickle could not be used.

6:2 / **what is unlawful**: "What is lawful" or "unlawful" is an expression which may refer either to the law of Moses or to the oral laws and traditions of the scribes and Pharisees. The issue in the minds of the Pharisees was the work involved in picking and rubbing the grain. Among some rabbis even picking and rubbing grain was considered "harvesting" and so was forbidden, as was all other work, on the Sabbath (see m. *Shabbath* 7.2; b. *Shabbath* 73b).

6:3 / **what David did**: Luke wisely omits Mark's reference to "Abiathar the high priest" (Mark 2:26) since according to 1 Sam. 21:1–6 Ahimelech, not Abiathar, was high priest when David and his men entered the house of God. Reference to David would emphasize further Jesus' messianic status, for his action was comparable to that of Israel's most famous king, from whom would descend the Messiah (see Isa. 11:1, 10; Jer. 23:5; Zech. 3:8).

6:5 / **Lord of the Sabbath**: Luke has derived this verse from Mark 2:28, but he did not, however, retain Mark 2:27, which reads: "The Sabbath was made for man, not man for the Sabbath." In the Marcan context the point seems to be that since the Sabbath is intended primarily for man's benefit (and not vice versa), Jesus as "Son of Man" is therefore Lord of the Sabbath. Luke may have sensed that Mark 2:27 implied that the expression, "Son of Man," meant no more than "human" (for whom the Sabbath was made). Luke, however, probably understood "Son of Man" as more of a messianic or even divine title (see note on 5:24 above); he therefore elected to omit the saying in Mark 2:27. Luke seems to conclude that since Jesus is Son of Man (in a messianic and probably even a divine sense), he is therefore Lord of the Sabbath (as well as Lord of everything else) and can dictate what is acceptable Sabbath activity and what is not. According to Tiede (p. 131), Jesus "is the embodiment of the reign of God, and his authority supersedes the Law itself."

In the Greek ms. Codex D, following Luke 6:5 is this brief episode that some scholars think may be genuine: "On the same day he saw a man performing a work on the Sabbath. Then he said to him: 'Man! If you know what you are doing, you are blessed. But if you do not know, you are cursed and a transgressor of the law.' " Presumably, if a person works on the Sabbath for proper reasons, or in a proper spirit, much as Jesus had done in healing the man with the paralyzed hand, then he is not guilty of violating the Sabbath laws. For a discussion of other potentially authentic sayings found outside of the canonical Gospels see J. Jeremias, *Unknown Sayings of Jesus* (London: SPCK, 1958), pp. 49–87.

6:6 / The **right hand** was thought of as the hand needed for work, and therefore the man's condition of paralysis represented a serious disability. Again, it is likely that the man's condition would have been thought of as brought on by sin.

6:9 / **Is** it **lawful on the Sabbath . . . to save life . . . ?** Lachs (pp. 199–200) notes that the rabbis permitted healing on the Sabbath only if life is in danger (see m. *Yoma* 8.6). In the case of the man with the withered hand, Jesus could have—and from the Pharisaic point of view should have—waited until the next day.

6:11 / **they were furious**: The word translated "furious" connotes "mindless rage" and probably contributes to the theme of the hardened heart that stubbornly refuses to believe.

Mark 3:6 reads, "how to destroy him," but Luke has elected to write, **what they might do to Jesus**. Luke's modification probably reflects his desire to hold the reader in suspense a little longer before revealing the murderous plans of Jesus' opponents. (It might also be noted that although the Pharisees in Luke appear as Jesus' opponents, they are not presented as those who clamor for Jesus' death.)

§14 *Instruction for the Disciples (Luke 6:12–49)*

Luke's account of the choosing of the Twelve (6:12–16) is based on Mark 3:13–19, while his summarizing account of Jesus' healings on the "level place" (6:17–19) is based loosely on Mark 3:7–12. Luke reversed the order of these Marcan units to accommodate the sermon that follows (6:20–49). As it now stands in Luke, Jesus goes up on a mountain (v. 12) to appoint the Twelve, then he descends to a plateau to teach and heal crowds (vv. 17–18), which leads quite naturally into the sermon. (Mark has no equivalent sermon.) The sermon seems to be derived primarily from the sayings source utilized by Luke and Matthew. Thus, we may say that Luke 6:12–49 is based on material taken from Mark and from the sayings source.

6:12–16 / As we have seen previously, in Luke, prayer often precedes an important task (3:21–22; 5:16), and so on this occasion **Jesus . . . spent the night praying to God** (v. 12). **When morning came** Jesus **called his disciples to him and chose twelve of them** as **apostles** (v. 13). Here Luke's reference to "apostles" anticipates the missionary work which will be described in the Book of Acts (so Matt. 10:2; Mark later calls them "apostles" in 6:30). Luke records twelve names, but comparison with other apostolic lists (Matt. 10:2–4; Mark 3:16–19; Acts 1:13) suggests that there were more than twelve among the Twelve. Moreover, if the eight names given in the Gospel of John are taken into consideration (Peter, Andrew, Philip, Bartholomew, Thomas, Judas [not Iscariot], Nathanael, and Judas Iscariot) there could be as many as fifteen or sixteen apostles. We have in the Gospels and Acts the following names of men considered among the Twelve:

(1) **Simon Peter**	Matt. 10:2; Mark 3:16; Luke 6:14; John 1:42; Acts 1:13; see also 1 Pet. 1:1; 2 Pet. 1:1
(2) **Andrew**, the brother of Peter	Matt. 10:2; Mark 3:18; Luke 6:14; John 1:40; Acts 1:13
(3) **James**, son of Zebedee	Matt. 10:2; Mark 3:17; Luke 6:14; Acts 1:13
(4) **John**, son of Zebedee	Matt. 10:2; Mark 3:17; Luke 6:14; John 1:35–40?; Acts 1:13; see also Rev. 1:9; 22:8
(5) **Philip**	Matt. 10:3; Mark 3:18; Luke 6:14; John 1:43; Acts 1:13
(6) **Bartholomew**	Matt. 10:3; Mark 3:18; Luke 6:14; Acts 1:13
(7) **Matthew**	Matt. 10:3; Luke 6:15; Acts 1:13
(8) Levi	Mark 2:14; Luke 5:27
(9) **Thomas**	Matt. 10:3; Mark 3:18; Luke 6:15; John 11:16; Acts 1:13
(10) **James**, son of Alphaeus	Matt. 10:3; Mark 3:18; Luke 6:15; Acts 1:13
(11) Thaddaeus (or Lebbaeus in some mss)	Matt. 10:3; Mark 3:18
(12) "Simon the Cananaean"	Matt. 10:4; Mark 3:18
(13) **Simon the Zealot** (Gk. *zēlōtēs*)	Luke 6:15; Acts 1:13
(14) **Judas**, son of James	Luke 6:16; Acts 1:13; John 14:22, "Judas, not Iscariot"

| (15) **Judas Iscariot**, the betrayer | Matt. 10:4; Mark 3:19; Luke 6:16; John 12:6; Acts 1:16 |
| (16) Nathanael | John 1:45 |

Since it is likely that "Levi" and "Matthew" are one and the same (cf. Matt. 9:9 and Mark 2:14 and see commentary on 5:27–32 above) and that "Simon the Cananaean" and "Simon the Zealot" refer to the same person ("Cananaean" is Aramaic for "zealous") our list of sixteen names is reduced to fourteen. It is also assumed that the "Judas, not Iscariot" of John 14:22 is the same as "Judas, son of James" in Luke 6:16 and Acts 1:13. Other names among the remaining fourteen may refer to one individual, but we have no sure way of knowing. Some efforts have been undertaken in the past to reduce the list to twelve, but ingenuity and desperation have been more in evidence than actual fact. For example, the suggestion put forward several centuries ago that the "Bartholomew" of the Synoptic tradition is the "Nathanael" of the Gospel of John rests on pure conjecture and lacks any evidence whatsoever. Other even more improbable suggestions have been made. Consequently, it is impossible to reduce these names to twelve.

The solution to the difficulty lies in recognizing that whereas the number twelve had symbolic value, and probably represented the approximate number of those men who were regarded as Jesus' closest followers, the actual number of apostles fluctuated. Evidence for this view is seen in the Book of Acts. Not only is Judas Iscariot replaced by Matthias (Acts 1:26), but Paul *and* Barnabas are also numbered among the apostles (see Acts 14:14; also implied in 1 Cor. 9:6). (Paul calls himself an apostle in Rom. 1:1; 11:13; 1 Cor. 1:1; 9:1, 2; 15:9; 2 Cor. 1:1; 12:12; Gal. 1:1; see also Eph. 1:1; Col. 1:1; 1 Tim. 1:1; 2 Tim. 1:1; Titus 1:1.) In 1 Cor. 15:5–7 Paul seems to make a distinction between the "eleven" (the Twelve minus Judas Iscariot) and other apostles. From his argument in 1 Cor. 3:1–15 it would also seem that Paul regarded Apollos as an apostle. Finally, in Rom. 16:7 Paul extends his greetings to "Andronicus and Junias . . . outstanding among the apostles and . . . in Christ before I was." (Note that the name Junias could either be masculine or feminine.)

Since it is accepted that there were more than twelve apostles, it would appear best to understand the number "twelve" as a general designation with a symbolic meaning. Because of the historic significance of this number, it is not difficult to imagine why this number was utilized by Jesus and retained as a tradition by the early church. A few of the most important examples should be noted. Abraham is told that Ishmael, his son by Hagar the slave girl (Gen. 16:15–16), shall become "the father of twelve rulers" (Gen. 17:20) of twelve tribes (Gen. 25:16). Undoubtedly, this is a counterpart to the "twelve sons" of Jacob (Gen. 35:22) who became the fathers of Israel's (i.e., Jacob's) "twelve tribes" (Gen. 49:28). (Although there is no evidence that Luke has exploited the "twelve princes" of Ishmael, the idea of there being *twelve Gentile* patriarchs in addition to the twelve Jewish patriarchs would have been very suggestive to a predominantly Gentile church.) Moses builds an altar to the Lord with "twelve pillars representing the twelve tribes of Israel" (Exod. 24:4). Twelve men are sent as spies into the "promised land" (Deut. 1:23, in reference to Num. 13:1–16). Interestingly, the names of the twelve spies are listed (Num. 13:4–15). In his effort to bring about religious reform Elijah built an altar with twelve stones according to the number of the tribes of the sons of Jacob (1 Kings 18:31).

New Testament references to the twelve other than those to the apostles seem to have symbolic meaning. For example, in James 1:1 Christians are called "the twelve tribes scattered among the nations." Similarly, the Seer John enumerates the chosen people as 12,000 from each of the twelve tribes (Rev. 7:3–8). Moreover, he writes that the new Jerusalem will have "twelve foundation stones" on which will be inscribed the twelve names of the twelve apostles (Rev. 21:14; which twelve names he has in mind is anybody's guess; see also the other references to twelve in Rev. 21:12, 16, 21), while in heaven there will be a "tree of life, bearing twelve crops of fruit, yielding its fruit every month" (Rev. 22:2). The most insightful reference, however, comes from the sayings source ("Q") utilized by Matthew and Luke. Luke 22:29–30 reads: "I confer on you a kingdom . . . so that you may eat and drink at my table in my kingdom and sit on thrones ["twelve thrones" according to Matt. 19:28], judging the twelve tribes of Israel." The twelve apostles symbolize the foundation of God's new people of faith, or in Luke's terms, that part of Israel that has believed in Messiah Jesus (see Introduction, pp. 6–12). Just as the twelve patriarchs fathered the twelve tribes of (old) Israel, so the twelve apostles are the spiritual fathers of the "twelve tribes" (as in James 1:1) of repentant and believing Israel. What has become formally fixed in the Gospel tradition is the number "twelve," not an exact and unvarying list of twelve names (see notes below).

6:17–19 / This paragraph serves as a transition from the appointing of the Twelve and the giving of the sermon that follows. In appointing the Twelve and so laying the foundation upon which will be built a repentant and believing people of God, Jesus is now ready to teach his people. As in Luke 5:17, where the "power of the Lord was present for him to heal the sick," so now again **power was coming from him and healing them all** (v. 19). Luke understands this power as very real, for **people** were trying **to touch him** (see 5:13; 7:14; 8:44; 18:15; 22:51; cf. Acts 5:15–16). The emphasis, however, falls on the people who came **to hear him** (an element not found in the Marcan parallel), which prepares the reader for the sermon. That some of these people had come from **Tyre and Sidon** may be a hint of Gentile presence.

6:20–49 / Called the "Sermon on the Plain" because of the reference to the "level place" (6:17), this section parallels Matthew's better known, and much longer, "Sermon on the Mount" (5:3–7:27; see notes below). This sermon teaches not what must be done to *enter* the kingdom of God, but what is expected of one who is already *in* the kingdom. This is seen not only in the sermon's actual contents, in what it seems to presuppose, but also in the fact that Jesus' sermon is intended primarily for his apostles and **disciples** (see vv. 17, 20). This sermon calls for the implementation of those ideals contained in Isa. 61:1–2, the passage which Jesus quoted at the beginning of his Nazareth sermon (Luke 4:16–30). The major thrust of the sermon is found in the four "beatitudes" (or blessings) introduced with the adjective **blessed** (vv. 20–22) and the four "woes" introduced with the interjection **woe** (vv. 24–26).

On the one hand, Jesus teaches his disciples that though they are **poor** and **hunger now**, they really are rich because the **kingdom of God** belongs to them; though they **weep** and **men hate** and **insult** them, the day will come when they will **laugh** and receive a great **reward in heaven**. The last part of v. 23 summarizes why the disciples should respond to such insult and abuse in this way: **For that is how their fathers treated the prophets**. Luke advises that the followers of Christ should **rejoice and leap for joy** when they experience such treatment, for it puts them into the company of some of the greatest OT heroes of the faith. On the other hand, woes are pronounced upon those who are wealthy and too concerned with worldly affairs to be bothered about the **kingdom of God** (see also Luke 14:15–24). They may be **rich** and **laugh now**, but the day will come when they **will go hungry** and **will mourn and weep**. Though **all men speak well of** them, it means nothing, **for that is how their fathers treated the false prophets**.

Unlike Matthew's version, the Lucan sermon is referring to those who suffer from real poverty and hunger, not to those who are "poor in spirit" (Matt. 5:3) or who "hunger and thirst after righteousness" (Matt. 5:6). The Lucan form of the sermon reflects and contributes to Luke's overall concern with poverty and wealth. Jesus' disciples may experience deprivation and persecution, but they are truly **blessed**. In vv. 27–36 Jesus gives the proper response to those who hate, reject, and insult his people (v. 22). His disciples are to **love** their **enemies, do good to those who hate** them; they are to **bless those who curse** them, to **pray for those who mistreat** them, and to **turn** the other **cheek**. The disciples are to be generous and giving with their resources and to **be merciful, just as** their heavenly **Father is merciful**.

In vv. 37–42 Jesus warns his disciples to take care in the way that they evaluate other people. The command **not** to **judge** others refers to fault-finding and criticism, but it should not be understood as prohibiting constructive criticism and assistance, as is verified by the humorous exaggeration concerning the **speck** and the **plank** (vv. 41–42). The sayings in vv. 39–40 refer to the necessity of proper preparation if the disciples are to be leaders. If they are **blind** then they cannot **lead** another, but when they are **fully trained**, they will be like their **teacher** (Jesus). Verses 43–45 illustrate metaphorically how people can be evaluated: **Each tree is recognized by its own fruit**.

Verses 46–49 draw the sermon to a close with an exhortation to obedience and with a parable contrasting the wise man **who hears** Jesus' **words and puts them into practice** with the foolish man **who hears** Jesus' **words and does not put them into practice**. This parable evokes a vivid picture of a flash flood that comes upon all without warning. Although some will be prepared, because they have obeyed the words of Jesus, others will not be prepared, and so will experience **destruction**, for they disregarded Jesus' warning. Since the whole sermon seems directed to Jesus' disciples, it is likely that this parable refers to his disciples as well. Thus understood, it is an exhortation to all disciples to hear and obey Jesus' teachings and so remain firmly founded in the faith.

Additional Notes §14

6:12 / It is significant that **Jesus went out to a mountainside** (lit. "up a mountain"), for a mountain was often the site for special encounters with God (see Exod. 19:1–6, where Moses meets God on Mount Sinai; and 1 Kings 18:17–40, where God sends fire down on Mount Carmel). Later in Luke, Jesus is transfigured on the mountain (9:28–36).

to pray: Before selecting his apostles and before delivering the Sermon on the Plain, Jesus prayed. This is characteristic of the Lucan portrayal of Jesus; see note on 5:16.

6:13 / **he called his disciples to him and chose twelve**: The earliest sources know of the tradition of the Twelve Apostles (Paul and the Synoptics), even if they are not in exact agreement as to the names. According to one rabbinic tradition in the Babylonian Talmud (ca. A.D. 500) "Jesus had five disciples: Matthai, Nakai, Nezer, Buni, and Todah" (b. *Shabbath* 104b). Although the first name approximates Matthew's name, these names are no more than symbolic and are the basis for the critical comments that follow in the Talmudic passage. Neither the number five nor the names themselves are of any historical value.

6:14–16 / **Simon (whom he named Peter)**: Simon is a shortened form of Simeon, which means "hearing with acceptance." In Luke, Peter is a fisherman and the first disciple to be called (5:1–11; in v. 8 he is called "Simon Peter"). Although Luke does not present his own version of Matt. 16:16–19, where Jesus gives Simon the name "Peter" (Greek for "rock"), he was obviously aware of the tradition that it was Jesus who had named him. Simon is also called "Cephas" (Aramaic for "rock"; see John 1:42; 1 Cor. 1:12; 3:22; 9:5; 15:5; Gal. 2:9). See *HBD*, pp. 776–78. According to Papias, a second-century church father, John Mark, the kinsman of Barnabas (see Acts 12:12; 15:37–39), based his Gospel (of Mark) account on Peter's memoirs. This is at best a dubious tradition. The prominence of Peter among the Twelve prompted many to name writings after him.

The so-called Petrine epistles are probably examples within the NT, while the apocryphal *Gospel of Peter* is one of the better known extracanonical works. For the text of this writing see E. Hennecke and W. Schneemelcher, *New Testament Apocrypha*, 2 vols. (Philadelphia: Westminster, 1974), vol. 1, pp. 185–86. Peter's name has also been associated with some of the gnostic writings: the *Acts of Peter and the Twelve Apostles* (Nag Hammadi Codex VI,1), the *Apocalypse of Peter* (NHC VII,3), and the *Letter of Peter to Philip* (NHC VIII,2). For English translations see James M. Robinson, ed., *The Nag Hammadi Library* (San Francisco: Harper & Row, 1977). For Jewish legends about Peter see J. Greenstone, "Jewish Legends about Simon Peter," *Historia Judaica* 12/2 (1950), pp. 89–104.

James and John: James is actually the OT name "Jacob" (Hebrew for "supplanter"), the great patriarch. His death is reported in Acts 12:1–2. He and his brother John (from the Hebrew *Yôḥānān* meaning "the Lord has shown favor") were the sons of Zebedee (Luke 5:10), and in Mark 3:17 they are dubbed "the Sons of Thunder." Tradition ascribes authorship of the Fourth Gospel to this John and identifies him as the "disciple whom Jesus loved" (John 13:23; 19:26; 20:2; 21:7, 20), the disciple who leaned against the breast of Jesus and inquired who the betrayer was (John 13:21–27). The sons of Zebedee and Peter were apparently Jesus' closest followers, for Jesus is often in their company (see Luke 9:28–36).

Philip: a Greek name meaning "lover of horses." He figures prominently in the Gospel of John (1:43–45; 12:21–22; 14:9). His name appears in the gnostic *Letter of Peter to Philip* (see note on Peter above).

Bartholomew: His name (from Aramaic *bar-Tolmai* meaning the "son of Tolmai") occurs only in the formal lists of the Synoptic Gospels and Acts. We know nothing of him. There is no evidence that he is the same person as "Nathanael" (John 1:45–46), though this suggestion has been made from time to time.

Matthew: The name is from the Hebrew and means "the gift of the Lord." He is probably the same person as "Levi, son of Alphaeus" (Mark 2:14), however the "Alphaeus" coincidence or confusion is to be explained, for reasons mentioned in the commentary above. In Matt. 10:3 Matthew is identified as a tax collector. Tradition ascribes authorship of the Gospel of Matthew to this apostle. Papias says that Matthew wrote down the *logia* ("oracles") of the Lord in Hebrew, and everyone translated them as best as he could. Many regard this tradition as unreliable. Even if the tradition were accepted, there is doubt that Papias has in mind the canonical Gospel of Matthew. For a different assessment of Papias' testimony and a thorough defense of Matthean authorship of the Gospel of Matthew see Gundry, pp. 609–22.

Thomas: The name comes from Aramaic meaning "twin" (Heb. *te'om*). Hence he is called "Didymos," which is Greek for "twin," in John 11:16; 20:24; 21:2. Only in the Gospel of John are we told anything about this apostle. Legend had it that Thomas was Jesus' twin. Probably for this reason the name of Thomas was associated with a variety of apocryphal writings. There is an *Infancy Gospel of Thomas* that tells of Jesus' infancy and boyhood. According to this work, Jesus performs several astounding and often ostentatious miracles. His touch restores a man who had been transformed into a donkey; his diapers purify a poisoned well; idols bow down before him; clay pigeons fashioned by the boy Jesus fly away at the clap of his hands; the hand of an angry rabbi withers when raised to strike Jesus; a classmate drops dead when he elbows Jesus during a race; the dead boy is raised after angry parents protest and beseech Jesus' parents. In some ways no less bizarre is the gnostic *Gospel of Thomas* (NHC II,2). Its prologue reads in part: "These are the secret sayings which the living Jesus spoke and which Didymos Judas Thomas wrote down." Although some of the materials in this writing may be early, even authentic, most of it reflects ideas, gnostic or otherwise, that emerged in the second and third centuries. And, in any case, the Apostle Thomas had nothing to do with it.

James son of Alphaeus: Other than his mention in the apostolic rosters we know nothing of this "son of Alphaeus" (from the Hebrew meaning "chief ox"). He is not to be confused with "James the Lord's brother" (Mark 6:3; 1 Cor. 15:7; Gal. 1:19) or with "James the Smaller" (Mark 15:40). Because Levi (Matthew) in Mark 2:14 is called the "son of Alphaeus" there is the slight possibility that he and James were brothers. The Tosefta tells of one "Jacob" [= James] who healed in the name of Jesus the Nazarene (t. *Hullin* 2.22). This tradition, whether it is reliable or not, could refer to almost anyone.

Simon who was called the Zealot: In Mark 3:18 and Matt. 10:4 this apostle is called "Simon the Zealot" (or "Cananaean," see commentary above). In what sense he was a "zealot" is difficult to say. It would probably be anachronistic to associate Simon with the "zealots" who banded together a few decades later to fight Rome (A.D. 66–70). The epithet may have had nothing to do with political views but with personal piety and zeal.

Judas son of James: The name is the Greek form of the Hebrew name "Judah" meaning "praised." Nothing is known of this Judas, although in John 14:22 he is probably the "Judas (not Iscariot)" who asks Jesus a question. He is sometimes referred to as "Jude" or "Judah" to avoid confusion with the better known Judas Iscariot, but he should not be confused with the "Jude, brother of James," to whom is ascribed the Letter of Jude. The suggestion that is sometimes made (in the interest of reducing the apostolic roster to no more than twelve names in all) that Jude and Thaddaeus (Matt. 10:3; Mark 3:18) are names of the same person is without any evidence.

Judas Iscariot, who became a traitor: In John 6:71 and 13:26 he is called Judas son of Simon Iscariot. It has been suggested that "Iscariot" is Hebrew for "a man from (the town of) Kerioth," a "village about twelve miles S[outh] of Hebron in Judea" (Fitzmyer, p. 620). Suggestions that "Iscariot" comes from Aramaic words meaning "liar" or "dagger" are not convincing and probably represent later Christian speculation. The reference to him as traitor anticipates, of course, his betrayal of Jesus into the hands of the religious authorities (Luke 22:3–6, 47–48). For more on the names of the twelve apostles see Fitzmyer, pp. 613–20; Marshall, pp. 236–41; Ellis, p. 110; *HBD*, pp. 40, 222, 1101.

6:20–49 / Most of the material in the Matthean and Lucan sermons is derived from the sayings source (Q) that is common to these Gospels. The Matthean sermon is about three times as long as the Lucan sermon. This is due primarily to Luke's having placed many of the parallel components outside his sermon (Luke 8:16; 11:2–4, 9–13, 33–35; 12:22–34, 58–59; 13:24, 26–27; 16:17–18). In a couple of instances Luke places parallel material in his sermon that is found outside the Matthean sermon (Luke 6:39 = Matt. 15:14b; Luke 6:40 = Matt. 10:24–25a). Several Matthean components have no parallel in Luke (5:17, 19–24, 27–30, 33–39a, 43; 6:1–8, 16–18; 7:6, 15). Finally, Luke has a few components not found anywhere in Matthew (6:24–26, 27b, 28a, 34–35a, 37b, 38a, 39a).

There have been attempts to harmonize the contents and the respective settings of these two sermons. The most plausible explanation is that Matthew and Luke have freely adapted what was probably an extended sermon (of twenty verses or so) in the sayings source. Since both Matthew and Luke relate their sermons to a "mountain," there could very well have been reference to a mountain in the sayings source as well. Efforts have also been made to harmonize Matthew's statement that Jesus "went up into the mountain" (5:1) with Luke's statement that Jesus "descended to a level place" (6:17). Probably the simplest solution is to recognize that each evangelist utilized the mountain setting for his own purpose. Whereas Matthew is content to leave the impression that Jesus taught the crowds on the mountain (though exactly where the people were supposed to be seated is not clear, nor does it really matter), Luke is more concerned with where the people were to sit for this sermon and so mentions the **level place**. On Jesus' descent to teach the people, Ellis (p. 112) thinks that there might be a parallel with Moses in Exod. 19:25.

6:20–22 / **Blessed**: Beatitudes also occur in the OT (Pss. 1:1; 2:12; 34:8; 41:1; 84:4; 94:12; 119:2; Prov. 8:34; Jer. 17:7) and intertestamental writings (Sir. 14:1; 25:8, 9; 28:19; *Pss. Sol.* 5:18; 6:1; *1 Enoch* 48:9; 62:1). Fitzmyer (p. 633) notes that "they usually stress a reversal of values that people put on earthly things. . . . A paradox is often involved in them." Talbert (pp. 69–71) explains that the Beatitudes do not confer blessings; they are expressions of congratulations.

poor: Lachs (p. 71) suggests that the "poor" equals the righteous (*Pss. Sol.* 10:7; b. *Berakoth* 6b). This is likely what Matthew means when he adds "in spirit" (Matt. 5:3). Luke may have thought of the "poor" as literally poor.

6:31 / The so-called Golden Rule has many parallels in antiquity. The "negative" version is found in Tob. 4:15: "And what you hate, do not do to any one" (RSV). For references to other pagan and Jewish parallels see Talbert, p. 73.

6:46–49 / Lachs (p. 151) cites this interesting rabbinic parable that parallels Jesus' Parable of the Wise and Foolish Builders: "He used to say: 'One in whom there are good works, who has studied much Torah, to what may he be likened? To lime poured over stones: even when any number of rains fall on it, they cannot push it out of place. One in whom there are no good works, though he studied much Torah, is like lime poured over bricks: even when a little rain falls on it, it softens immediately and is washed away' " (*Aboth de Rabbi Nathan* 24; see also m. *Aboth* 3.18).

This section consists of three parts that are loosely related to Jesus' answer to the messengers of the imprisoned John the Baptist. Another factor uniting these stories together are the parallels with the Elijah/Elisha stories in 1 and 2 Kings. The first of Luke's episodes is about the healing of the officer's servant (7:1–10); the second is about the raising of the widow's son (7:11–17); and the third is John's question and Jesus' answer (7:18–35).

7:1–10 / The episode of the healing of the **centurion's servant** parallels Matt. 8:5–13 (though there are some differences) and may perhaps be related to the similar account in John 4:46–53. The emphasis of this account lies not on the miracle itself, which is performed at a distance, nor on the centurion's humility, but on his **great faith**. Even Jesus was amazed and said to the crowd: **"I tell you, I have not found such great faith even in Israel"** (v. 9). The point is obvious enough: Gentile faith can be just as great, sometimes even greater, than Jewish faith. Hinted at here is Israel's unbelieving response to the gospel in contrast to the joyous reception among the Gentiles. Perhaps intended as a parallel to the healing of the Centurion's servant, in which the Gentile shows such great faith, is the conversion of Cornelius in Acts 10. Cornelius' eager acceptance of the gospel contrasts with the rejection and unbelief on the part of so many in Israel.

Brodie (pp. 134–47) detects parallels between Luke's story of the healing of the centurion's servant and Elijah's provision of food for the widow and her son in 1 Kings 17:7–16. He suggests that a major common element concerns the power of the spoken word. (That Luke may have had this OT passage in mind is quite possible in view of the earlier allusion to it in Luke 4:25–26 and the numerous parallels between the Elijah/Elisha narratives and the pericope that follows.) Elsewhere in Luke–Acts the story parallels the account of Cornelius in Acts 10 (Leaney, p. 141; Fitzmyer, p. 650; Tiede, p. 149).

7:11–17 / This story, found only in Luke's Gospel, reveals several points of contact with the Elijah/Elisha stories as well (Tiede, pp. 151-52). The most noteworthy parallels include: (1) the setting in **Nain** (Luke 7:11), which may be an allusion to the ancient city of Shunem (2 Kings 4:8; see note below); (2) arrival at **the town gate** (Luke 7:12; 1 Kings 17:10); (3) a grieving **widow** (Luke 7:12; 1 Kings 17:9, 17); (4) the death of **the only son** (Luke 7:12; 1 Kings 17:17; 2 Kings 4:32); (5) the speaking or crying out of the resuscitated son (Luke 7:15; 1 Kings 17:22); (6) the expression, borrowed verbatim from the LXX, "he **gave him back to his mother**" (Luke 7:15; 1 Kings 17:23); and (7) the recognition that "a great prophet has appeared among us" (Luke 7:16; 1 Kings 17:24). Although the widow in 1 Kings says, "Now I know that you are a man of God" (RSV), the Aramaic version (i.e., the Targum) inserts the word "prophet," thus bringing the Lucan and Kings passages into closer agreement. (For further details see Brodie, pp. 147-52.)

Despite the parallels there is a major difference, however. Whereas Elijah must pray to God and stretch himself upon the dead lad three times before he revives, Jesus merely speaks the word of command and the dead one is raised up. Jesus' demonstration of superior power sets the stage for his response to the messengers of John: the hopeless now have hope, for Jesus, acting as the Lord's anointed, has begun to fulfill his messianic task, just as he had earlier announced (Luke 4:18-21). In this particular episode Jesus has remedied the worst possible tragedy, for with the death of her only son the widow has been left alone and the family line has come to an end (Ellis, p. 118). This is indeed an example of the Good News of the Lord's "favorable year." Such a story contributes significantly to Luke's theology of messianic blessings being extended to the weak and the outcast.

7:18–35 / This section may be subdivided into: (1) the question of John the Baptist (vv. 18-20), (2) Jesus' answer, both in action and in word (vv. 21-23), (3) Jesus' brief discourse about John (vv. 24-28), (4) the response of different groups of people (vv. 29-30), and (5) Jesus' response to those who have not heeded the Baptist (vv. 31-35).

The question of the Baptist is very significant, for it highlights the differences between John's expectations of Jesus' min-

istry and Jesus' actual ministry. That John actually understood
Jesus to be the Messiah is not at all certain (Fitzmyer, pp. 663–65,
does not think so), but from what he said earlier in his ministry
he obviously expected the one who followed him to be a fiery
reformer (Luke 3:15–18). As Fitzmyer notes, "Jesus . . . carries
no ax or winnowing-fan, cleans no eschatological threshing-floor,
and burns no chaff. Instead, he cures, frees, resuscitates; he cares
for the blind, cripples, lepers, deaf, and even the dead; and he
preaches good news to the poor" (p. 664). John's growing doubt
had to do with his understanding of what the "last days" would
bring for the righteous and unrighteous. For John it was to be
a "day of vengeance" and house-cleaning. People like Herod and
Pilate would have to go. Instead, while John languishes in prison,
Jesus ministers to the poor and the sick. In essence, John's own
understanding of what God was expected to do through the return of Elijah or the appearance of the Messiah was quite similar
to the understanding of the audience in the synagogue in Nazareth (Luke 4:24–29). John had called the people to repentance,
to make the nation ready for the Lord to purge out the unrighteous and exalt the righteous.

Jesus' answer is seen in what he was doing. Verse 21 summarizes the healing ministry and thus sets the stage for his answer: **"Go back and report to John what you have seen and heard
. . . "** (v. 22). Jesus then recapitulates his ministry in terms of
Isa. 61:2 and the related passages of Isa. 29:18–19 and 35:5 (with
the notable addition of the clause, **the dead are raised**, which
refers back to Luke 7:11–15 and looks forward to 8:49–56). Verse
23 provides further evidence that **John's messengers** (v. 24) were
sent because the Baptist had doubts about Jesus. Brodie (pp. 153–
73) believes that Luke intends this controversy between Jesus and
John to be understood against the controversy between Micaiah
and the false prophets in 1 Kings 22. As he sees it, the main theme
in both Luke and 1 Kings is the search for true prophecy. If
Brodie's analysis is correct, then there is more evidence for seeing an essential difference in (the prophet) John's understanding
of what should characterize (the prophet) Jesus' ministry.

But even if John has not fully comprehended or anticipated
the nature of Jesus' ministry, the following verses (vv. 27–28) show
that Jesus regards the ministry of John as fulfilling Scripture. By
identifying **John** with the **messenger** of Mal. 3:1 (who is later iden-

tified as "Elijah" in Mal. 4:5) Jesus acknowledges that the Baptist was indeed his precursor. Because John was his precursor, Jesus declares that he is much **more than a prophet**. Indeed, according to Jesus, **among those born of women there is no one greater than John** (v. 28a). But because John is identified with the period of the "Law and the Prophets" (Luke 16:16), as great as he is, **the one who is least in the kingdom of God is greater than he** (v. 28b). This implies that the new era brought about by Jesus is vastly superior to the period of (old) Israel. John is the "prince" among the prophets, the climax of the old era, but in comparison to the new age that has dawned he is a minor figure.

Luke summarizes in vv. 29–30 the differing reactions among the people who had heard the preaching of John (Luke 3:7–17) and had heard and witnessed the ministry of Jesus. Whereas **all the people, even the tax collectors** recognized God's righteous demands (see note below) and so **had been baptized by John** (v. 29; see 3:10–14), the **Pharisees and experts in the law rejected God's purpose for themselves, because they had not been baptized by John** (v. 30). In response to this rejection Jesus utters the words found in vv. 31–35, words which are tinged with exasperation and sarcasm. Jesus wonders **to what** he can **compare the people of this generation. What are they like?** In answer to his questions Jesus tells the proverb of the children who will neither **dance** nor **cry**. The exact meaning of this proverb is elusive (and many interpretations have been offered), but Jesus has applied it to the general lack of response to his and John's differing ministries (as vv. 33–34 would seem to indicate). But even then there are two possible interpretations. It may be that the people who **did not dance** are the people who refused to respond to Jesus' Good News and the people who **did not cry** are the people who refused to mourn and repent in response to John's preaching. The problem with this interpretation is that the responses do not correspond to the order of John first, Jesus second. (Although this is not necessarily a major problem.) Another interpretation contends that the **children** represent **the people of this generation** (v. 31) who ask John to **dance** (instead of calling for repentance) and ask Jesus to **cry** (instead of celebrating the presence of the kingdom). (See Marshall, pp. 300–301.) The second interpretation enjoys the advantage of presenting its components in the proper sequence. Taken either way, the point of the parable is that the people of Israel (particularly the religious authorities) have not been satisfied either with John or with Jesus.

In vv. 33–34 Jesus further clarifies his point by illustrating the obstinate nature of his contemporaries. In response to John's message and lifestyle they say, **"He has a demon."** In response to the alternate style of Jesus' message and ministry they say, **"Here is a glutton and a drunkard, a friend of tax collectors and 'sinners.' "** Jesus concludes his remarks with the proverb: **"But wisdom is proved right by all her children."** The proverb means that God's purposes in John and Jesus will be vindicated by their results, that is, by the many who come to faith and become part of the people of God. "They see the 'purpose of God' at work in John and Jesus" (Tiede, pp. 158–59).

Additional Notes   §15

7:1–10 / L. C. Crockett ("Luke 4:25–27 and Jewish-Gentile Relations in Luke–Acts," *JBL* 88 [1969], pp. 177–183; see also Tannehill, p. 72) suggests that Luke 7:1–10 mirrors Elisha's healing of Naaman the Syrian (2 Kings 5:1–14), an episode alluded to in Luke 4:27, just as Luke 7:11–17 mirrors Elijah's raising up of the widow's son (1 Kings 17:8–16, 17–24), alluded to in Luke 4:25–26.

7:2 / **a centurion**: This officer is not necessarily a Roman soldier, for Galilee was not a Roman province until A.D. 44. He (a Gentile according to v. 5) is probably a captain in Herod's provincial militia.

7:11 / The **town called Nain** (from the Latin *Naim* and/or from Hebrew *Na'im* meaning "pleasant") may possibly be traced back to the pre-exilic city of Shunem, the original site of which is quite close to the newer city. Nain is perhaps derived from the second half of the name Shunem. Lachs (p. 207) notes that the modern Arab village Nein may stand on the site. Even if such an identification cannot be made with certainty (Fitzmyer, p. 656, thinks that it cannot), it is entirely possible that Luke saw a connection. The various other parallels between the raising of the widow's son and the similar episodes in 1 and 2 Kings would suggest that Luke did see a connection.

7:16 / **God has come to help his people**: Lit. "God has visited his people." This exclamation makes the reader recall the similar words of praise uttered by Zechariah after the naming of his son John (Luke 1:68; see commentary on 1:68). Although many of the people recognize in Jesus' ministry God's visitation, the religious establishment, particularly as it is represented by Jerusalem, does not recognize such a "visitation." For this reason, when Jesus reaches Jerusalem he weeps over the city, "because you did not recognize the time of God's coming to you [lit. "your visitation"]" (Luke 19:44). This reflects an OT concept that God comes near to inspect the human condition (whether Israelite or Gentile) to determine what action ought to be taken. The visitation may involve judgment (Exod. 32:34; Pss. 59:5; 89:32; Isa. 23:17; Jer. 14:10) or it may involve deliverance (Gen. 50:24, 25; Exod. 13:19; Ruth 1:6; Ps. 80:14; Jer. 15:15). [Note that many of the modern English translations do not use the word "visit."]

7:18–19 / According to Josephus (*Antiquities* 18.119), John was imprisoned (see Matt. 11:2) in the fortress of Machaerus, east of the Dead Sea; see Lachs, p. 189.

7:22 / Jesus' reply to the Baptist reflects the belief that people would experience healing in the messianic age (*Midrash Tanhuma* B, tractate *Mezora* 7: "all who suffer affliction will be cured in the world-to-come"); see Lachs, p. 190.

7:29 / This verse, particularly the second part, is difficult to translate and interpret. It may be translated literally: "And all the people having heard (this) and the tax collectors justified God, having been baptized with the baptism of John." The first problem has to do with what is "heard." It may refer to Jesus' remarks about John in vv. 24–28 (so Marshall, p. 298). Fitzmyer (p. 676; see his translation on p. 670) thinks that "heard" really means "listening to John's preaching (and accepting his baptism)." Another problem concerns what Luke means by saying that the **people** and the **tax collectors** "justified God" (so RSV; NIV: **acknowledged that God's way was right**). Ellis (p. 120) understands it as meaning "accepted his [God's] judgments as right" (so also Marshall, p. 298). Fitzmyer states that the expression means that they "acknowledged God as righteous, or acknowledged God's way of righteousness. The sense is that, in listening to John's preaching and in accepting his baptism for the remission of sins, people were acknowledging what God had done to establish righteousness in the world of human beings and to enable them to attain it in his sight. Their actions, in effect, rendered a verdict of approval on God's plan of salvation" (p. 676).

7:32 / **We played the flute . . . we sang a dirge**: Playing the flute and dancing probably allude to the celebration at a wedding. It is a happy and festive occasion. Singing a dirge and weeping allude to mourning that takes place at a funeral (see Luke 8:52). Jesus' contemporaries (v. 31) are like children who refuse to participate, no matter what is offered. They wish neither to celebrate nor to mourn. They are dull and insipid, oblivious to the presence of the kingdom of God.

7:33 / **neither eating bread nor drinking wine**: John's abstention was a sign of mourning and repentance (see Luke 1:15).

"He has a demon": Some people apparently regarded John's peculiar lifestyle as evidence of insanity or actual demon-possession.

7:34 / **eating and drinking**: Unlike John, Jesus did not live the life of an ascetic. Jesus celebrated the presence of the kingdom and welcomed sinners who wished to enter.

7:35 / **her children: Wisdom** calls to her "sons" in Prov. 8:32 and Sir. 4:11.

§16 *Jesus Ministers to Some Women* (*Luke 7:36–8:3*)

7:36–50 / The episode of the sinful woman who anoints the feet of Jesus bears some interesting similarities to the accounts of Jesus' anointing just prior to his arrest and crucifixion (see Matt. 26:6–13; Mark 14:3–9; John 12:1–8). Since Luke does not have a later anointing episode and since there are several specific parallels between the Lucan episode and the other Gospel accounts (see Fitzmyer, pp. 684–85), some commentators suggest that Luke 7:36–50 is nothing more than a variation of Jesus' anointing during passion week. There are, however, numerous differences (in Galilee instead of Judea; feet anointed instead of head; in the presence of a Pharisee instead of disciples). This suggests that Luke saw this episode as distinct from the one he would have seen in Mark 14:3–9. It also suggests that some of the Marcan details may have influenced Luke's account, while his tendency to avoid repetition may explain why there is no anointing episode later, during passion week (for further discussion see Marshall, pp. 306–7).

There are certain curious aspects about Jesus' visit to the house of Simon the Pharisee. That Jesus would be invited to a dinner and then be denied customary courtesies seems odd. How the sinful woman managed to enter the dining area of a Pharisee's house seems odder still. But these and other questions that might be raised need not detain us.

In the previous section Jesus referred to himself as one who "ate and drank" and as one who is a "friend of sinners" (v. 34). It may be, then, that Luke understood this episode to be an illustration of this description, for in this episode Jesus is seen eating and drinking and in the company of a sinner (Talbert, p. 85). For Luke the main issue emerges in the Pharisee's comment in v. 39: **If this man [Jesus] were a prophet, he would know who is touching him and what kind of woman she is—that she is a sinner.**

The Pharisee assumes that Jesus, as a holy man not wishing to be defiled, would shrink back from her and perhaps order her away. It can only be, so he reasons, that Jesus must not be aware of the true character of the woman (see note below). He concludes, then, that this Galilean preacher may not be a prophet after all. Jesus' response evidences his prophetic capacity, for he has perceived his host's thoughts. Simon's address to Jesus as **teacher** may indicate newly found respect for Jesus (see note below). Jesus next tells the parable of the **moneylender** who **canceled the debts** of the two debtors (vv. 41–42), and then he applies it to the love that the woman has shown for him. This stands in vivid contrast to the minimal respect that Simon has shown. Because the woman has experienced forgiveness for **her many sins** (it is likely that the woman had experienced forgiveness prior to her coming to Simon's house), she shows great love and gratitude. But self-righteous people like Simon, who believe that their sins are few and therefore have been **forgiven little**, have only a **little** love (vv. 44–47).

A second issue is raised in vv. 48–50 when **Jesus** assures the woman: **"Your sins are forgiven."** The **other guests** react, wondering **who** Jesus could be to forgive **sins**. Jesus' further words to the **woman** in v. 50 show that her **faith** was what made forgiveness and salvation possible. In these last three verses Luke brings his readers back to his major concern, and that is that Jesus has the authority to forgive sins, and this authority must be accepted in faith (see Luke 5:20–26).

8:1–3 / One of the astonishing features in Jesus' ministry was the presence of women disciples and associates among his followers. Women accompanying Jesus and his disciples would have been completely contrary to Jewish customs (see Tannehill, pp. 137–39). In this brief section Luke identifies by name three of the **women** who traveled through Galilee with the **Twelve** (see note below). He also notes that there were **many others** who **were helping to support them out of their own means** (v. 3). Luke probably had three reasons for mentioning these women: (1) to show that the women who witnessed the crucifixion (Luke 23:49) and the empty tomb (24:10, 22, 24) had been with Jesus from the time of his Galilean ministry (which in effect meets the qualifications for apostleship in Acts 1:21–22); (2) to show that women may (and will) have influential roles in the church (see Acts 1:14; 8:12; 16:13–15; 17:4, 12; 18:24–26); and (3) to show that financial liberality is a mark of discipleship and is essential for the continuation of the ministry.

Additional Notes §16

7:36–50 / Brodie (pp. 176–89) suggests that the Lucan version of this story has been influenced by the story of the Shunammite woman and Elisha's ministry to her in 2 Kings 4:8–37. He believes that the theme common to both passages is that of receiving new life from God's prophet (as Jesus is called in Luke 7:39).

7:37 / **a woman who had lived a sinful life**: Lit. "a woman who was a sinner." It is likely this woman had been a prostitute, although adultery could be in view. Matthew Black (*An Aramaic Approach to the Gospels and Acts*, 3rd ed. [Oxford: Clarendon, 1967], pp. 181–83), however, has suggested that the Greek has misunderstood the original Aramaic which had described the woman as a "debtor." If he is correct, then the Parable of the Two Debtors (7:41–42) fits the context better. Leaney (p. 147) is correct in noting that there is no evidence that the sinful woman was Mary Magdalene (see also Tiede, pp. 164–65).

7:40 / **teacher**: To be called "teacher" (usually understood as the equivalent of "rabbi," see John 1:38) was a mark of reverence and respect.

7:41 / **denarii**: The singular form is denarius. A denarius is a Roman coin worth a day's wage. Even the smaller debt of the parable is significant, but the larger debt represented an almost unimaginable sum to the average Palestinian peasant in the first century.

8:2 / **Mary, called Magdalene**: She is so named because she is from the town of Magdala (possibly meaning the "city of the tower"). She figures prominently in the Gospel tradition, particularly at the crucifixion and resurrection (Matt. 27:56, 61; 28:1; Mark 15:40, 47; 16:1, [9]; Luke 24:10; John 19:25; 20:1, 11, 16, 18). Only Luke mentions that **seven demons had come out** of this woman (the later ending affixed to the Gospel of Mark repeats the Lucan statement [Mark 16:9]). The number of demons indicates the severity of the possession (Ellis, p. 128; Fitzmyer, p. 698). According to a rabbinic tradition the Angel of Death "said to his messenger, 'Go, bring me Miriam [Mary] the Women's hairdresser!' He went and brought him Miriam" (b. *Hagiga* 4b). "Hairdresser" is *megaddela*, which could be a pun with Magdalene. The wider context of this rabbinic tradition reveals that Magdalene has been confused with Mary the mother of Jesus.

8:3 / Joanna the wife of Cuza, the manager of Herod's household: The reference to Herod is to Herod Antipas. Fitzmyer (p. 698) thinks that her husband should be understood as a manager of Herod's estate. That the wife of such a person was a follower of Jesus suggests that not all of Jesus' followers were of humble means and origin. Outside of this verse and Luke 24:10 there is no mention of this woman anywhere else.

Susanna: Besides this reference in Luke, nothing is known of this woman. This is the name of the beautiful heroine of one part of the apocryphal additions to Daniel.

their own means: Lit. "from their own possessions." The word translated "possessions" occurs frequently in Luke (11:21; 12:15, 33, 44; 14:33; 16:1; 19:8; Acts 4:32) and reflects the Lucan concern with wealth and the proper attitude toward it.

§17 The Parable of the Sower (Luke 8:4–21)

This section is comprised of three parts: (1) the Parable of the Sower (vv. 4–15), (2) the Parable of the Lamp (vv. 16–18), and (3) Jesus' definition of his true family (vv. 19–21). What unites these three parts is the theme of hearing and obeying the Word of God (see vv. 8, 15, 18, 21). Luke has obtained these materials from Mark.

A comparison of the parallel passages in Matt. 13:3–50 and Mark 4:2–34 highlights the different emphases that the three Synoptic evangelists are able to bring out of what is essentially the same material. The Marcan collection begins with the Parable of the Sower and its interpretation (4:2–20), to which is added the Parable of the Lamp (vv. 21–25) and two kingdom parables (vv. 26–32). The main point of this collection seems to be the concern to show how the kingdom will *grow*. Despite obstacles, failures, and a small beginning, through the preaching of the Word, the kingdom will grow and succeed. The Matthean collection also begins with the same Parable of the Sower (13:3–23), omits Mark's Parable of the Lamp (but see Matt. 5:15) and the Parable of the Seed that grows secretly (Mark 4:26–29), and adds five new kingdom parables to Mark's Parable of the Mustard Seed (Mark 4:30–32; Matt. 13:24–50). The focus of the Matthean collection is on the kingdom's *membership* (note especially the Parable of the Wheat and Tares, vv. 24–30, and its explanation in vv. 36–43). Luke, however, has gathered together no collection, electing to retain the Sower and Lamp parables only (8:4–17), to which he appends Jesus' warning to heed his words (v. 18) and his pronouncement concerning his true family (vv. 19–21, taken from Mark 3:31–35). The Lucan theme has nothing to do with the kingdom. Instead, its focus is upon Jesus' word and the urgent need to obey it.

8:4–8, 11–15 / Luke's version of the Parable of the Sower follows the Marcan version fairly closely. Most changes have to do with style and economy. The most notable modification is the insertion of **his seed** in v. 5. The effect of this addition is to shift the reader's attention away from the **farmer who went out to sow** to the **seed** that is sown (= **word of God**; see v. 11), a shift that may be observed in the general thrust of the whole Lucan section. The seed has fallen on a variety of soils with varying results. But the **good soil** (= **those with a noble and good heart, who hear the word**) will **retain it, and by persevering produce a crop** (v. 15). Luke's version does not seem concerned with why there are different responses to the proclaimed Word (as it seems to be in Mark). Rather, the emphasis is on what will happen when someone hears and obeys the Word. "In the face of various and persistent obstacles, the proclamation of the kingdom will yet produce an astonishing yield" (Tiede, p. 166).

8:9–10 / These verses are taken from Mark 4:10–12, a passage that has perplexed interpreters since the time the evangelists Matthew and Luke took up their pens (see note below). Luke has retained part of the Marcan text, since it provides a link between the parable (vv. 4–8) and its interpretation (vv. 11–15). Probably because he did not fully understand (or fully share) Mark's view of the purpose of the parables, Luke has shortened the last part (v. 10b), which consists of a paraphrase of Isa. 6:9. (In omitting the last part of the paraphrase Luke leaves out Isa. 6:10.) Moreover, the Marcan question "concerning the parables" (4:10) has become in Luke a question concerning **what this parable meant** (v. 9). As it stands in Luke the **disciples** want to know what the Parable of Sower (or "Sowed Seed" in light of Luke's emphasis on Word) means and not "why Jesus speaks in parables," as Matt. 13:10 puts it. However, the Marcan answer that Luke retains does not answer the question as Luke has reformulated it. The explanation of the parable comes in vv. 11–15. In the Lucan form of the answer (v. 10) Jesus' immediate reply is to be understood more as a general statement of principle and not as an answer at all. His followers are given the **secrets of the kingdom of God**, by which is meant the plain, non-parabolic **word of God**, or gospel; **others** are given parables. The reason for this is so that **"though seeing, they may not see; though hearing, they may not understand"** (v. 10, paraphrasing Isa. 6:9). There have been numerous attempts to mitigate the severity of this statement, but it should be taken at face value (see note below). The secrets of the kingdom have been given to Jesus' disciples (and here Luke means everyone who will, or has ever, become a follower of Jesus), but for the rest (i.e., those who will not heed the word of God) Jesus' words remain enigmatic parables so that they will understand even less (see v. 18). This is in essence a statement of judgment and all the more reason to listen (vv. 8, 15, 21).

8:16–18 / Verses 16–18 contain three sayings which probably were originally independent but were pulled together by Mark (4:21–25) or the tradition before him. In Mark 4:21–22 the idea seems to be that what remains secret during Jesus' ministry (i.e., who Jesus really is, what his ministry is really all about; see Luke 4:35, 41) will eventually become public. But in the Lucan version (vv. 16–17) the sayings have more to do with the reason why someone should heed Jesus' words. When one is enlightened by the message of Jesus (or **lights a lamp**) one does everything one can to receive more illumination. Therefore, the lamp is placed **on a stand** to increase the light. Similarly, what had not been known before (what is **hidden** or **concealed**) must now be investigated carefully (i.e., **be disclosed** or **brought out into the open**). The Lucan warning in v. 18 (see note below) has the same meaning as its counterpart in Mark 4:23–25 and fits into the theme of the whole passage nicely. Listening carefully and heeding the words of Jesus results in more understanding; but failing to pay attention may result in forfeiting whatever understanding one may have had (as in the warning in v. 10 above).

8:19–21 / These verses come from Mark 3:31–35 and have been placed here because Luke discerned a useful example of the point of the preceding verses. (Probably because of his lofty assessment of Mary [see Luke 1:30; Acts 1:14], Luke omits Jesus' negative rhetorical question found in Mark 3:33.) Those who are part of Jesus' true family **are those who hear God's word and put it into practice** (v. 21); they are not part of his family simply because of physical descent from Abraham (Luke 3:7–9; Tiede, p. 171).

Additional Notes   §17

8:4–8 / Outside of the NT there is some tradition that parallels the Parable of the Sower. Jer. 4:3 ("Break up your fallow ground, and sow not among thorns"; RSV) and Isa. 55:10–11 ("For as the rain and the snow . . . water the earth, making it bring forth and sprout, giving seed to the sower . . . so shall my word be . . ."; RSV) may have contributed to the parable's theme and imagery. Perhaps a closer parallel is 2 Esdras 8:41: "For just as the farmer sows many seeds upon the ground and plants a multitude of seedlings, and yet not all that have been sown will come up in due season, and not all that were planted will take root; so also those who have been sown in the world will not all be saved" (RSV).

Birger Gerhardsson ("The Parable of the Sower and Its Interpretation," *NTS* 14 [1967–68], pp. 165–93) has suggested that the three soils that failed to bring forth fruit are meant to correspond to the three requirements of loyalty found in Deut. 6:4–5, the "Great Commandment" (Matt. 22:37; Mark 12:29–30; Luke 10:27). The first fruitless soil represents the person who does not "love the Lord" with all his "heart" (see Matt. 13:19 where "heart" appears); the second fruitless soil represents the person who does not "love the Lord" will all his "soul" (endurance); and the third fruitless soil represents the person who does not "love the Lord" with all his "might" (i.e., wealth). Gerhardsson is suggesting that the fourth soil represents the person who does "love the Lord" with all his heart, soul, and might. Gerhardsson further suggests that the Matthean order of the three temptations in the desert (Matt. 4:1–11=Luke 4:1–12) corresponds as well. He believes that it is in the Gospel of Matthew that these parallels with Deuteronomy are the clearest.

8:8a / **a hundred times more than was sown**: Luke has omitted two of Mark's yields ("thirty," "sixty," Mark 4:8) probably to avoid an interpretation which would attach the degrees of fruitfulness to various members of the church (Jews, Samaritans, Gentiles), something that might undermine his portrayal of the church's unity. See Marshall, p. 320.

8:8b / **He who has ears to hear, let him hear**: This saying appears to "float" in the sayings tradition, appearing in a variety of places (Matt. 11:15; 13:43; Mark 4:23; Luke 14:35; cf. Rev. 2:7, 17; 3:6, 13, 22). It is a call to the spiritually discerning to pay close attention to what is about to be said.

8:9–10 / These verses, especially as they are found in Mark 4:10–12, have provoked more debate and scholarly discussion than any other two or three verses in all the Gospels. The chief difficulty lies in what appears to be a very harsh and judgmental reason for speaking in parables. This harshness is most explicit in Mark's version, which literally reads: "When he was alone, those around him with the Twelve asked him about the parables. He told them, 'The secret of the kingdom of God has been given to you. But to those who are outside everything is said in parables in order that, "they may be ever seeing but never perceiving, and ever hearing but never understanding; lest they repent and be forgiven!" ' " Two specific elements make this text so harsh: (1) its paraphrase of Isa. 6:9–10, itself a harsh, judgmental passage; and (2) its citation as Jesus' *purpose* for speaking parables (as seen by its introduction, "in order that").

Although influenced by the Aramaic version of Isa. 6:9–10 (as is especially seen in the last clause, "and be forgiven"), the Marcan paraphrase retains the telic, or final, sense of Isaiah's terrible word of prophetic judgment: "And he said, 'Go, and say to this people: "Hear and hear, but do not understand; see and see, but do not perceive." Make the heart of this people fat, and their ears heavy, and shut their eyes; lest they see with their eyes, and hear with their ears, and understand with their hearts, and turn and be healed' " (RSV). Jesus' parables could have been interpreted by Mark (or the tradition before him) as analogous to Isaiah's strange message (Isa. 6:9, an instance of a riddle or parable). (In Hebrew the word *māšāl* could mean riddle, proverb, parable, or any sort of enigmatic or paradoxical saying; see Raymond E. Brown, "Parables and Allegory Reconsidered," *NovT* 5 [1962], pp. 36–45.) Just as Isaiah's parabolic word was to produce obduracy (for that was its purpose, as is attested in Isa. 6:10: "Make the heart of this people fat . . . "), so the parables of Jesus would have a similar effect. Frank Eakin ("Spiritual Obduracy and Parable Purpose," in James M. Efird, ed., *The Use of the Old Testament in the New and Other Essays* [Durham, N.C.: Duke University Press, 1972], pp. 87–107) has suggested that it is very probable that Jesus regarded himself and his rejected message as parallel to the rejection of Isaiah and his message centuries earlier. But the parallel may extend even further. Just as Isaiah's word of judgment would result in actual judgment (Isa. 6:11–13b, originally in reference to the Assyrian invasion, but later probably understood in reference to Jerusalem's first destruction at the hands of the Babylonians) and the emergence of a "holy seed" (Isa. 6:13c), so Jesus' word of judgment would result in actual judgment (the second destruction of Jerusalem at the hands of the Romans?) and the emergence of a fruitful seed (i.e., his followers). John Bowker ("Mystery and Parable: Mark iv. 1–20," *JTS* 25 [1974], pp. 300–317) has suggested that Mark's entire passage (4:1–20) is a unified interpretation based on the "holy seed" of Isa. 6:13c; see Craig A. Evans, "A Note on the Function of Isaiah, VI, 9–10 in Mark, IV," *RB* 88 (1981), pp. 234–35. The parable may reflect Isa. 55:10–11 and Jer. 4:3 as well. Note that Isa. 6:9–10 is employed in the same telic sense in John 9:39 and 12:40; see Craig A. Evans, "The Function of Isaiah 6:9–10 in Mark and John," *NovT* 24 (1982), pp. 124–38.

In his version of the question concerning the meaning of the Parable of the Sower (Matt. 13:10) Matthew makes numerous modifications, mostly by way of addition. First, he takes Jesus' answer in Mark 4:11–12 to be more of an answer to why he spoke in parables at all (as opposed to plain, non-parabolic speech); hence Matt. 13:10 asks: "Why do you speak to them in parables?" Second, Matt. 13:13 introduces the paraphrase of Isa. 6:9–10 with "because" (not Mark's "in order that"). Jesus speaks parables to people *because* they will not see, etc. He does not speak parables *in order that* they will not see, etc. Third, Matt. 13:13 omits the second half of the Isaiah paraphrase that begins "lest"; and, fourth, Matt. 13:14–15 is a formal, verbatim quotation of Isa. 6:9–10 according to the LXX, not the Hebrew (whose meaning Mark in essence has captured). In comparison with the Hebrew there are noticeable and significant differences in the LXX of Isa. 6:9–10: "You shall indeed hear but never understand, and you shall indeed see but never perceive. For this people's heart has grown dull, and their ears are heavy of hearing, and their eyes they have closed, lest they should perceive with their eyes, and hear with their ears, and understand with their heart, and turn for me to heal them" (as cited in Matt. 13:14b–15, RSV). There are three major differences between the LXX and the Hebrew: (1) The verbs of Isa. 6:9 (=Matt. 13:14b) are in the future tense and not in the imperative mood. Thus Isa. 6:9 is no longer interpreted as an attempt to prevent hearing and seeing, but it is now recognized as a *prediction* of the refusal to hear and see. (2) The causative imperatives of Isa. 6:10 ("Make the heart . . . fat . . . close their ears . . . shut their eyes . . .") have been transformed into passives ("their heart has become dull . . . their ears are heavy . . . their eyes they have closed . . ."); and (3) the word "for" has been added signifying that the prediction of v. 9 will come true *because* of the dull and insensitive nature of the people. Matthew replaces Mark's "in order that" with "because," drops Mark's "lest" clause in Matt. 13:13, and quotes the LXX (instead of the Hebrew) of the OT in order to show that Jesus spoke parables *because* people would not listen. The idea in Matthew, just as it is in the LXX of Isa. 6:9–10, is that the people make themselves insensitive; God does not (nor does Jesus).

Rather than producing an elaborate expansion of the Marcan material, as Matthew does, Luke elects to abbreviate. Although he does retain Mark's conjunction meaning "in order that," he drops the second half of the paraphrase in Isaiah (the equivalent of Isa. 6:10), which begins in Mark 4:12 with "lest" (NIV: "otherwise"). The way that Luke presents the passage, however, suggests that his understanding of Mark's Isaiah paraphrase is virtually the same as Matthew's: Jesus speaks parables in order that those who refuse to heed Jesus' words will become even more blind. For a full discussion of Mark's parables and how Matthew and Luke understand them, see Charles E. Carlston, *The Parables of the Triple Tradition* (Philadelphia: Fortress, 1975).

Lachs (p. 220) cites an interesting rabbinic tradition that alludes to Isa. 6:9: "Since the day that Joseph was stolen, however, the Holy Spirit departed from him [Jacob], so that he saw yet did not see, heard yet did not hear" (*Genesis Rabbah* 91.6). The significance of this saying lies in the idea that without the Holy Spirit there can be no spiritual perceptivity.

8:13 / **Those on the rock are the ones who . . . have no root**: Compare Sir. 40:15: "The children of the ungodly will not put forth many branches; they are unhealthy roots upon sheer rock" (RSV).

8:18 / Lachs (pp. 219–20) cites rabbinic sayings that parallel Luke 8:18: "The Holy One . . .puts more into a full vessel but not into an empty one" (b. *Berakoth* 40a and b. *Sukkah* 46a); "what they desired was not given to them, and what they possessed was taken from them" (*Genesis Rabbah* 20.5).

8:19–21 / Leaney (pp. 153–54) suggests that Luke removed the implicit criticism of Jesus' mother and family because in the Marcan context from which Luke had taken this material (Mark 3:21, 29–35), Jesus had warned of blasphemy against the Holy Spirit. Perhaps, thinks Leaney, Luke wished to avoid leaving the impression that Jesus' family was guilty of such blasphemy.

For more on the theme of preaching the word in this section, see William C. Robinson, Jr., "On Preaching the Word of God (Luke 8:4–21)," in Leander E. Keck and J. Louis Martyn, eds., *Studies in Luke–Acts* (New York: Abingdon, 1966), pp. 131–38.

§18 Jesus Calms a Storm (Luke 8:22–25)

The stilling of the storm is taken from Mark 4:35–41 (and is also found in Matt. 8:23–27). Luke's account is the shortest and most succinct. By omitting and modifying a few of the Marcan details and by inserting the episode immediately after the section on hearing and obeying the word of Jesus, Luke has drawn out a slightly different emphasis. Whereas in Mark the story underscores the mysteriousness of the person and ministry of Jesus (particularly as seen in the question of the disciples, Mark 4:41; Luke 8:25), in Luke the main point seems to be that Jesus' word is so authoritative that even the natural elements heed it. Also, in Mark the disciples are portrayed as not yet having faith (see 4:40), but in Luke the disciples apparently have only suffered a momentary lapse (see 8:25a: **"Where is your faith** [i.e., at the moment]?").

Luke sees in this episode a dramatic illustration of obedience to the spoken word of Jesus. In 8:4–21 the emphasis falls on the need to hear and obey Jesus' message (esp. vv. 15, 18, 21). In the stilling of the storm Luke shows that even nature obeys Jesus. It is as though the underlying implication is, "If even **the winds and the water . . . obey him**, who are we not to?"

Additional Notes §18

According to 2 Macc. 9:8, Antiochus IV, the ruler who oppressed Israel for a time (175–164 B.C.), had boasted that "he could command the waves of the sea" (RSV). In stark contrast, Jesus makes no boast, he simply does it. There is some possible OT background against which we should read the stilling of the storm, as seen in Pss. 65:7; 89:9; 104:6–7; 107:23–30. Just as the Lord God was Lord over the sea, so Jesus is its Lord. In ancient Israel the violent sea sometimes symbolized the forces of chaos, forces which the Lord subdued. Sometimes ancient Israel likened its enemies to flood waters that threatened to overwhelm the small kingdom (see Isa. 28:2, 17).

8:23–24 / There is a certain amount of correspondence with Jonah 1:4–6: Jonah embarked on a boat, fell asleep, a great storm arose, and he was awakened by a frightened crew fearing that they were about to perish.

Lachs (p. 161) cites a rabbinic tradition which tells of the calming of a raging storm by the prayer of Rabbi Gamaliel (b. *Baba Mes'ia* 59b).

A squall came down on the lake: Lit. "a hurricane of wind." Gennesaret Lake (or the "Sea of Galilee") lies 600 feet below sea level, and strong cold winds blowing through the deep gorges that feed into this basin often cause sudden and violent storms. See Jack Finegan, *The Archaeology of the New Testament* (Princeton: Princeton University Press, 1964), pp. 47–48.

Before moving into chap. 9, where Jesus begins his preparations for his journey to Jerusalem (which begins in 9:51), Luke furnishes three more examples of Jesus' healing ministry in Galilee, all of which have been taken from Mark. They are the exorcism (and healing) of the demon-possessed man from Gerasa (vv. 26–39); the raising of Jairus' daughter (vv. 40–42, 49–56); and the healing of the woman with the hemorrhage (vv. 43–48). In the Lucan context these miracles, together with the preceding episode (the stilling of the storm, vv. 22–25), represent all four types of Jesus' miracles: (1) exorcism, (2) healing, (3) resuscitation, and (4) nature miracle. In view of the transitional nature of Luke 9 (see commentary on 9:1–9), it may be that Luke provides his readers with this sampling of miracles as a way of rounding off Jesus' Galilean ministry.

8:26–39 / Like Matthew (8:28–34), Luke has abbreviated this story, which he has taken from Mark 5:1–20. Like Mark, however, Luke describes only one demon-possessed man and not two, as does Matthew (8:28). This story is certainly the strangest episode in the Synoptic tradition (with the possible exception of Matt. 27:52–53). The setting, the principal characters, and the grotesque outcome create an eerie atmosphere. Jesus and his disciples enter the predominantly Gentile **region of the Gerasenes** (see note below), where they are encountered by a demon-possessed man (probably a Gentile) who was unclothed and who **lived in the tombs**. With a graphic description of this miserable person, Luke relates that even though the man had been kept under guard, **he had broken his chains and had been driven by the demon into solitary places**. Mark adds that he used to cry out and cut himself with stones (5:5).

When this tormented person saw Jesus **he fell at his feet** and cried out in the voice(s) of the demon(s). His recognition of **Jesus** as **Son of the Most High God** is reminiscent of the demonic

cries in Luke 4:34, 41. When **Jesus asked** his name, he answered,
"**Legion**" (see note below), which would suggest that this time
Jesus had taken on a whole army of demons. Up to this point
Jesus has cast out individual demons, but here was the opportunity to demonstrate his power over a demonic army, whose col-
lective power would have been viewed as awesome and extremely
dangerous. Why Jesus **gave them permission** to enter the **pigs**,
instead of consigning them to the **Abyss** is uncertain (see note
below). It could be that since the day of judgment had not yet
actually arrived, as the demons apparently thought (at which time
demons would be consigned to hell, or the "Abyss"), the demons'
fear, as expressed in v. 31, was premature. Nevertheless, Jesus
does send them into a nearby herd of swine with the result that
they stampede into the Gennesaret Lake (see note below) and
so are destroyed in a manner that may very well foreshadow the
final day of judgment when demons will be cast into the Abyss
(for a similar suggestion see Ellis, p. 129).

The man, now **dressed and in his right mind**, was **sitting
at Jesus' feet** (a phrase not found in Mark's account) as an indication of his faith and discipleship (so Fitzmyer, p. 739). As a
disciple he wishes **to go with** Jesus, but **Jesus sent him away** to
tell how much God has done for him. The conclusion of this episode foreshadows the church's missionary outreach to Gentiles
in the Book of Acts.

8:40–56 / The stories of the resuscitation of Jairus' daughter and the healing of the woman with the hemorrhage are also
derived from Mark (5:21–43). As often is the case, Luke has
abbreviated his Marcan material. (Matthew's version is the briefest; 9:18–25.) The emphasis of both of these episodes is the need
to have faith in Jesus. In view of what Jesus has just accomplished
on the lake (vv. 22–25) and among the Gerasene people (vv. 26–
39), the need to have faith in him becomes all the more compelling. The two stories are linked by the reference to **twelve years**
v. 42, 43), the age of Jairus' daughter and the length of time that
the woman had suffered. The resuscitation of Jairus' daughter is
a counterpart to the earlier resuscitation of the widow's son (7:11–
17). Jesus has raised the only son of a woman and now he will
raise the only daughter of a man.

Jesus is approached by **a man named Jairus** (see note below). Like the demon-possessed man in v. 28, he **came and fell**

at Jesus' feet, pleading with him to come to his house and heal
his only daughter who **was dying**. While going to his home, Jesus
is delayed in the throng of people by the touch of the **woman**
who **had been subject to bleeding for twelve years**. At the moment that she **touched the edge of his cloak** she was healed, for
power had gone out of Jesus (see also Luke 4:14; 5:17). Jesus asks,
"Who touched me?" in order to bring the **woman** forward so that
he might make the pronouncement: **"Your faith has healed you.
Go in peace"** (lit. "Your faith has saved you"; see note below).

Meanwhile, a messenger **came from the house of Jairus** in-
forming them that his **daughter is dead**. To Jairus all hope was
now apparently lost; Jesus was too late (cf. the similar episode
in John 11, esp. v. 21). But Jesus assures him with the same words
spoken to the woman only moments before: **"Don't be afraid;
just believe, and she will be healed"** (lit. "she will be saved").
When he entered the **house** and described the girl as **not dead
but asleep**, he may have been hinting at the resurrection (so Fitzmyer, p. 749; cf. John 11:23–24). Because the mourners misunder-
stand his reference to "sleep" (cf. John 11:11–14), **they laughed
at him, knowing that she** really **was dead**. But with the command, **"My child, get up!"** Jesus restores her life and silences
his mockers.

In these two miracles we see a touch of irony. Whereas the
woman with the hemorrhage would have been regarded as ritually "unclean" (Lev. 15:25–30), and so out of place at the synagogue, Jairus, an official of the local synagogue, who would have
been regarded as ritually "clean," also needed the ministry of
Jesus. These episodes graphically illustrate humankind's universal
need for Jesus.

Additional Notes §19

8:26–39 / This story of the healing of a demon-possessed person has raised many questions. The most problematic have to do with
why Jesus would accommodate the demons' wish in the first place, why
he would send the demons into the herd of swine, and why the herd
stampeded into the lake. It has been suggested that the demons (whether
real or imagined) were mistakenly thought to have entered the swine;

that the swine stampeded when frightened by the loud cries of the tormented man. But this explanation and others like it are hardly plausible. The fact of the matter is that we really do not know just exactly what happened. What adds to the difficulty is that many mental illnesses were (mis)interpreted as being brought on by demon possession or some other form of demon influence. Beliefs about leprosy may provide an analogy. Virtually every serious skin disorder was thought to be leprosy, when in reality actual cases of leprosy were much smaller in number. So it was with respect to mental illness or epilepsy. It was usually assumed that the demonic world had something to do with it. Thus, many of the so-called exorcisms may have had absolutely nothing to do with demons.

8:26 / **Gerasa**: Some mss. read "Gadara," others "Gergesa." On the significance of these variant readings see the note on v. 33 below.

8:27 / The demoniac's behavior matches that of what the rabbis regarded characteristic of the insane: "Our rabbis taught: 'Who is considered to be an imbecile? He who goes out alone at night, and he who spends the night on a cemetery, and he that tears his garments' " (Lachs, p. 164).

8:30 / **Legion**: A Greek form of the Latin *legio*. The picture is that of an army, emphasizing power and fierceness.

8:31 / **Abyss**: It was believed that at the final judgment Satan (the devil) and all demons would be gathered up and cast into a bottomless abyss (see Rev. 20:3; *1 Enoch* 16:1; *Jub.* 10:5–11). Water, into which the swine plunged, was often associated with the Abyss (see Ellis, pp. 128–29). Note also that it was believed that demons sought "waterless places" (Luke 11:24).

8:32 / That a whole **herd** of swine (Mark 5:13 tells us that there were 2,000 in all) would be destroyed would scarcely be a cause for concern among Jews for whom the animal was unclean and forbidden (Lev. 11:7; Deut. 14:8). Naturally enough, however, the local (Gentile) residents were upset (v. 37).

8:33 / Since Gerasa (v. 26) is more than thirty miles from Gennesaret Lake, the pigs' stampede would have been a long one. Fitzmyer (p. 736) remarks humorously: "The stampede of the pigs from Gerasa to the Lake would have made them the most energetic herd in history!" No doubt sensing this difficulty some early Christian scribes wrote "Gadara" instead, a town only a few miles from the lake (but still making for a long stampede!). Following Origen's suggestion (mid-second century), other Christian scribes wrote "Gergesa," a town that actually borders the lake. (Origen himself, however, knew of no mss. that actually read "Gergesa.") Ellis (p. 128) suggests that the episode actually occurred in Kersa, a town on the Eastern shore of the lake where nearby there is a steep bank, but that the name became confused with the similar sounding Gerasa. This may be the case. All that Luke says, however, is that Jesus and his disciples entered "the region of the Gerasenes" (see v. 26) not necessarily the town of Gerasa itself. This seems to be indicated by v. 26, which says that the demon-possessed man had been driven into the "wilderness" (and thus out of town) and had met Jesus near the "shore." It is quite possible that this "region" was understood to extend to the very edge of the Gennesaret Lake.

8:37 / Talbert (p. 98) thinks that the people wanted Jesus to leave because of the (economic) loss of the herd. That is unlikely, and, in any case, Luke himself adds that the people asked Jesus to leave "because they were overcome with fear" (cf. Mark 5:17).

8:40 / **when Jesus returned**: Jesus returned to Galilee, Jewish territory, on the west side of Gennesaret Lake.

8:41 / **a ruler of the synagogue**: Ellis (p. 130) calls this person a "synagogue president" and notes that "he is to be distinguished from a civic official and from a Sanhedrin member."

8:43 / **subject to bleeding for twelve years**: According to Lev. 15:19–30 the woman would have been considered unclean, and all that she touched would be unclean (Tiede, p. 175).

The clause, **and she had spent all she had on doctors** (read only in a footnote in the NIV), is not found in the most important mss. That Luke "the physician" would not wish to repeat it seems understandable. Even if it is authentic, however, Luke's omission of Mark's caustic remark, "and had suffered a great deal under the care of many doctors . . . yet instead of getting better she grew worse" (Mark 5:26), probably was motivated by his desire to deflect criticism from his medical colleagues.

8:44 / **the edge of his cloak**: Lachs (p. 172) notes that Jewish men of Jesus' time wore fringes at the corners of their garments (Num. 15:38–40). It was believed that the fringe of a holy man possessed magical powers (see b. *Ta'anit* 23b).

8:48 / **Daughter**: "An affectionate term is used to reassure her that she is now to be recognized as part of Israel" (Fitzmyer, p. 747; Tiede, p. 176). Her "uncleanness" has been removed; she is no longer an outcast. See also Jesus' statement to Zacchaeus in 19:9.

your faith has healed you: Lit. "Your faith has saved you." For Luke faith is the basis and requirement for forgiveness of sins (see 5:20) and salvation (physical or otherwise, see 7:50; 17:19; 18:42).

Go in peace: An OT expression of farewell (from Hebrew *šālôm*); see 1 Sam. 1:17; cf. Luke 2:29. In the present context, in which a person has just been healed, it is particularly appropriate, for the *šālôm* also connotes the sense of wholeness. See note on 10:5 below.

8:51 / **Peter, John and James**: This is the first time in Luke these three disciples are singled out from the rest of Jesus' followers. See Luke 9:28; Acts 1:13; Gal. 2:9.

8:52 / **"She is not dead but asleep"**: Jesus was not suggesting that the young girl only appeared to be dead. His was not a remarkable medical diagnosis, but an authoritative word of assurance: God can restore life as easily as one might awaken a sleeper.

8:53 / **They laughed at him**: That is, they ridiculed Jesus. If Jesus was supposed to be a great teacher and healer, then how is it that he cannot recognize death when he sees it?

8:55 / **Her spirit returned**: The Greek may only mean that the girl's "breath" returned (Fitzmyer, p. 749). The episode parallels the resuscitation stories in the ministries of Elijah (1 Kgs. 17:17–24) and Elisha (2 Kgs. 4:32–37).

8:56 / **not to tell anyone**: Luke has carried over this prohibition from Mark 5:43.

This section is made up of the sending of the Twelve (vv. 1–6) and Herod's perplexity about Jesus' identity and the meaning of his ministry (vv. 7–9). It is probably legitimate to combine these two parts (derived from Mark 6:7–29 and portions of the sayings source) since Luke may have intended Herod's question to be viewed against Jesus' Galilean ministry as it reaches its climax in the sending of his men to preach and to heal, the very things that Jesus has been doing since Luke 4.

Luke 9 is for the evangelist a transitional chapter. In it we see the Galilean phase of Jesus' ministry draw to a close. We also see the inauguration of his Jerusalem ministry at his transfiguration, where the heavenly voice speaks again (9:35) as it had at his baptism (3:22). The journey to Jerusalem is finally launched in 9:51. Ellis (p. 131) has discerned in this chapter "alternating notes of exaltation (9:6, 17, 20, 32, 43) and rejection (9:9, 22, 44)" as Jesus begins the next major phase of his ministry.

Jesus has made his messiahship known in Galilee in Luke 4–8. Having been anointed by the Spirit (3:22; 4:1, 18), he has gone about in the "power of the Lord" (5:17), healing, exorcising, and forgiving sins. During this time his disciples have been in training. Now it is time for them to take a more active role in Jesus' ministry, for the day will come when they will have to assume a much fuller responsibility.

9:1–6 / **When Jesus had called the Twelve together, he gave them power and authority to drive out all demons and to cure diseases.** This authority should not be understood as extending to the forgiving of sins (as in 5:24). The disciples, sent out as apostles, were to heal and to exorcise as Jesus had done. Now they, too, were **to preach the kingdom of God**, as Jesus earlier had done (4:43). Jesus lays down the guidelines for their mission in vv. 3–4. They are to **take nothing for the journey**. It has been pointed out (see Fitzmyer, pp. 753–54; Ellis, p. 137) that the Essenes often traveled without any provisions in anticipation of being received by fellow believers as one of the family (see Josephus, *War* 2.124; and note below). So it is in the case of the Twelve; they are not to carry provisions, but are to enjoy the hospitality of those who are repentant and yearn for the kingdom of God. Where they are **not welcome**, however, the apostles are to **leave** and to **shake the dust off** their **feet** as a **testimony against them**. This warning would be understood as a statement of reciprocal rejection: the people who reject the apostles, the apostles will reject (see note below). Having received this commission they depart, traveling **from village to village** (in a sense retracing Jesus' steps), **preaching the gospel and healing people everywhere**.

This commission will be repeated at the beginning of the journey to Jerusalem in the form of the sending of the Seventy (10:1-12) and, of course, it anticipates the Great Commission (24:45-49; see also Acts 1:8).

9:7-9 / This episode has a different purpose for Luke than it has for Mark (6:14-16), where it describes the execution of John the Baptist (6:17-29). In Luke, John's death is assumed but not described (v. 7). The emphasis, however, falls upon the question of who Jesus is, an aspect that is thematic throughout much of Luke 9, climaxing in the transfiguration scene (9:28-36). One point that is being made is that even **Herod** has **heard about all that was going on**. Jesus' ministry has had such an impact in Galilee that the Galilean **tetrarch** has become **perplexed, because** no one around him apparently knew just what to make of Jesus. It was conjectured that Jesus might be a resurrected **John** or the awaited **Elijah**. Out of curiosity (or fear?) Herod wanted **to see** Jesus (perhaps to kill him, 13:31), which he eventually will be able to do (see 23:8).

Additional Notes §20

9:3 / Although the parallel to the practice of the Essenes seems close enough, the following rule in the Mishnah, tractate *Berakoth* 9.5, is worth citing: "A man should not behave himself unseemly while opposite the Eastern Gate [of the temple] since it faces the Holy of Holies. He may not enter into the Temple Mount with his staff or his sandal or his wallet, or with dust on his feet . . ." (trans. from H. Danby, *The Mishnah* [Oxford: Oxford University Press, 1933], p. 10).

no staff: The parallel passage in Mark 6:8 reads: "Take nothing for the journey *except a staff*—no bread, no bag . . ." (my emphasis). The staff is also forbidden in Matt. 10:10, a passage from the sayings source that Luke has used in composing his second commissioning in 10:1–12. In this passage Luke makes no reference to a staff (see 10:4). Marshall (p. 352) suggests that in Luke 9:3 the evangelist is influenced by the sayings source (where the staff is prohibited) and is not intending to correct Mark (where the staff is permitted). This is possible, but it scarcely removes the difficulty. The first suggestion of Norval Geldenhuys (*The Gospel of Luke*, NIC [Grand Rapids: Eerdmans, 1951], p. 266, n. 8) that Mark's "except" and Luke's "no" may result from two Aramaic words that sound alike and possibly were confused (*'ella* and *wella*, respectively) is no real solution (though it might explain the difference between the traditions in Mark and the sayings source). Luke is not translating Aramaic or utilizing in this instance some unknown parallel Gospel tradition. He is making use of Mark and for some reason, perhaps for consistency, has excluded the staff along with the other items. Geldenhuys's second suggestion that Mark and Luke should be read together ("take no staff, except one only") is more a sign of desperation than a plausible solution. Fitzmyer (p. 754) suggests that the Lucan Jesus forbids the staff because it "suits the Lucan view of detachment from earthly possessions which is otherwise characteristic of his writings" (similarly Schweizer, p. 152). Perhaps.

9:5 / **shake the dust off your feet**: Ellis (p. 137) states: "Upon re-entering Palestine religious Jews would 'shake off the dust' of unclean Gentiles. Here it signifies an abandonment to judgment" (see Luke 10:11–12). In Acts 13:51 Paul and Barnabas shake the dust from their feet in protest against the Jews who persecuted them and drove them out of town. Tiede (p. 178) suggests that the gesture means no more than that the disciples have taken nothing from those whom they had visited.

9:7 / On **Herod** Antipas see note on 3:1 above. Luke correctly refers to him as **tetrarch**, whereas in Mark 6:14 he is called "king." It was Herod's ambition to be recognized as king that led to his exile in A.D. 39.

9:8 / On **Elijah** see note on 1:17 above.

one of the prophets of long ago: According to 2 Esdras the Lord promised: "I will send you help, my servants Isaiah and Jeremiah" (2:18, RSV). The passage goes on to describe the blessings of the end time, including the resurrection (vv. 19–32). See also 2 Macc. 2:4–7; 15:13–14; Matt. 16:14.

§21 *Jesus Feeds 5,000 People (Luke 9:10–17)*

Luke's account of the feeding of the 5,000 is based on the Marcan account (Mark 6:30–44) and is the only miracle found in all four Gospels (Matt. 14:13–21; John 6:1–15). Luke omits, however, Mark's feeding of the 4,000 (Mark 8:1–10 and see Matt. 15:32–39). Such an omission is due to (1) Luke's avoidance of repetition and to (2) the fact that the evangelist has omitted a large section of Mark (6:45–8:26, sometimes called Luke's "Big Omission") in which the second feeding story occurs (see note below).

Verse 10 takes up where 9:1–6 left off. In 9:1–6 the Twelve had been sent to heal and to preach. The news of their activities spread throughout Galilee so that its ruler, Herod, began to wonder who this person Jesus was. With the return of the **apostles** and the withdrawal to **Bethsaida** the stage is set for the miraculous multiplication of the loaves and fish, which perhaps in Luke's mind was a partial answer to Herod's question in v. 9 (so Fitzmyer, p. 763; Tiede, p. 181) and was the cause for the question in v. 18 (so Marshall, p. 357).

The account is interesting because the apostles themselves are challenged to **give** the people **something to eat**. Only shortly before they had received the authority to "drive out all demons and to cure diseases" (9:1); now they are given the opportunity to meet the needs of the hungry **crowd**. The **Twelve** wanted Jesus to **send the crowd away** to **find** their own supply of **food**. But **Jesus** wanted his disciples to feed them. For them, however, the task seemed impossible, since all they had were **five loaves of bread and two fish** (in John 6:9 we are told that this food belonged to a young lad). But for Jesus this was sufficient, for with it he was able to feed all the people and even have **twelve basketfuls of broken pieces that were left over** (see note below).

This story teaches that Jesus is more than sufficient to meet every need, even the needs of a large crowd. Whereas the disciples had received authority and power and therefore could do many of the things that Jesus had done, the power of Jesus, nevertheless, far overshadowed their own. Just as God provided bread for the wandering Israelites (Exod. 16:1–36) and to one hundred men in the days of Elisha (2 Kings 4:42–44) so Jesus, in an even mightier way, is able to feed a multitude (see note below).

Although it is not certain that Jesus himself may have intended such a meaning to be attached to the feeding of the 5,000, it is quite possible that for Luke and his readers this miracle foreshadowed the institution of the Lord's Supper (Luke 22:14–23). This can be seen most clearly in the words found in v. 16: **Taking the five loaves and the two fish and looking up to heaven, he gave thanks and broke them. Then he gave them to the disciples to set before the people**. These words are quite similar to those found in Luke 22:19: "And he took some bread, gave thanks and broke it, and gave it to them [the disciples]" (see also 1 Cor. 11:23–24). Moreover, the eucharistic-like discourse that follows John's account of the feeding of the 5,000 (John 6:30–58) would suggest clearly that at least in one segment of the early church the miracle had been related to the Lord's Supper.

Additional Notes §21

A major question that always arises from the study of this particular miracle concerns the presence of two feeding miracles in Mark (6:30–44; 8:1–10; both are also found in Matt. 14:13–21; 15:32–39). It is often wondered if what we have in Mark (and in Matthew who has followed Mark) are two accounts of the same miracle story. It is usually suggested that the feeding of the 4,000 is a variant of the feeding of the 5,000, the version that is found in both Luke and John. (Recently, however, Robert M. Fowler [*Loaves and Fishes: The Function of the Feeding Stories in the Gospel of Mark*, SBLDS 54 (Chico: Scholars, 1981)] has argued that the feeding of the 4,000 was the original story.) At least four reasons argue that Mark's two feeding stories are actually two accounts of the same episode. First, in view of the first feeding (Mark 6:30–44) the question of the disciples just prior to the second feeding (Mark 8:1–10) seems quite odd: "But where in this remote place can anyone get enough bread to feed them?" (8:4). That the disciples could ask such a question so soon after Jesus had multiplied loaves and fish seems almost beyond comprehension. Thus, for this reason alone one could argue that the feeding of the 4,000 is no more than another version of the feeding of the 5,000. Second, both feeding episodes have numerous points of similarity: (1) large numbers of people with Jesus and his disciples out in the wilderness; (2) a handful of loaves are multiplied (plus two fish in the first account); (3) the multitudes are made to recline; (4) Jesus blesses, breaks, and multiplies the food; and (5) several baskets of scraps are left over. The similarity of these details could suggest that the accounts are two versions of the same miracle story. Third, immediately after the feeding miracles Jesus enters a boat and crosses over Lake Gennesaret (Mark 6:53–54; 8:10, 13). Fourth, after both feeding accounts the disciples find themselves in their boat, either afraid or confused, because they had not understood the significance of the "loaves" (6:45–52; 8:14–21). These last two parallels place the miracle stories in almost identical historical contexts thus suggesting, once again, that these stories are really two versions of the same episode. Therefore, it is possible that the feeding accounts are indeed two accounts of the same incident. But of equal plausibility is the possibility that Mark (or, less likely, the tradition before him) has deliberately underscored many of the points of similarity that have been observed, thereby creating the impression that the two episodes were virtually identical. It could be that because of the great significance that the evangelist Mark attached to the feeding miracles, understood as revealing something crucial about the nature of Jesus and his messiahship, he wished to emphasize certain common features (such as the disciples' inability to understand who Jesus really was).

Another interesting aspect to be observed in the comparison of the Marcan and Lucan versions of the feeding of the 5,000 is Luke's omission of Mark's allusions to the Moses/wilderness-wandering theme (a theme which becomes prominent in John 6, in which explicit comparison between the multiplied loaves and the manna is made). First, the general setting (out in the wilderness, no food) and the miraculous provision of bread and meat may very well have been an allusion to God's provision of manna (see Exod. 16:1–36) and meat (see Num. 11:4–32) during the time of Israel's wilderness wanderings. Tiede (p. 180) suggests that the miracle may have answered the question of Ps. 78:19–20: "Can God spread a table in the wilderness? . . . Can he also give bread, or provide meat for his people?" (RSV). The Psalmist is referring, of course, to Israel's experience in the wilderness. Second, the phrase, "like sheep without a shepherd" (Mark 6:34), may allude to Num. 27:17 where Moses prays that the people have a leader so that they "will not be like sheep without a shepherd." Third, the direction that the people recline "in groups of hundreds and fifties" (Mark 6:39–40) may be an allusion to Moses' similar division of the people, over which his appointed leaders would supervise (see Exod. 18:21). In the Lucan account most of these details drop out, but it is not because of the evangelist's lack of interest in Moses, as can be seen in the place of prominence Moses receives in the transfiguration episode (Luke 9:30–31) and the correspondence between Luke 10:1–18:14 and Deuteronomy 1–26. Luke probably sees the feeding of the 5,000 against the backdrop of Elisha's ministry. It has already been shown that there are numerous points of contact between Jesus and the Elijah/Elisha stories of 1 and 2 Kings (Luke 4:25–27; 7:11–17, 18–35, 36–50; 8:1–3) and more will be seen shortly (9:51–56, 57–62).

In the feeding of the 5,000 Luke may have been thinking of Elisha's multiplication of the barley loaves for one hundred men (2 Kings 4:42–44; Fitzmyer [pp. 766–67] and Tiede [p. 180] allow for some possible influence). There are several points of contact worth noting: (1) a specific number of loaves (2 Kings 4:42; Luke 9:13); (2) the command to give to the people so that they may eat (2 Kings 4:42; Luke 9:13); (3) food is "set before" the people (2 Kings 4:43; Luke 9:16); (4) having eaten, there was food "left over" (2 Kings 4:44; Luke 9:17); and (5) the food was either taken from or placed into a "basket" (lit. "sack"; 2 Kings 4:42; Luke 9:17). Two other interesting parallels can be seen in John's account of the feeding: (1) the puzzled question of those told to feed many with a few loaves (2 Kings 4:43; John 6:9) and (2) the specific designation of the loaves as "barley loaves" (2 Kings 4:42; John 6:9). Besides the parallels (which may be due only to their presence in the account taken from Mark), the fact that Luke alludes to Elisha passages immediately surrounding the feeding episode (the raising of the Shunammite widow's son, 2 Kings 4:29–37; Luke 7:11–17; and the cleansing of Naaman the Syrian, 2 Kings 5:1–14; Luke 4:27) makes it quite plausible to suppose that he had this OT text in mind as he produced his own version of the feeding of the 5,000.

9:10 / **they withdrew by themselves to a town called Bethsaida**: This statement is curious in light of the wilderness setting of the miracle that follows (v. 12). Mark says nothing of a town (6:31, 32, 35). Why Luke mentions a town at all is difficult to understand. Some mss. read "a wilderness place" to bring the Lucan version closer to the Marcan version and to avoid the awkwardness of going to a town and then ending up in a "remote [i.e., uninhabited] place." In any case, the reference to Bethsaida (Aramaic for "house of hunting" or "fishing") is probably original. Bethsaida is on the northern shore of Lake Gennesaret, just East of the Jordan River. It is actually not in Galilee as John 12:21 states (the town from which the "Galilean" disciples Peter, Andrew, and Philip come according to John 1:44), but is in the neighboring province of Gaulanitis, at that time ruled by Philip the tetrarch (see Fitzmyer, pp. 765–66).

9:14 / **About five thousand men**: Matt. 14:21 adds, "besides women and children." No doubt this was Luke's understanding as well. Thus, the multitude was indeed a large one.

9:16 / **he gave thanks**: Lit. "he blessed them" (the loaves). The parallel verse in Mark (6:41, which is followed by Matt. 14:19) reads: "he blessed" (with "God" as the understood object). The Marcan version is in keeping with the Jewish prayer formula, *Baruch Adonai* ("Blessed be the Lord"). Fitzmyer (p. 768) cites m. *Berakoth* 6.1, as an example of such a prayer that Jesus may have uttered on such an occasion: "Blessed be you, O Lord our God, King of the world, who causes bread to come forth from the earth" (for more references see Lachs, p. 242). Since Luke has added "them" to the verb "he blessed," Fitzmyer suspects that Luke has misunderstood the idiom, not knowing that it is God who is blessed (or praised) for the food, not the food itself. Marshall (p. 362), however, suggests that Luke has not misunderstood the usage of the word "bless" and that the text really should be translated, "he blessed [God] for them" (see also Luke 24:30).

9:17 / **They all ate and were satisfied**: Perhaps Luke perceived this as a fulfillment of the beatitude in Luke 6:21, where the same word (lit. "were filled") is used. Lachs (p. 241) notes that the phrase comes from Deut. 8:10.

twelve basketfuls of broken pieces that were left over: Fitzmyer (p. 769) suggests that the "twelve" baskets (or sacks) constitute a symbolic reference to the twelve disciples who "now have enough to feed still others." Perhaps. With regard to the basket (Greek *kophinos*) Lachs (p. 241) cites Juvenal (*Satires* 3.114), who states that Jews carried their kosher food in baskets (Latin *cophinus*).

The question of Jesus' identity, brought out into the open with Herod's question in 9:9, is now answered. Whereas the Lucan account of the feeding of the 5,000 comes from Mark 6:30–44, Luke's version of Peter's confession has been taken from Mark 8:27–29. All of the Marcan material between these two episodes (Mark 6:45–8:26; Luke's "Big Omission") has been omitted by Luke not simply because of the appearance of certain repetitious materials, such as a second feeding miracle, but because of the evangelist's desire to produce a unified section revolving around the theme of Jesus' identity. This theme is seen especially in Herod's question (9:9) and in Peter's answer (9:20).

Luke 9:18–36 is made up of three parts: (1) Peter's acknowledgment of Jesus' messiahship (vv. 18–20), (2) Jesus' prediction of his suffering and death and the hardships of following him (vv. 21–27), and (3) the transfiguration (vv. 28–36). In all three parts we learn something more about who Jesus is.

9:18–20 / Once again **Jesus was praying** before a special event took place (see also 3:21; 6:12). The question that Jesus asked of his **disciples, "Who do the crowds say I am?"** recalls Herod's question in 9:9, "Who, then, is this? . . . " The disciples' answer repeats what the **others** had been saying in 9:8. Jesus was thought to be **John the Baptist, Elijah,** or **one of the prophets of long ago** (see note on 9:8 above). But the question is now put to the disciples: **"Who do you say I am?"** Is Jesus just one more prophet, or is he something more? **Peter,** as spokesman for the disciples, replies: **"The Christ of God"** (on the meaning of Messiah see note on 2:11 above). Peter's confession is crucial, for it attests that in Jesus' ministry the disciples (not just the readers who have been informed in advance) were able to recognize Jesus' messianic identity. Others had recognized Jesus as a "great prophet" (7:16), perhaps even as Elijah (9:8). Even Herod had become interested. But the disciples, who had been appointed to preach, and upon whom power and authority had been conferred to cast out demons and to heal, had come to recognize that Jesus was none other than the long-awaited Christ (or Messiah).

9:21–27 / Peter's confession is followed immediately by the command of secrecy and by Jesus' announcement of his impending suffering, death, and resurrection (derived from Mark 8:30–9:1). The point that is being made here is defining what it means to be the Messiah. For Jesus, being Messiah has little to do with popular expectations; hence the command **not to tell . . . anyone** that he was the Messiah. Jesus is not about to become a popular hero, a champion of the Jewish cause against foreign domination. He has no plans to start a war for the liberation of Israel. His plans, instead, call for his own rejection and humiliation at the hands of the religious authorities, for his own trial and crucifixion by the authority of the Roman governor. Peter's rejection of this idea and his rebuke in turn by Jesus (Mark 8:32–33) are omitted by Luke so that the evangelist may provide a closer link between Jesus' passion pronouncement in vv. 21–22 and his teaching in vv. 23–26 on the suffering involved in being his follower. (It is also omitted because Luke wishes to present Peter and the other apostles in the best light possible.) Following Jesus means taking up one's **cross** and being willing to **lose** one's **life for** Jesus. Jesus is the Messiah, a Messiah who must suffer and die, and a Messiah whose followers must also be willing to suffer and even to die. All of these ideas are part of the question of who Jesus is.

Although the statement in v. 27, **"some . . . standing here will not taste death before they see the kingdom of God,"** may have been understood as a reference to Jesus' return and establishment of the kingdom (or the establishment of the kingdom shortly after the resurrection), it is possible that the primary reference is to Jesus' resurrection, at which point the power of the kingdom of God is released upon earth through the Spirit (see Acts 2). The context suggests, however, that the transfiguration is in view (Leaney, p. 166), which is probably meant to be understood as a foreshadowing of the resurrection which Jesus had predicted in v. 22 (see note below).

9:28–36 / Several features of the transfiguration have led commentators to conclude that this passage has some sort of typological connection to Exodus 24 and 33–34, passages which describe Moses' ascent up the mount where he meets God and then descends with a shining face. The following specific parallels between Mark's account (9:2–8) and Exodus are evident: (1) the reference to "six days" (Mark 9:2; Exod. 24:16); (2) the cloud that covers the mountain (Mark 9:7; Exod. 24:16); (3) God's voice from the cloud (Mark 9:7; Exod. 24:16); (4) three companions (Mark 9:2; Exod. 24:1, 9); (5) a transformed appearance (Mark 9:3; Exod. 34:30); and (6) the reaction of fear (Mark 9:6; Exod. 34:30). Another suggestive item that should be mentioned is that in Exod. 24:13 Joshua is singled out and taken up the mountain with Moses. Since "Joshua" in the Greek OT is "Jesus," the early church may have seen in Exod. 24:13 a veiled prophecy, or typology, that came to fulfillment in the transfiguration, where once again Moses and Jesus are together.

There are several noteworthy modifications in Luke's version of the transfiguration, modifications which only enhance and strengthen the connection between the transfiguration and Moses. (1) In v. 30 Luke reverses the order of the names of the two heavenly visitors by mentioning the name of Moses first. This reversal is likely designed to place more emphasis upon the Law-giver. (2) That Luke intends such emphasis is confirmed when it is noted that in v. 31 the two visitors speak with Jesus of "his departure." The word "departure" translates the Greek word *exodos*, the very word that gives the Book of Exodus its name. (3) Only Luke mentions Jesus' "glory" seen by his disciples (v. 32). Luke may very well intend this to recall Moses' request to see God's glory (Exod. 33:18–23). Also, in Exod. 24:16 we read that the "glory of the LORD rested on the mount." This glory not only looks back to the glory manifested upon the mount in Exodus, but also anticipates the glory into which the Messiah will enter at his resurrection (see Luke 24:26). (4) Luke notes in v. 29 that Jesus' face was changed, which may recall more specifically the change in Moses' face (Exod. 34:30, 35). (5) Luke introduces the episode by saying "about eight days after" (v. 28), instead of Mark's "six days later" (9:2). There is seemingly only one plausible explanation for this alteration. The rules for observing the Feast of Booths are laid down in Lev. 23:33–44. According to Lev. 23:36 there are to be offerings for seven days and then on the eighth day there is to be "a holy convocation" or gathering. During this time the people are to dwell in booths (tents or tabernacles) (Lev. 23:42), the purpose of which is to remind the people of the exodus long ago (Lev. 23:43). (6) Finally, Luke has slightly modified the wording of the heavenly voice in v. 35. Instead of Mark's "My beloved Son" (9:7), Luke has "My chosen Son." This modification is likely meant to recall the chosen servant of Isa. 42:1 (see notes and commentary on 3:22 and 4:18 above).

What are we to make of all of this? I would suggest that Luke has taken the raw materials that he found in the Marcan version of the transfiguration and has enriched the parallels in such a way as to enhance the presentation of Jesus as God's Son (and Servant) whose authority and significance greatly surpass those of Moses and Elijah. Luke shows his readers that the two greatest OT figures appeared in order to discuss with Jesus his own impending "exodus." Moses, who may represent the Law, and Elijah, who may represent the Prophets, bear witness to Jesus' identity and to his destiny awaiting him **at Jerusalem**. Even the heavenly voice is probably meant to allude to both major parts of the OT. The first part of the voice's declaration, **This is my Son whom I have chosen**, echoes Isa. 42:1 and so represents the Prophets. The second part, **listen to him**, is a phrase taken from Deut. 18:15 (where Moses commands the people to listen to the great prophet that God would some day raise up) and so would represent the Law. This idea of the "Law and the Prophets" bearing witness to Jesus is seen explicitly in Luke 24:27 (and 24:44). Moses and Elijah bear witness to Jesus and then fade away from the scene, leaving Jesus **alone**, because the era of the "Law and the Prophets" is over (Luke 16:16a). Now it is the era of the "good news of the kingdom of God" (Luke 16:16b). Just as God's glory appeared on Mount Sinai, so now God's Son, in all of his glory, has appeared on the mount (cf. John 1:14–18). Whereas only the face of Moses shone, Jesus' entire personage is transfigured. Finally, because the disciples wish to build **three shelters** (i.e., "tents" or "booths") for Jesus and the two visitors, Luke has likely seen the connection with the Feast of Booths, a festival in commemoration of the exodus. Hence, Luke begins his episode on the eighth day, the day on which a "holy convocation" was to take place (Lev. 23:36, 42). Undoubtedly, in the evangelist's mind there could be no holier convocation than the meeting of Moses, Elijah, and Jesus; God's Law-giver, Prophet, and Son. The cli-

mactic feature in the transfiguration episode is the declaration of
the heavenly voice. Here at last is the dramatic answer to Herod's
question in 9:9: "Who, then, is this I hear such things about?"
He is the Son of God.

Additional Notes §22

9:19 / **Some say . . .** : Various prophetic figures from the past
were viewed as candidates to appear on the scene to announce the dawn
of the messianic kingdom; see note on 9:8 above.

9:21 / This verse is derived from Mark 8:30 and is part of the
so-called messianic secret in Mark's Gospel (see note on 4:41 above). In
the Lucan context (and probably in the Marcan as well) the prohibition
applied only to the time of Jesus' pre–Easter ministry. After the resurrection the disciples will be commanded to preach Jesus as God's Messiah and humankind's Savior (Luke 24:46–48; Acts 1:8; 2:36).

9:22 / This is the first announcement of Jesus' impending passion (two others are found in 9:43–45; 18:31–34). There is the possibility
that the reference to "suffering" may be an allusion to the Suffering
Servant Song of Isa. 52:13–53:12 (esp. 53:3–8, 11; so Ellis, p. 140). Fitzmyer
(p. 780) notes that the Targum to Isaiah cannot be dated any earlier than
A.D. 500 and therefore its identification of the Servant as the "Messiah"
(in 52:13; 53:5) tells us nothing of how this Isaianic Servant Song was
understood in the first century, much less whether or not Jesus (and/or
the early church) applied it to himself. However, in a recent study on
this Targum, Bruce D. Chilton (*The Glory of Israel: The Theology and Pro-
venience of the Isaiah Targum*, JSOTSup 23 [Sheffield: JSOT, 1982]) has concluded that although containing traditions well into the Middle Ages,
most of this Targum may be traced back to the period between the two
Jewish wars against Rome (i.e., A.D. 70 and 135). Thus, the suggestion
that a messianic interpretation of Isaiah 53 was known in the first century is more plausible than Fitzmyer has allowed. Moreover, Luke's references to this Servant Song elsewhere in his writings (Luke 22:37; Acts
3:13; 8:32–33) add further support to the idea that he at least, if not the
Gospel tradition before him, saw a connection between Jesus' suffering
and the suffering of the Lord's Servant in Isaiah 53.
    Many interpreters believe that Jesus' passion predictions derive not
from Jesus but from the early church as it struggled to explain the crucifixion; see E. Käsemann, *New Testament Questions of Today* (Philadelphia:
Fortress, 1969), pp. 77–78. Others, however, think that Jesus did anticipate his suffering and death; see Raymond E. Brown, "How Much Did
Jesus Know?—A Survey of the Biblical Evidence," *CBQ* 29 (1967), pp. 315–

45; I. Howard Marshall, "The Son of Man in Contemporary Debate," *EvQ* 42 (1970), pp. 12–21. Tiede (pp. 182–83) notes that Jesus would have had to have been "naive or ignorant" not to have been aware of the peril that he faced as he approached Jerusalem. His proclamation of the reign of God would have represented a direct challenge, in the minds of Romans and Palestinian Jews alike, to Rome's imperial authority.

9:23 / **take up his cross**: Some commentators think that this saying could have originated only in the early church, after Jesus' death on the cross. For example, Fitzmyer (p. 786) suspects that the saying was originally, "Take up my yoke" (Matt. 11:29); but after the crucifixion it became, "Take up my cross." If Jesus had anticipated his death, however, and there is no compelling reason that would preclude such a possibility, he most likely would have had in mind Roman crucifixion and its practice of making the condemned person carry the main beam on which he would be hanged. This debate revolves around the larger question of whether or not Jesus anticipated his death and whether or not he spoke of it. If one assumes that Jesus could not or did not anticipate his death, then the passion predictions are usually rejected out of hand (but see above note).

9:27 / **some who are standing here will not taste death**: This curious statement is really an idiom of emphasis, meaning "most surely," and is not a prediction of some sort. It is quite possible, however, that this saying was understood among early Christians as a prediction that some of Jesus' contemporaries would still be living when Jesus returned to inaugurate the kingdom (see John 21:21–23; Schweizer, p. 158).

9:29 / **his face changed, and his clothes became . . . bright**: The closest parallel is probably to the shining face of Moses (Exod. 34:30), but the faces of other saints are describes as shining; see 2 Esdras 7:97, 125; *1 Enoch* 37:7; 51:5. The clothing of the saints also will shine; see Dan. 12:3; Rev. 4:4; 7:9; *1 Enoch* 62:15; *Ecclesiastes Rabbah* 1.7.

9:30–31 / **Moses and Elijah . . . talking with Jesus . . . about his departure**: This "departure" (or exodus) probably has in view Jesus' death, resurrection, and ascension (see commentary and note on 9:51 below). Moses and Elijah are often paired up. The two witnesses of Rev. 11:3–12 could very well be Moses and Elijah (on Moses cf. v. 6 with Exod. 7:17, 19; on Elijah cf. vv. 5–6 with 2 Kings 1:10). (However, Elijah is sometimes paired with Enoch; see 2 Esdras 6:26; *Apocalypse of Elijah* 4:7–19, which appears to be dependent on Revelation 11.) According to one rabbinic midrash, God promises in the future to bring Moses with Elijah (*Deuteronomy Rabbah* 3.17). The rabbis compared Moses and Elijah at many points: "You find that two prophets rose up for Israel out of the tribe of Levi; one the first of all the prophets, and the other the last of all the prophets: Moses first and Elijah last, and both with a commission to redeem Israel. . . . You find that Moses and Elijah were alike in every respect. . . . Moses went up to God [cf. Exod. 19:3]; and Elijah went up to heaven [cf. 2 Kings 2:1]. . . . Moses: 'And the cloud covered the mountain six days' [Exod. 24:16]; and Elijah went up in a whirlwind [cf. 2 Kings 2:1]" (*Pesiqta Rabbati* 4.2); translation based on William G. Braude, *Pesikta Rabbati*, 2 vols., Yale Judaica 18 (New Haven: Yale University, 1968), vol. 2, pp. 84–85.

In Luke's account of Jesus' ascension (Acts 1:2–11), there are possible points of contact with both the Elijah and Moses ascension traditions. Just before the risen Christ ascends, his apostles asks: "Lord, are you at this time going to restore the kingdom to Israel?" (v. 6). This question probably echoes Elijah tradition (see Mal. 4:5–6, where Elijah will "restore the heart of the father to the son"; and Mark 9:12, where Elijah is to "restore all things"); see Michael D. Goulder, *Type and History in Acts* (London: SPCK, 1964), p. 148. According to Acts 1:2, Jesus "was taken up," the same expression used of Elijah when he was taken up by the chariot (2 Kings 2:9; a word from the same root occurs in Luke 9:51). When Moses ascended the mountain and entered the cloud, he was with God for "forty days" (Exod. 24:15–18). Similarly, after "forty days" Jesus is taken up into a cloud (Acts 1:3, 9). If Luke 9:51 does allude to these ascension traditions, then the passage undoubtedly anticipates Jesus' ascension which the evangelist later recounts (Luke 24:51; Acts 1:2, 9–11, 22).

9:32 / Only the Lucan account tells us that **Peter and his companions were very sleepy**. This may be Luke's way of explaining why Peter would not know "what he was saying" (v. 33). It also could have more to do with providing a contrast with v. 29: that is, while Jesus prayed, the disciples slept. The same contrast will occur again in Luke 22:44–45.

9:33 / **three shelters**: In all likelihood **Peter** had concluded that the Last Day had arrived when some of the great events of the first exodus would be repeated (such as manna in the wilderness and God's presence among the people). To commemorate the exodus Jews celebrated the Feast of Booths by living in small booths or huts ("shelters," NIV) for seven days (Lev. 23:42–44; Neh. 8:14–17). But the feast was also understood by many as looking ahead to the glorious day of Israel's deliverance (Ellis, p. 143; Marshall, p. 386; Tiede, 189–90).

9:35 / The heavenly voice interrupts Peter (v. 34) and may be partially intended as a rebuke (**listen to** Jesus, not to Moses or Elijah). The time of Moses and Elijah is over. It is time to heed the words of Jesus.

9:36 / **The disciples kept this to themselves, and told no one**: What they had experienced was to be kept secret until Easter. This idea comes from Mark and is part of Mark's secrecy theme (see note on 4:41 above), but for Luke it probably meant that because the transfiguration foreshadowed Easter, it would not be appropriate to tell of it until Easter. **At that time** (lit. "in those days") refers to the time of Jesus' pre-Easter ministry.

§23   Jesus Heals an Epileptic Boy (Luke 9:37–43a)

Luke's story of the exorcism and healing of the epileptic boy is taken from Mark 9:14–27. Luke has abbreviated and refined the story in such a way that it ties in more closely with the transfiguration episode and contributes in a general way to the overriding question of Luke 9 concerning the identity of Jesus. Having just descended from the mountain, Jesus has the opportunity to define his messiahship in terms of ministry to the sick and needy.

The **man in the crowd** who **called out** in desperation reminds us of Jairus (8:40–42), while the fact his afflicted son is his **only child** reminds us of the widow of Nain (7:11–17). According to the description, the boy was an epileptic, although the cause of the condition is attributed to a **spirit** (v. 39) and, later, an **evil spirit** (v. 42; lit. "demon"). The curious feature of this incident is the inability of his **disciples to drive it out**. Since Peter, James, and John were with Jesus on the Mount of Transfiguration, the reference, at least in the Lucan context, would have to be to some of the other disciples. What is puzzling is that in 9:1 Jesus had given his disciples "power and authority to drive out all demons," and yet in this case they were unable to effect a cure. It is unlikely that disciples other than the Twelve are in view. Fitzmyer (p. 809) wonders if the power given to the Twelve in 9:1 was only for the mission itself and so was temporary. This may be, for it is in the context of the later mission of the Seventy that the disciples of Jesus once again experience authority over demons (see 10:17). (Although, in 9:49–50 others apparently are able to cast out demons in Jesus' name.)

The disciples' inability to exorcise the demon and cure the boy prompts Jesus' outburst in v. 41. His questions, in all likelihood, refer to everyone, not just to his disciples (in Mark the emphasis lies very much on the lack of faith). In asking, **how long?** . . . Jesus is hinting at the nearing end of his earthly ministry. By referring to the **generation** as **unbelieving and perverse** Jesus is setting the stage for his own rejection. His generation is not yet prepared to receive him. Because of their unbelief and perversity they are not yet ready to repent and receive God's blessing.

Additional Notes §23

9:38 / **Teacher**: See note on 7:40 above.

9:40 / **but they could not**: The inability of the disciples to cast out the demon only heightens the picture of Jesus' power. Fitzmyer (p. 809) and Lachs (p. 263) point to the example of Gehazi's inability apart from his master Elisha (2 Kings 4:31).

9:41 / **O unbelieving and perverse generation**: Possibly an allusion to Deut. 32:5b.

9:42 / The sudden convulsion is depicted as the result of the demon being brought into the presence of Jesus (cf. 4:35). Jesus both exorcised the demon and **healed the boy**. The phrase, **gave him back to his father**, echoes 7:15 (see 1 Kings 17:23).

9:43a / **And they were all amazed at the greatness of God**: In view of the fact that it was Jesus who had just displayed his power, could this statement be a hint at the deity of Jesus? Compare Luke 8:39; Acts 20:28.

§24 On Discipleship (Luke 9:43b–50)

This section is loosely tied together by the theme of discipleship and represents three successive units from Mark 9:30–40. The section consists of: (1) Jesus' second passion prediction (vv. 43b–45); (2) the question of who is the greatest among the disciples (vv. 46–48); and (3) the question of how other disciples relate to the disciples of Jesus (vv. 49–50).

9:43b–45 / Because he omits Mark 9:28–29 (the discussion concerning why the disciples could not exorcise the demon) and greatly modifies Mark 9:30, Luke is able to move immediately from the amazed crowd that had witnessed the miracle of the healing of the epileptic boy (v. 43a) to Jesus' second passion prediction (v. 44), a prediction that is to be read against the background of the people who were still **marveling at all that Jesus** had done (v. 43b). (In fact, the transition from the healing to the second passion prediction is so abrupt that only one verse [v. 43], instead of two, concludes the former episode and introduces the latter.) The effect is one of contrast. Jesus has demonstrated great power, such that the people see it as a display of God's mighty power (v. 43a); and yet he reminds his disciples that rejection, humiliation, and suffering are what lie ahead for him. Luke has presented the paradox as sharply as possible. It is no wonder, then, that the disciples **did not understand what this meant**. Mark's account leaves the impression that the disciples were incredibly dull in their understanding (which is Mark's intended effect), but here in Luke the disciples' lack of comprehension seems quite understandable. In view of his mighty power what does this statement mean? How can he, who possesses the power of God, **be betrayed into the hands of men**? Although now the disciples cannot understand it, they will come to realize that all these things were according to the Scriptures (24:25–27).

9:46–48 / Because Luke has omitted geographical references (to Galilee in v. 43; cf. Mark 9:30; to Capernaum in v. 46;

cf. Mark 9:33), the question about greatness and the question about rival disciples (vv. 49–50) are more closely linked to the transfiguration and the larger questions of who is Jesus and what does it mean to be his disciple? It may be that their concern with greatness prevented the **disciples** from comprehending Jesus' statement about his fate. Jesus summarizes the essence of Christian fellowship in v. 48. Everyone, even the weak and lowly, is to be considered great. To welcome the insignificant and the humble is to welcome Jesus himself. This idea is part of Jesus' unusual and unexpected criteria of evaluation, criteria which were unacceptable to many of the religious authorities of his time. The notion that the weak and the lowly will more readily gain admission into the kingdom of God than the rich and the mighty is stressed throughout Luke's Gospel (e.g., 14:15–24).

9:49–50 / From openness and tolerance for the weak and humble (vv. 46–48) Luke moves to an example of openness and tolerance for the outsider who does work in Jesus' **name**. Although it is hard to reconstruct the historical background of this brief episode, it is likely that for Luke such a saying would be applied to those who believe in Jesus and in his name carry on ministry. Understood this way the saying implies that Christian leaders (such as Gentiles) are not to be prohibited or prevented from ministry just because they were not part of the original Jewish group of believers.

Additional Notes   §24

9:45 / **hidden from them**: Luke has added this phrase (see Mark 9:32) to explain why the disciples **did not understand** the meaning of Jesus' statement. It was God's purpose that they not fully understand until the resurrection. Luke may be reacting to Mark's negative portrayal of the disciples.

they were afraid to ask him about it: This probably means that the disciples feared that further questioning and explanation would only confirm the grim pronouncement.

9:47 / **Jesus . . . took a little child**: A quaint and completely unfounded tradition arose during the Middle Ages that this child was none other than the church father Ignatius.

9:49 / On **Master** see note on 5:5 above.

driving out demons in your name: Rabbis often attempted exorcisms in the name(s) of various OT worthies (such as Solomon). See the episode in Acts 19:13–16. Fitzmyer (p. 820) has noted that "underlying the phrase is the Hebrew use of [the name of the Lord] in the sense of a source of power" (he cites Pss. 54:1; 124:8).

9:50 / **whoever is not against you is for you**: The reverse of this statement occurs in Luke 11:23a (=Matt. 12:30a): "He who is not with me is against me." Leaney (p. 170) and Lachs (p. 267) think that these two sayings contradict one another. This is hardly the case. The saying in 9:50 provides the proper attitude toward outsiders, while the saying in 11:23 challenges the follower of Jesus to total obedience; see Fitzmyer, p. 821.

§25 The Beginning of the Journey to Jerusalem (Luke 9:51–62)

In 9:51 Luke begins his account of Jesus' journey to Jerusalem (9:51–19:27), which is sometimes called the "Travel Narrative" or simply the "Central Section." Luke breaks away from his Marcan source in this section until 18:15 (see Introduction, pp. 3–5 and commentary on 10:1–24 below). During this section the reader is reminded of Jesus' journey by references to the verb "to go" (9:51–53, 56–57; 10:38; 13:31, 33; 17:11; 19:28) and the noun "road" or "way" (9:57; 10:4).

We shall examine 9:51–62, which is comprised of: (1) Jesus' rejection by a Samaritan town (vv. 51–56) and (2) three exchanges with would-be followers (vv. 57–62). The first part launches the journey; the second part reviews the requirements for making the trip. There is no doubt that Luke intends a certain amount of symbolism. The journey symbolizes in a limited way the "way of the Lord," that is, the pattern that a disciple of Jesus must emulate (see commentary on 10:1–24 below). The journey is the actual working out of Jesus' "exodus" (see 9:31).

9:51–56 / This first passage sets the pace for the journey that follows and cannot be adequately appreciated without a grasp of the several OT themes that underlie it. The opening phrase, **As the time approached for him to be taken up to heaven**, should draw the readers' attention back to the account of the transfiguration (9:31), where Jesus spoke with Moses and Elijah of his impending "exodus" (or departure). The word **heaven** is not found in the Greek, but almost certainly Luke's word translated "taken up" (lit. "going up" or "ascension") refers to Jesus' literal uphill climb to Jerusalem as well as his ascension to the Father following his passion (see Luke 24:51; Acts 1:9). Quite possibly Luke was familiar with the legendary account known as the *Assumption* [or *Ascension*] *of Moses*, in which Moses is depicted as giving his final teaching while journeying to the place where God would take him up (see notes below). If such a parallel were intended, then Luke's account would only be enriched and the interest of his first-century readers would be heightened. Just as the great Law-giver Moses, after giving the law a second time (Deuteronomy), was taken up by God, so Jesus, after giving his "law" (Luke 10:1–18:14), is taken up by God.

The second half of v. 51, **Jesus resolutely set out for Jerusalem**, may be rendered literally: "He set his face to go to Jerusalem." The expression "to set one's face" recalls an OT figure of speech often used in the context of someone's being commissioned and dispatched with a message of judgment (see Num. 22:4–25; 24:1–9, where King Balak commissions the prophet Balaam to curse the approaching tribes of Israel). The best example of this idea, and the one that probably has most directly influenced Luke, comes from Ezek. 21:2–3: "Son of man [cf. Luke 9:44], set your face toward Jerusalem and preach against the sanctuaries; prophesy against the land of Israel and say to the land of Israel, Thus says the LORD: Behold, I am against you, and will draw forth my sword out of its sheath . . . " (RSV). This is in fact very similar to the message that Jesus will deliver to Jerusalem. In 19:41 and 21:20–24, in language reminiscent of the OT prophets' description of the first destruction of Jerusalem and the temple (see Isa. 63:18; Jer. 6:6; Ezek. 4:2), Jesus woefully predicts a second destruction of the city and the temple (see notes below).

The clause in v. 52, **he sent messengers on ahead**, may recall the prophecy of Mal. 3:1: "Behold, I will send my messenger who will prepare the way before me." Later in Malachi, of course, we are told that the Lord will send the prophet Elijah (Mal. 4:5–6). The messengers (probably his disciples) **went into a Samaritan village . . . but the people there did not welcome him, because he was heading for Jerusalem**. Since Jesus has business with Jerusalem, especially of a religious nature, the Samaritans, who have little liking for Jews (see John 4:9), refuse to receive him into their village (see notes below). Reacting in righteous indignation, **the disciples James and John** ask to **call fire down from heaven to destroy them**. Some ancient mss. add: "as Elijah did." Although this addition is probably not authentic, it does correctly see in the question of the disciples an allusion to the incident in 2 Kings 1:9–16, where Elijah twice called down fire from heaven to destroy the soldiers sent by Ahaziah, the king of Samaria. James

and John may have thought that if Elijah called fire down upon
the obstinate Samaritans, should not Jesus, who is greater than
Elijah, do no less in this case? However, **Jesus . . . rebuked them**.
It has already been observed (see commentary on 4:25–27 above
and 9:61–62 below) that despite Elijah's great reputation Jesus does
not feel bound to follow the former prophet's precedent. Since
Jesus has come not to judge and punish (see commentary on 4:16–
30) but to save the lost (19:10), the request of the disciples is completely inappropriate. The addition in some mss., "You do not
know what kind of spirit you are of, for the Son of Man did not
come to destroy men's lives, but to save them" (see NIV footnote),
is probably inauthentic, but it certainly does capture the essential point in this passage.

We shall see throughout the Travel Narrative examples that
illustrate how Jesus views people and their religious assumptions.
The episode just examined portrays a loving and gracious Lord
who does not seek vengeance, while the passages that follow depict Jesus extending God's summons to those who appear outcast and left out of the kingdom.

9:57–62 / The first two exchanges with would-be followers are also present in Matt. 8:19–22 and so are derived by Luke
in all likelihood from the sayings source ("Q"). The third saying,
appearing nowhere else in the Gospel tradition, may also have
been part of the sayings source, but in view of its affinities with
the Elijah/Elisha tradition, this third exchange may be unique to
Luke. Fitzmyer (p. 833) suggests that all three exchanges likely
derive from "independent contexts in the ministry of Jesus." But
because of their similar form and function it was only natural to
group them together.

These exchanges drive home the point that it *costs* to follow Jesus. In the first exchange (vv. 57–58) **a man** offers to **follow**
Jesus **wherever** he should **go**. **Jesus** tells him that he has little to
offer by way of material security. To follow Jesus requires radical
commitment. In the second exchange (vv. 59–60) Jesus summons
another man with the words, **Follow me**. He is willing, but **first**
he must return and **bury** his **father**. In view of the commandment to honor one's mother and father (Exod. 20:12) and the importance placed upon loyalty to one's parents in Jewish society
(including Jesus himself, see Matt. 15:3–6; Mark 7:9–13), the man's
request would have seemed only reasonable. But Jesus tells him

to **let the dead bury their own dead** (see note below) and **go and proclaim the kingdom of God**. This reiterates that following Jesus requires radical commitment. The third exchange (vv. 61–62) intriguingly makes a deliberate allusion to Elijah's summons of Elisha (see 1 Kings 19:19–21). When Elijah approached Elisha, the latter was plowing, and when Elijah extended his call by throwing his mantle upon him, Elisha requested permission to bid his parents farewell. All that the man had asked of Jesus was to do something similar, but for Jesus it was asking too much: **No one who puts his hand to the plow and looks back is fit for service in the kingdom of God**. To follow Jesus required severing one's self from one's family (see Luke 8:19–20). Again the requirements for following Jesus are cast into the most radical of terms.

These exchanges teach that commitment to Jesus and to the kingdom of God must be a matter of first priority for anyone to be his disciple. In order to drive home the point, exaggeration is employed, for there is nothing wrong with having a house or a bed, and there is nothing wrong with taking care of one's parents; neither is there anything wrong with showing love and respect to one's family. What Jesus is teaching, however, is that if these things mean *too much* to a person, then that person will find discipleship too demanding and too costly.

Additional Notes §25

William C. Robinson, Jr. ("The Theological Context for Interpreting Luke's Travel Narrative [9:51ff.]," *JBL* 79 [1960], pp. 20–31) believes that Luke has produced the Central Section as exemplifying the "way" (see Acts 9:2) that Christians should live, based on Jesus' teaching and conduct. Robinson's view comports well with the possibility that the Central Section's teaching component (10:1–18:14) corresponds to the order, contents, and themes of Deuteronomy 1–26 (see commentary on 10:1–24 below).

9:51 / As the time approached: Compare the phrase with the similar "hour" theme in John (e.g., John 17:1).

to be taken up to heaven: Jesus' ascension may be viewed against the OT background of the ascension of Enoch (Gen. 5:24) and Elijah (2 Kings 2:11). Luke might also be alluding to ascension traditions concerned with Moses. Because of the mystery surrounding his death (Deut. 34:5–6) there was speculation that perhaps Moses, too, like Enoch and

Elijah, had been taken up into heaven (see Pseudo-Philo, *Biblical Antiquities* 32:9). Josephus states that while Moses was bidding Joshua farewell a cloud suddenly descended upon him and he disappeared (*Antiquities* 4.326). The word "disappeared" is the same one that Josephus later uses to describe the ascension of Elijah (*Antiquities* 9.28). According to Clement of Alexandria (*Stromateis* 6.15.132), Joshua saw Moses ascend with the angel. According to Jerome (*Homilies on Amos* 9:6), "the Lord ascended in a cloud with Enoch, ascended with Elijah, ascended with Moses." Later rabbinic writings preserve similar traditions. According to *Sipre Deuteronomy* §357 (on Deut. 34:5), "Moses never died, but stands and serves on high." Finally, *Midrash Haggadol* on Deuteronomy states that Enoch, Moses, and Elijah are the three who were taken up to heaven alive. That Luke actually does have Jesus' ascension in mind here in 9:51 is seen in the similar vocabulary that he uses later in the ascension accounts themselves (Luke 24:51; Acts 1:9, 11).

Jesus resolutely set out: Lit. "he set his face." The expression to "set one's face" may be an idiom of dispatch, against which the Lord's commands to Ezekiel should probably be viewed (see Ezek. 6:2; 13:17; 15:7; 21:2; 25:2) and against which Luke may also be understood (see William H. Brownlee, "Ezekiel," *ISBE* [1982], vol. 2, pp. 254–55; Craig A. Evans, " 'He Set His Face': Luke 9:51 Once Again," *Biblica* 68 [1987], pp. 80–84; Tiede, p. 197). Marshall (p. 405) believes, however, the expression means no more than "determination to do something." This idea lies behind the NIV's translation.

9:53 / Because of Jewish-Samaritan hostilities, Jewish pilgrims from Galilee would often cross over to the East Bank of the Jordan River in order to skirt around Samaria. Josephus provides a graphic description of these hostilities: "Hatred also arose between the Samaritans and the Jews for the following reason. It was the custom of the Galileans at the time of the festival to pass through the Samaritan territory on their way to the Holy City [Jerusalem]. On one occasion, while they were passing through, certain of the [Samaritan] inhabitants of a village . . . joined battle with the Galileans and slew a great number of them" (*Antiquities* 20.118; see also *War* 2.232. See J. D. Purvis, "Samaritans," *IDBSup*, pp. 776–77). According to 2 Kings 17:24–34, the people of Samaria were Gentiles, not Israelites, brought into the land from Cutha (hence they are frequently called "Kutim" or "Cutheans"). Jews regarded the Samaritans with contempt, considering them as fools (Sir. 50:25–26; *Testament of Levi* 7.2) and idolaters (*Genesis Rabbah* 81.3), who were killed with divine approval (*Jubilees* 30:5–6, 23). Brodie (pp. 207–15) works out numerous points of contact between Luke 9:51–56 and 2 Kings 1:1–2:1.

9:54 / **to call fire down from heaven**: In addition to 2 Kings 1:9–16, cf. 1 Kings 18:36–38, where fire falls upon the altar at Mount Carmel, and Gen. 19:24, where fire and brimstone fall upon the cities of Sodom and Gomorrah.

9:60 / **Let the dead bury their own dead**: Even though the OT did not permit a Nazirite to bury anyone, including his own parents

(Num. 6:6–7), and only makes allowance for his parents in the case of the high priest (Lev. 21:1–3, but v. 11 seems to forbid it), Fitzmyer (p. 835) notes that later rabbinic tradition came to view it as obligatory even for the Nazirite and, indeed, came to view it as an act of meritorious service (see Tob. 4:3; 12:12 where burial of the dead is viewed as one of Tobit's great demonstrations of piety). Jesus' peculiar saying surely must mean: "Let the (spiritually) dead bury the (physically) dead" (so Fitzmyer, p. 836; Tiede, p. 199).

9:62 / **who puts his hand to the plow and looks back**: Marshall (p. 412), rightly commenting that Jesus' demands are "more stringent than those of Elijah," cites this interesting parallel from Hesiod, *Works and Days*, 443: "one who will attend to his work and drive a straight furrow and is past the age for gaping after his fellows, but will keep his mind on his work." On the parallels between Luke 9:61–62 and 1 Kings 19 see Brodie, pp. 216–27.

§26 The Mission of the Seventy-two (Luke 10:1–24)

Luke 9:51–18:14 represents material that Luke has inserted into his Marcan narrative (often called Luke's "Big Interpolation"). C. F. Evans (see abbreviations) observed that the teaching part of the Central Section (10:1–18:14), beginning with the sending of the Seventy-two (10:1–20), corresponds to the teaching section of Deuteronomy (chaps. 1–26). Several compelling reasons support this observation. (1) In Luke 9:52 and 10:1 Jesus sends messengers "before his face" (the Greek rendered literally) as he begins his journey to Jerusalem. Similarly, in Deut. 1:21 Moses tells the people that the Lord has set the promised land "before your face" (literal rendering of both Hebrew and Greek versions) and then in 1:22–23 he reminds them of the "twelve" whom he had sent "before our face." Jesus appoints and sends out the Twelve in Luke 9:1–6. In Luke 10:1, however, Jesus appoints and sends out seventy-two. Although Deuteronomy makes no mention of a sending of seventy (-two; see discussion in note below), "seventy elders" accompany Moses up to the holy mountain (Exod. 24:1, 9); they share in God's Spirit (Num. 11:16) and are enabled to prophesy (Num. 11:24–25). Jesus enjoins his appointed seventy to preach the kingdom (Luke 10:9) and later tells them that the "spirits" are subject to them (Luke 10:20). Another important aspect of the word "seventy" is that this is the name of the Greek version of the OT (from the Latin *septuaginta* or LXX). The mere reference to "seventy" may very well have been intended as a hint at the presence of the Greek version of Deuteronomy underlying Luke's Central Section.

(2) The reference to Jesus' "days of his ascension" in 9:51 (again literally rendered) may very well be an allusion to the legendary traditions about the ascension of Moses (see commentary and notes on 9:51 above). In the *Assumption of Moses*, Moses relates to Joshua (=Jesus in the Greek) his final prophecies and teachings and appoints him as his successor. It is quite possible,

and I believe quite probable, that Luke sees "Jesus" as this successor to Moses (as promised in Deut. 18:15–18). Most commentators believe that the reference to "ascension" has in mind Jesus'
actual ascent to Jerusalem and his death, resurrection, and heavenly ascension (see J. H. Davies, "The Purpose of the Central Section of St. Luke's Gospel," in *Studia Evangelica II*, TU 87 [Berlin:
Akademie-Verlag, 1964], pp. 164–69, esp. p. 168. Luke, then, sees
the journey as the first part of that ascent to heaven via death
and resurrection.) David P. Moessner ("Jesus and the 'Wilderness
Generation': The Death of the Prophet like Moses according to
Luke," in *SBL Seminar Papers* [1982], pp. 319–40) pursues this parallel even further by concluding that just as Moses had to die in
behalf of his people, before they could enter the promised land,
so Jesus had to die "to effect deliverance for his people" (p. 339;
see also D. P. Moessner, "Luke 9:1–50: Luke's Preview of the Journey of the Prophet like Moses of Deuteronomy," *JBL* 102 [1983],
pp. 575–605; for more on Exodus typology in Luke–Acts see Luke
T. Johnson, *The Literary Function of Possessions in Luke–Acts*, SBLDS
39 [Missoula: Scholars, 1977], pp. 70–76).

(3) Virtually all modern commentators have come to recognize the Central Section as yielding little or no chronology (see
Ellis, p. 147: "The Lord is no nearer Jerusalem in 17:11 than in
9:51."). Since elsewhere the evangelist shows the interest and
ability to produce a logical and ordered account (as he in fact
claims in his preface, Luke 1:1–4), the question of what order
underlies the Central Section becomes acute. We must either conclude that the Central Section has no discernible order or arrangement, which would be inconsistent with this evangelist, or we
must look for clues as to its order and arrangement, even if these
clues are not particularly obvious.

(4) C. F. Evans has, I think, detected such clues that answer the question of the Central Section's arrangement. He noted
the following parallels (pp. 42–50):

Deut. 1:1–46	Luke 10:1–3, 17–20
Deut. 2:1–3:22	Luke 10:4–16
Deut. 3:23–4:40	Luke 10:21–24
Deut. 5:1–6:25	Luke 10:25–27
Deut. 7:1–26	Luke 10:29–37
Deut. 8:1–3	Luke 10:38–42
Deut. 8:4–20	Luke 11:1–13

Deut. 9:1–10:11	Luke 11:14–26
Deut. 10:12–11:32	Luke 11:27–36
Deut. 12:1–16	Luke 11:37–12:12
Deut. 12:17–32	Luke 12:13–34
Deut. 13:1–11	Luke 12:35–53
Deut. 13:12–18	Luke 12:54–13:5
Deut. 14:28	Luke 13:6–9
Deut. 15:1–18	Luke 13:10–21
Deut. 16:1–17:7	Luke 13:22–35
Deut. 17:8–18:22	Luke 14:1–14
Deut. 20:1–20	Luke 14:15–35
Deut. 21:15–22:4	Luke 15:1–32
Deut. 23:15–24:4	Luke 16:1–18
Deut. 24:6–25:3	Luke 16:19–18:8
Deut. 26:1–19	Luke 18:9–14

(5) Whereas Evans understood Luke's purpose for this arrangement as attempting to show that Jesus was the promised prophet like Moses (pp. 50–51), James A. Sanders ("The Ethic of Election in Luke's Great Banquet Parable," in J. L. Crenshaw and J. T. Willis, eds., *Essays in Old Testament Ethics* [New York: Ktav, 1974], pp. 247–71) has pointed out that the reason Deuteronomy is followed is because Luke is interacting with the theology of election. Sanders has sensed that underlying every paragraph of the Central Section is some question having to do with election. Deuteronomy clarifies who is obedient (and thus elect) and who is not obedient (and thus non-elect) and promises blessings for the former and curses for the latter. In Jesus' day this theology was often understood in an inverted sense: Those who are blessed must be obedient, while those who are cursed are evidently disobedient. Because of a materialistic interpretation of these ideas (as Deuteronomy itself essentially is), "blessings" were thought of as health and wealth, while "curses" were thought of as sickness and poverty. Underlying all of this was the assumption that the wealthy and healthy (the "blessed") were obedient and righteous, while the sick and poor (the "cursed") were disobedient and sinful. It is against these assumptions that Jesus taught, and because of his interest in questions of poverty and wealth, it is not at all surprising that Luke chose to develop this as a major theme in his Gospel. Another reason that Luke is interested in this theme is because Gentiles were lumped together with those considered

non-elect. By showing that God's mercy and blessings extend to the supposedly non-elect, Luke paves the way for the missionary outreach to the Gentiles, as related in Acts (see Introduction, pp. 6–12).

In view of these reasons the Central Section (or Travel Narrative) will be worked through, exploring what relationship, if any, each component has to a parallel component in Deuteronomy. As has already been pointed out, the parallels are not always readily apparent, and since it would be beyond the scope of the present commentary to explore the technical details that make for comparison, certain parallels, owing to their complexity, will not be discussed.

10:1–12 / The sending of the **seventy-two others** parallels the sending of the Twelve in Luke 9:1–6. Though the number seventy (or seventy-two, see note below) is rich with meaning (see discussion above), it is quite possible that Luke understands it symbolically, as he may have understood the number twelve. Whereas the Twelve may represent the reconstitution of the twelve tribes of Israel, the Seventy may represent the seventy Gentile nations of the world, founded by the sons of Noah after the flood (Genesis 10; so Talbert, p. 115; and Tannehill, p. 233). Thus, the appointed Twelve and the Seventy would represent the Jewish-Gentile foundation of the church.

The instructions given to the Seventy are derived for the most part from the sayings source (see Matt. 9:37–38; 10:7–16; 11:21–23), and in Matt. 10:7–16 some of these instructions appear in the Matthean version of the appointing and sending of the Twelve. Like Matthew (see 10:5–42), Luke has assembled these related sayings and has produced a minor discourse. Like the sending of the "messengers" on ahead (9:52), the Seventy are sent before Jesus **to every town and place where he was about to go**. They are sent out **two by two** in order to provide a legally acceptable testimony (Lev. 19:17; Deut. 19:15; see note below). They are sent out as **workers into** God's **harvest field** (cf. John 4:35). The saying in v. 2 looks ahead to the missionary task of bringing in God's elect before the Day of Judgment arrives. But the task is a dangerous one, for Jesus' emissaries will be **like lambs among wolves**. This saying anticipates the persecution and opposition to be endured by the early Christians. As in the sending of the Twelve (9:1–6), the Seventy must travel light to travel swiftly, not even stopping to **greet anyone on the road** (cf. 2 Kings 4:29; Leaney, p. 177; Marshall, p. 418). The greeting of **Peace to this house** is probably an offer to accept the peace and well-being that the Messiah Jesus has to offer. If a person is a **man of peace** (lit. "son of peace"), that is, a son or daughter of the messianic kingdom (Ellis, p. 156), that one will receive the message of the apostles gladly and will enjoy its blessing. But **if** he is **not** a son of peace, the offer of peace is to be withdrawn. The messengers are to **stay** in the **house** where they are received, and they are to eat and drink **whatever** is offered. They are not to **move around from house to house**, thereby taking advantage of generous hospitality. Such table-fellowship would provide evidence of faith and acceptance of the message of the kingdom. As the Twelve had done (9:6) the Seventy were to **heal the sick** and proclaim the **kingdom of God**; and when they were rejected they were to **wipe off** the **dust** as a testimony of coming judgment (instead of peace). Finally, Jesus warns that the judgment coming upon those who reject his message of peace will be a terrible one, as indicated by the reference to **Sodom**, a city which had been utterly destroyed by fire (Gen. 19:24–28; Marshall, p. 424: "If there is no hope for Sodom, there is even less for a city which rejects the gospel.").

Evans (p. 42) compares Luke 10:1–3, 17–20 with Deuteronomy 1:1–46, where Moses leads Israel away from the mountain (cf. Luke 9:37 where Jesus leaves the mountain) toward the promised land, a land where there is a bountiful harvest (cf. Luke 10:2).

10:13–16 / The next four verses elaborate on the grim warning of v. 12. Three cities of Galilee and Gaulanitis (**Chorazin, Bethsaida**, and **Capernaum**) are singled out for special mention, for apparently in them Jesus had **performed** works that should have led these cities to repent, but they had not. **Tyre and Sidon**, in contrast, would have responded in repentance, and therefore they will receive more mercy **at the judgment**. The section concludes with the statement that **he who rejects** his messengers **rejects** him and, consequently, **rejects him** (God) **who sent** Jesus. In this statement the person of Jesus is closely identified with his message. (See the similar sayings in Matt. 18:5; Mark 9:37; John 5:23; 13:20.)

Evans (pp. 42–43) compares Luke 10:4–16 with Deut. 2:1–3:22, where Moses sends messengers ahead to inquire about food and drink (cf. Luke 10:7) and about whether or not the foreign peoples will receive Israel in peace (cf. Luke 10:5–6a). If the people will not receive Israel in peace there will be war (cf. Luke 10:6b, 11–14; cf. also Deut. 2:36; 3:5 ["no city too high for us"] with Luke 10:15: **Capernaum, will you be lifted up to the skies? No, you will be thrown down to the depths**).

10:17–20 / In startling contrast to the essentially negative and judgmental point of view of the previous verses, the **seventy-two returned** to Jesus **with joy**. What is even more odd is that their report has nothing to do with the success (or lack of success) of their preaching, but has to do with their authority over the **demons** (see note below). To this Jesus adds that he **saw Satan fall like lightning from heaven** (see note on 10:15 below), but he reminds his disciples that although they have been given **authority to trample on snakes and scorpions, and to overcome all the power of the enemy** (see note below), their real reason for rejoicing lies in the fact that their **names are recorded in heaven**.

The general lack of continuity from vv. 1–12, where the disciples are to preach the kingdom, to vv. 17–20, where there is no mention of such preaching, strongly suggests that what we have here is a collection of related missionary sayings. This conclusion is confirmed when it is noted that the parallel sayings are scattered in diverse contexts in Matthew (see comments on 10:1–12 below).

10:21–24 / Luke obviously intends this paragraph as Jesus' response to the joy of the disciples who have returned. It may be inferred from the general tenor of vv. 17–24 that the disciples' experience was a positive one, one that has enabled them to grasp the truth of Jesus and the kingdom more clearly. Jesus rejoices (see note below) and thanks God the **Father** for having **revealed . . . to little children** (lit. "infants," i.e., those who are quite unsophisticated) what he has **hidden . . . from the wise and learned** (cf. the similar ideas in 1 Cor. 2:4–9). Verse 22 (=Matt. 11:27) represents a saying reminiscent of the phraseology in the Gospel of John (John 3:35; 10:15) and teaches that the **Son** reveals the true identity of God (cf. John 14:7, 9). Verses 23–24 are also derived from the sayings source. Matthew (13:16–17) places this saying in the context of the discussion of the Parable of the Sower (Matt. 13:3–23; cf. Luke 8:4–10). Nevertheless, the respective Matthean and Lucan contexts are quite similar. In both Gospels Jesus' saying is private (Matt. 13:10; Luke 10:23) and in both Gospels the saying is applied to the great privilege that the disciples enjoy in being able to witness the messianic ministry of Jesus and the dawning of the kingdom of God, something that **many prophets and kings wanted to see** and **hear** (cf. Isa. 52:15).

Evans (p. 43) compares Luke 10:21–24 to Deut. 3:23–4:40, where Moses prays and thanks God for his law, which enables his people to be more wise and discerning than all other people (cf. esp. Deut. 4:6; Luke 10:21, 24).

Additional Notes §26

In all probability Luke has presented us in 10:1–20 with a blend of Moses/Elijah-related themes (see commentary and notes on 9:30, 51 above). Various OT and legendary sources contain traditions of both Moses and Elijah undertaking journeys before finally being removed from the scene (Deut. 34:1–5/2 Kings 2:8–11); both give their final teachings and instructions to their respective successors (to Joshua, Deut. 31:14–23; 34:9; Josh. 1:5; Sir. 46:1/to Elisha, 1 Kings 19:16; 2 Kings 2:1–14; Sir. 48:12); and both had experienced theophanies (appearances of God) on Mount Horeb (=Sinai) (Exod. 24:9–11; Sir. 45:3, 5/1 Kings 19:8–18). In Luke it is Jesus who experienced a theophany, which included the appearance of Moses and Elijah (9:29–31), and it was shortly after this episode that Jesus "set his face" for Jerusalem (9:51) and began to give his final teaching to those who would succeed him (10:1–18:14). For more on the Elijah/Elisha background see Brodie, pp. 227–53.

10:1 / seventy-two others: Though technically this is a mission of the Seventy-two, I—because of conventional tradition—prefer to use "Seventy." The decision in no way affects the sense of the text or its interpretation. The ms. tradition is almost evenly divided over whether Luke 10:1 should read seventy-two or seventy. The reference may allude to the nations mentioned in Genesis 10 or to the number of persons who made up Jacob's family (Gen. 46:27). However, in the Hebrew there are only seventy, while in the Greek version there are seventy-two. Since it is the Greek version that Luke has followed, seventy-two is probably the original reading. For a fuller discussion see Bruce M. Metzger, *A Textual Commentary on the Greek New Testament* (New York: United Bible Societies, 1971), pp. 150–51. On the significance of this number see Fitzmyer, p. 847; Schweizer, p. 174; Tiede, pp. 200–201.

two by two: Brodie (p. 229) thinks that the reference to two is an allusion to the two prophets Elijah and Elisha as they undertook their final journey together to the cities Jericho and Bethel (2 Kings 2:2–7). Perhaps, but I suspect that the primary reference is to the idea of a testimony being confirmed by two witnesses (Lev. 19:17; Deut. 19:15), an idea which reappears elsewhere in Luke (see 24:13–27 where the resurrected Jesus appears to the two on the road to Emmaus; and 24:27, 44–48 where Jesus twice appears and points to the Scriptures as confirmation of the things that have happened).

10:2 / Lachs (p. 178) notes this interesting parallel: "R. Tarfon said: 'The day is short, the work is great, and the laborers are sluggish, and the wages are great and the householder is urgent' " (m. *Aboth* 2.15).

10:3 / Lachs (p. 181) and Fitzmyer (p. 847) note that Israel and the nations are sometimes compared to sheep and wolves, respectively: "Great is the sheep which stands amidst seventy wolves" (*Tanhuma Toledoth* 5; see also *1 Enoch* 89:14, 18–20). Jewish tradition held that there were seventy Gentile nations (Gen. 10:2–31).

10:4 / **sandals:** The prohibition applies to the taking of an extra pair of shoes within one's **bag.** Jesus has not commanded his messengers to travel barefoot.

10:5 / **peace:** In the Bible the idea of "peace" (Hebrew: *šālôm*) means much more than the absence of conflict, but it expresses the idea of completeness or well-being (see 1 Sam. 1:17; Ps. 37:11; 85:8; Isa. 9:6–7; Luke 2:14; 7:50; 8:48; John 14:27; 16:33; 20:19, 21, 26).

10:12 / **Sodom:** It is speculated that the ruins of Sodom lie beneath the Dead Sea.

10:13 / **Korazin:** A small town in Galilee, a few miles north of Lake Gennesaret. On **Bethsaida** see note on 9:10 above.
Tyre and Sidon: Two famous cities of antiquity (situated on the southern coast of modern Lebanon), upon which prophetic oracles of doom were pronounced (Isa. 23:1–18; Jer. 47:4; Ezek. 26:3–28:24). See *HBD*, 949–50, 1101–2.
sackcloth and ashes: In times of mourning and/or repentance, Israelites (and other peoples of the ancient Near East) would wear sackcloth (a coarse material usually made of camel's hair, comparable to modern burlap) and either sit in ashes (Esth. 4:3; Job 2:8; Jonah 3:6) or place ashes upon their heads (2 Sam. 13:19; Matt. 6:16).

10:15 / On **Capernaum** see note on 4:31 above. The image of being **lifted up** and then thrown **down** is probably an allusion to Isa. 14:13, 15, part of a prophetic oracle pronounced against the city of Babylon (Isa. 14:4). The suggestion is confirmed when it is noted that Satan's "fall like lightning from heaven" (v. 18) is certainly an allusion to Isa. 14:12, a passage sometimes understood as describing Lucifer's (Satan's) fall from heaven (see Rev. 12:7–10, 13).

depths: Lit. "Hades" (which the NIV cites in a footnote), a Greek word which in pagan circles referred to the god of the underworld. The word usually translates the Hebrew word *šeʾôl*, a place where all humans went at death (see Ps. 89:48). In later Judaism it was understood that there were two compartments, one for the righteous and the other for the unrighteous (see Luke 16:22–25). The negative part of Sheol eventually came to be called "Gehenna" (after the infamous Valley of Hinnom, a place where the heathen offered human sacrifice to the god Molech), which is usually translated "hell." The fires of Gehenna burn forever (from Isa. 66:24).

10:19 / **Snakes and scorpions** were names for demons (v. 17) and evil spirits. Satan himself is called a snake (or serpent) in 2 Cor. 11:3; Rev. 12:9, 14–15; 20:2. The snake whose head is crushed in Gen. 3:15 was sometimes understood as Satan (as may be the case in Rom. 16:20). To **trample on** these powers is to exercise dominion over them. Marshall (p. 429) cites a good parallel from the *Testament of Levi* 18:12: "And Beliar [Satan] shall be bound by him [the coming priest], and he shall give power to his children to tread upon the evil spirits." On demons see *HBD*, pp. 217–18.

10:21 / **through the Holy Spirit**: Some mss. read "in his [i.e., Jesus'] spirit." It is probably the former in light of Luke's interest in being filled or moved by the Holy Spirit before speaking (see Luke 2:27; 4:1, 14; Acts 2:4).

10:23 / **Blessed are the eyes that see what you see**: Lachs (p. 221) cites several passages where this beatitude is found (*Pss. Sol.* 4:23; 5:16; 6:1; 17:44; b. *Hagiga* 14b).

§27 The Good Samaritan (Luke 10:25–42)

This section may be divided roughly into three parts: (1) the question of the teacher concerning eternal life, a question which occasions the "Great Commandment" (vv. 25–29); (2) the Parable of the Good Samaritan (vv. 30–37); and (3) Jesus' visit with Martha and Mary (vv. 38–42). A theme common to all of these parts is setting proper priorities. To the teacher of the law, Jesus places priority on love for one's neighbor (vv. 25–37), while in his visit to Martha and Mary (vv. 38–42), Martha learns that Jesus takes priority over all other matters. Talbert (p. 120) has suggested that the Parable of the Good Samaritan and the visit with Martha and Mary illustrate the twofold Great Commandment. That is, the Good Samaritan loves his neighbor, and Mary loves the Lord more than anything else.

10:25–29 / This incident parallels (and possibly is derived from) Mark 12:28–34, where it is Jesus, not the **expert in the law**, who cites the commandments to love God and one's neighbor (although in Mark 12:32–33 the expert repeats similar commandments). In Luke 10:25 Jesus is put to the **test**. (This test is not necessarily "trap," as some versions translate, for there is no indication of hostility in the balance of the episode.) The legal expert is interested in Jesus' theology. He wants to know **what**, in Jesus' opinion, is required **to inherit eternal life**. In rabbinic style Jesus answers the question with a question of his own: **"What is written in the Law?"** and, **"How do you read it?"** The expert then cites Deut. 6:5 and Lev. 19:18 (see note below). He understands the chief requirement of the law to be summarized in the commandments to love God and one's neighbor. Jesus agrees with his answer (**"You have answered correctly"**), for it is the answer that he himself has given elsewhere (Matt. 22:37; Mark 12:29–31). It is, however, easier to profess love for God and to observe religious rituals as proof of this love than it is to show love for one's neighbor. The legal expert must have sensed this and so, wishing **to justify himself,** asked Jesus, **"And who is my neighbor?"** Implicit in his question is an excuse for failing to keep the second commandment, that is, one must love only one's neighbor (when properly identified and qualified) and not others. (According to Lev. 19:18 only Israelites are "neighbors.") But this is not how Jesus understood the commandment. The commandment to love one's neighbor is to be applied universally, not selectively. As the Parable of the Good Samaritan will illustrate, it is the man who treats a stranger as a neighbor that really keeps the commandments of the law. The legal expert, by his qualifying question, may have been trying to find a loophole.

Evans (p. 43) naturally sees a correspondence between this section of Luke and Deuteronomy 5–6, where the Ten Commandments are repeated (5:6–21) and the summarizing commandment (called the "Shema" from the first word "hear") is found (6:4). Evans notes that Israel was told to keep the law, "so that you may go in and take over the good land" (6:18) and "so that we might be kept alive" (6:24). The question of the legal expert (Luke 10:25) and Jesus' allusion to Lev. 18:5 (in Luke 10:28) contain language that Evans thinks is either derived from, or at least alluding to, these verses in Deuteronomy. Deuteronomy 5–6 emphasize the need for "complete devotion to God" (Evans, p. 43), and this is the thrust of Luke 10:25–28.

10:30–37 / To answer the legal expert's question Jesus tells the well-known Parable of the Good Samaritan (see note below). The man who proves to be the **neighbor** (and who really keeps the spirit of the law, as seen in 10:27) is the **Samaritan** who cared for the wounded **man.** Ironically, those who were most concerned with keeping every requirement of the law (as seen through the grid of many oral laws and traditions), the **priest** and **Levite,** were unable to aid a fellow human being in great need for fear of becoming ceremonially "unclean." Because of their religious duties there was no room left for the duty that every person, especially a priest, has as neighbor to another. The Samaritan, however, was viewed as "unclean," as one with no concern for the oral laws and traditions (indeed, as one not worthy himself of receiving assistance from a Jew; see b. *Sanhedrin* 57a; Talbert, p. 123), and yet he is the one who fulfills the law, as expressed in the quotation of Lev. 19:18 (cf. the similar context of Mark 12:33 where Hos. 6:6 is quoted; see also Matt. 9:13; 12:7). The irony is intensified by Jesus' command that the **expert in the law** follow the example of the Samaritan.

Evans (p. 43) finds a parallel between this parable and Deuteronomy 7, in which Israel is commanded to have "no mercy on" foreigners. In this instance the parallel is one of contrast. Note that the legal expert admits that the Samaritan, by having "mercy on" the wounded man, kept the commandment. Unlike the Israelites who were to hate the foreigner (lest they become ensnared in the religions of the foreigners), the Lucan passage teaches that the commandment to love one's neighbor extends to foreigners as well. The Parable of the Good Samaritan contributes significantly to Luke's overall concern to show that foreigners, outcasts, poor, and humble may all receive God's mercy.

10:38–42 / The point of this episode is simple and relates in some ways to the parable that precedes it: It is more important to hear and obey the word of Jesus than to be busy with other matters, even though they may be commendable of themselves. It would have been far better for **Martha** to have made simpler and less time-consuming preparations in order, like her sister **Mary**, to learn from the **Lord**. Likewise, the priest and the Levite of the Parable of the Good Samaritan needed to learn that God and people are better served by deeds of mercy than by religious rituals. Evans (p. 43) suggests that Luke intends this passage to parallel Deut. 8:1–3 where people are to learn that they are to live not by bread alone, but by every word that comes from God (see Luke 4:4). This could very well be the case. By choosing to listen to Jesus' teaching (v. 39), Mary is an example of one who knows that "man does not live by bread alone, but . . . by everything that proceeds out of the mouth of the Lord" (Deut. 8:3b, RSV). In contrast, Martha busies herself with the food that perishes (v. 40; Deut. 8:3a). For further discussion of this pericope, see R. W. Wall, "Martha and Mary (Luke 10.38–42) in the Context of a Christian Deuteronomy," *JSNT* 35 (1989), pp. 19–35.

Additional Notes §27

10:25 / **an expert in the law**: Lit. "lawyer," virtually identical to "scribe" (Mark 12:28). See note on 5:21 above.

Teacher (referring to Jesus): See note on 7:40 above.

10:27 / The combination of the Two Great Commandments (Deut. 6:4 and Lev. 19:18) appears in writings before the time of Jesus; see *Testament of Issachar* 5:2; *Testament of Dan* 5:3.

10:28 / **Do this and you will live** echoes Lev. 18:5. The one who obeys God's law will have eternal life. For the Christian this is realized through Christ who fulfilled the law.

10:29–35 / This parable, as the other parables, is not to be allegorized. The **man** leaving **Jerusalem** does not represent fallen Adam's exit from Paradise (Gen. 3:22–24); the **robbers** do not represent Satan and his demons; **stripped him** does not refer to humanity's loss of immortality; the **priest** does not represent the Law nor the **Levite** the Prophets or some other part of the OT or Jewish practice; the **Samaritan** is not Jesus; the **oil and wine** do not represent the Holy Spirit and/or gifts of the Holy Spirit; the **inn** is not the church; the **innkeeper** is neither the Apostle Paul nor the Holy Spirit; and the **two silver coins** refer neither to the sacraments of baptism and the Lord's Supper nor to anything else. For a discussion of the allegorical abuses of this parable see Robert H. Stein, *The Method and Message of Jesus' Teaching* (Philadelphia: Westminster, 1978), pp. 45–55.

The Parable of the Good Samaritan has its roots in Scripture itself. Consider 2 Chron. 28:8–15 where, after Samaria has defeated Judah in battle, the Samaritans, acting on the advice of a prophet, treated their captives with mercy. They clothed the naked, provided them with food and drink, anointed them, carried the feeble on donkeys, and brought them to Jericho (v. 15).

J. T. Sanders (pp. 182–84) believes that the Parable of the Good Samaritan evidences Lucan anti-Semitism. He assesses the parable accordingly: "By no Jewish prescribed practice, but by behaving like a Samaritan, can salvation be obtained. . . . Jesus' final words [vv. 36–37] mean not only that the hearer should behave in a certain way, but that the legalist should behave like a Samaritan, *not* like the Jewish religious leaders" (pp. 183–84, his emphasis). This is not correct; Sanders has read something into the parable that is simply not there. (Fitzmyer [p. 885] says that to read the parable in an anti-Semitic way "is just another subtle way of allegorizing it.") The point of the parable is that anyone (even a lowly Samaritan), not just a religious expert, can show love and so keep the Great Commandment (Luke 10:25–28); not that it is necessary to avoid being Jewish or to attempt to imitate a Samaritan.

10:30 / **A man**: Lit. "a certain man." Lachs (p. 282) wonders if Jesus might not have been referring to himself in the indefinite third person.

Jericho: East of Jerusalem some 17 miles (and about 3,300 feet lower), in the Jordan Valley. "It is not the Jericho of Old Testament times, . . . but the town founded by Herod the Great about a mile and a half to the south of the western edge of the Jordan plain" (Fitzmyer, p. 886). See *HBD*, pp. 458–61. According to Josephus (*War* 4.451–475) the road from Jerusalem to Jericho was dangerous.

10:33 / **Samaritan**: See note on 9:53 above.

10:34 / **bandaged his wounds, pouring on oil and wine**: This was not an uncommon practice for those times. Fitzmyer (p. 888) notes that the oil would soften the wounds (see Isa. 1:6), while the wine, with its acidic and alcoholic content, would "serve as an antiseptic"; see m. *Shabbath* 19.2.

10:42 / **what is better**: According to the rabbis, learning Torah is better than any other activity; see m. *Aboth* 2.8; 3.2.

This section is made up of three parts: (1) the Lord's Prayer (vv. 1–4), (2) the Parable of the Persistent Friend (vv. 5–8), and (3) the exhortation to trust God for meeting needs (vv. 9–13). The first and third parts evidently come from the sayings source and appear in Matthew's Sermon on the Mount, though not together as they are here (see Matt. 6:9–13; 7:7–11). The Parable of the Persistent Friend occurs only in Luke. Evans (p. 43) suggests that Luke may have seen a parallel with Deut. 8:4–20 where Moses reminds the Israelites of God's adequate provision of food and clothing during their years of wandering in the wilderness.

11:1–4 / Some commentators have suggested that Luke's version of the Lord's Prayer is derived from a source other than one utilized by Matthew (or that Luke adapted and modified Matthew's version). More plausible, however, is the theory that the Lucan and Matthean versions are derived from a common written source (usually designated as "Q") with Luke's version closer to the original wording. (Matthew has in all probability expanded his version of the Lord's Prayer; see Gundry, pp. 105–9; Marshall, pp. 456–57.) The original setting of the prayer was probably not known to the evangelists, although this cannot be categorically ruled out. Matthew placed it in his Sermon on the Mount in order to illustrate the correct way to pray, as opposed to the ostentatious prayers of the hypocrites (Matt. 6:5) and the meaningless repetitions of the Gentiles (Matt. 6:7). Luke did not place the Lord's Prayer in his equivalent sermon (the "Sermon on the Plain," 6:20–49), but chose to place it in the Central Section (or Travel Narrative) in order to illustrate the need for faith and persistence in prayer.

The first part of the prayer is concerned with God's **name** being kept sacred (or **hallowed**, a traditional Jewish concern of first importance) and with the inauguration of his **kingdom**. (Matthew adds: "Your will be done on earth as it is in heaven";

see Gundry, p. 106.) The second part of the prayer is the petition
that God **give us each day our daily bread**. "Bread" could refer
to the messianic feast that was anticipated whenever the kingdom would come (Ellis, p. 165). For the kingdom to come and
for this bread to be supplied, there must be repentance (which
is implied) and forgiveness. This entails the third part of the
prayer. We may ask God to **forgive our sins** because we **forgive
everyone who sins against us**. The idea is that it would be impossible for one to ask God properly for forgiveness if at the same
time one harbored grudging and unforgiving feelings toward another person (cf. Matt. 5:23-25). The prayer closes with the petition that God **lead us not into temptation**. What is probably in
view here is the temptation that will come upon all of those who
follow Jesus, particularly during the days that precede the coming of the kingdom of God. These temptations (or testings) would
include persecution and violence and, perhaps, the allurements
and enticements of false teaching and worldly living. These temptations, probably understood as of Satanic origin, pose the danger
of leaving the faithful unprepared for the kingdom and, at worst,
of disqualifying the faithful altogether. Matthew's version confirms
this idea, for it adds: "but deliver us from the evil one" (6:13b;
see Gundry, p. 109).

11:5-8 / The Parable of the Persistent (or Importunate)
Friend teaches that prayer will be answered. If a person will
answer the summons of a **friend**, though not eagerly because of
extreme inconvenience, certainly God, for whom there is no in-
convenient time, will answer the prayers of his children (see also
Luke 18:1-5).

11:9-13 / These sayings expound upon the point of the
previous parable. Because God will answer our prayers, we should
go to him and **ask**, expecting that **it will be given**. Would a father
give his **son** a **snake** (something evil) instead of a **fish**? Thus, Jesus
drives home the point. If imperfect (or **evil**, see note below)
people usually do the right things for those they love, will not
our **Father in heaven give the Holy Spirit** (the giver of "good
things," cf. Matt. 7:11) **to those who ask him**?

Additional Notes §28

11:1 / **teach us to pray, just as John taught his disciples**: Jesus' disciples wanted to have their own distinctive community prayer, as other groups had (such as John's group of disciples, and other groups of disciples who followed various rabbis and teachers). Lachs (pp. 118–19) points out that the Lord's Prayer is best compared to the Jewish "Short Prayer," not to the longer prayers (such as the Eighteen Benedictions). One of the short prayers that he cites begins, "Perform your will in heaven and bestow satisfaction on earth upon those who revere you . . . " (t. *Berakoth* 3.2).

11:2 / **Father**: In the OT the people of Israel are often referred to as God's children (Deut. 14:1; Hos. 11:1–3).

11:3 / **daily bread**: The meaning of the word that is translated "daily" is obscure. Fitzmyer (p. 896), following Origen (*De oratione* 27.7), translates, "bread for subsistence." Appealing to a short prayer in t. *Berakoth* 3.11, Lachs (p. 120) comes to a similar conclusion: It is the bread that is sufficient for our needs.

11:4 / **Forgive us . . . for we also forgive**: Compare Sir. 28:2: "Forgive your neighbor the wrong he has done, and then your sins will be pardoned when you pray" (RSV).
lead us not into temptation: Lachs (p. 122) cites the following rabbinic parallel: " . . . do not accustom me to transgression, and bring me not into sin, or into iniquity, into temptation, or into contempt" (b. *Berakoth* 60b). In light of this parallel Talbert (p. 130) suggests that the idea is not that no temptation ever come upon Jesus' follower, but that God not allow his follower to be overcome by temptation.

11:5 / **midnight**: The lateness of the hour is not intended as parabolic exaggeration. Such a detail is quite plausible, for people often traveled at night to avoid the heat of the day (Marshall, p. 464).

11:7 / **my children are with me in bed**: It is not at all uncommon in small Palestinian homes ("huts," Ellis, p. 165) for the entire family to sleep together "on a mat which serves as a bed" (Marshall, p. 465). Consequently, for the man to rise would disturb his whole household.

11:9 / **seek and you will find**: We may ask: seek and find what? The reference is probably to seeking entrance into the kingdom (Luke 13:24). Knocking and having a door open may have in view the same idea of being admitted into the kingdom. In any case, Marshall (p. 468) is surely correct in seeing it as a guarantee that God will respond.

11:11–12 / Water snakes were sometimes caught in the fishing nets. When rolled up the **scorpion** would resemble an **egg**.

11:13 / **though you are evil**: Lachs (p. 142) suspects that underlying "evil" is the Hebrew word *biša*, which originally was intended only as an abbreviation for *bāśār vādām* ("flesh and blood"). He notes that to describe one as "flesh and blood" is to call someone mortal, and he cites a rabbinic tradition that parallels the logic of Jesus' saying very closely: "If this man, who is flesh and blood, cruel and not responsible for her [his divorced wife's] maintenance, was filled with compassion for her and gave her [aid], how much more should You be filled with compassion for us who are the children of Your children Abraham, Isaac, and Jacob, and are dependent on You for our maintenance" (*Leviticus Rabbah* 34.14).

Holy Spirit: Gundry (pp. 124–25) suspects that Luke's "Holy Spirit" may be original, while Matthew's (literally) "good things" (7:11) is a Matthean modification. I do not agree. Given Luke's pronounced interest in the Holy Spirit (recall 1:35, 41, 67; 2:25; 3:16, 22; 4:1, 14, 18) it is much more probable that it was Luke who changed the original "good things" (as is read in Matthew) to "Holy Spirit" (so Schweizer, p. 192).

§29 Jesus and Beelzebub (Luke 11:14–26)

This section consists of two parts: (1) the accusation that Jesus is empowered by Beelzebub and Jesus' reply (vv. 14–23), and (2) Jesus' teaching on the return of an evil spirit to the person from whom it had gone out (vv. 24–26). The first part is derived from Mark 3:20–27, which is also adopted by Matthew (12:22–30). The second part is found elsewhere only in Matthew (12:43–45) and so probably is derived from the sayings source. Evans (p. 44) finds a few interesting parallels with Deut. 9:1–10:11 ("greater strength," Deut. 9:1 and Luke 11:22; "by the finger of God," Deut. 9:10 and Luke 11:20). An important thematic parallel is seen in Moses' entreaty that now that God has delivered his people from bondage he not destroy them, and in Jesus' warning that although a person may be delivered from an evil spirit, he may still be in danger of yet a worse fate.

11:14–23 / The accusation that Jesus casts out **demons** by **Beelzebub, the prince of demons**, stands in stark contrast to the preceding passage where Jesus concluded with reference to the Holy Spirit. In the minds of some of those who disbelieved and opposed Jesus, his power over demons could be explained only by assuming that he was in league with Satan, or Beelzebub as he was sometimes called (see note below). What occasioned this accusation was the exorcism of a demon which, apparently, had rendered its host mute. When the **man who had been mute spoke**, it became apparent to all that the demon had been driven out. It was useless to deny the reality of Jesus' power, but its source could be questioned. This is the reason why some **tested him by asking for a sign from heaven**. Only for those who had faith, or were at least sincere in their appeals to Jesus, were miracles performed. Jesus was not interested in entertaining crowds or dazzling opponents (see Luke 23:8–9 where Herod hopes for a miracle, but receives none). The healing of the mute man was proof enough for those sensitive to the presence of God.

Jesus answers his accusers by revealing the illogicality of their charge on two grounds. (1) Surely Satan (or Beelzebub) would not work against his own followers (the demons). (2) If it is true that Jesus casts out demons by the authority of Satan then perhaps it is true that the **followers** of his accusers cast out demons by Satanic power also. This second point reveals the inconsistency of their accusation. On what grounds can they charge Jesus? Is there any reason to suppose that Jesus' power is derived from an evil source? No, Jesus drives **out demons by the finger of God** and so demonstrates the **kingdom of God has come to** Israel (see note below). For those with faith and a receptive heart, the exorcisms and miracles of Jesus are perceived as signs of the presence of the kingdom, but for those who are insensitive and unbelieving, the miracles have little or no effect.

In vv. 21–22 the point is made that the **strong man** (in this context it must refer to Satan) is defeated by **someone stronger** (Jesus). In defeating the enemy Jesus is able to ransack his stronghold and carry away the **armor** and the **spoils**, which is probably to be understood as Jesus' activity of freeing those possessed by Satan's agents, the demons. No one is able to assault the domain of Satan so aggressively unless he has in fact defeated Satan who now stands by helplessly. This Jesus has done and hence the frequency of his miracles of healing and exorcism.

Verse 23 summarizes the argument by saying there is no middle ground. Either one is **with** (i.e., believes in) Jesus, or one is **against** (i.e., rejects) Jesus; either one helps Jesus **gather** the things of the kingdom, or one **scatters** (or hinders) the kingdom.

11:24–26 / Although this was originally an independent but related saying, Luke has put it to good service by making it a concluding statement of the Beelzebub controversy. Almost certainly Luke sees the reference to the **evil spirit** who has been cast **out**, but later returns, as relating to the "followers" of Jesus' accusers who cast out demons (v. 19). Whereas other Jewish exorcists may have enjoyed some success in casting out demons, theirs is but a temporary victory, for the spirit is able to **return**. Indeed, the situation may even become worse, for the spirit may bring along **seven other spirits more wicked than itself**. The number seven indicates the severity of the possession (see note on 8:2 above). The combined strength of eight demons was thought to be too powerful for exorcism (Marshall, p. 480). The implication seems to be that only if the cure comes through the power of Jesus will it last, for the purpose of the cure is not the cure itself, but the purpose is to bring the person into the kingdom.

Additional Notes §29

11:15 / **Beelzebub, the prince of demons**: Beelzebub (some mss. read Beelzebub or Beelzebul) is taken from "Baal-zebul" the Canaanite god whose name means "Lord of the high place." In 2 Kings 1:2-6 he is sarcastically called "Beel-Zebub," which means "Lord of the flies." Hence, this name appears in two forms. The name probably refers to Satan himself (as v. 18 seems to assume) and not to a subordinate demon. In all likelihood he is the same one called "Belial" and "Beliar" in some of the intertestamental writings, including the Qumran scrolls from the Dead Sea area. Early Jewish tradition regarded Jesus as a sorcerer empowered by Beelzebul. Typical is this statement: "Jesus practiced magic and led Israel astray" (b. *Sanhedrin* 107b; see Lachs, p. 211, for additional references). For more on Beelzebul see *HBD*, p. 86.

11:20 / **by the finger of God**: Evans (p. 44) places Luke 11:20 opposite Deut. 9:10. But in what sense does God's writing upon the stone tablets with his finger relate to Jesus' casting out demons? Robert W. Wall (" 'The Finger of God': Deuteronomy 9.10 and Luke 11.20," *NTS* 33 [1987], pp. 144-50) recently has argued that Luke intends to compare Jesus and Moses in that on the brink of bringing their people to salvation both faced a stubborn and rebellious Israel. Just as Moses had to remind Israel that the law had been written "by the finger of God," so Jesus too has to point out to his opponents that Satan has been cast out by God's finger. In both cases, the "finger of God" reveals God at work, advancing his kingdom. Tiede (p. 217) suggests that Luke's phrase may parallel Exod. 8:19, where the Egyptian magicians, despite the evidence of the power of the finger of God, remain hardened. Later Jewish exegesis (as seen in the midrash) concluded that the magicians were able to perform their miracles through demonic power (see Leaney, p. 189).

11:23 / **he who does not gather with me, scatters**: Lachs (p. 213) notes the following relevant parallels from the *Psalms of Solomon*: "And he [the Messiah] shall gather together a holy people, whom he shall lead in righteousness" (12:28); and "He [the wicked one] never ceases to scatter" (4:13).

11:24 / **I will return to the house I left**: Lachs (p. 215) notes that this language is typical of demonic speech. The person inhabited by the demon is viewed as a "house"; see b. *Gittin* 52a and b. *Hullin* 105b.

§30 Jesus Challenges the Pharisees (Luke 11:27–54)

The four parts of this section are loosely tied together around the theme of conflict, conflict between the views of Jesus and his opponents, the Pharisees. The four parts are (1) a saying about true happiness (vv. 27–28); (2) the demand for a sign (vv. 29–32); (3) sayings about light (vv. 33–36); and (4) a lengthy diatribe against the Pharisees (vv. 37–54). Other than the saying about true happiness and some of the sayings in the diatribe, Luke has derived his material from the sayings source (vv. 29–32=Matt. 12:38–42; vv. 33–36=Matt. 5:15; 6:22–23; vv. 39, 42, 44, 46–52=Matt. 23:4, 14, 23–27, 29–31, 34–36). Evans (pp. 44–45) suggests a parallel between Deut. 10:12–11:32 and Luke 11:27–12:12, which contain such ideas as "blessing" (Deut. 11:26–27; Luke 11:27–28), "eye(s)" (Deut. 11:7, 12; Luke 11:34), stranger or alien (Deut. 10:19; Luke 11:30–32). The most impressive parallel has to do with laws pertaining to clean and unclean (cf. Deut. 12:1–16 with Luke 11:37–12:12). Here again is further evidence that Luke has indeed ordered his teaching portion of the Central Section (10:1–18:14) after Deuteronomy 1–26 (see commentary on 10:1–24 above).

11:27–28 / The exclamation of the **woman in the crowd** probably means how happy the mother of Jesus must be for having such a wonderful son. B. S. Easton suggests that the implicit thought was, "If only I could have had such a son" (cited by Marshall, p. 481). This may be. But the heart of the incident is reflected in Jesus' reply. Those who are truly **blessed . . . are those who hear the word of God and obey it**. In view of the fact that a sign from a skeptical crowd had been asked for above in v. 16 and that Jesus will make a pronouncement of judgment upon his generation for craving for signs, Luke may regard the saying on true happiness as a blessing on those who hear and obey but who do not demand dramatic proof, such as a miracle would afford.

11:29-32 / The pronouncement, **This is a wicked generation**, starkly contrasts the pronouncement in the preceding verses. The request for the sign in v. 16 is now finally addressed. Jesus calls his generation wicked because it refuses to believe and obey Jesus, asking instead for a new sign. The request for a sign betrays their unbelief, not a willingness to learn more and become fully persuaded. No sign will be given this generation **except the sign of Jonah**. What is in mind is very likely Jonah's "miraculous deliverance from death" (Marshall, p. 485). (Some think that Jesus intends no more than a comparison between his proclamation of judgment and that of Jonah's; see Ellis, pp. 167-68; Tiede, pp. 219-20.) If the **Queen of the South** was willing to travel to **listen to Solomon's wisdom** (1 Kings 10:1-10), and if the **men of Nineveh** saw their need to repent because of the **preaching of Jonah** (Jonah 3:4-5), then Jesus' generation is utterly without excuse if it does not heed him. For he is greater than both Solomon and Jonah. On the day of **judgment** these people **will stand up and condemn** Jesus' generation for its lack of faith.

11:33-36 / Verse 33 contains a saying on light, while vv. 34-36 contain an extended saying based on a similar metaphor. The **lamp** that is lit and then placed **on its stand** is probably to be understood as referring either to Jesus himself or his proclamation of the kingdom. When one hears Jesus (=**one lights a lamp**), one is to respond in obedience (=**he puts it on its stand**). The second metaphor is slightly different. Jesus equates the **eyes** with the **lamp**. If one's **eyes are good** then one is **full of light**. The "eyes" probably represent one's moral disposition. The one inclined to hear and obey Jesus (=**eyes are good**) will be full of truth (=**light**). If one's moral disposition is to disregard Jesus and his proclamation (=eyes **are bad**), then one will be left in ignorance (=whole body **is full of darkness**). Verse 35 is an exhortation to examine one's self carefully, to make sure that the **light** is truly light and not **darkness**. Verse 36 promises that whoever **is full of light** can be assured of the complete transformation (=**it will be completely lighted**) at the last day.

11:37-54 / This lengthy section begins by a Pharisee's observation that **Jesus did not first wash before the meal** (see note

below). The reference is to Pharisaic ritual, as expressed in their
oral laws and traditions. In response to this, Jesus addressed the
issue (ritualistic washing) in vv. 39–41, but then goes on to deliver a diatribe revolving around the theme of Pharisaic hypocrisy. The first example of hypocrisy that Jesus cites is a take-off
on the Pharisaic concern with washing. In actual practice the
Pharisees did clean the inside of the cup and dish (see Lev. 11:32;
15:12), but Jesus' figurative remark suggests "that the Pharisaic
ritual of only washing the outside of a man is as foolish as only
washing the exterior of a dirty vessel" (Marshall, p. 494). If God
made both the outside and the inside of a person, then both are
important. Indeed, it is really the inside (the attitude of the heart)
that is most important.

In his next example (v. 42) Jesus notes that although the
Pharisees were careful to give God a tenth of everything, even
of the smallest of produce (see Lev. 27:3–33; Deut. 14:22–29; 26:12–
15), they neglect justice and the love of God, the most basic things
that God expects. (For similar expression in the prophetic tradition see 1 Sam. 15:22; Hos. 6:6.) Verses 43–44 offer a pair of
contrasting sayings. In v. 43 the Pharisees are criticized for their
desire to sit in the most important seats in the synagogues and
to receive greetings in the marketplaces. The idea is that the Pharisees want to be seen, recognized, and treated preferentially. The
metaphor shifts in v. 44 to the idea of being unseen. The Pharisees (as is implied) are like unmarked graves, which people walk
over without knowing it. That is, they are like graves that have
become overgrown and so are able to hide their corruption and
uncleanness from people. Because of their mask of religiosity
people do not realize that they have come into contact with corruption (Fitzmyer, p. 949).

With vv. 45–46 (which Luke alone has) the diatribe shifts
its attention from the Pharisees to the **experts in the law** (lit.
"lawyers") who have felt the sting of Jesus' words also. Through
their numerous, complicated, and strict rules these legal experts
have placed heavy burdens upon the people, but they have been
unwilling to **lift one finger to help them**. Although this may have
meant that the legal experts were able themselves to escape the
burden of their rituals (so Marshall, p. 500), these people often
had little concern or compassion on those who struggled, and
usually failed, to keep the oral laws (and probably the written

ones too) and traditions. Rather than helping their own people, they build **tombs for the prophets** (whom, according to Matt. 23:30, they would never have murdered had they lived then—or so they claim!). By tending to their tombs the Pharisees and scribes show themselves to be accomplices in the murders of the prophets. Their **forefathers** murdered them; they **build their tombs**. Neither their ancestors nor they themselves responded to the message of the prophets. Because of this sad history and tradition of rejecting, persecuting, and murdering the prophets, from **Abel** (Gen. 4:8) to **Zechariah** (2 Chron. 24:20–21), future prophets and messengers (i.e., Christian apostles and evangelists) will be mistreated as well. Although the warning of judgment and punishment that were to come probably originally had in view the Last Day, it is quite possible that Christians in Luke's time believed the warning to be fulfilled, perhaps only partially, at the time of Jerusalem's destruction in A.D. 70 (see note below).

The diatribe concludes with the summary of v. 52. Although the **experts in the law** possess the **key to knowledge** (i.e., they are able to read and understand the Scriptures), they themselves **have not entered** (i.e., they do not obey the Scriptures), and they **have hindered those who were entering**. Thus, a double condemnation falls upon them. They are condemned because of their unbelief and hostility toward God's messengers and what the Scriptures really teach, and they are condemned because they have failed in their responsibilities as true experts in the law. After this harsh accusation the **Pharisees and the teachers of the law began to oppose him fiercely and besiege him with questions**. With this acrimonious exchange the plot begins to thicken.

Additional Notes §30

11:27–28 / This unique Lucan saying is also found in the *Gospel of Thomas*, an apocryphal Gospel originally composed in Greek and later translated into Coptic, and now conveniently available in James M. Robinson, ed., *The Nag Hammadi Library* (San Francisco: Harper & Row, 1977), pp. 118–30. Saying 79 (p. 127) reads: "A woman from the crowd said to Him, 'Blessed are the womb which bore You and the breasts which nourished You.' He said to her, 'Blessed are those who have heard the word of the Father and have truly kept it.' " Although some scholars have concluded that some of the synoptic-like tradition in *Thomas* may be as early as the canonical tradition (and even earlier in a few instances), this particular saying appears to be dependent on Luke (see also Luke 23:29). Lachs (p. 287) cites the following rabbinic saying that is spoken in reference to the Messiah: "Blessed is the womb from which he came forth" (*Pesiqta de Rab Kahana* 22 [149a]).

11:38 / **Pharisee**: See note on 5:17 above.

did not first wash before the meal: The Pharisee's surprise at Jesus' failure to wash his hands is clarified by the following rabbinic parallel, where one Jewish man says to another: "When I saw that you ate without washing your hands and without (saying) a blessing, I thought that you were an idolater" (*Numbers Rabbah* 20.21).

11:44 / **unmarked graves**: Lit. "unseen tombs." Matt. 23:27 has "whitewashed tombs," which advances the idea of looking impressive on the outside, but of being corrupt on the inside (see Gundry, pp. 466–67). It is not easily decided if Luke represents a variant version of the same saying or if he has given us a distinct saying.

11:45 / **experts in the law**: See note on 5:21 above.

11:46 / **you yourselves will not lift one finger to help them**: Contrast Jesus' offer in Matt. 11:28–30: "Come to me, all you who are weary and burdened, and I will give you rest. . . . For my yoke is easy and my burden is light."

11:49 / **God in his wisdom said**: Lit. "the wisdom of God said." "Wisdom" in Scripture is sometimes presented as a person (a literary device called personification; see Prov. 1:20–33).

11:49–51 / **from the blood of Abel to the blood of Zechariah**: Ellis (pp. 171–74) thinks that the Zechariah of v. 51 is not the Zechariah of 2 Chron. 24:20–21, but a Christian prophet, a "Zechariah son of Bareis" (the Zechariah son of Berekiah of Matt. 23:35?), who was murdered in the temple courts in A.D. 67–68 (see Josephus, *War* 4.335). Therefore, vv. 50–51 would fit v. 49 better; that is, obstinate Jews have always murdered God's messengers, from the time of Abel down to the time of the Christian message about Jesus. It is probably better to understand the reference to Zechariah as the priest of 2 Chronicles 24, at least when the saying was first uttered. (Of course, when Luke writes a connection with the "son of Bareis" may have been seen.) In the OT, however, it is the prophet Zechariah who is the "son of Berekiah" (Zech. 1:1). Gundry (in commenting on Matt. 23:35, p. 471) suggests that the Synoptic tradition may have conflated the two Zechariahs. In any case, the two murders, that of Abel and that of Zechariah, are taken from Genesis, the first book of the Hebrew Bible, and from 2 Chronicles, the last book of the Hebrew Bible (whose order differs from that of the Christian

Bible). It is a way of saying, "This has been the practice from beginning to end."

J. T. Sanders (pp. 186–88) thinks that the polemic of this passage is thoroughly anti-Semitic. Again, however, he has failed to distinguish intramural polemic from racial hatred. Tiede (p. 225) is correct when he says: "This is not anti-Jewish polemic. It is classic prophetic indictment and call to repentance. Israel knew well that the struggle of wills between God and the people had a long history."

§31 Lessons for the Disciples (Luke 12:1-59)

Luke 12 may be divided into 11 brief units, all of which provide lessons for the disciples: (1) a warning against hypocrisy (vv. 1-3); (2) a saying concerning whom to fear (vv. 4-7); (3) confessing Jesus (vv. 8-12); (4) the Parable of the Rich Fool (vv. 13-21); (5) sayings on the need to trust God (vv. 22-31); (6) a saying concerning riches (vv. 32-34); (7) an exhortation to watch and wait (vv. 35-40); (8) the Parable of the Faithful Servant (vv. 41-48); (9) a saying on family division (vv. 49-53); (10) a saying on recognizing the times (vv. 54-56); and (11) a saying on the need to settle disputes (vv. 57-59). Much of this material is scattered in Matthew (5:25-26; 6:19-21, 25-33; 10:19-20, 26b-36; 12:31-32; 16:2-3, 6; 24:43-51) and thus should be understood as being derived from the sayings source utilized by Matthew and Luke. Luke's Parable of the Rich Fool (vv. 13-21) and the saying on watching and waiting (vv. 35-40) are unparalleled (though cf. the latter with Matt. 24:43-44). Evans (pp. 45-46) relates most of Luke 12 to Deuteronomy 12-13, where Israel is commanded to tithe faithfully and to serve God alone. No one, not even brother, son, daughter, or wife is to come between the faithful person and God (cf. Deut. 13:6-10 with Luke 12:49-53).

Probably to a certain extent Luke 12 is the counterpart to the diatribe against the Pharisees and scribes in the preceding chapter. In the diatribe the faults of Jesus' critics and opponents were exposed, but in this chapter the emphasis falls upon the virtues that Jesus' disciples are to develop and strengthen. Whereas the Pharisees and scribes have no faith, but impatiently demand signs, the disciples of Jesus are to watch and serve faithfully while they wait for their Master.

12:1-3 / This paragraph provides the transition from the diatribe against the Pharisees (11:37-54) to admonitions to the disciples. Jesus' disciples are to beware of the **yeast** (or leaven) **of the Pharisees**, that is, their **hypocrisy**. It is their hypocrisy that has blinded them to the reality of God's presence among his people through his anointed one, the Messiah Jesus. The reference to "yeast" connotes something that spreads throughout whatever it comes in contact with (see Matt. 13:33). In other words, hypocrisy characterizes the Pharisaic approach to religion, and the disciples are warned not to adopt their ways of thinking. The essence of the warning is given in vv. 2–3. The truth will eventually be known. The "hypocrites will be unmasked" (Marshall, p. 512). The truth of the gospel is to be proclaimed openly (**from the roofs**), and through it will come the exposure of false religion and hypocritical motives.

12:4–7 / Jesus' concern now shifts away from the subject of Pharisaic hypocrisy to words of warning (vv. 4–5) and reassurance (vv. 6–7) for the disciples. He tells his **friends** (see note below) not to fear those **who kill the body**, for they cannot do any further harm (Matt. 10:28: "but cannot kill the soul"). God is the one whom all should fear, because he **has power to throw** people **into hell**. This saying follows vv. 1–3 as a warning not to practice hypocrisy of the Pharisees out of fear or out of a felt need to impress those who have authority. It is far wiser to please (or **fear**, which means to hold in respect) God, whose authority greatly exceeds that of any mortal, than it is to please people and thereby incur God's wrath.

The second saying (vv. 6–7) is a word of reassurance. Though the lives of the disciples may have little value in the eyes of those who would persecute and kill them, they are to know that they are precious in God's sight. If **five sparrows sold for two pennies** are **not forgotten by God**, his disciples can know most assuredly that God cares for them. The extent of God's care is expressed by the idea that God is aware of the number of **hairs of** one's **head**. Such knowledge would seem trivial even to the person whose hairs have been numbered. Thus, God's love and concern for his people extend to every facet and dimension of our being.

12:8–12 / The preceding sayings have a more general application. The religion of the Pharisees is judged hypocritical; Jesus' disciples are not to follow their example. Moreover, the disciples are not to fear those who would persecute them for their faith, for they are to rest assured knowing that God cares for them.

Now Jesus' teaching narrows its focus. True religion is not simply avoiding Pharisaic hypocrisy, but confessing one's allegiance to Jesus, the **Son of Man**. Those confessing Jesus **before men** are assured that Jesus will confess them **before the angels of God**. Likewise, if one **disowns** Jesus, that one will in turn be **disowned**. The final judgment is in view (as is probably indicated by the designation Son of Man). All trials and persecution for the sake of allegiance to Jesus are worth it when it is realized that the day will come when Jesus will **acknowledge** before God in heaven the faith of his follower.

The saying in v. 10 may very well have been originally independent of the present context. Its location is appropriate, however, for it answers the question that very naturally arises from vv. 8–9. What about those who not only denied Jesus, but actively sought his death, and then later regretted it? Verse 10 declares that forgiveness is possible; but not when someone **blasphemes against the Holy Spirit**. Attempts to interpret the meaning of this sin, for which apparently there is no forgiveness, has led to several different interpretations. Whatever the original context and meaning of this saying, the present context suggests that Luke sees it as referring to the rejection of the gospel. The gospel, as the Book of Acts attests, was proclaimed with great conviction through the power of the Holy Spirit (Acts 1:8). What we are to understand is that the rejection of Jesus himself during his earthly ministry can be forgiven, but for those who reject the proclamation of his resurrection, a proclamation inspired by the prompting of the Spirit of God (see v. 12 below), there can be no forgiveness. In Acts 2–3 many of those (indirectly) responsible for Jesus' death are confronted with the good news of Jesus' resurrection (2:22–23, 36; 3:17). The Holy Spirit is present in a mighty way (Acts 2:4–18), thus making rejection of Jesus this time inexcusable (see Acts 7:51, which says that the religious leaders "always resist the Holy Spirit").

This interpretation receives additional support when it is observed that vv. 11–12 also reflect the experience of the early church, as seen in the Book of Acts. The disciples are assured that when the day comes that they are **brought before synagogues, rulers and authorities**, the **Holy Spirit will teach** them **at that time what** they **should say**. Examples of this occur in Acts. For example, after he is arrested and brought before the high priest and other religious leaders, Peter is "filled with the Holy Spirit" and is able to speak the Good News boldly (see Acts 4:8 and context).

12:13–21 / The disciples also must learn not to be diverted from their commitment to Jesus by greed for wealth and material possessions, a theme that is important to the evangelist Luke. The transition to this topic, presented as the Parable of the Rich Fool (found only in Luke), is effected by **someone in the crowd** who wants Jesus to **tell** his **brother to divide** his **inheritance**. Jesus had no legal authority to arbitrate in such a matter (a matter often settled in the synagogue), as his answer in v. 14 indicates. More importantly, and what is probably the real point underlying Jesus' answer, Jesus' mission is too urgent and too important for a task that just as easily could be settled by a rabbi (Ellis, p. 178; Fitzmyer, pp. 968–69). But the concern with a fair and proper division of the inheritance leads Jesus to tell a parable calculated to illustrate the folly of laying up treasures on earth (cf. vv. 15–21). Because of an abundant harvest the rich man finds it necessary to replace his **barns** with **bigger ones**. The man is implicitly selfish. He does not see this abundance as an opportunity to help those needing food (see 16:19–25). Rather, he hoards his plenty and then relaxes under the assumption that his troubles are over. Herein lies his folly. The day will come, often sooner than expected, when all persons will have to stand before God and give an account. All that the **fool** will have to show for his life will be bigger barns crammed with food, food that will be enjoyed by others now that he is dead. Rather than giving away his surplus, and so laying up treasure in heaven, he has selfishly and greedily hoarded his worldly goods with the result that in the end he does not even benefit from them.

12:22–31 / The applications of the Parable of the Rich Fool are now driven home. Jesus wants the lives of his disciples to be guided by interests other than worldly, material ones. The disciple is not to worry about **food** and **clothes**, which is not only a distraction, but betrays a lack of faith in God (see v. 28). There is more to **life** than food and clothing. **God** will supply food for his children just as surely as he provides for the **ravens** of the sky; and he will furnish clothing as surely as he arrays the **lilies** of the fields. If **God** cares for such relatively insignificant things as birds and flowers, **will he** not feed and **clothe** his own beloved children? To worry about such things is fruitless according to v. 25. What did the Rich Fool gain by his extra labors designed to prolong his life of ease? All of the stored food in the world would not add an extra day to his life (see note below).

Verses 29–31 summarize the teaching. In view of these truths, Jesus is saying there is no need to **worry about** what **you will eat or drink**, things that are of great concern to those who know no better (like the **pagan world**). The disciples are to know that God their **Father knows that** they **need them**, and he, better than they, is able to provide. Rather, the disciples are to be concerned with the things of God's **kingdom**.

12:32–34 / In vv. 32–34 we come to a vital theme of the Lucan Gospel. Although somewhat paralleling Matt. 6:19–21, Luke 12:32–33a is unique to Luke. The disciples are to be ready and willing to **give to the poor**, because the **Father has been pleased to give** them **the kingdom**. The kingdom of God outweighs everything else in value. Nothing should stand in the way of entering and advancing the kingdom. Proper disposition towards one's earthly possessions will result in the acquisition of heavenly riches. Treasures laid up in heaven will not be given away to others, as was the treasure of the Rich Fool. In heaven the **purses** will have no holes that will allow their contents to fall out and be lost; in heaven the **thief** will not be able to break in and steal, nor will the **moth** be able to destroy. The essence of the issue is summarized in v. 34. Wherever one's **heart** is, will inevitably be found one's **treasure**. People put their time, energies, and resources into those things they value, those things dear to their heart. Resources invested in material things are a sure sign that the things of this world are valued and not the things of God's kingdom. The disciple willing to use personal resources to help those in need and to further the work of the kingdom, however, demonstrates a heart inclined to God's work.

Jesus' assuring words in v. 32 constitute the high point of the section (so Tiede, pp. 226, 237). Despite the threats and persecutions endured by the "flock" (see Acts 20:29), God's people should know that they have been given the kingdom (see Luke 22:29). Having this assurance, Christ's disciples should have the courage to follow their Master's example.

12:35–40 / Luke may have placed this material here because of the catchword "thief" in v. 39 (see also v. 33). In any case,
the transition is smooth enough. If the disciples are free from
worldly cares, then they are in a position to be ready and watch-
ful. The disciples are to be like servants **waiting for their master
to return from a wedding banquet**. They have no idea at what
hour he will come, but whenever he does they will be glad that
they are **watching**. The theme of the need for preparation and
the unexpectedness of Jesus' return is furthered by the image of
the **thief** who breaks into the **house** at a time when the **owner**
least expects it. The import of these illustrations is captured in
v. 40. The disciples of Jesus are to **be ready**, for Jesus the **Son of
Man will come** suddenly, and then there will no longer be opportunity for further preparation.

12:41–48 / The question of **Peter** (v. 41) surfaces only in
Luke. (The parallel material in Matt. 24:43–51 moves from the admonition to be ready to the Parable of the Faithful Manager, without
Peter's question.) To what **parable** Peter refers is unclear. Curious,
too, is that Jesus never directly answers the question. In the Lucan
context the question probably calls for a distinction between church
leaders and Christians in general (Marshall, p. 540; Ellis, p. 181).
Thus, the answer of the question is only implied. As church leaders,
Peter and the apostles are especially to be alert and ready, teaching
the other disciples to be prepared as well. The Parable of the Faithful
Manager illustrates this. The **wise manager** will run the household well by properly delegating the work to the other **servants**.
When the **master** of the house returns he likely will promote the
faithful **servant** (=when Jesus returns his faithful servant-leaders
will be given assignments of prominence in his kingdom). However, if the **servant** is irresponsible and abuses his position of authority (mistreating the other **servants**, getting **drunk**), the **master**
will punish him severely when he returns (=Jesus will condemn
false leaders in the church who have abused their positions of
authority). The additional sayings in vv. 47–48 explain that punishment will be meted out according to one's knowledge of God.
This idea is summarized in the second half of v. 48. Naturally,
from those who had been the actual disciples of Jesus, or the disciples of those disciples, and who had therefore acquired much
learning and insight, much more would be expected than from
those whose training had been meager in comparison.

12:49-53 / These related sayings suggest that Jesus is almost impatient for the crisis of division to come that his death and resurrection will instigate. Jesus understands his mission in terms of setting the **earth** on **fire**, which he wishes **were already kindled**. Ellis (p. 182) and other commentators think that the fire refers to the outpouring of the Holy Spirit, as seen in Acts 2:3, where the Spirit manifests itself as "tongues of fire." This may be, but it seems hardly suitable for the context here. The context seems to call for an understanding of this fire in terms of judgment (recall 3:16-17). Jesus' life, death, resurrection, and subsequent proclamation by his followers will bring about a crisis. In v. 50 Jesus refers to his **baptism**, undoubtedly a reference to his impending death. It is ironic to recall that Jesus' ministry commenced with baptism.

In vv. 51-53 Jesus clarifies the nature of this crisis that will be achieved through the "baptism" of his death. His coming to the world will result in **division**, not **peace**. This should not be understood as a contradiction to the idea of peace that Jesus does in fact represent and bring (see 2:14; 7:50; 10:5), but in this particular context Jesus teaches that on account of him divisions will occur. The division that Jesus specifically has in mind is within families. Verse 53 alludes to Mic. 7:6, a passage that describes the social disintegration of the prophet's day, which later came to be associated with the turbulence that was believed would precede the appearance of the Messiah (as seen, for example, in m. *Sotah* 9.15; and *Jubilees* 23:16, 19). Whereas the Micah passage describes only the hostility of the young against the old, the Gospel version (see also Matt. 10:36) sets the old against the young as well.

12:54-56 / Jesus' address now shifts from the disciples to the **crowd**. The theme of the end times continues, however. People are able to recognize changes in the weather (**rain** from **west**, that is, the Mediterranean Sea; heat from the **south**, that is, the Negev Desert), but as **hypocrites** they are oblivious to the meaning of **this present time**. Discerning the weather may pose no problem, but they are completely undiscerning when it comes to recognizing that God has made salvation possible through Jesus. To receive Jesus means salvation, but to reject him means judgment.

12:57-59 / This brief section may be understood as Jesus' advice to those who have not believed in him. He urges them to settle affairs in this world before God settles with them in the next. Verses 58–59 suggest that if people are liable for commitment to debtor's prison for debts and crimes against people, how much more serious will their judgment be before God? Jesus' warning, if taken seriously, should jolt people to the realization of their need to turn from their sins and to seek God's forgiveness, the very thing that Jesus urges his hearers to do in the next paragraph, 13:1–5.

Additional Notes §31

12:1 / **yeast** (or leaven): The term is not always negative (as seen in Matt. 13:33), though the requirement to have no leaven in one's bread for Passover may have created a negative association, so that the mere reference to leaven could connote something that was to be avoided (see 1 Cor. 5:6).

12:2–3 / **There is nothing concealed that will not be disclosed**: Lachs (p. 185) cites the following rabbinic parallel: "In the end everything in this world which is done in secret will be publicized and made known to mankind, and for this reason, fear the Lord" (Targum to Eccl 12:13).

12:4 / **friends**: This is the only time in the Synoptic Gospels that the disciples are called "friends" (see John 15:13–15).

12:6 / **sparrows**: Lit. "small birds" (sparrows were not actually eaten). The reference is to small birds sold for food. A "penny" (lit. *assarion*) was the smallest of Roman coins, worth 1/16 of a denarius (which in turn was equivalent to a day's wage). Lachs (p. 185) cites the following rabbinic saying: "R. Simon ben Yohai said: 'No bird perishes without God, how much less man' " (*Genesis Rabbah* 79.6; *Pesiqta de Rab Kahana* 10 [88b]).

12:8 / On **Son of Man** see note on 5:24 above.

12:10 / The early church applied this verse to apostates who later returned to the faith. The saying, however, has nothing to do with apostasy, but with the initial rejection of Jesus. The rabbis considered blaspheming the Divine Name an unforgivable sin: "Five shall have no forgiveness . . . and he who has on his hands the sin of profaning the Name" (*Abot de Rabbi Nathan* 39); "He who profanes the Name of Heaven [i.e., God] in secret, they exact the penalty from him openly. Ignorant and willful are all one in regard to profaning the Name" (m. *Aboth* 4.5); see Lachs, pp. 213–14.

12:11 / **Synagogues** had the authority to whip people for holding to views considered heretical. See commentary and notes on 4:16–30.

12:13-14 / The *Gospel of Thomas* (see note on 11:27-28 above) 72 also contains this unique Lucan passage: "[A man said] to him, 'Tell my brothers to divide my father's possessions with me.' He said to him, 'O man, who has made Me a divider?' He turned to His disciples and said to them, 'I am not a divider, am I?' " The *Thomas* form of the saying probably derives from Luke. Compare Exod. 2:14: "Who made you [i.e., Moses] a prince and a judge over us?" (RSV; see also Acts 7:27).

12:15 / Jesus' warning about the danger of greed is commonplace in Jewish literature (see Lachs, p. 291). His Parable of the Rich Fool reflects the words of the Psalmist: "Be not afraid when one becomes rich, when the glory of his house increases. For when he dies he will carry nothing away; his glory will not go down after him" (Ps. 49:16–17, RSV; see also Job 31:24–28). Compare also the wisdom of Sirach: "There is a man who is rich through his diligence and self-denial, and this is the reward allotted to him: when he says, 'I have found rest, and now I shall enjoy my goods!' he does not know how much time will pass until he leaves them to others and dies" (Sir. 11:18–19, RSV).

12:16–20 / The Parable of the Rich Fool also surfaces in *Thomas* 63: "Jesus said, 'There was a rich man who had much money. He said, "I shall put my money to use so that I may sow, reap, plant, and fill my storehouse with produce, with the result that I shall lack nothing." Such were his intentions, but that same night he died. Let him who has ears hear.' " Fitzmyer (p. 971) concludes that the *Thomas* version is secondary and "has lost the cutting edge of the Lucan parable, viz. God's verdict." Since most Gnostics were ascetic, and so opposed to wealth, it is not surprising that they found much of the material unique to Luke (who also was concerned with wealth) useful for their own purposes.

12:24 / **Consider the ravens**: Compare Ps. 147:9: "He gives to the beasts their food, and to the young ravens which cry" (RSV); Job 35:11: " . . . who teaches us more than the beasts of the earth, and makes us wiser than the birds of the air?" (RSV).

12:25 / **add a single hour to his life**: Lit. "to add a cubit to his lifespan [or stature]." The reference is undoubtedly to lifespan, as is indicated by the context, particularly by the Rich Fool's death shortly after building his new barns. A cubit is 18 inches (which would be quite an addition to one's height!), but it can be used, as it is here, with reference to time (Marshall, p. 527). Lachs (p. 132) notes that the cubit might refer to an increase in the height of one's crop (i.e., the height of standing corn, perhaps in references to the Rich Fool's good crops in vv. 16–17).

12:27 / **Solomon** was considered Israel's wealthiest monarch; 2 Chron. 9:13–22: " . . . thus King Solomon excelled all the kings of the earth in riches . . . " (RSV); Sir. 47:18: " . . . you gathered gold like tin and amassed silver like lead" (RSV); see also 1 Kings 10:4–5, 21, 23; 2 Chron. 9:4, 20.

12:28 / On using **grass** as an illustration cf. Isa. 37:27; 40:6–8; Job 8:12; Pss. 37:2; 90:5–6; 102:11; 103:15–16.
you of little faith: Lachs (p. 133) cites this rabbinic parallel: "Whoever has a morsel of bread in a basket and says, 'What shall I eat tomorrow' is one of those who has little faith" (b. *Sotah* 48b).

12:31 / **seek his kingdom**: Compare Matt. 6:33: "But seek first his kingdom and his righteousness. . . . " Righteousness is a major theme in the Matthean Gospel.

12:32 / **to give you the kingdom**: Jesus' words are probably understood as the fulfillment of the scene in Daniel 7, where the Son of Man and the saints "receive the kingdom" (Dan. 7:13–14, 18, 22, 27).

12:33 / **no moth destroys**: With regard to the wicked, Isaiah says: "For the moth will eat them up like a garment, and the worm will eat them like wool" (51:8a, RSV).

12:34 / Fitzmyer's paraphrase (p. 983) expresses the point succinctly: "If you put your treasure in heaven, then your heart will be set on heavenly things."

12:35–36 / **ready for service . . . like men waiting for their master**: Lachs (p. 294) notes that the rabbis believed that the coming of Messiah would be sudden and unexpected: "Three things come unexpectedly: the Messiah, the discovery of treasure, and the scorpion" (b. *Sanhedrin* 97a). On the instructions for readiness, compare Exod. 12:11: "In this manner you shall eat [the Passover]: your loins girded, your sandals on your feet, and your staff in your hand" (Tiede, p. 240). A wedding banquet might end late at night.

12:37 / The master serving his servants is unusual and does not reflect the culture of Jesus' day. Jesus' point is that when he returns in glory his faithful servants will be rewarded.

12:38 / **second or third watch in the night**: Assuming Luke is following the Roman practice of dividing the night into four watches (6–9 p.m., 9–12 p.m., 12–3 a.m., 3–6 a.m.), then the "second or third watch" extends from 9 p.m. to 3 a.m.

12:39 / **not let his house be broken into**: Lit., "not let his house be dug through." The adobe-like walls of Palestinian homes could be dug through, and probably quietly enough not to arouse the household.

12:40 / **the Son of Man**: See note on 5:24.

12:42 / **the faithful and wise manager**: Compare the dishonest manager of 16:1–8. Fitzmyer (p. 989) suspects that Luke may have thought of the faithful managers as leaders of the church. Distributing **food allowance** does reminds us of the activity in Acts 6:1–6 (see also Acts 2:44–45).

12:44 / **in charge of all of his possessions**: The idea is similar to that of receiving the kingdom (see note on 12:32). The master's faithful servants will share in his kingdom and in his possessions as well.

12:46 / **cut him in pieces**: Such a severe judgment was not unknown in antiquity. Some scholars, however, think that the Greek tradition, upon which Luke is of course based, has taken the Semitic phrase, "to be cut off" (i.e., excommunicated), too literally. This may be, for if the worthless servant has literally been "cut in pieces" he can scarcely be assigned **a place with the unbelievers**; see Lachs, p. 294.

12:48 / Fitzmyer's explanatory paraphrase (p. 992) is helpful: "Much will be required (by God) of the gifted servant, and even more of the really talented one."

12:49 / The *Gospel of Thomas* (see note on 11:27–28 above) 10 reads: "Jesus said, 'I have cast fire upon the world, and see, I am guarding it until it blazes.' " Fitzmyer (p. 994) regards this *Thomas* saying as "almost certainly a derivative of the Lucan v. 49."

12:54 / **a cloud rising in the west . . . rain**: Compare 1 Kings 18:44: " 'Behold, a little cloud like a man's hand is rising out of the sea [i.e., out of the west].' And he said, 'Go up, say to Ahab, "Prepare your chariot and go down, lest the rain stop you" ' " (RSV).

12:58–59 / Jesus' warning fits a Gentile setting, not a Jewish one. In the latter setting there would be at least three judges (and not a single judge or **magistrate**) and **prison** would not be the sentence of a debtor; see Lachs, pp. 93–94.

This section contains materials that teach the urgency of repentance: the death of some Galileans during a time of sacrifice
(vv. 1–3); the death of some upon whom a tower collapsed (vv.
4–5); and the Parable of the Barren Fig Tree (vv. 6–9). The incidents reported here, in which reference is made to the murder
of some Jews from Galilee and the death of 18 people in Siloam,
is unique to Luke. Neither of the episodes is mentioned in secular histories (though some scholars point to two or three inex-
act parallels to the incident of the murdered Galileans; see
Marshall, p. 553). Concerning theme, Evans (p. 46) points to a
parallel with Deut. 13:12–18, where the emphasis on turning to
the Lord in order to live is quite similar to the Lucan passage
under consideration (cf. the similar expression, "all who live in
that town," Deut. 13:15, with "all the others living in Jerusalem,"
Luke 13:4).

13:1–5 / **Some** people who presumably have just arrived
from Jerusalem **told Jesus about the Galileans whose blood Pilate had mixed with their sacrifices**. For some unknown reason
Pilate had slain a few Galileans while they were offering their sacrifices. Since laymen were allowed to perform their own Passover sacrifices, this may very well have been the occasion. The
report that Pilate had "mingled their blood with their sacrifices"
is not literally the case, for such an action would have incited the
populace to a possible insurrection; but it is probably meant in
a proverbial sense, that is, not only was the blood of the sacrificial animals shed, but the blood of the Galileans was as well.
Passover time was often a time of political unrest, a time when
Jewish patriotic feelings ran high and Roman concerns were justi-
fiably aroused. (Jesus was crucified under precisely such circumstances.) These Galileans (how many is unknown) were seemingly
caught up in some sort of plot or activity deemed treasonable by
Pilate. Whatever the circumstances, the death of these unfortu-

nate pilgrims evokes the question that Jesus asks in v. 2, a question that reflects the Pharisaic belief that misfortune was often brought on by God in retaliation for sin (see John 9:1–2). Did their murder prove that they **were worse sinners than all the other Galileans**? Their death proved no such thing. But their death should remind all who hear of it of the need to **repent**. Similar is the case of the **eighteen** people **who died when the tower of Siloam fell on them** (see note below). Their accidental death most certainly does not indicate that they **were more guilty than all the others living in Jerusalem**. From this episode Jesus draws the same lesson: **Unless you repent, you too will all perish**.

13:6–9 / The Parable of the Fig Tree illustrates that people will not always have an opportunity to repent and turn over a new leaf. Just as the reports concerning those who died (vv. 1–5) should awaken one to the realization of the nearness of judgment, so the present parable underscores that judgment cannot be put off forever.

Additional Notes §32

13:1 / Various historical incidents that have been proposed as underlying the murder of the **Galileans** include: (1) the riot that ensued Pilate's posting of imperial ensigns in A.D. 26 (Pilate's first year in office); and (2) riots resulting from the work on an aqueduct; however, as Marshall (p. 553) has noted, "this incident involved the murder of Judaeans [not Galileans] with cudgels outside the Temple" and had nothing to do with sacrifices; and (3) the murder of some Samaritans. But since this incident involved Samaritans, not Galileans, and occurred in A.D. 36 (Pilate's last year in office), it is scarcely the event alluded to in Luke. It was probably a less noteworthy incident. We may ask why the report was delivered to Jesus. Although by no means certain, it is possible that the messengers thought the news worthy of Jesus' attention because of his fame and following. Had many regarded him as a or *the* Messiah in the popular sense they might have hoped that Jesus' movement would gain additional support by spreading the news of this fresh outrage. According to his contemporaries Philo (*Embassy to Gaius* 38) and Josephus (*Antiquities* 18.55–62; *War* 2.169–174), Pontius Pilate was a cruel and violent man. The Roman historian Tacitus (*Annals* 15.44; ca. A.D. 115) mentions Pilate in connection with the crucifixion of Jesus.

13:4 / **Siloam** was the name of the reservoir which supplied Jerusalem (Isa. 8:6, where it is spelled "Shiloah"; John 9:7). The aqueduct referred to in the preceding note could have had something to do with this accident (see Josephus, *Antiquities* 18.60). Otherwise, we have no record of any such accident (nor should we really expect to have any, for the episode would scarcely have been deemed historically significant). Marshall (p. 554) notes that there is a rabbinic statement that no building "ever collapsed in Jerusalem" (the reference is found in *Aboth de Rabbi Nathan* 35). This statement is not conclusive (nor is it likely accurate). The **tower** may have been no more than some temporary scaffolding.

13:6 / Marshall (p. 555) states that "there is nothing strange about a fig-tree being planted . . . in a vineyard . . . since fruit trees of all kinds were regularly planted in vineyards." It is not certain whether Jesus meant the **fig tree** to represent Israel (though see Jer. 8:13; Mic. 7:1; Tiede, p. 247), but it is probable that Luke's contemporaries would have understood it this way.

13:7 / **three years**: Evans (p. 46) has pointed to Deut. 14:28–29, where every third year a special tithe of produce (fruit) has to be brought out for widows and orphans. If Luke has seen this connection he may have wished the parable to be understood as suggesting that on the third year there is to be special evidence of fruitfulness (which for Luke is seen chiefly in terms of sharing wealth with the poor, widows, orphans). Disgusted, the owner of the vineyard wants to **cut it down**, but his question (**Why should it use up the soil?**) may hint at the replacement of this fruitless tree.

13:8 / **one more year**: The implication is that judgment will be postponed, but only for a brief period. When the parable was originally told, the **man** who pleaded for the tree probably represented no one, but it is possible that later he came to be understood as symbolizing Jesus in his intercessory role (see Marshall, p. 556).

Lachs (p. 297) cites the Syriac version of the *Story of Ahikar* as a possible parallel to the Parable of the Barren Fig Tree: "My son, thou hast been to me like that palm tree that stood by a river, and cast all its fruit into the river, and when its lord came to cut it down, it said to him, 'Let me alone this year, and I will bring thee forth carobs.' And its lord said unto it, 'Thou has not been industrious in what is thine own, and how wilt thou be industrious in what is not thine own' " (35).

§33 Healing on the Sabbath (Luke 13:10–17)

The healing of the woman with a crooked spine occurs only in Luke. Like earlier episodes in Luke (6:1–5, 6–11), the controversy centers around Jesus, who allegedly violates the law by healing someone on the Sabbath. The episode exposes yet another example of Pharisaic hypocrisy, while it also furthers the general theme of the growing hostility that eventually will result in Jesus' arrest and crucifixion.

To this point in his Gospel account Luke has frequently presented Jesus as **teaching in one of the synagogues** (4:15, 16, 33, 44; 6:6). This story, however, represents Jesus' last teaching experience in any synagogue. The synagogue has come to symbolize the source of opposition to Jesus (12:11; 21:12). The **woman** had been **crippled by a spirit for eighteen years**, resulting in a condition probably involving a fusion of the bones in her back (Marshall, p. 557). It is not necessary to assume that some form of demonic possession is implied. The Greek reads literally: "a woman having a spirit of sickness. . . . " What is probably in view is not a case of possession itself, but one of affliction ultimately sourced in Satanic influence (as illness was often understood), as indicated in v. 16 (**whom Satan has kept bound**). **When Jesus saw her,** he pronounced her cured and placed **his hands on her. And immediately she straightened up and praised God**. (See the similar reaction of the healed lame man in Acts 3:8.) The **synagogue ruler**, however, challenges the legality of Jesus' act, for he regarded it as a violation of the **Sabbath**. Herein lies the irony of the whole episode. Jesus has healed a woman who has suffered for many years. But does the synagogue ruler rejoice and praise God, as the woman did? No. He has found something wrong with Jesus' "religion." The ruler is utterly blind to the significance of what has happened. The gracious and mighty act of God was completely lost on him. That a fellow Israelite has been **set free** from a horrible oppression seems to him to be of little consequence in comparison to a violation of one or more of the oral laws and stipulations set up to protect the sanctity of the Sabbath. After all, he reasoned, **"There are six days for work. So come and be healed on those days, not on the Sabbath."**

The hypocrisy (and absurdity) of the ruler's attitude was immediately exposed by Jesus. He notes that his oral laws and traditions allowed the man to **untie his ox or donkey . . . to give it water,** so why should not a **daughter of Abraham,** one who is worth much more than an ox or donkey, be untied (or **set free**) **on the Sabbath** (the day of "rest," in this case a day of rest and relief from one's oppressive affliction)? What better day is there than the Sabbath to demonstrate God's power over Satan? Jesus' answer was not lost on his enemies, for they **were humiliated** (but were still angry at Jesus); while in stark contrast, the **people were delighted**.

Additional Notes §33

13:10–16 / According to C. G. Montefiore (*The Synoptic Gospels*, 2 vols. [New York: Ktav, 1968], vol. 2, p. 501), "The argument which Jesus employs is scarcely sound. The ox must be watered every day, or it would suffer greatly. Cruelty to animals was abhorrent to the rabbis. But the woman, who had been rheumatic for eighteen years, could well have waited another day. Unsound arguments of this kind would have been speedily detected by the trained Rabbis." Montefiore's assessment is wanting. Jesus is not trying to justify doing work on the Sabbath. (If he were, then the rabbis certainly would have had no problem exposing the fallacy of his logic.) To think this is to miss the crux of the issue. The healing of the woman was not just another chore that could have been done on another day. It represented a victory over Satan (see Tiede, p. 251). Since the Sabbath is special, sanctified by God himself, why should not such a triumph of God over Satan—one which, by the way, will give the woman relief and rest from her affliction for the first time in years— take place on this day? This is why Jesus reproaches the synagogue ruler. The issue is not over what kind of work is or is not permitted on the Sabbath. The issue has to do with the spirit and true intent of the law. Jesus may have regarded such a healing **on the Sabbath** as especially appropriate, in that God's act of power in effect consecrated the day. Evans (p. 46) has suggested a parallel with Deut. 15:1–18, where every Sabbath (seventh) year is proclaimed a time of "release" from debt for all fellow Israelites. The healing of the woman might then be understood as an example of an Israelite released or **set free**.

13:13 / **put his hands on her**: See note on 4:40 above.

13:14 / The comment of the **synagogue ruler** echoes Exod. 20:9–10 (=Deut. 5:13–14) where work on the **Sabbath** is prohibited. The Mishnah tractate, *Shabbath*, is concerned with what is and is not lawful for the Sabbath and contains many of the oral laws and traditions that Jesus and the early church encountered.

13:17 / Marshall (p. 559) comments that this verse echoes Isa. 45:16 and "may perhaps imply that for the narrator the messianic promises are being fulfilled in Jesus" (so also Fitzmyer, p. 1014).

§34 Parables of the Kingdom (Luke 13:18–30)

In this section Luke has gathered three of Jesus' parables that teach something about the kingdom of God: (1) the Parable of the Mustard Seed (vv. 18–19), (2) the Parable of the Yeast (vv. 20–21), and (3) the Parable of the Narrow Door (vv. 22–30). The first parable is found in Mark 4:30–32 and Matthew 13:31–32, while the second and third parables appear only in Matthew (13:33; 7:13–14, including verses elsewhere in Matthew). Originally these parables were delivered in different contexts, but they are here grouped together topically. Of the three, the third one fits in especially well with Luke's theological interests (see esp. vv. 29–30).

13:18–19 / The point of the Parable of the Mustard Seed is simple enough. The **kingdom of God** is like a **mustard seed** (which is quite small) that **grew** into a **tree**, a tree large enough for **birds** to perch **in its branches**. In other words, the kingdom may have a small and insignificant beginning, but it will grow and become very large. The reference to the birds perching or making their nests in the tree's branches is an allusion to Dan. 4:12, 21, a passage in which the "birds" probably refer to the nations that were dependent on Nebuchadrezzar, the king of the Babylonian Empire (Leaney, p. 207; Marshall, p. 561; Fitzmyer, p. 1017). It is possible, then, that the birds are therefore meant to refer to the Gentiles (nations) that become part of the kingdom. They may contribute, however, no more to the parable than the idea that the mustard tree becomes so big that even birds find it suitable for nesting. (The suggestion sometimes made that the "birds" refer to heretics who infiltrate the church is completely unfounded.)

13:20–21 / The point of the Parable of the Yeast (or leaven) is similar to the preceding parable, though a slightly different aspect of the growth of the kingdom is illustrated. The **kingdom of God** is **like yeast** which, when kneaded into dough, spreads throughout all the dough. The action of the yeast (fermentation) is unseen, but its effect is pervasive. This parable suggests that the kingdom of God will come to have significant influence throughout the world (see note below).

13:22–30 / Verses 22–23 disrupt the flow of thought somewhat. Some see in these verses (particularly the reference to Jesus' going **through the towns and villages . . . as he made his way to Jerusalem**) the beginning of a new major sub-section in the Central Section (see commentary on 9:51–62 and 10:1–24 above). This could be the case, but the Parable of the Narrow Door does relate to the previous parables, especially since it is a parable concerned with entry into the **kingdom of God** (v. 28). The question of v. 23 (**are only a few people going to be saved?**) occasions the parable. According to the parable, the answer is "yes." But the parable does not merely affirm the question; it explains why only a few enter the kingdom. This explanation takes place primarily in v. 24. There are **many** people who simply cannot (or will not) **enter through the narrow door**, the door which is difficult and unpopular (i.e., Jesus' teaching). In Matthew the false alternative is referred to as the "wide gate" and "broad road" (7:13), that is, the way that is popular and seems easiest and most desirable. Jesus' teachings, as we have seen already, ran counter to popular expectation (see commentary on 9:57–62). Verses 25–26 imply that many who are unable to enter by the narrow door were people who knew Jesus and who had heard him and had fellowshipped with him. However, a casual acquaintance with Jesus, even hearing his teaching, is insufficient. Jesus calls people not to hear, but to hear and to obey. Those who obey him (or "follow him") are those who will enter the narrow way and join **Abraham, Isaac and Jacob and all the prophets in the kingdom of God**. Although many persons who had acquaintance with Jesus and had firsthand knowledge of his teaching will be **thrown out**, there will be people from the four corners of the earth who **will take their places at the feast in the kingdom of God**. These people are certainly meant to be Gentiles, the very people who were never imagined to be included among those destined for a place in the kingdom. (Indeed, in some zealous Jewish writings the Gentiles were expected to become fuel for the fires of hell.) Thus, **those who are last** (Gentiles, Jewish "sinners," Samaritans) **will be first** (i.e., admitted into the kingdom, perhaps with special standing), while those who are **first** (persons of what seems to be good religious standing) **will be last** (last to enter kingdom, perhaps unable to enter the kingdom at all). The idea of "first" originally referred to those of honor or privilege, while the "last" referred to those of no honor. The literal idea of sequence is secondary, although it may have been part of the saying's original meaning. For Luke, however, the idea of sequence has likely become more significant. That is to say, the last to hear the gospel (the Gentiles and other religious outcasts) will become the first (in honor and status in the kingdom), while the first to hear the gospel (many religiously devout persons) will become the last (in honor and status in the kingdom).

Additional Notes   §34

13:18 / **the kingdom of God**: See notes and commentary on 4:43 above, and 17:20-21 below.

13:19 / The average **mustard** tree (or bush) grows to about four feet in height, although some may reach the height of nine feet (Marshall, p. 561).

13:21 / **a large amount of flour**: Lit. "three *sata* [or pecks] of meal" (about a bushel, as noted in an NIV footnote). This is an enormous amount of dough, sufficient for many loaves of bread. Nevertheless, the amount is not unusual (see Gen. 18:6; 1 Sam. 1:24) and would probably be intended to supply a large family for a week or so. The reference to "three" should not occasion allegorizing.

13:24 / **Make every effort to enter through the narrow door**: This suggests that entry is not gained without a struggle. Compare 2 Esdras 7:11-14: "For I made the world for their sake, and when Adam transgressed my statutes, what had been made was judged. And so the entrances of this world were made narrow and sorrowful and toilsome; they are few and evil, full of dangers and involved in great hardships. But the entrances of the greater world are broad and safe, and really yield the fruit of immortality. Therefore unless the living pass through the difficult and vain experiences, they can never receive those things that have been reserved for them" (RSV). Lachs (p. 146) cites the following rabbinic parallel: "It is like the one who sat by a crossroad and before him were two paths of which one was smooth to start with, and ended in thorns, and the other was thorny to start with but became smooth" (*Sipre Deut.* 53 [on Deut. 11:26: "Behold, I set before you this day a blessing and a curse"]).

13:25 / **"I don't know you or where you come from"**: Not only is the door narrow, which makes entry difficult, but one must also be recognized by the **owner of the house** (=Jesus) in order to be permitted entry.

13:27 / **"Away from me, all you evildoers"**: Part of this expression has been borrowed from the Greek translation of Ps. 6:8.

13:28 / Whereas Matt. 8:11 also mentions **Abraham, Isaac and Jacob**, Luke's version includes **all the prophets**. Gundry (p. 145) thinks that Matthew has omitted the phrase. However, because of Luke's interest in the OT prophets (see Luke 6:23, 26; 13:31–35), who provide a major witness to Jesus as the Messiah (Luke 24:25, 27, 44), I am more inclined to view the phrase as a Lucan addition.

13:29 / **People will come from east and west and north and south**: The expression is borrowed from Ps. 107:2–3, where the Lord gathers the "redeemed" from the east, west, north, and south.

and will take their places at the feast in the kingdom of God: See the commentary on 14:15–24 below.

13:30 / The saying is probably derived from Mark 10:31 (see also Matt. 19:30; 20:16).

§35 Lament for Jerusalem (Luke 13:31-35)

We come now to the first of four laments for Jerusalem (see note below) in Luke's Gospel (13:31-35; 19:41-44; 21:20-24; 23:27-31). The first, second, and fourth laments are found only in Luke, while the third one, although somewhat parallel to and dependent upon Mark 13:14-23 (=Matt. 24:15-28), affords many distinctive features. It is clear from these passages that the fate of the city of Jerusalem is of major interest to the evangelist Luke (see Charles Homer Giblin, *The Destruction of Jerusalem according to Luke's Gospel*, Analecta Biblica 107 [Rome: Biblical Institute, 1985]). The main point seems to be that because the city has rejected God's messenger (Jesus), God will abandon the city to its enemies (see esp. commentary on 19:41-44). According to Giblin, the destruction of Jerusalem is due to the people's unbelieving response to Jesus and to their toleration of injustice.

13:31-35 / The section is linked together somewhat awkwardly, particularly with respect to vv. 32-33, which seem almost to contradict one another. However, there is a basic overall unity to the passage. **Jesus** is warned in v. 31 that **Herod wants to kill** him. This threat leads Jesus to utter the saying on the necessity that a **prophet die** in **Jerusalem**. The anticipated rejection and death in Jerusalem then leads to the lament for Jerusalem, the city which has had a long tradition of killing the **prophets** that God has **sent**.

The first question that immediately confronts the reader is why the **Pharisees**, elsewhere presented as Jesus' enemies (5:17, 21, 30; 6:2, 7; 7:30; 11:38-54; 14:1-6), warn **Jesus** of **Herod's** desire to kill him. Herod had already executed John the Baptist (9:9) for the latter's condemnation of the former's immorality. In Jesus' case, however, Herod may have feared a messianic uprising in Galilee and so sought to put an end to Jesus. (Although it is possible that Herod's threats were no more than threats designed to frighten Jesus out of Galilee.) Traditionally commentators have

interpreted the warning of the Pharisees as devious and hypocritical, either to incite Jesus into acting rashly or to scare him
out of Galilee and toward Jerusalem where he might meet his end.
There is, however, no hint of animosity in this passage. These
particular Pharisees (**some Pharisees**) may very well have been
supportive of Jesus' ministry and wished to warn Jesus of a very
real danger. This piece of synoptic tradition is probably very early
and has not yet been filtered through the lens of anti-Pharisaic
polemic that is otherwise pervasive in the Gospels (see Fitzmyer,
p. 1030). However the warning is understood, the central concern occurs in the following verses. Jesus has tasks to perform
today and tomorrow and then he **will reach** his **goal**. (It is not
likely that the expression, **on the third day**, is meant to be a veiled
reference to the resurrection; nevertheless, Ellis [p. 190] believes
that Luke's readers would have seen an allusion to the resurrection.) Jesus will not be distracted or intimidated. He must be on
his way for the time being (the meaning of **today and tomorrow**),
for **surely no prophet**—one who bears God's message for God's
people—**can die outside Jerusalem**. Jesus has "set his face" for
Jerusalem (see 9:51) and it will be in that great city of biblical history that Jesus' destiny will be worked out. As a true prophet,
that is, one who truly speaks God's word, Jesus knows what fate
awaits him in Jerusalem, for no true prophet is "acceptable" (see
4:24) to his own people.

Knowing what lies ahead, Jesus is filled with anguish and
utters the lament found in vv. 34–35. **Jerusalem** is the city which
had a long tradition of rejecting, persecuting, and killing the
prophets and **those sent to** it (see note below). Jesus' statement
that many times he wanted to gather Jerusalem's people may
imply previous visits (see John 2:13; 6:4; 11:55 where three Passover visits to Jerusalem seem to be implied). The idea is that Jesus
had longed to gather all of Israel into the kingdom of God. Within
this kingdom (and not the one of popular expectation) would salvation be found. But Jesus and his message had been rejected
and so Jerusalem's **house** (perhaps the temple, see note below),
the center of worship and the symbol of God's abiding presence
in Israel, will be **left . . . desolate**, that is, left uninhabited and
vulnerable to destruction (see 19:41–44; 21:20–24). By rejecting
Jesus, Jerusalem's chances for peace and safety are nonexistent.
The day of reckoning will come. This is Jesus' last visit, after which

his people **will not see** him **again until** they **say, "Blessed is he who comes in the name of the Lord"** (v. 35). This statement of blessing is taken from Ps. 118:26, a passage which will be cited later during Jesus' Triumphal Entry into Jerusalem (19:38). At that time the "multitudes" will shout this, not the religious leaders who reject Jesus. Therefore it is unlikely (against Schweizer, p. 230) that Luke 13:35b is uttered in anticipation of the Triumphal Entry, though it is paralleled by it to a certain extent; but rather, the passage looks forward to Jesus' return (the Parousia) when a religious leadership, as well as the people in general, softened by the pounding blows of defeat, will be ready and eager to receive their true Messiah. (Fitzmyer [p. 1035] thinks that the reference is to both Jesus' Triumphal Entry and his Parousia.)

Additional Notes §35

13:32 / **fox**: The designation may imply a person of no significance or consequence, or a person of cunning and treachery. In either case the designation is derogatory and in today's parlance might be better rendered as "rat."

13:33 / **I must keep going**: Lachs (p. 300) suggests that Jesus' expression might be an allusion to the words of the dying David in 1 Kings 2:2: "I am about to go the way of all the earth" (RSV).
surely no prophet can die outside Jerusalem: Lit. "it is impossible that a prophet perish outside Jerusalem." It is impossible in Jesus' case, because "the Son of Man will go as it has been decreed" (22:22).

13:34 / Few clear examples exist in the OT of prophets who were either stoned or killed by other means. In 2 Chron. 24:20–21 Zechariah, son of the priest Jehoiada, is stoned to death for speaking the word of the Lord (which is a prophetic activity; 2 Chron. 24:20 also says the "Spirit of God came upon Zechariah"). Jeremiah is placed in stocks (Jer. 20:1–2) and cast into a pit (38:6). There was a tradition that the prophet Isaiah was placed in a hollow log and sawed in two by order of Manassah, a tradition possibly alluded to in Heb. 11:37. The general tradition of the unpopularity of the prophets' messages is seen throughout the OT, from Elijah down to the post-exilic prophets. In Jesus' day the idea of the persecuted and stoned prophet had become commonplace. See also the account of the stoning of Stephen in Acts 7:54–60. Evans (p. 47) compares Luke 13:31–34a with Deut. 17:2–7, where the Israelites are commanded to stone those who teach and practice false religion. Obviously, in the eyes of his opponents, Jesus taught a false religion.

as a hen gathers her chicks under her wings: The language re-calls the imagery of God's care and protection; see Deut. 32:11; Ruth 2:12; Pss. 17:8; 36:7; 57:1; 61:4.

13:35 / your house is left to you desolate: Ellis (p. 191) thinks that this statement implies the movement of "God's presence to a new temple, a 'house not made with hands' " (see Acts 7:48; 1 Cor. 3:16–17). This interpretation is rightly questioned by Marshall (p. 576). Jesus' words may better allude to Jer. 22:5: "this house shall become a desolation" (RSV; see also Jer. 12:7; 4QFlor 1.5–6); Leaney, p. 210.

Jerusalem: See 19:42 and note on 2:22 above.

§36 *Doing Good on the Sabbath (Luke 14:1–6)*

This episode is part of a section unique to Luke (14:1–24); the section is loosely tied together by the setting of Jesus being invited to the house of a Pharisee. The episode is the fourth and final episode in which controversy over Sabbath laws emerges. Previously Jesus has been accused of breaking the Sabbath by doing what the Pharisees regarded as work, such as picking grain to eat (6:1–5) or healing someone (6:6–11; 13:10–17). This time the controversy revolves around the question of healing on the Sabbath, an activity that was viewed as work (i.e., practicing medicine).

Apparently **Jesus** was invited to have dinner following a Sabbath service at the local synagogue. The dinner was held **in the house of a prominent Pharisee** (lit. "one of the rulers of the Pharisees"), which could possibly mean that this Pharisee was a member of the Sanhedrin (Marshall, p. 578 ; Ellis, p. 193). If he were a member of the Sanhedrin (see 22:66), then the story's setting would have to be close to Jerusalem where the Sanhedrin convened and where (or nearby) its members lived.

The direction the story will take is hinted at in the last part of v. 1: **he was being carefully watched**. Jesus was being observed closely to see if he would do anything unlawful, such as heal someone on the Sabbath. In view of this it has been suggested that the man **suffering from dropsy** (see note below) was a "plant," a person asked to the house as part of the Pharisees' attempt to put Jesus to the test. This may be the case, but the fact that after healing the sick man Jesus **sent him away** would suggest that he had not been one of the invited guests. In any case, the Pharisees are afforded the opportunity for which they had been seeking. Jesus, knowing that he was being watched carefully and knowing what was in the minds of his critics, put a question to the **Pharisees and experts in the law**. Jesus does not ask if work is permitted on the **Sabbath**, but if healing is permitted. His critics, however, do not offer an answer (vv. 4, 6). Implicit in this question is the recognition that ultimately it is God alone who heals. If God is willing to heal someone on the Sabbath, then who were the Pharisees to object? Present also is the idea, expressed explicitly in 6:5, that Jesus is "Lord of the Sabbath" and can act as God's anointed representative.

Jesus then takes the man, heals him, and sends him away. What reaction to this the Pharisees had we are not told. Jesus himself, however, pursues the matter further by putting a second question to them, a question which recalls 13:15 (the saying about helping one's ox or donkey on the Sabbath). The answer to this question (unlike the first one) is more readily apparent, even to his opponents. They would quite naturally rescue **a son or an ox** (see note below) that happened to fall into a well on a Sabbath. Such a rescue operation would in most cases involve far more work than any healing involves for Jesus. Moreover, such a rescue is very much the same idea as healing, for in both cases one's health is endangered and the rescue/healing removes the danger. The implication of the question is unmistakable and apparently was perceived by Jesus' critics, for **they had nothing to say.** The fact that they could offer no answer at this point answers in part the first question (v. 3). The logic of the passage runs thus: Is it legal to heal on the Sabbath? Yes, it is legal to do so (see 13:15; Marshall, p. 558), since the rescue of a son or ox on the Sabbath is always permitted.

Additional Notes §36

14:2 / The **man suffering from dropsy** would have swollen arms and legs. The swelling is caused by excessive fluids in various parts of the body (not just arms and legs) and, as Fitzmyer (p. 1041) remarks, "is usually symptomatic of more serious problems." Marshall (p. 579) comments that dropsy was regarded by some rabbis as resulting from immorality.

14:3 / **experts in the law**: Lit. "lawyers," who were legal experts on the law of Moses. See note on 5:21 above.

14:5 / **a son or an ox**: A variety of textual readings of this verse is found in the manuscript tradition. Some mss. read "donkey and ox" (or "ox and donkey") or "sheep and ox." These variant readings are likely due to 13:15 ("ox and donkey") and to the strangeness of linking "son" with "ox." Had Jesus said "donkey or ox" then his implied argument would be: If you are concerned enough to rescue a dumb animal on the Sabbath, then surely you should have as much concern for a fellow human being (see commentary on 13:10–17 above). However, by referring to a "son" (which is most likely the original reading) the argument is somewhat different and would run as follows: If you are concerned to rescue your own son (or even an ox) on the Sabbath, then surely there is nothing wrong with rescuing the son of someone else. By way of contrast, it is interesting to note that the members of the desert community of Qumran applied the Sabbath laws so strictly that they believed that it was wrong to "assist a beast in giving birth on the Sabbath day," much less to pull it out of a pit (Fitzmyer, p. 1040; see CD 11.13–17).

Although the three parables of Luke 14:7–24 are closely related, the connection with the preceding unit (14:1–6) is not nearly
as close. In the Lucan context the reader, one should suppose,
is to imagine the three parables of vv. 7–24 as being uttered at
the same house to which Jesus had been invited and at which
he had healed the man afflicted with dropsy. Originally, however, the incidents of vv. 1–6 and 7–24 were probably separate.

By combining the healing episode and the three parables,
Luke has produced a larger section that deals with the theme of
God's mercy, a mercy that extends far beyond the limits to which
those who are most religious usually restrict it. In the healing episode we see a man whose pitiful physical condition may very well
have been viewed as resulting from divine punishment. In contrast to the religiously significant man, called a "prominent Pharisee" (14:1), this religiously insignificant man is the one who
experienced God's gracious healing power. Similarly, in the parable that follows (vv. 7–11) it is the unassuming man that is
honored, while in the remaining parables (vv. 12–14, 15–24) the
invitation to dine at the (messianic) table is to be extended to those
considered by many religious notables of Jesus' day to be unworthy. The net effect of this section is to proclaim loudly and
clearly that those least expected to share in the blessings of the
kingdom of God will in fact share in them, while in contrast, and
surprisingly, those most expected to be participants may very well
be among those who will be excluded.

14:7–11 / The saying of vv. 8–10 reflects the advice of Prov.
25:6–7, while the summarizing saying in v. 11 apparently alludes
to Ezek. 21:26. Ironically, by their behavior, the **guests** (probably
meant to be understood as the Pharisees and experts in the "law"
mentioned above in v. 3) have not only ignored the wise counsel
of Proverbs (and Sirach), but they have failed to heed the various warnings against arrogance and presumption throughout the

OT (Isa. 13:11; Jer. 13:15; 50:29–32; Prov. 15:25; Sir. 3:17–20). (Jesus also criticizes the Pharisees for their pride in Luke 11:43; 20:45–47.)

Jesus' **parable** is simple enough on the face of it. **Guests** at a **wedding feast** would be wise not to assume that the host considers them to be as important as they may be in their own eyes. But Jesus intends far more than mere advice for proper behavior at dinner parties. In view of the meaning of the Parable of the Great Banquet that follows in vv. 15–24, it seems reasonable to interpret the wedding feast as a veiled reference to the kingdom banquet of the last times. Invitation to attend this banquet means that one has been graciously chosen to enter the kingdom. The response, however, is to be one of humility, not one of self-exaltation. The Pharisees presume upon their invitation and find in it a cause for arrogance and pride. They are to be reminded, however, that the proud are humbled and the humble are exalted (Ezek. 21:26). Luke quite possibly sees in this parable a further application for his own community. Those who have been invited into the kingdom of God should enter with all humility, assuming that they are worthy of nothing more than the lowly positions. For there will be some (perhaps the Gentiles) who enter the kingdom later and yet receive positions of greater honor. Thus, the lesson that Jesus intended for his fellow countrymen becomes a lesson for the church as well.

14:12–14 / Just as it is like human nature to seek places of honor, so it is a human tendency to do good things for one's friends (or those whom one hopes to make a friend) in anticipation of having the favors returned. Jesus advises **his host** that kindness shown to those who will repay with kindness does not impress God. Again, when seen in the broader context of Luke 14, it is probable that an allusion to the concern over the question of who will enter the kingdom of God (thought of as a **dinner** or feast) is intended. Jesus' advice not to invite one's **friends, brothers, relatives,** or **rich neighbors** probably implies that one cannot assume that only those whom we respect (or envy) are also respected by God. Others, such as **the poor, the crippled, the lame,** and **the blind,** are valued and respected by God and will be among those invited to the great feast of the last days. If one is to be like God, one should extend one's kindness and mercy to those people as well. But Jesus' immediate point is in v. 14. If one invites those who by religious standards of the day are viewed as outcasts from the kingdom, one **will be blessed** (truly happy) and accordingly will receive a reward from God **at the resurrection of the righteous**.

Such advice would have sounded quite strange to the ears of many of Jesus' contemporaries. To their way of thinking the poor, the crippled, the lame, and the blind are those from whom God has withheld his blessing. In all likelihood, it was thought that their afflictions were the result of sin. These people, along with the Gentiles, would be the last people to enter the kingdom of God. Why should anyone invite them to a feast? To eat with such people could result in religious defilement. Therefore, the pious Israelite would quite naturally desire table fellowship with others of similar piety. Jesus, however, does not share this narrow, self-righteous view. His proclamation of the Good News declares that even the lowly and outcast may be included in the kingdom of God. Nowhere is this idea seen more vividly than in the parable that follows.

14:15–24 / Jesus' advice on inviting the lowly to one's feast leads one of the guests to pronounce a beatitude (**blessed**) upon those **who will eat at the feast in the kingdom of God**. For Luke this beatitude surely strikes at the very heart of the question with which he is most concerned. Who really are those who will be included in the kingdom of God? To those surrounding Jesus at table the answer probably seemed clear enough. Those virtually guaranteed admission would be those in whose lives God's blessing seemed most apparent: one's friends, relatives and rich neighbors (v. 12 above), the very sort of people with whom anyone would most wish to associate. However, Jesus' Parable of the Great Banquet (vv. 16–24) suggests that those who enter the kingdom and enjoy the great banquet may be more like those usually not invited to feasts (cf. list in v. 13 with that of v. 21).

In a recent study James A. Sanders ("Banquet Parable"; see Introduction, pp. 10ff.) suggested that the Parable of the Great Banquet represents the theological high-point in Luke's Central Section (10:1–18:14), a lengthy section which apparently has been composed so as to correspond to Deuteronomy 1–26 (see commentary on 10:1–24 above). Sanders ("Banquet Parable," pp. 255, 258, 265) points out that certain religious assumptions concerning election (i.e., who is acceptable before God and on what grounds) were founded upon a distortion of the biblical teaching on the subject. The distortion ran as follows: Since Deuteronomy promises blessings (such as health and wealth) for those who are obedient (as seen by their religious devotion) and curses (such as sickness and poverty) for those who are disobedient (as seen by their lack of religious devotion), then it may be assumed that those who are healthy and wealthy are righteous and so are enjoying God's blessings, while those who are sick and poor are sinners and so are suffering God's curses. This distortion is in effect an "inversion" of Deuteronomy's teaching and is questionable on at least four grounds: (1) It assumes that health and wealth are always signs of God's favor and that sickness and poverty are always signs of God's wrath; (2) it assumes that health/wealth and sickness/poverty correspond to righteousness and sinfulness; (3) it inverts Deuteronomy's promises and warnings; and (4) it particularizes the general, that is, it applies Deuteronomy's nationally directed promises and warnings to individuals.

This distortion and its attendant faulty assumptions Jesus has challenged. And nowhere is Jesus' challenge to these popular beliefs more dramatic and forceful. In the Parable of the Great Banquet those who end up enjoying the feast are the very persons not expected to participate. The parable thus refers to the great eschatological banquet when the righteous (or elect) enjoy God's fullest blessing and reward. The **man** who **was preparing a great banquet** equals God himself. The banquet alludes to the eschatological (or messianic) banquet. The invited **(guests)** represent those of Jesus' contemporaries who assumed that their election ("invitation") was secure (i.e., the "relatives," "rich neighbors," etc.). Quite unexpectedly, however, the guests decline the summons to come to the banquet. It is not that they are uninterested in the feast (or in the awaited kingdom); they are simply too busy with worldly concerns to respond promptly and with commitment when the invitation is given. These worldly concerns are very similar to three of the conditions that disqualify an Israelite from participation in holy war, as seen in Deuteronomy 20 (Evans, pp. 47-48; James A. Sanders, "Banquet Parable," pp. 256-58). Deuteronomy 20:5-7 gives three reasons why one should not go to war, reasons which roughly approximate the three excuses of Luke 14:18-20 (cf. the excuses in Luke 9:57-62). (The fourth excuse, cited in Deut. 20:8, is fear. This excuse, however, presupposes one's initial willingness to answer the call to battle and thus a Lucan

parallel to it would scarcely fit the banquet parable. That Luke
was aware of the holy war context of Deuteronomy is possibly
indicated in 14:31–32.) James A. Sanders argues ("Banquet Parable," pp. 257–58) that there is a very close relationship between
the idea of preparation for holy war and the preparation to enter
the great feast celebrated when the kingdom of God finally comes,
for those qualified to participate in the war are the very ones qualified to enjoy the feast. But the relationship between the holy war
stipulations of Deuteronomy 20 and the persons invited to the
great banquet runs even deeper. In the Lucan parable, those who
finally enter the banquet hall are **the poor, the crippled, the blind
and the lame** (v. 21; see also v. 13). According to Lev. 21:17–23,
however, these people could never be qualified for priestly service
(even if they were Levites). The list in Leviticus 21, as Sanders
("Banquet Parable," p. 262) has shown, inspired the stipulations
in at least two of the writings of Qumran, which prohibited such
"defective" persons from participation in the final great holy war
(1QM 7.4–6) and the feast (1QSa 2.5–22). Sanders correctly suspects that Jesus (or Luke at the very least) has intentionally contradicted this popular, but strict, interpretation. Jesus' parable
suggests that the very persons thought to be disqualified (basically
according to the stipulations of Lev. 21:17–23) from the final holy
battle of the last days and from the messianic feast that follows
would end up being the very people who will participate in this
celebration, while ironically and tragically **none of those** people
who were invited will get a taste of my banquet. A closer examination of related texts from Qumran also reveals that the members
of Qumran believed that seats of honor would be assigned to the
most holy and zealous of the community (1QSa 2.11–21). This
idea is also challenged by Jesus' advice regarding choosing one's
seat at a dinner (Luke 14:7–10).

Thus, Luke 14:7–24 forms a unified section that sharply contrasts popular views, including those held by many Pharisees and,
in their extremest forms, those of members of the wilderness community of Qumran. Jesus' parable teaches that the **invited** (see
note below) may miss the opportunity of entering the kingdom,
while the seemingly "uninvited" will be given the opportunity.
It is interesting to note that after **the poor, crippled, the blind
and the lame** enter the banquet hall (vv. 21–22) the **master** commanded **his servant** to **go out to the roads and country lanes and**

make more people **come in**. This additional invitation to enter
the feast was evidently meant to be understood as the summons
to the Gentiles to enter the kingdom. Such a thought, of course,
would be utterly contrary to popular Jewish assumptions about
kingdom membership (see commentary on 4:16–30 above).

In Luke 14:7–24 it would seem that Luke's election theology
has reached its clearest and most forceful expression. Whereas
earlier passages depicting Jesus' compassion for the poor, the sick,
the needy, and the sinner have suggested all along that the kingdom of God is meant for these people as well as for those of more
obvious and more impressive religious qualifications, in Luke
14:7–24 the messianic invitation to those thought unqualified is
made explicit. There can be no mistaking Jesus' message now.
In the concluding words of the Central Section: Jesus has come
to seek and to save the lost (see 19:10).

Additional Notes §37

14:7-11 / Lachs (p. 303) cites this interesting rabbinic parallel:
"R. Simeon ben Azzai said: 'Stay two or three seats below your place
[i.e., where you feel you should sit], and sit there until they say to you,
"Come up!" Do not begin by going up because they may say to you,
"Go down!" It is better that they say to you, "Go up," than that they
say to you, "Go down!" ' " (*Leviticus Rabbah* 1.5). Compare Prov. 25:6-7:
"Do not put yourself forward in the king's presence or stand in the place
of the great; for it is better to be told, 'Come up here,' than to be put
lower in the presence of the prince" (RSV).

**everyone who exalts himself will be humbled, and he who humbles
himself will be exalted**: Compare Ezek. 21:26: "exalt that which is low,
and abase that which is high" (RSV).

14:16-24 / Luke's Parable of the Great Banquet is similar but not
identical to Matt. 22:1-10 (the Parable of the Wedding Feast). Fitzmyer
(p. 1052) concludes that Luke and Matthew derived their respective parables from their common sayings source. The Matthean form of the parable concludes with a much harsher note of judgment. According to
Matthew the rebuffed king sends his armies to burn the city of those
ungrateful persons who, although having been properly invited, had
acted in a disgraceful and murderous way. The Matthean version could
well reflect the Roman destruction of Jerusalem, an event no doubt interpreted by many first-century Christians as divine retribution for the re-

jection of Jesus and the Christian proclamation (see Gundry, pp. 432–39, for a different view).

J. T. Sanders (pp. 133–34) believes that the Parable of the Great Banquet advances Lucan anti-Semitism. He thinks that those who are rejected are most likely Jews, while those who are admitted to the banquet are Gentiles. Again his interpretation misses the mark. The Lucan parable has *three* groups of persons in mind, not two, and therefore it resists the simplistic interpretation that Sanders has given it. Taken at face value, the parable seems to be saying that the well-to-do (presumably Jewish) ignore the invitation (vv. 18–20), whereas the **poor** and the sick **of the town** (v. 21; also presumably Jewish), and those out in the **roads and country lanes** (v. 23; presumably Gentiles, though not necessarily to the exclusion of Jews) accept the invitation and so enjoy the banquet. As in 4:16–30, the thrust of the Parable of the Great Banquet is found in its challenge to assumptions about election; that is, those who are well off and apparently blessed may be excluded from the kingdom, while those who are not well off and apparently cursed may be included in the kingdom. The differentiation seems to be between the apparent blessed and the apparent lost, not between Jews and Gentiles.

14:16 / **a great banquet**: Matt. 22:2 reads: "a marriage feast for his son." This version would also be understood as an allusion to the great feast of the last days.

14:17 / **those who had been invited** (see also 14:24): Herein lies a word-play that contributes significantly to the meaning of the parable. The word translated "invited" may just as correctly be translated "chosen" or "elected." Thus, Luke undoubtedly means more than merely that some people were invited to dinner. Rather, the evangelist is talking about those who are the (apparently) *chosen* or *elect* people of God. Seen in this way the irony of the parable is enhanced. The apparent elect, chosen to enter the kingdom, failed to heed the summons, and so the apparent non-elect (the poor, the crippled, etc.) enter instead.

14:18–20 / I cannot agree with Fitzmyer (p. 1056) who regards the link with Deut. 20:5–7 as "eisegetical." Because Fitzmyer disregards the significance of the Central Section's correspondence with the contents and themes of Deuteronomy 1–26, he is not always able to explain the rationale behind the Lucan sequence (see commentary on 16:1–13 and 16:14–18 below) and, in this instance, fails to appreciate the interpretive significance that Deuteronomy 20 has for Luke 14. See Tiede, pp. 266–67.

14:23 / **make them come in**: These words contain no suggestion of force or violence (as was sometimes erroneously supposed in the church of the Middle Ages). The idea is persuasion, and in the parable such persuasion would be necessary and understandable before persons acutely aware of how much they were out of place would be willing to enter the banquet hall.

This section consists of two parts: (1) a brief discourse on the cost of following Jesus (vv. 25–33) and (2) the saying on worthless salt (vv. 34–35). Part of the section on counting the cost has to do with the king who plans for war (vv. 31–32), which may provide a link with the preceding Parable of the Great Banquet (vv. 15–24), since Deuteronomy 20 apparently has conceptual and verbal parallels to these Lucan passages (so Evans, pp. 47–48; see commentary on 14:15–24 above). The main point of the section is that the would-be follower of Jesus had better count the cost carefully and, according to v. 33, be willing to give up everything.

As with most of Luke 14 already considered, this section is for the most part unique to Luke. Only a few verses are found in Matthew and so presumably were derived from the sayings source (Luke 14:26a=Matt. 10:37; Luke 14:27=Matt. 10:38; Luke 14:34–35=Matt. 5:13b; see also Mark 9:50).

14:25–33 / The audience has shifted from the Pharisees and dinner guests of 14:1–24 to **large crowds** of people who **were traveling with Jesus**. Apparently Jesus has resumed his journey toward Jerusalem (9:51) and now will address the crowds. Jesus made it plain in vv. 1–24 that many more were eligible for entry into the kingdom than the legalistic Pharisees (or even stricter people of Qumran) were willing to allow. Now Jesus addresses those people who may enter the kingdom. Entry is not easy, however; it has a price. Jesus cites two stipulations (vv. 26–27) and two examples (vv. 28–32) of the costs involved in following him.

First, whoever would be a **disciple** of Jesus must love Jesus more than his or her own family; indeed, more than his own **father and mother**, the very persons one is commanded to honor (Exod. 20:12). This is a radical requirement and only underscores the place of preeminence that Jesus must occupy in the life of anyone who would be his follower. Second, Jesus requires that one who would follow him must **carry his cross** (see comment on 9:23 above). Anyone who would follow Jesus must be prepared to endure the same fate that Jesus himself endured. Although Jesus means for his words to be taken quite seriously, there must be recognized a certain amount of hyperbole (exaggeration intended to emphasize a point). According to v. 26: Whoever . . . **does not hate his own father and mother**. . . . Jesus does not demand actual hatred of one's own parents (which would directly contradict and violate the commandment of Exod. 20:12), but his forceful exaggeration makes it clear that one's love for Jesus must outweigh all other loyalties. Similarly, not all who follow Jesus will be put to death, but one's commitment to Jesus should be such that if faced with the threat of death one would not abandon Jesus.

To illustrate the need for assessing the cost of discipleship carefully, Jesus tells two brief parables. The man who wishes **to build a tower** (or anything, for that matter) must first calculate the cost of the total project. Failure to do so could result in the embarrassing (and financially ruinous) situation in which the project is left unfinished. Equally foolish would be the person who declares his intention to follow Jesus, but who then gives it up when he discovers that the cost of following Jesus exceeds his commitment. In the second parable Jesus likens the need to assess carefully to a **king** who **is about to go to war against another king** and then finds out that his army is only half the size of his opponent's. He must **sit down** and carefully calculate to see if he can still win the battle. If he cannot, he should ask for terms. Otherwise, the king may foolishly go out against a much stronger opponent and suffer a terrible defeat. In this example Jesus does not intend to offer advice for military strategy, nor should the particular details of the parable be allegorized. The point that Jesus is making is that whenever one sets out to undertake a difficult (or dangerous) task one should carefully assess one's resources. In these parables one's money (first parable) or one's soldiers (second parable) should be understood as one's level of commitment to Jesus. If one lacks adequate commitment then one should not follow. Rather, if one is to follow Jesus, then a total commitment is expected, a commitment arising out of careful, thoughtful consideration.

14:34–35 / The saying on salt is only loosely connected to the discourse on counting the cost of discipleship, but there is a definite connection, nevertheless. The follower of Jesus is likened to **salt**, which is **good** as long as it retains its flavor. However, **if it loses its saltiness**, it is of no value and must be **thrown out**. This is like the person who fails to count the cost. He begins, but then quits. In the Matthean context (5:13b) the saying is applied to the influence that Jesus' followers have upon a corrupt world. As long as his followers are "salty" (righteous) they have a beneficial influence, but if they have lost their "saltiness" then they no longer have a beneficial influence in the world and so are no longer of any use to God (see further Gundry, pp. 75–76). In contrast, however, Luke has applied the saying to the idea of the need for an enduring commitment. Although the Matthean and Lucan applications are not identical, they are not contradictory either. The disciple who retains his "saltiness" (i.e., righteousness) is the disciple who endures.

Additional Notes   §38

14:26 / **my disciple**: "Disciple" is a favorite Lucan designation for the followers of Jesus (first used in 5:30), and in Acts it is virtually the equivalent of "Christian" (Acts 6:1, 2, 7; 9:1, 10, 19, 26, 38, and many more). The word comes from a root meaning "to learn." A disciple, therefore, is a "learner." But the word connotes more than the idea of a student/teacher relationship. A disciple is one who follows the lifestyle, habits, and way of thinking of his teacher (or master). The goal of the disciple is to become as much like his teacher as possible (see Luke 6:40).

14:28 / **a tower**: a look-out for the purpose of guarding a vineyard (see Isa. 5:2), the land, or a house. If the tower is only half finished, that is, if only the **foundation** is laid, the construction would be of no use. Thus, the labor and expense would be entirely in vain.

Will he not . . . estimate the cost: Lit. "will he not calculate?" Fitzmyer (p. 1065) cites this interesting parallel from Epictetus, *Discourses* 3.15.8: "Reckon, sir, first what the task is, then your own nature, what you are able to carry."

14:31–32 / It has been suggested (see Fitzmyer, p. 1066) that Jesus' parable contains an allusion to 2 Sam. 8:10, where Tou, king of Hamath, sent an envoy to King David. Perhaps.

14:35 / **He who has ears to hear, let him hear**: See note on 8:8 above.

§39 God's Attitude toward the Lost (Luke 15:1–32)

This section contains three parables that return to the theme of the inclusion of the lowly and the outcast in the kingdom of God: (1) the Parable of the Lost Sheep (vv. 1–7); (2) the Parable of the Lost Coin (vv. 8–10); and (3) the Parable of the Lost Son (vv. 11–32). These parables more or less pick up where the Parable of the Great Banquet (14:15–24) left off. The Parable of the Great Banquet taught that the least expected people would be included in the kingdom, while the three parables of Luke 15 reveal God's attitude toward the lost and, in the case of the Lost Son, the unworthy. Other than the Parable of the Lost Sheep, which is found in Matt. 18:12–14, the passage is unique to Luke.

15:1–2 / Luke establishes the context for the following three parables by noting that **tax collectors and "sinners" were all gathering around to hear** Jesus. Their interest in hearing him links this passage to the preceding passage which contains the injunction to hear (Luke 14:35; Tiede, p. 273). Because of Jesus' association with "rabble," the **Pharisees and the teachers of the law muttered** their disapproval. In their thinking Jesus' association (as seen in such phrases as **welcomes . . . eats with**) with such people suggests that Jesus himself is no better than they. If Jesus is truly a teacher of proper Jewish piety and theology (much less Messiah or Son of God), he should not associate with such people. It is in response to this attitude, therefore, that Jesus tells the three parables.

15:3–7 / The first parable tells of a man who **has a hundred sheep**. If **one** of the **sheep** becomes **lost**, what will the man do? By asking the question, Jesus forces his hearers to answer it. Undoubtedly all will answer: "I shall look for it until it is found." This is the natural human response when something of value is lost. In this case the shepherd is even willing to **leave**

the other **ninety-nine in the open country** (at some slight risk to them) in order to search for the **lost sheep. When he finds it, he** is overjoyed and ready to celebrate. The point of the parable is that if one values something, when it is lost, one will seek it out diligently, and when it is found one will rejoice. Jesus applies the parable to God's attitude toward the lost who repent. **There will be more rejoicing in heaven over one sinner who repents than over ninety-nine righteous persons who do not need to repent**.

15:8–10 / The Parable of the Lost Coin makes the same point. When the **woman** lost **one** of her **ten silver coins**, she turns the **house** upside down in search of it. **When she finds it, she** is delighted. As in the case of the Parable of the Lost Sheep, there is joy in heaven whenever one who is lost (sinful) is found (repents). Both of these parables drive home the point that it is natural to respond with joy when something (or someone) is recovered. This joy stands in sharp contrast to the Pharisees and other "respectable" religious people who grumbled because Jesus spent time with those whom the Pharisees would regard as "lost."

15:11–32 / The section reaches its climax in the Parable of the Lost (or Prodigal) Son. This time it is not a lost sheep or coin but a lost son. Unlike the lost sheep and the lost coin, which were not responsible in any way for being lost, the lost son is lost because of his own wayward actions. If anyone deserved what he got, it would have to be this ungrateful, selfish, and wasteful young man. Jesus graphically portrays the ingratitude, sin, and degradation of this person. He requests his **share of the estate**. He apparently has no concern for the well-being of his **father** (or family). He has not chosen to stay nearby; rather, he liquidates his inheritance and leaves home. He then went to a **distant country and there squandered his wealth in wild living**. In the minds of respectable first-century Jewish people the behavior of this son would be considered disloyal and outrageous. But the parable advances from the son's selfishness to his degradation. He ends up working for a Gentile (as implied by the reference to the "distant country") for whom he feeds the **pigs**. Not only does he feed swine, he even eats the very **pods that the pigs were eating**. From a Jewish point of view his disgrace and degradation have reached their lowest level. (Fitzmyer [p. 1088] cites b. *Baba Qamma* 82b: "Cursed be the man who raises pigs.") Eventually **he came to his**

senses. As the context suggests, the younger son has finally come to a true understanding of himself and of his situation. He recognizes that he has fallen to a low estate (indeed, one lower than that of his father's servants) and recognizes that he has **sinned against heaven and against** his father. He knows that he is **no longer worthy to be called** his **son**. Having thus repented, he returns to **his father**.

The parable reaches its dramatic conclusion when the **father** sees his **son**, hears his confession of sin, and receives him with joy. Rather than being angry with his wasteful, wayward son, the father is filled with joy and commands that he be dressed in the **best robe** and that a **feast** be held. The **father** cries out, as did the shepherd (v. 6) and the woman (v. 9), **"Let's . . . celebrate"** (v. 23).

Had the parable ended with v. 24 it would have been complete. However, with v. 25 a new issue emerges. The **older son**, who apparently was at work **in the field**, hears the celebration and so inquires about what is going on. (To ask why the older son was not invited to the feast misses the point of this part of the parable. The point here is to provide contrast. Unlike his irresponsible younger brother, the older brother has remained at home faithfully going about his work.) When he discovers the cause for the celebration he is indignant and refuses to be a part of it. He feels cheated, for no feast has even been given in his honor, and yet he has always been faithful. He reminds his father of his brother's wasteful and sinful adventures and protests against what he regards as an unwarranted and undeserved celebration. The father explains to his older son that all the blessings and rewards for his faithfulness and loyalty are undiminished: **"You are always with me, and everything I have is yours"** (v. 31). The joyous celebration illustrates the joy of recovering what was lost (as in the preceding parables). The older son must understand this. He too should share in the father's joy.

In its original context the two sons very likely would have been understood as referring to irreligious Jews (the "sinners," tax collectors, harlots), symbolized by the younger son, and religiously strict Jews (priests, Pharisees, teachers of the law), symbolized by the older son. The attitude of the Pharisees in 15:2 is quite similar to the attitude of the older son. Rather than celebrating Jesus' successful ministry among the outcasts of Jewish religious society, the Pharisees "mutter." The Third Evangelist, however, may have regarded the parable as applying to the resentment expressed over the entry of Gentiles into the church. It is possible also that, whereas the younger son symbolized the Gentiles and the disenfranchised of Jewish society, the older son represented religious Jews (perhaps even Christians) whose stricter standards made it difficult to accept Gentiles as part of the new community (see Acts 11), or at least difficult to have fellowship with them (see Acts 15).

Additional Notes §39

Evans (p. 48) suggests that Deut. 21:15–22:4 corresponds to Luke 15, especially vv. 11–32, which make up the Parable of the Lost Son. The parallels are remarkable and are worthy of brief comment. Deuteronomy 21:15–17 is concerned with the status of the firstborn son. He is to be regarded as firstborn and honored over a second-born son, even if the father loves the second-born son more. The firstborn son is to retain his proper place in the family and receive a "double portion" of the inheritance. Deut. 21:18–21 is concerned with what to do with a wayward and disobedient son. A son who does "not obey his father" and who is "a glutton and a drunkard" is to be taken out of the city and stoned. Jesus' parable stands in stark contrast to this legislation. The wayward young son, who squandered his inheritance on prostitutes and riotous living, is not expelled and stoned when he returns (as his older brother might have expected, and perhaps even hoped) but is lovingly received into his father's house. Whereas the emphasis falls on severity in Deuteronomy 21, in Luke 15 the emphasis falls on mercy and forgiveness. Jesus is not contradicting the law of Moses; he is only correcting a false ethic, possibly derived from such a passage as Deuteronomy 21. By laying down civil law, Deuteronomy 21 does not intend to exclude the possibility of repentance, forgiveness, and restoration. Such legislation, however, could be appealed to as grounds for viewing in a very judgmental and unforgiving way those regarded as unrighteous and disobedient. Such thinking lies behind the grumbling of the Pharisees: How could Jesus, supposedly a man of God, have fellowship with those who by all rights should be excluded from Jewish society, perhaps even stoned?

Jack T. Sanders ("Tradition and Redaction in Luke xv. 11–32," *NTS* 15 [1969], pp. 433–38) has argued on form-critical grounds that vv. 25–32 were not part of the original parable, but that Luke composed the second part of the parable in order to direct polemic against the Pharisees and so provide for a smoother transition into the next chapter. Other scholars disagree (for example, see John J. O'Rourke, "Some Notes on

Luke xv. 11–32," *NTS* 18 [1972], pp. 431–33). The main objection to J. T. Sanders's proposal is that it is not at all clear why polemic against the Pharisees should not be traced back to Jesus himself in this instance. Indeed, the parable actually places the Pharisees (assuming that they are alluded to in the character of the older son) in a rather surprisingly positive light. It is true that the older son expresses dismay over the joyous reception of his younger brother, but the consoling words of his father in vv. 31–32 imply that the older son has a place in his father's heart. If Luke freely composed the second part of this parable (vv. 25–32), as Sanders claims, and did so as a polemic against the Pharisees of his day (who were bitterly opposed to Christianity), it seems strange that the evangelist did not take the opportunity to paint a much more unambiguously negative picture of the older son. The same point may be raised against Luise Schottroff's view that Luke himself wrote the entire parable (vv. 11–32), not just the second part, as polemic against Pharisaism ("Das Gleichnis vom erlorenen Sohn," *ZTK* 68 [1971], pp. 27–52). A major problem with Sanders's interpretation is that it is based on and is part of his view that Luke's theology is essentially anti-Semitic (see Jack T. Sanders, pp. 197–98; idem, "The Salvation of the Jews in Luke–Acts," *1982 SBL Seminar Papers* [Chico: Scholars Press, 1982], pp. 467–83; idem, "The Parable of the Pounds and Lucan Anti-Semitism," *TS* 42 [1981], pp. 660–68), a view which I regard as totally erroneous. Luke's Parable of the Lost Son extends an offer of reconciliation to the Jews, the "older sons" of the Father (see Tiede, p. 280). They are invited to accept their new siblings and to rejoice in their reclamation. In no sense is this parable anti-Semitic.

15:1 / On **tax collectors and "sinners"** see note on 5:30 above. For more on tax collectors see notes on 3:12 and 19:2. Talbert (p. 148) cites several scriptures to which the Pharisees could have appealed in justifying their displeasure over the company which Jesus kept (Prov. 1:15; 2:11–15; Psalm 1; Isa. 52:11). Lachs (p. 306) quotes from *Mekilta* on Exod. 18:1: "Let not a man associate with the wicked, not even to bring him nigh to the Law." Even if this statement represents an extreme view on this matter, it does help us to understand the misgivings the Pharisees had with respect to Jesus' habit of associating with people Jewish society regarded as sinful.

15:2 / On **Pharisees** see note on 5:17; on **teachers of the law** see note on 5:21.

15:3–6 / Jesus' Parable of the Lost Sheep may have been inspired by Ezek. 34:11–16: "For thus says the Lord God: Behold, I, I myself will search for my sheep, and will seek them out. As a shepherd seeks out his flock when some his sheep have been scattered abroad, so will I seek out my sheep. . . . I will seek the lost, and I will bring back the strayed" (RSV). See also Isa. 40:11; Tiede, p. 274.

15:4 / A shepherd who has one **hundred sheep** would be relatively well off in first-century Palestine. Fitzmyer (p. 1077) notes that it was in search of a stray goat that an Arab goatherd discovered the first cave in the Dead Sea area, containing the now-famous Dead Sea Scrolls. Although the shepherd has **ninety-nine**, his concern for the one lost sheep impels him to search.

15:6–7 / These verses reflect the greatest variation with the Matthean version. Whereas the Lucan context has the parable illustrate God's joy over receiving a repentant sinner into his kingdom, the Matthean version (18:12–14) illustrates reconciliation within the church itself (see Gundry, pp. 364–67).

15:8 / **ten silver coins**: Lit. "ten drachmas," only a modest sum. Although the **woman** has nine other coins, she values the **one** lost coin enough to search for it diligently. Lachs (p. 306) cites an interesting rabbinic parallel: "If a man loses a coin in his house he kindles many lights, and seeks till he finds it. If for something which affords only an hour's life in this world, a man kindles many lights, and searches till he finds it, how much more should you dig as for hidden treasure after the words of the Law, which gives life both in this world and in the world-to-come" (*Song of Songs Rabbah* 1.9).

15:12 / Since Deut. 21:17 requires the firstborn son to receive a "double portion" of his father's inheritance, we may assume that the younger son's share of the estate was about one third. Income from this property, however, was due the father as long as he lived.

15:13 / **the younger son got together all he had**: Jewish law permitted property to be sold, but the income of the land was still due the father (the original owner) as long as he lived. To liquidate his portion of the estate and then to leave his family amounted to an act of the grossest disregard and disloyalty.

squandered his wealth in wild living: Lit. "scattered his substance living loosely." Thus, "loose living" is described by his older brother as wasting money on prostitutes (v. 30). The noun form of "loosely" occurs in Eph. 5:18, "Do not get drunk on wine, which leads to debauchery."

15:15–16 / **Pigs** were "unclean" and forbidden as food for Jews (Lev. 11:7; Deut. 14:8). No occupation would have been more disgraceful for a Jewish man of respectable family.

pods: According to Lachs (p. 308) these are the pods of the carob tree, and they were traditionally regarded as the food of the poor. He cites an interesting rabbinic parallel: "When Israelites are reduced to eating carob-pods, they repent" (*Leviticus Rabbah* 13.3; *Song of Songs Rabbah* 1.4).

15:17 / **When he came to his senses**: "When a son [abroad] goes barefoot [through poverty] he remembers the comfort of his father's house" (*Lamentations Rabbah* 1.7; from Lachs p. 308).

15:18, 21 / **I have sinned against heaven**: "Heaven" is a substitute for "God," out of pious reluctance to name God directly.

15:20 / **He ran to his son, threw his arms around him and kissed him**: Compare Gen. 29:13: "He [Laban] ran to meet him [Jacob], and embraced him and kissed him, and brought him to his house" (RSV). The kiss is a sign of reconciliation and forgiveness (Talbert, p. 150).

15:22 / The **best robe, ring**, and **sandals** signify the younger son's treatment as an honored guest. All the son had asked for was to be taken on as one of the hired men (v. 19). Talbert (p. 150) states that the best robe was a sign of honor, the ring a sign of authority, and the sandals a sign of a free man (for servants went barefoot).

15:23 / The **fattened calf** would provide a banquet table with the very best feast possible in first-century Palestine.

15:24, 32 / The references to being **lost** and **found** links the Parable of the Lost Son quite closely to the two preceding parables.

15:29 / The older son grumbles that not even a **young goat** has ever been prepared in his honor. A goat would be considered quite inferior to the "fattened calf" of v. 23.

15:30 / **this son of yours**: By calling his brother "this son of yours," instead of "my brother," the older son reveals his contempt for his brother. Likely it reflects the idea that such a disloyal son had been regarded as "dead" to the family (see vv. 24, 32) and so the older brother would have said that he had no brother. See Leaney, p. 218.

15:32 / **we had to celebrate**: The refrain of "celebration" (or rejoice) is heard at the conclusion of all three parables of the lost (see vv. 6, 9, 23, 32).

§40 The Shrewd Manager (Luke 16:1–13)

This section includes the Parable of the Shrewd Manager (vv. 1–8a) and various sayings of Jesus related to the parable or to the topic of money in general (vv. 8b–13). This material is for the most part unique to Luke (although Luke 16:13=Matt. 6:24) and contributes to the Lucan concern over proper use of wealth.

16:1–8a / Few of the parables of Jesus have puzzled readers of the Gospel more than the Parable of the Shrewd Manager. The main question has to do with why the **rich man** would **commend** his **dishonest manager**. A second question has to do with why Jesus cites the actions of the dishonest manager with approval, using him as an example for his disciples. The first question may be answered only when the actual action of the dishonest manager is fully understood. An old interpretation of this parable held that the rich man was impressed with the shrewdness of the manager because the latter, after being served notice of dismissal, dishonestly reduced the bills owed the rich man so as to ingratiate himself with these various clients and business associations. Although the rich man has been cheated yet again by the scoundrel, he is, nevertheless, impressed with his manager's cleverness (see Tiede, pp. 282–83). Related to this interpretation is the suggestion that the manager has eliminated the interest part of the bill in conformity to the Old Testament's law against usury (see Deut. 15:7–8; 23:20–21). Thus, the idea is that the dishonest manager has finally done a proper, biblical thing. This approach to the parable, however, is not satisfying. Why should the **master** praise the **dishonest manager**? Would he have anything good to say about someone who had not only wasted his money (v. 1), but then after being fired (v. 2) further cheated him? This seems highly unlikely. More plausible is the suggestion of J. Duncan M. Derrett ("Fresh Light on St Luke xvi: I. The Parable of the Unjust Steward," *NTS* 7 [1961], pp. 198–219), followed by Fitzmyer (pp. 1097–98), that what the dishonest manager has done is to cancel out the profit that was due him (sort of a commission). By canceling the commissions, the debts were reduced, an action that would no doubt result in future kindness being shown the dishonest manager. Thus, the rich man has not at all been cheated by this final action of the fired manager. The master is still owed what is due him, while his former employee, by foregoing a few commissions, now has a brighter future. Having understood the parable thus, it is now much easier to understand why Jesus sees in the action of the dishonest manager a worthy example for his disciples. They, like the dishonest manager, should be able to recognize the advantage in giving up a little now so that some day in the future they may receive much more.

16:8b–13 / Several lessons are drawn from the Parable of the Shrewd Manager (16:1–8a). The implication is that the shrewd, but dishonest, manager is praiseworthy because of the shrewd steps taken to guarantee his future. Jesus' disciples should learn a lesson from the manager's cleverness. Verse 8b suggests that many **people of this world are more shrewd in dealing with their own kind than are the people of the light**. Therefore, "Christians can learn something from the prudence of such people" (Fitzmyer, p. 1106). One lesson from the parable is drawn from v. 9. Jesus' disciples are enjoined to **use worldly wealth to gain friends for** themselves (lit. "make friends from the mammon of unrighteousness"). Jesus (or Luke) is not urging his disciples to acquire wealth dishonestly but to make good use of the resources (particularly financial resources) of this world (see note below). Jesus is not recommending compromise and he is certainly not recommending dishonesty, but he is urging his followers not to overlook opportunities and resources that will sustain his people and advance the Christian mission. By using the resources of this world wisely, Christians can be assured that **when it is gone** (the Vulgate reads: "when you give out" [i.e., die]) they **will be welcomed into eternal dwellings**. While Jesus' followers are on earth they should make use of the world's available resources in order to maintain themselves and the work of the church. When, however, these resources are exhausted and life's work is finished, the followers of Christ can look forward to entering a home that is eternal, not temporary, a home whose resources will never give out.

In vv. 10–12 a second lesson is drawn from the Parable of
the Shrewd Manager. The principle of v. 10 is that by the way
a person handles himself **with very little** it is evident how such
a person handles himself **with much**. We come to what for Luke
is probably the heart of the matter in v. 11. If the followers of Jesus
cannot properly handle worldly wealth, then they cannot expect
to be trusted **with true riches**. That is, if Christians cannot man-
age their money, property, and other possessions properly (such
as supporting the poor and the ministry), they cannot expect to
be entrusted with the rewards and wealth that last forever (cf.
Matt. 6:25–34). Implicitly, one's stewardship in this life will form
the basis for future reward and responsibility in heaven (see Matt.
25:14–30). Verse 12 adds a new thought to this second lesson: **If**
Jesus' disciples **have not been trustworthy with someone else's
property** (i.e., God's "property"), **who** (God) **will give** them **property** (rewards) **of** their **own?**

Verse 13 provides a third lesson drawn from the Parable of
the Shrewd Manager. In Matthew this verse occurs in a much fuller context (6:24) concerning the need to be loyal to God over
against the things of the world. Here in Luke the saying brings
out one more truth with respect to wealth that every follower of
Jesus should know, a truth that has been presupposed in vv. 9–
12. Christians owe their total allegiance to **God** and not to **Money**
(lit. "mammon"; see note below). This saying thus prevents one
from misunderstanding vv. 8b–9 above. Whereas Christians are
to put wealth to good purposes, they are not to become enslaved
to it. Herein lies a grave danger for many Christians. What often
passes for "good stewardship" or "God's blessing" is really nothing
short of greed and materialism.

Throughout his Gospel Luke reveals concern over the attitude toward and the use of possessions. Luke 16 probably represents the high point for this theme. The basic issue on which
the passage closes is that whereas every Christian is to be concerned about wealth and how it is utilized, it is never to become
a god in itself.

Additional Notes §40

16:1 / **told his disciples**: The audience has now shifted from the muttering "Pharisees and teachers of the law" in 15:2 to the disciples of Jesus. In Luke 15 the Pharisees were taught about God's attitude toward the lost, while in Luke 16 the disciples are taught about God's attitude toward wealth.

manager: Fitzmyer (p. 1099) remarks that the Greek word for manager (or "steward") often refers to a slave born in the household of his master. The Hebrew equivalent translates literally "a son of the house" (see Gen. 15:3). It is not clear in the parable that the manager was necessarily a slave; but slave or free, his mishandling of his master's property would have been viewed as a serious breach of loyalty. In light of his dismissal, the dishonest manager's chances of securing new employment would be very slight (as implied in v. 3). Evans (p. 48) sees a possible parallel to Deut. 23:15–16, where instructions regarding household slaves are given.

wasting his possessions: Lit. "scattering his master's property." The Lost Son had also "wasted his money" (15:13).

16:2 / By receiving **an account of** the manager's **management** the rich man will learn the extent of the waste and theft, while at the same time a new manager will more easily be able to take over the task of management.

16:3–4 / If the dishonest manager can no longer be a manager, he is left with two basic options: physical labor or begging. Neither occupation, however, would be acceptable, so the shrewd manager contrives a scheme that will permit him to continue in the capacity of manager, although for another employer. This is what is meant by the expression, **people will welcome me into their houses**. The manager hopes to win over someone among his master's debtors who, in gratitude, will hire him.

16:6 / **Eight hundred gallons**: Lit. "one hundred baths." The NIV translators apparently understand one "bath" as equivalent to eight gallons. Fitzmyer (p. 1100), however, suggests that it was closer to nine gallons.

16:7 / **A thousand bushels of wheat**: Lit. "one hundred kors of grain." It is uncertain how many bushels a single *kor* represents, but the NIV's "thousand bushels" is probably close enough.

16:8 / **people of the light**: Lit. "sons of the light." See the similar expressions in John 12:36; 1 Thess. 5:5; Eph. 5:8. Members of the wilderness community of Qumran referred to themselves as sons of light (1QS 1.9; 2.16; 3.13; 1QM 1.3, 9, 11, 13).

16:9, 11, 13 / **worldly wealth**: Lit. "mammon." The word comes from either Hebrew *māmôn* or Aramaic *māmônā'* (Fitzmyer, p. 1109). Although not found in the Old Testament, the word occurs in a few of the Dead Sea Scrolls and in the Aramaic paraphrase of the Old Testament, known as the Targum. Fitzmyer (p. 1109) suspects that the best explanation for the meaning of the word is that it is from the root which means "firm" or "certain" (from which "amen" is derived). Therefore, mammon is "that in which one puts trust," which could be money, property, wealth (so also Marshall, p. 621).

16:10 / **trusted with very little**: This lesson does not fit the context of the Parable of the Shrewd Manager very well, since the manager, as it turned out, could not be trusted with anything. Therefore, this saying probably originated in a separate context (Leaney, p. 223).

Luke 16:14–18 represents a cluster of sayings of Jesus from the sayings source that Luke had in common with Matthew (Luke 16:16=Matt. 11:12–13; Luke 16:17=Matt. 5:18; Luke 16:18=Matt. 5:32; cf. also Matt. 19:9; Mark 10:11–12). The passage is loosely related to the wider context in which the proper attitude toward wealth is thematic (Luke 16:1–13, 19–31) by the opening verse (v. 14). How vv. 16–18 relate to the theme of money will be seen in the commentary that follows.

16:14–15 / Although Luke 16:1 indicates that Jesus' Parable of the Shrewd Manager was addressed to his disciples, v. 14 indicates that the **Pharisees** had overheard Jesus' teaching (16:1–13). The Pharisees sneer at Jesus' teaching because they **loved money**. There is evidence that not only the aristocratic and wealthy Sadducees, but even the Pharisees, were fond of money (see Marshall, p. 625). In the Lucan context the point may be that Pharisees assumed that wealth was a sign of God's blessing, as well as the means for practicing one's piety in an ostentatious manner (such as almsgiving or giving large gifts to the temple or a local synagogue). Perhaps in the minds of some Pharisees the poverty of Jesus and most of his followers was a sign that they lacked God's blessing. (This false assumption is sharply challenged in the Parable of the Rich Man and Lazarus found in vv. 19–31 below). This seems to be the idea in v. 15 where Jesus criticizes the Pharisees for knowing how to **justify** themselves **in the eyes of men**. Jesus warns them that, unlike people who look on the outward appearance, **God knows** their **hearts** (cf. Prov. 21:2). The things that are considered to be of great value (in the case of the Pharisees, their oral laws and traditions) are **detestable in God's sight** (lit. "an abomination before God"; see Prov. 16:5).

16:16–18 / Contained in these three verses are three sayings, originally independent in all likelihood (as comparison with Matt. 11:12–13; 5:18, 32 would seem to indicate). What connection these sayings have with the surrounding context is not immediately clear. In view of Jesus' teaching about proper standards for living in the new age, Luke possibly wished to clarify how the law, the rule and guide for the old era, should be understood. In the first saying (v. 16) Jesus declares that the **Law and the Prophets were proclaimed until John.** John the Baptist is both the end of the old era and the beginning of the new. His was a ministry of preparation for the coming of the Messiah (see 1:57–80; 3:1–20). **Since** John's **time, the good news of the kingdom of God is being preached,** that is, it is being preached by Jesus and his apostles (on the last part of v. 16 see note below). As discussed in the Introduction (see pp. 8ff.), Luke 16:16 is an important verse for understanding the evangelist's concept of God's saving work in history. Luke seemingly understood history as consisting of three eras or epochs (see Fitzmyer, p. 185). The first epoch is referred to in Luke 16:16a, from creation to the appearance of John. This is the period of the "Law and the Prophets." With the appearance of John this era is ended and a new one is inaugurated. This second epoch, referred to in v. 16b, is the period of Jesus, during which time the "good news of the kingdom of God" is proclaimed. The third epoch is the period of the church, as can be seen in Acts 1:6–8, during which time the followers of Jesus preach the Easter faith (see Acts 2:16–39). During this period of time the church is commanded to preach the Good News throughout the world (Acts 1:8).

In declaring that the old era is now past, the era of the law of Moses, Luke is anxious to avoid leaving the impression that the law is either irrelevant or, worse yet, broken. The second saying (v. 17) reaffirms the eternal validity of the moral, or ethical, aspects of the law. Acts 15 shows that the Gospel writer believed that the sacrificial aspects of the law were no longer in force, but the ethical commandments were still binding. This idea was seen earlier in 10:25–28, where Jesus is asked what one must do in order to inherit eternal life. Jesus asks his questioner what is written in the law. The commandment to love God (Deut. 6:5) and to love one's neighbor (Lev. 19:18) is cited, to which Jesus replies: "Do this and you will live" (Luke 10:28; see Lev. 18:5). For Luke, this is the essence of the ethical requirements of the law. In Luke 24:26–27, 44–47, however, the evangelist makes it plain that the "Law and the Prophets" speak of Christ, foretelling his suffering, death, and resurrection. Viewed from this angle, then, it is easier to see how v. 17 would have been understood.

The third saying (v. 18) supplies an example of the ethical aspect of the law that is never to "drop out" (see v. 17b). This saying on divorce upholds God's perfect will for marriage (that it is not to be broken), as implied in Gen. 2:24. (In Matt. 19:3–9 Jesus acknowledges that Deut. 24:1–4 allows for divorce, but he views this part of the law negatively, as necessary to control and limit a practical evil.) Jesus' view on divorce captures the spirit of the law and stands in contrast to the Pharisaic interpretation, which by its many rules and regulations made generous allowance for divorce. The real reason Jesus condemns divorce is because divorce is often sought for the purpose of remarriage, and such remarriage is viewed as adulterous (see note below).

With the third saying it appears as if Luke has wandered a bit from the theme of riches. However, the prohibition against divorce would have its readiest application to the wealthy among whom divorce, adultery, and polygamy were more frequent. Thus, in a certain sense, we are not completely unprepared for the Parable of the Rich Man and Lazarus that follows (16:19–31; see also note below).

Additional Notes §41

16:14–18 / Ellis (p. 201) suggests that the Parable of the Rich Man and Lazarus (16:19–31) mirrors the sayings found in 16:14–18. Verses 14–15 parallel vv. 19–26 (contrasting divine and human values), while vv. 16–18 parallel vv. 27–31 (obeying Moses). Talbert (p. 156) accepts the suggestion, since it gives unity to the section.

16:14 / On **Pharisees** see note on 5:17 above. Fitzmyer (p. 1113) has noted that T. W. Manson thought that Jesus originally addressed the Sadducees rather than the Pharisees, since the former were aristocratic and wealthy and would have indeed sneered at the idea of pursuing heavenly wealth rather than earthly wealth. There is no evidence, however, that Jesus (or Luke) had anyone else in mind. Moreover, the Parable of the Rich Man and Lazarus, with its emphasis on the afterlife, would hardly be meaningful to Sadducees who did not believe in an afterlife. Thus, the context would argue that the Pharisees were in fact those addressed.

16:15 / **You are the ones who justify yourselves in the eyes of men**: Fitzmyer (p. 1113) has aptly remarked: "Jesus' words imply that the Pharisaic attitude toward money is rooted in something deeper, in a quest for an image of uprightness before others." Such "uprightness" would include ostentatious almsgiving, prayer, and fasting (see Matt. 6:1–18).

God knows your hearts: In the Bible the "heart" is the seat of one's emotions, desires, and loyalty. The heart reveals a person's character. So when the Bible says that God knows the heart, it means that God knows what a person really is like, what he or she really thinks.

detestable in God's sight: The language is actually much stronger: "an abomination before God." Evans (pp. 48–49) suggests that Luke 16:1–18 parallels Deut. 23:15–24:4. It is worth noting that the word "abomination" comes from Deut. 24:4 in reference to divorce and re-marriage. Thus, it is possible that Luke's reference to "abomination" in v. 15 and his later inclusion of the saying on divorce (v. 18), often thought of as curious, may been suggested to the evangelist by the contents of Deuteronomy. (Because he has dismissed the Deuteronomistic parallels proposed by Evans, Fitzmyer [p. 1121] is at a loss to explain why the evangelist has placed the saying on divorce in this part of the Central Section.)

16:16 / **The Law and the Prophets**: The phrase actually refers to the first two parts of the Old Testament, the Law (Torah or Pentateuch) and the Prophets. (See Luke 24:44 where the Law, the Prophets, and *Psalms* are mentioned, the latter representing the third part of the Old Testament, the Writings.) The reference here in Luke 16, however, is probably meant to be understood as referring to the whole Old Testament (see 16:29 below).

the good news of the kingdom of God is being preached: What Luke has in mind here is probably the twofold idea that Jesus proclaimed in his Nazareth sermon in 4:16–30. First, the time of the kingdom is at hand. The prophetic Scriptures are fulfilled. The Anointed One, the Messiah, is present. The call to repent and to enter the kingdom now sounds forth. Second, the call to enter the kingdom is an inclusive one; it summons not only the righteous but the unrighteous, the lowly, the downtrodden. Those who by Pharisaical standards are thought unworthy of the kingdom of God are invited to enter. Thus, the "good news of the kingdom" is that it has appeared in the person of Jesus and that it is offered to all who will receive it.

everyone is forcing his way into it: This statement is not easily interpreted, for the meaning of the word translated "forcing" is not readily determined. The fuller parallel in Matt. 11:12 suggests that *violent entry* is in mind. In the Matthean context, Jesus discusses the ministry and fate of the imprisoned John the Baptist (Matt. 11:2–19). The Matthean parallel reads: "The kingdom of heaven has suffered violence [*or* is forcibly entered; *or* has been forcefully advancing, NIV], and men of violence take it by force" (RSV). Commenting on the form of the saying in Matthew, Gundry (pp. 209–10) thinks that the point is that the persecuted and imprisoned John the Baptist serves as an example of the fate many who enter the kingdom will experience. It is unclear, however, if this is the meaning that Luke has intended in his abbreviated and modified form of the saying. If the picture is negative, the Lucan form may have in mind militant messianic figures who advocate bringing the kingdom through violence; two such characters are mentioned in Acts 5:36–37. But the picture may also be positive, that is, all who enter the kingdom are being *urged* or *pressed* into entering (recall 14:23; see Fitzmyer, p. 1117; Tiede, p. 287). Leaney (p. 223) suggests the reading, "everyone one oppresses it."

16:17 / **the least stroke of a pen**: Lit. "a serif" (RSV, "dot"; KJV, "tittle"), the small point that distinguishes certain Hebrew letters from one another. (In Matt. 5:18 there is mention of a "yod" as well, which the smallest letter in the Hebrew alphabet.) The point of the saying is that nothing in the law of Moses is insignificant. All of it must be fulfilled.

16:18 / Matthew 19:9 gives unchastity (adultery or any other form of sexual sin) as the only acceptable grounds for divorce. There is some debate as to whether or not Jesus actually made this allowance. Quite possibly Jesus himself saw no legitimate grounds for divorce, but Matthew, or the tradition before him, added the exception clause (which also occurs in Matt. 5:32). There is also some debate as to what actually is being "excepted." Although it has usually been assumed that unchastity provides the grounds for a divorce, the exception clause may only mean that one is not guilty of causing one's spouse to commit adultery through divorce, if that spouse has already committed a sexual sin. If this latter interpretation is correct, then the exception clause really does not permit divorce. The question may be asked why Jesus was so strict on the question of divorce and remarriage. A. Isaksson (cited by Fitzmyer, p. 1121) has suggested that Jesus' high standards reflected the rule for priests (Lev. 21:7; Ezek. 44:22), and since his followers had an even higher calling than the priests, their standards could not be any lower. The suggestion is plausible.

§42 The Parable of the Rich Man and Lazarus (Luke 16:19–31)

Although perhaps not quite as popular as the Parable of the Lost Son (15:11–32), Luke's Parable of the Rich Man and Lazarus is another favorite. This parable, like so many others, drives its point home with crystal clarity. This parable brings the theme of wealth in Luke 16 to a fitting conclusion: wealth or poverty in this life is no measure of God's blessing. The parable may be divided into two parts: (1) the reversal of the conditions of this life in the next (vv. 19–26) and (2) the lesson that nothing can persuade the wealthy to take heed (vv. 27–31).

16:19–26 / The first half of the parable is the part that is best remembered, for it illustrates the theme of reversal, a theme which appears in the Gospels in a variety of forms (e.g., "the first shall be last, and the last first"; "he who exalts himself shall be humbled, and he who humbles himself shall be exalted"). Scholars have pointed out that in all likelihood there were similar fables of wealthy and poor people whose roles were reversed in the afterlife known to Jesus and his contemporaries, and so Jesus' parable, containing its own unique features, would have been readily understood and appreciated.

Jesus portrays the different circumstances of the **rich man** and **Lazarus** in the most graphic terms. The rich man **was dressed in purple** (see note below) **and lived in luxury** (i.e., feasted and partied) **every day**. From a worldly point of view the rich man had every creature-comfort that life had to offer. In stark contrast was the **beggar named Lazarus**, who was **covered with sores** (see note below) and who longed **to eat what fell from the rich man's table**. The picture of Lazarus is pitiful. What is not stated but probably implied is the insensitivity of the rich man toward his poor neighbor. He who enjoyed feasts and every comfort had no concern for one nearby who suffered and finally died from starvation and ill heath. But at death the picture changes dramatically.

The **beggar** is carried by **angels** to **Abraham's side**. When the **rich man** dies, however, there is no angelic escort. The rich man enters **hell**, the world of the dead (see note below). There he agonizes in pain and in desperation begs for a drop of moisture to **cool** his parched **tongue**. The agony that the rich man now experiences by far exceeds the misery that poor Lazarus had ever experienced in life, while the bliss Lazarus now enjoys far exceeds the pleasure that the rich man had ever experienced. Their roles are not only reversed; their new conditions are intensified. The hearer of the parable now learns the lesson that the rich man unfortunately had not learned in his lifetime. After death there is no longer any opportunity to change one's condition. Although Lazarus may not have borne the rich man any grudge and would have been willing to aid his former neighbor, there is no opportunity (in contrast to the rich man who had had every opportunity to aid the poor Lazarus).

Once again Jesus' teaching strikes at the heart of theological assumptions held by many of his contemporaries. Surely the rich man, they would reason, exemplified a man who was blessed of God while the poor man has only suffered what he deserved. But it is the poor man who is received by **Father Abraham**, and it is the rich man who enters hell. The "religious" assumed that health and wealth evidenced God's blessing, while sickness and poverty evidenced God's cursing. As the parable indicates, such assumptions can be hazardous.

16:27–31 / The parable continues by developing a second idea. The rich man has learned his lesson, albeit too late. Now he hopes to warn his **five brothers** so that they will not suffer the same eternal fate. But he is told that his brothers—as he had also—have every opportunity to hear and obey **Moses and the Prophets**. If they will not listen to the commandments of Scripture, then they will not listen to one who had been raised from the dead.

This last part of the parable, in which reference to being raised from the dead is made, has given rise to a number of interpretations. Assuming that Jesus' parable originally contained this part (and there is no convincing reason why it did not), we may inquire as to what special significance, if any, the reference would have had for Jesus and his hearers. Almost certainly Jesus did not originally refer to his own resurrection. As it stands in the context of the parable the reference seems to mean no more than the idea that if one is not convinced by Scripture (i.e., "Moses and the Prophets"), then a warning from the next world will have no greater effect. The implication is that Scripture is the greatest authority and carries (or should carry) the greatest conviction. If one's heart is too insensitive to hear and obey its warnings, then no testimony, no matter how authoritative or dramatic it may be, will be persuasive. If one is deaf to God's words, one will scarcely be able to hear the words of another.

In the later period of Luke and his readers, however, the reference to being raised from the dead was understood as an allusion to Jesus' resurrection. Just as his opponents had refused to hear and obey the words of Moses and the Prophets, so too would they reject the message of the risen Christ (as the Book of Acts gives eloquent testimony). (On the relation of the name Lazarus to the raising of Lazarus in John 11 see note on v. 20 below.)

Additional Notes §42

Evans (p. 49) suggests that the injunctions regarding the treatment of the poor and the needy found in Deut. 24:6-7, 10-15 parallel Luke's Parable of the Rich Man and Lazarus. The rich man's lack of concern for his poor neighbor would surely violate the spirit of the laws of Deuteronomy.

16:19 / In most of the oldest manuscripts there is no name given to the **rich man**. However, in the very oldest manuscript (P^{75}) the phrase, "by the name of Neues," is found. Fitzmyer (p. 1130) suspects that it is intended as a shortened form of "Nineveh." That a name would be assigned to the rich man is understandable, since a name is assigned to the poor man. But why "Neues" (or "Nineveh") is anybody's guess. The name "Dives" comes from the Vulgate, but there it is not intended to be a name.

dressed in purple and fine linen: This is the clothing of royalty. The inference, as Fitzmyer (p 1130) has pointed out, is that the rich man lived like a king (see Prov. 31:22). Consequently Leaney (p. 225–26) wonders if the rich man was supposed to have been Herod Antipas. According to v. 28 the rich man had five brothers, as had Herod when the parable was originally told.

16:20 / There are at least two issues related to the name of the **beggar**. (1) It is sometimes wondered why a figure in a parable would be assigned a proper name. In no other parable of Jesus is this the case. It has been suggested that there was understood, or intended, a connection with the Lazarus of the Fourth Gospel, the one raised up in John 11. This possibility leads to the next issue and that is, (2) if there is a connection between the **Lazarus** of the Lucan parable and the Lazarus of John 11, what is the nature of this relationship? There are at least two possible explanations. First, it has been argued that the Johannine account of the raising of Lazarus is in fact a fictional illustration based upon the Lucan parable: Lazarus was indeed raised from the dead (as the rich man had requested) as a witness, yet even then Jesus' opponents did not believe (as Abraham had predicted). A second explanation, and one that is preferred to the first, is that because of the rough similarity between the point of the Lucan parable and the experience of Lazarus in John 11, early in the manuscript tradition a certain Christian scribe (or scribes) inserted the name Lazarus. Although this suggestion must remain speculative since there is no early manuscript evidence of the parable without the name, it provides a reasonable explanation to the two questions raised above, for it explains why a proper name has appeared in the parable and why this name was Lazarus of all names.

covered with sores: Lit. "ulcerated." The condition of the poor man is not only serious but quite painful.

16:21 / **longing to eat**: This phrase is identical to the lost son's wish to fill himself with the bean pods that the swine ate (15:16).

16:22 / Although the **rich man** is honored by burial (and with his burial ends his honor), the **beggar** is apparently not buried and honored (by people), but the **angels carried him to** Paradise.

Abraham's side: Lit. "Abraham's bosom," that is, the place of intimacy with Abraham, the father of the Jewish people. Such a place was considered the place of greatest honor and security (see Fitzmyer's references, p. 1132).

16:23 / **hell**: Lit. "Hades"; see note on 10:15 above.

16:24 / By calling Abraham **Father Abraham** (similarly, see vv. 27, 30), the rich man is appealing to his kinship with the father of his race. Such physical kinship, however, especially in Lucan theology (see 3:8), means nothing. According to Jewish legends, Abraham will sit at the entrance to hell to make sure that no circumcised Israelite is cast in (cf. *Genesis Rabbah* 48.8). However, even for those Israelites who are sentenced to spend some time in hell, Abraham has the authority to take them out and receive them into heaven (b. *Erubin* 19a). It is probably against the background of traditions like these that the rich man believed that Abraham could give him comfort.

dip the tip of his finger in water: Whereas Paradise has an abundance of water, hell is dry and hot: " . . . so the thirst and torment which are prepared await them" (2 Esdras 8:59).

fire: The idea of fire in Hades probably goes back to Isa. 66:24 (see note on 10:15 above), which is quoted in Mark 9:48 (see also Rev. 20:14–

15). The anguish now experienced by the rich man is similar to (but more severe than) the burning pain the poor man had experienced because of his ulcerous condition.

16:26 / **great chasm**: This chasm is "an unbridgeable gulf between the locale of bliss and that of torment" (Fitzmyer, p. 1133).

16:27 / Recall that the dead Samuel was raised up to warn King Saul (1 Sam. 28:11–19).

16:28 / **Let him warn them**: Lit., "Let him witness to them." This is the same word that is used in Acts 2:40: "With many other words he warned them [*or* witnessed to them], 'Save yourselves from this corrupt generation.' "

16:29 / **Moses and the Prophets**: The resurrected Jesus will later tell his disciples that "Moses and all the Prophets" spoke of him (Luke 24:27, 44).

16:31 / **they will not be convinced**: For the evangelist Luke this word implied conversion and salvation, as seen in Acts 17:4: "Some of the Jews were persuaded [*or* convinced] and joined Paul"; and in Acts 28:24: "Some were convinced by what he said."

§43   Lessons on Faith (Luke 17:1–19)

This section consists of five units tied loosely together by the theme of faith: (1) a warning against causing someone to stumble (vv. 1–3a); (2) a saying on forgiveness (vv. 3b–4); (3) a saying on faith (vv. 5–6); (4) a saying on duty (vv. 7–10); and (5) the cleansing of ten lepers (vv. 11–19). The idea of faith is seen most clearly in the third and fifth units (vv. 5, 6, 19). However, when the concept is broadened in terms of *faithfulness* it becomes more apparent that the idea of faith runs throughout the section. Only the first six verses are paralleled in the other Gospels (Matt. 18:6–7, 15, 21–22; 21:21; Mark 9:42; 11:22–23).

17:1–3a / Jesus now turns his attention away from the Pharisees and speaks **to his disciples**. The first saying is a warning against causing **one of these little ones** (disciples) **to sin** (lit. "to stumble"). The idea is not simply to cause someone to sin, but rather to become less faithful disciples, or to stop following Jesus altogether (see note below). **Jesus** recognizes that such **things** will happen, but **woe to that person through whom they come**. In what sense is it terrible for the disciple who causes another to stumble? In v. 2 Jesus states that **it would be better for him to be thrown into the sea with a millstone tied around his neck than for him to cause one** to stumble. Elsewhere Jesus states that it would be better to lose an eye or a limb in order to gain heaven than to go to hell (see Mark 9:43, 47). Although this language may be hyperbolic, Jesus warns of the danger of judgment upon anyone who would destroy the faith of the one who believes in him. The final warning of v. 3a, **so watch yourselves**, probably concludes the stumbling-block saying and is not the introduction for the saying on forgiveness that follows (though it may have been intended as a transition linking the sayings; Fitzmyer, p. 1139).

17:3b–4 / This saying, coming as it does immediately after the frightening warning above, may point to the way out of some of the problems associated with causing someone to stumble. The person who is sinned against (offended, or possibly caused to stumble) is to **forgive** his errant **brother**. Even **if he sins against you seven times in a day**, he is to be forgiven. (See Matt. 18:22 where Jesus tells Peter to forgive the sinner seventy times seven; Gundry [pp. 370–71] suspects that this variation of the saying is a Matthean creation based upon Gen. 4:24.) Although this saying is addressed apparently to the stronger disciple who does not falter in his faith on account of some offense, the idea of forgiveness is, nevertheless, relevant to the above warning against causing someone to stumble. But the saying also applies to the weaker disciple as well. God expects everyone to be forgiving toward another who repents.

17:5–6 / The **faith** that the disciples (or here, **apostles**) wish Jesus to **increase** is the kind of faith that will not waver in the face of opposition but is a faith that will expect great things from God (such examples can be seen in the Book of Acts). It may be that in light of the saying's context, Luke understands this faith as the kind of faith that will not cause other disciples to falter (vv. 1–2), but it is a faith that will readily forgive those who sin and then repent (vv. 3b–4). What is curious is that Jesus does not actually grant (or at least obviously) the request of the apostles. They have asked for an increase in faith, but in response Jesus merely describes what great faith is. Even a little genuine faith can do mighty things (see Matt. 17:20). Jesus does not miraculously strengthen the faith of his disciples on the spot (which is clear by their fear, betrayal, and denial of Jesus when their master is arrested). But through his further teaching, example, and provision of the Spirit, he produces in his apostles a mighty faith, one that will proclaim the Good News boldly and gladly will suffer persecution.

17:7–10 / This saying suggests that in serving God, God's people have only done what is expected; just as a **servant** does not deserve thanks for doing his **duty**, so the disciples of Jesus should not expect special reward for being obedient. Jesus does not mean to rule out heavenly reward for faithful service, but he means only to instruct his disciples as to how they should think. The point of the saying is concerned with attitude. An arrogant attitude views God as fortunate for having people like us in his

service (perhaps this was a Pharisaic attitude). The proper attitude, however, is thankfulness for having the privilege and opportunity to serve God. What reward we have for serving God is not
earned, but is given because God is gracious. No Christian can
boast before God (see Rom. 3:27). Faithful servants understand
this and thus go about their work for God, motivated by love for
God and not by a sense of self-importance or by a sense of greed
for reward.

17:11-19 / Another aspect of faith, or faithfulness, is
thankfulness. This idea is seen clearly in the episode of the cleansing of the ten lepers. In v. 11 Luke notes that **Jesus** was **on his
way to Jerusalem**, traveling **along the border between Samaria
and Galilee** (see note below). This introduction not only reminds
the reader of the journey to Jerusalem, originally announced in
9:51, but sets the stage for the appearance of the Samaritan leper.
Jesus is **met** by **ten men who had leprosy** (see note on 5:12 above).
According to custom and law **they stood at a distance** and cried
out to Jesus for help. Jesus makes no pronouncement of healing
(although one ancient manuscript adds: " 'I will [have pity on
you], be cleansed,' and immediately they were cleansed"), but
commands them, **"Go, show yourselves to the priests."** (Jesus
had given the same command to the leper in 5:14.) This command
alludes to the wording of Lev. 13:49 (see also Lev. 14:2-4), where
one whose leprosy or skin disease has cleared up must be in-
spected by a priest in order to be readmitted into society. In obedience the ten lepers depart, but while going they discover that
they had been **cleansed** (or had been healed; see note below).
One of them returns **praising God**, and **thanked** Jesus. Jesus' first
question (**Were not all ten cleansed?**) implies that there should
be ten, not one, praising God and giving thanks. His second question (**Where are the other nine?**) sets up the contrast between the
one who returned, who was a **Samaritan**, and the nine (who presumably were Jews) who did not return to give praise and thanks.
Jesus' third question (**Was no one found to return and give praise
to God except this foreigner?**) implies that the least religious or,
to put it differently, those presumably most deserving of judgment, are often the ones most thankful to God for his mercy (see
7:36-50). The Samaritan is a foreigner (lit. "a stranger"), one who
is not a pure descendant of "Father Abraham" (as the rich man of

16:19–31 had been). Jesus' question summarizes one of the major themes of Luke–Acts. It is the Gentile, the Samaritan, the outcasts and sinners, who respond enthusiastically to the offer of the Good News. Unlike the religious and proud, who assume that their piety guarantees their salvation, the outcasts and sinners assume no such thing (see 18:9–14) and eagerly accept God's gracious invitation (see 14:15–24). The foreigner is the only one who came back to give thanks to God, because only he recognized his sin and his need to repent. Unlike others whose hearts are hardened (another theme in Luke–Acts; see Acts 28:25–28), the Samaritan is receptive. Jesus then pronounces that it is his faith that has made him well (lit. "has saved you"). Although the "salvation" here may refer to no more than the leper's physical healing (which would then be true of the other nine lepers who had been healed), it is more likely that Jesus (or, if not Jesus, then very likely Luke) has understood his expression of gratitude as indicative of conversion. The leper has not only been healed from his dreaded **leprosy**, but he has gained entry into the kingdom of God.

Additional Notes §43

17:1 / **Things that cause people to sin**: Gk., *skandalon* or "stumbling-block." Fitzmyer (p. 1138) notes that "in Jesus' saying the 'scandal' has to be understood of an enticement to apostasy or abandonment of allegiance (to God or to his word as proclaimed by Jesus)."

17:2 / **a millstone**: Unlike the smaller millstone that could be manipulated by hand, the "millstone" to which Jesus refers is the larger variety that would be turned by an animal. Such a millstone would sink someone quickly and completely.

17:5 / **The apostles**: Luke likely means the Twelve (see 6:13). **Lord**: See commentary and note on 2:11 above.

17:6 / **mulberry tree**: Fitzmyer (p. 1144) suspects that in earlier tradition it was a "mountain" and not a "mulberry tree" that was to **be uprooted and planted in the sea**. How a tree was supposed to be planted in the sea does indeed seem strange. Perhaps there had been another similar saying in which the uprooted tree is planted on another patch of ground. At some point in the transmission of the tradition the two sayings merged.

17:7 / **a servant**: Fitzmyer (p. 1145, following Paul Minear, "A Note on Luke 7:7–10," *JBL* 93 [1974], pp. 82–87) believes that the word "servant" (or "slave"; see also vv. 9, 10) "could already have taken on the Christian nuance of the Pauline usage" (see Rom. 1:1; 1 Cor. 7:22; Gal. 1:10; and in Luke's writings see Acts 4:29; 16:17). Moreover, the activity of **plowing or looking after the sheep** is likened in Paul to Christian discipleship (1 Cor. 9:7, 10; Rom. 15:25), as well as elsewhere in Luke's writings (see Luke 9:61–62; Acts 20:28–29). The point of all this is to say that Jesus' parable would have come to be understood by early Christians as directly applicable to themselves. It is quite possible, however, that when originally uttered, the parable addressed not Jesus' disciples, but Pharisees (and Sadducees?), who owned farms on which servants worked. If so, then this would be another example of how a Palestinian saying or parable came to be applied to the later, wider Christian context.

17:10 / **So you also**: The parable (vv. 7–9) is applied to the disciples (or apostles). In another context the parable may have been applied to others, such as the Pharisees.

we have only done our duty: This is apparently a common theme in Jewish piety. Lachs (p. 318) and Tiede (pp. 294–95) cite a saying attributed to Yohanan ben Zakkai: "If you have achieved much in the Law, claim not merit for yourself; for this purpose you were created" (m. *Pirqe Aboth* 2.8).

17:11 / **Now on his way to Jerusalem, Jesus traveled along the border between Samaria and Galilee**: For geographical reasons this verse has stirred controversy. A glance at any map of first-century Palestine will reveal that Galilee lies to the north of Samaria and shares a border roughly running east to west. Judea (in which is located the city of Jerusalem) lies to the south of Samaria. Exactly how Jesus could make his way (south) toward Jerusalem, moving along the (east-west) border between Samaria and Galilee is not clear. Because of this statement Luke has been charged with an inadequate knowledge of Palestinian geography, to the effect that Luke apparently supposed that Galilee and Samaria were situated side-by-side to the north of Judea (see Hans Conzelmann, *The Theology of St. Luke* [New York: Harper & Row, 1960], pp. 68–73). Had Luke intended to convey this picture, then obviously his geographical knowledge was faulty. In the Greek, however, Luke actually says that Jesus passed "through the middle of Samaria and Galilee." Early Christian scribes sensed the confusion, as seen in the various readings they offered (e.g., "in the midst of," "between," "through the midst of"). Luke may not intend to say that Jesus was actually traveling south, along a north-south Samaritan-Galilean border (for if that is what he means then he is clearly in error), but only that while on his way to Jerusalem he was in the general vicinity of both provinces. As can be seen from the outset of the journey to Jerusalem, Luke's geographical references (indeed, the journey itself) are vague. The journey cannot be understood in a strict chronological or, for that matter, geographical sequence. All that Luke is saying is that while still many miles north of

Jerusalem (and Judea), Jesus was for a time in the general vicinity of Samaria and Galilee. We may infer from this vague geographical reference that Luke's knowledge was imprecise, but to accuse him of a gross inaccuracy is unwarranted.

Samaria: The region of Samaria in Old Testament times (tenth to eighth centuries B.C.) was inhabited by the ten northern tribes of Israel. Following the death of Solomon, the northern tribes seceded from the tribes of Judah and Benjamin in the south. The southern kingdom became known as Judah, while the northern kingdom was initially known as Israel, until it eventually came to be called Samaria after its capital city. In the eighth century Samaria was overrun by the Assyrians. Its inhabitants were exiled, and in their place foreign peoples were settled. In the centuries that followed a half-Jewish, half-Gentile race of people emerged with which the Jews of Judah to the south and of Galilee to the north frequently quarreled and whom the Jews loathed (see note on 9:53 above). That is why it is so ironic in a Jewish context that from time to time the "hero" of an episode or parable is a Samaritan. See *HBD*, pp. 895–900.

17:12 / **a village**: Lit. "a certain village." As explained in the note above, Luke's reference is intended to be general, in keeping with his vague geographical reference to Samaria and Galilee (see further in note on 17:16).

As was expected of lepers, they **stood at a distance** (Leaney, p. 228).

17:13 / **called out**: Fitzmyer (p. 1155) suggests that the cries of the ten lepers are not really shouts (although the Greek word allows for this translation), but they are more likely *prayers* (loud ones, to be sure).

Master: See note on 5:5 above.

have pity on us: Is it a request for charity or for healing? From the perspective of the lepers, it is not easy to say (perhaps they hoped for both). But from the point of view of the narrative a miracle is clearly anticipated. Hence, Jesus commands them to go and show themselves to priests in order to confirm their healing.

17:15 / Fitzmyer (p. 1155) suggests that the statement, **one of them, when he saw that he was healed**, should be understood as an opening of the eyes of faith. This may be the case (in light of Jesus' statement in v. 19; see note there). However, it may mean no more than when he realized that he had been healed *thanksgiving* and *praise* were awakened in him.

praising God: The phrase could possibly be an allusion to 2 Kings 5:15 where Naaman the Syrian leper glorifies the God of Israel for his cleansing. Allusion to Naaman is found in Luke 4:27.

17:16 / **and he was a Samaritan**: The reason for Luke's vague geographical reference in v. 11 above is now quite clear. In order to have a mixed group of lepers, one Samaritan and, presumably, nine Jews, it is necessary to locate the incident near Samaria and Galilee. Hence Luke's reference to the "middle of Samaria and Galilee."

17:19 / **your faith has made you well**: See commentary above. Since the leper's faith had something to do with his healing, it would appear that faith was present before he returned to give thanks. What has happened, however, is that his initial faith in Jesus has now become a much deeper faith ("Christian faith" for Luke); and thus Jesus' statement here in v. 19 very likely refers to total salvation, not just to the healing of his body. See Tiede, p. 298.

Contrary to Lachs (p. 318) and J. T. Sanders (p. 204), the healing of the ten lepers is not an example of Lucan anti-Semitism; it is another prophetic indictment. By singling out the thankful Samaritan, Luke is criticizing Israel for lacking insight and faith.

§44 *The Coming of the Kingdom (Luke 17:20–37)*

Unlike Matthew (24:3–25:46) and Mark (13:3–37), Luke scatters his materials concerning the destruction of Jerusalem, the last days, and the return of Jesus as Son of Man in at least five different locations (13:34–35; 17:20–37; 19:41–45; 21:7–36; 23:28–31). The passage presently under consideration (17:20–37) is paralleled at many points in Matthew (10:39; 16:21; 24:17, 18, 23, 26–28, 37, 39–41) and in Mark (8:31; 13:15–16, 21).

17:20–21 / The first part of this section is that part which actually relates directly to the **kingdom of God**. What follows in vv. 22–37 may more appropriately be regarded as material concerned with the return of the "Son of Man" and should be viewed, as Fitzmyer (p. 1158) has contended, as "something different" from the kingdom material in vv. 20–21. Nevertheless, because the evangelist has lumped the materials together, they are here treated as a unified discourse that has something to contribute to the general theme of the kingdom of God.

Elsewhere in Luke we have been told that the kingdom of God is something that can be seen and will be seen by some of Jesus' contemporaries (9:27). When Jesus sent out the Seventy he instructed them to proclaim that the kingdom of God has come near (10:9, 11), and similarly in 11:20 demonic exorcisms are seen as proof that the "kingdom of God has come to you." Therefore, when Jesus is **asked by the Pharisees when the kingdom of God would come**, it is clear that their conception of the kingdom does not correlate well with what has already been stated above. Undoubtedly underlying their question was the popular belief about the kingdom, i.e., the hope for a political redeemer through whom God would bless and exalt Israel above the nations. Jesus' immediate answer implies that he does not share this view (as could already be gathered by the statements mentioned above). **The kingdom of God does not come with . . . observation** (v. 20b). Initially this statement appears to contradict the statement found in 9:27. But

that is not so. Whereas the context in 9:27 anticipates the visible
manifestation of the kingdom's power, as seen in Jesus' transfiguration and consultation with the heavenly visitors (9:28–35), here
a different word is used (lit. "The kingdom of God does not come
with observation"), and the context suggests that what will not
be observed is a geographical, political kingdom, not the
kingdom's power. Such an observable kingdom is not coming, at
least not soon. Thus, Jesus states in v. 21 that no one will be able
to say with authority, **"Here it is,"** or **"There it is."** The kingdom of God is not a political, geographical entity; it is a power
within (or among) Jesus' disciples (see note below). The last part
of v. 21 refers to Jesus' presence upon the earth and the power
of God that is available to people because of that presence.

17:22–37 / The following verses were probably uttered on
a different occasion and are here addressed to the **disciples**, but
because of the close relationship between the appearance of the
kingdom and the appearance of the Son of Man (Jesus), these
materials are brought together by Luke. (The similar expressions
found in vv. 21 and 23 may have served as linking phrases.)

Whereas the kingdom of God is within (or possibly among)
people, which suggests a present reality, there yet remains a futur-
istic dimension. According to Acts 1:6–7, the kingdom has not yet
come in its fulness but is still awaited. What brings about the kingdom in its fulness will be the return of Jesus, the Son of Man
(Acts 1:11). It is with this return that vv. 22–37 are concerned.

This section may be divided roughly into three parts: (1)
the delay of the Son of Man (vv. 22–25), (2) the suddenness and
unexpectedness of the return of the Son of Man (vv. 26–30), and
(3) instructions in vigilance (vv. 31–37). Fitzmyer (p. 1167) summarizes the section as follows: "Jesus first tells the disciples that
the Son of Man will not come as soon as they wish (v. 22), instructs them about the way in which he will not come (v. 23) as
well as the way in which he will (v. 24), but also tells them about
what will happen first (v. 25), about the condition in which human beings will be when he does come (vv. 26–30), and about
the discriminating judgment which will be exercised on human
beings 'on that day' or 'on that night' (vv. 31–35)."

Jesus teaches his **disciples** in vv. 22–25 that **the time is coming when** they **will long to see one of the days of the Son of Man,**

that is, his second coming. **But** they **will not see it**. There will
be a delay. Jesus will not return for a long time. In the meantime
the disciples are to be vigilant, waiting with expectation, but not
fooled by those who say, **"There he is!"** or **"Here he is!"**
(Compare the similar warnings in vv. 20–21 about false predictions concerning the appearance of the kingdom itself.) There will
be false prophets (even false Christs; 21:8) who announce the appearance of a savior. But the disciples are **not** to **go running off
after them** (see note below). The reason for this prohibition is
that the appearance of the Son of Man will be sudden and un-
announced. Those who are heralded and announced are im-
posters; but Christ will appear as the lightning flashes across the
sky. Interrupting the flow of the idea, Jesus reminds his disciples
that this day of glorious revelation must be preceded by suffering and rejection (see 9:22) **by this generation**. For the people
who reject and crucify him are very much like those who will
be living on the earth when he returns.

In vv. 26–30 these people are compared to the people **in
the days of Noah**, people who did not heed the warning of the
coming judgment (Genesis 6–7). For these **people** life went on
as usual (v. 27). Jesus also compares them to the people of **Sodom**
and Gomorrah **in the days of Lot**, people who neither recognized
their sin nor expected God's judgment right up to the moment
when fire and sulfur rained down from heaven and destroyed
them all (v. 29; see Gen. 19:24). These unprepared peoples, those
in the days of Noah and Lot, perished when the day of judgment came upon them. From these comparisons it becomes quite
evident that the coming of the **Son of Man** is to be understood
not only as sudden and unexpected, but as bringing judgment
with it.

In light of these dangers, Jesus in vv. 31–36 instructs his disciples how to prepare for this time of upheaval. The first point
that Jesus makes is that at the moment of crisis one must be prepared. There will be no time to make provision. Exactly why there
is a prohibition against going into one's house is not clear. (Would
it be any safer outside?) The saying is probably meant to be taken
figuratively in the sense of the need to be mentally and spiritually
prepared. In the Lucan context true spirituality involves a correct attitude toward possessions. One who rushes back to a **house**
to get personal belongings is not ready to meet the Lord. That

one is like **Lot's wife**, who looked back longingly for the things that she had left behind in Sodom, and in so doing she lost her life (Gen. 19:26). Therefore, Jesus says, **whoever tries to keep his life** (by his own selfish means) **will lose it, and whosoever loses his life** (in service for Christ) **will preserve it**. The second point that Jesus makes is "the separation between closely related people" (Marshall, p. 667), an idea that is probably related to the saying on family division (Luke 12:49–53). The pair of examples (see note below) in vv. 34–35 is not explained. The fate of those **taken** or **left** behind is not explained in the passage. Those "taken" may be those rescued by the coming of the Son of Man, while those "left" would be those left for judgment and destruction. But then the opposite could be the sense: some taken for judgment, others left alive (Fitzmyer [p. 1172] prefers the latter; Marshall [p. 668] the former). In whichever way the illustrations are understood the point is clear: some will be ready, some will not be.

The section closes with an ominous saying in v. 37. Literarily question of the disciples (**Where, Lord?**) elicits Jesus' saying as an answer. But what "where" has to do with the preceding sayings is uncertain (for a survey of suggestions see Marshall, p. 669). In any case, the purpose of the question is to introduce Jesus' answer. The point of the saying seems to be that the appearance of the Son of Man "will be as unmistakable in its revelation as carrion is to the bird of prey" (Fitzmyer, p. 1168; see note below).

Additional Notes §44

17:20 / Fitzmyer (p. 1160) notes that nothing in the passage suggests that the Pharisees' question is a test or is asked in contempt; rather, the question arises from a genuine interest to know Jesus' opinion concerning the end time.

17:21 / The Lucan statement that **the kingdom of God is within you** (see note on 4:43 above), not paralleled in the other Gospels, is found in the non-canonical work, the *Gospel of Thomas* (late first or early second century in its original Greek form) saying 3: "Jesus said, 'If those who lead you say to you, "See, the Kingdom is in the sky," then the birds of the sky will precede you. If they say to you, "It is in the sea," then the fish will precede you. Rather, the Kingdom is inside of you, and it is outside of you'" (translation is from James M. Robinson, ed.,

The Nag Hammadi Library [San Francisco: Harper & Row, 1977], p. 118). The saying in *Thomas* appears to have been influenced by Deut. 30:11–14 and in no case represents an older or more original form of the saying than what is found in Luke. The phrase translated "within you" should probably be translated "among you," for the kingdom is not *within* people in some sort of mystical or spiritual sense (as Marshall [p. 655] supposes), but it is *among* people in the sense of Jesus' presence (so Fitzmyer, p. 1161; Tiede, p. 300).

17:22 / **Son of Man**: See note on 5:24 above.

17:23 / **Do not go running off after them**: Lit. "Don't go out, nor pursue [it]." Some manuscripts read: "Don't believe [it]." Such announcements regarding the kingdom are unfounded. The disciple will do well to ignore them. In Luke's church the tragic war with Rome (A.D. 66–70) may very possibly be in mind. Many Jews followed a would-be messiah named Simon bar Giora (as well as other leaders). Through his leadership it was hoped that Rome would be defeated and the kingdom of God inaugurated. These hopes and aspirations proved to be unfounded, and the city of Jerusalem, along with its temple, was destroyed.

17:26 / **in the days of Noah**: In the period between the Testaments, Noah was viewed as a righteous man who live among godless people (see 1 Pet. 3:20; 2 Pet. 2:5). See *HBD*, pp. 709–10.

17:27 / **up to the day Noah entered the ark**: See Gen. 7:7.

17:28 / **in the days of Lot**: Lot was the nephew of Abraham (Gen. 11:27), who chose to dwell in the Jordan Valley (Gen. 13:11). Eventually Lot and his family took up residence in Sodom, whose inhabitants were "wicked, great sinners against the Lord" (Gen. 13:13b, RSV).

17:29 / The verse recounts Lot's rescue in Gen. 19:16–26. Whereas the Genesis account does not put **Lot** in a very favorable light (in Gen. 19:16–17 angels have to drag him out of the city) in 2 Pet. 2:6–8 he is called a "righteous man, who was distressed by the filthy lives of lawless men." See *HBD*, p. 578. Both **Sodom** and Gomorrah were destroyed by **fire and sulfur** ("brimstone") (Gen. 19:24). See *HBD*, p. 974.

17:31 / **on the roof of his house**: The roofs of most Mediterranean houses were flat with exterior stairs. Hence one would have time only to run down the exterior stairs but not time also to run into the house. The phrase, **no one . . . should go back** (lit. "let one not turn to what is behind"), alludes to the wife of Lot, who turned to look at "what was behind" and perished (Gen. 19:26; Luke 17:32).

17:34 / In the *Gospel of Thomas* (see note on 17:21 above) we find this interesting parallel (61a): "Jesus said, 'Two will rest on a bed: the one will die, and the other will live.' " In all likelihood this saying is derived from Luke, but it is interesting to see how the Lucan saying has been interpreted. The person **taken** is the one who "will die," while the person **left** is the one who "will live."

17:37 / **Lord**: The title is probably to be understood as christological and not merely a title of respect (i.e., "sir"; see note on 2:11 above). For Luke and his community, the title probably was understood christologically in terms of Jesus' divine status.

the vultures: The word translated "vultures" could as easily be translated "eagles." Since there is reference to a dead body, most commentators and translations understand the word as referring to vultures, the carrion birds (Marshall, p. 669), but Fitzmyer (p. 1173) suspects that there may be an allusion to the Roman ensigns, which surround the image of an eagle (RSV translates "eagles"). Ellis (p. 212), however, doubts this interpretation.

Unlike much of the preceding material (17:20–37), the two parables that make up this section are found only in Luke: the Parable of the Widow and the Judge (vv. 1–8), and the Parable of the Pharisee and the Tax Collector (vv. 9–14). The two parables are linked by the theme of prayer (see vv. 1, 7, 10) and so make up a unit. The Parable of the Widow and the Judge, however, also relates closely to the preceding section (cf. 18:8b with 17:22, 26, 30), so much so that some commentators take 17:20–18:8 as a unified section. Nevertheless, it is probably best to understand the Parable of the Widow and the Judge as more closely related to the parable that follows (although it is quite possible that Luke has intended 18:1–8 to be a transition from one section to the next).

18:1–8 / Verse 1 is not part of the parable proper but is Luke's editorial introduction. Luke understands the parable as teaching Christian **disciples** that **they should always pray and not give up**. As the parable is later interpreted (vv. 7–8), however, it also teaches something about the faithfulness of God himself. The parable itself seems to drive home two points, as seen in the principal characters, the **judge** and the **widow** (Marshall, p. 671). We learn that the widow is persistent, and because of her persistence she receives **justice against** her **adversary**. On the other hand, the judge is fearless and uncaring, yet even *he* has his limits (even when his antagonist is nothing more than a mere widow) and so acquiesces to the pleas of the woman. The parable concludes with Jesus' (again called the **Lord**) exhortation to **listen to** (i.e., discern the significance of) **what the unjust judge says**. That is, Jesus' disciples are not to miss the point of the parable: persistence pays off.

Verses 7–8a clarify how the parable relates to **God**. (Fitzmyer [p. 177] notes that vv. 7–8a were probably added to the original parable in order to answer the natural question of how an unjust judge could possibly represent God.) The application is an instance of the form of argument *a minori ad maius* ("from minor to major"), in which it is argued that if a lesser case is valid (a dishonest, uncaring judge who finally sees that justice is carried out for an insignificant widow), then a greater case must be valid (a holy, caring God who will help his own people who ask him). But there is also another point of comparison as seen in vv. 7b–8a: **Will he keep putting them off? I tell you, he will see that they get justice, and quickly.** That is, whereas the unjust judge had to be nagged over a long period of time before he would finally, and grudgingly, act, God will not delay but will act promptly.

The presence of v. 8b is something of a puzzle. Commentators have pointed out that it would have found a more suitable context in 17:20–37, perhaps after v. 35 or 37, since that section is concerned with the end time and the return of the Son of Man (see v. 30). The appearance of v. 8b here provides a significant literary link to 17:20–37, but it is surely secondary to the original form of the Parable of Widow and the Judge. With its presence at this point a new application has been assigned the parable. Not only does the parable illustrate the need for persistence in prayer in general, but now the parable is made to illustrate the need to persist until Jesus (the **Son of Man**) returns. The implication is that when **he** returns he will **find** little **faith on the earth**. How does faith relate to prayer, the point of the parable in the first place (v. 1)? The implication is that persistent prayer is needed in order to maintain a healthy faith. This idea should work two ways: faith prompts prayer, while prayer strengthens faith. Thus, v. 8b also serves as a warning to the disciple to be persistent in prayer so that when his Lord returns he will be found faithful.

18:9–14 / With the Parable of the Pharisee and the Tax Collector, Luke's Central Section draws to a close (with v. 15 Luke resumes following his Marcan source [at Mark 10:13]). This parable "makes a fitting finale for the Lucan Travel Account" (Fitzmyer, p. 1183), for it illustrates with graphic clarity what Luke sees as the correct attitude one should have before God.

The Parable of the Pharisee and the Tax Collector is similar to the preceding parable in that its main point is seen in the individual responses of the two principal characters. In this parable the **Pharisee** provides an example of the wrong way to approach God, while the **tax collector** provides an example of the right way. The error of the Pharisee lies not in the fact the he has refrained from certain sins and has performed certain religious duties faithfully; his sin lies in his lofty self-esteem. Because he has remained legally and ritually pure, and because he has fasted regularly (a sign of religious seriousness) and has tithed faithfully (as required by the law of Moses), he assumes that he is acceptable before God. His estimation of his righteousness is greatly exaggerated. He thanks **God** that he is not like that tax collector standing nearby. Implicit in his offering of thanks is the delusion that he, and not the tax collector, is righteous. The Pharisee has no real sense of his own sinfulness and unworthiness before God, and therefore he has an inadequate appreciation of God's grace. Had he recognized his own sin, and God's gracious forgiveness, he would have viewed himself and the tax collector as equal before God. According to Talbert (p. 171), "the Pharisee's posture is unmasked as idolatry. He was usurping the prerogatives of God, which is how the devil acts. To judge is God's prerogative (cf. 1 Cor. 4:5), not ours. Proper thanks to God for one's lot in life never involves condescension toward others. Salvation by grace means one can never feel religiously superior to another. Faith never expresses itself as despising others. Spiritual arrogance is presumption, assuming that one stands in God's place, able to judge. It is this exaltation of oneself that God overturns." The tax collector, in vivid contrast, presumes nothing (as seen in his behavior, as well as in his prayer) but throws himself upon God's mercy. He confesses that he is a **sinner** and cries out for **mercy**. Jesus concludes the parable by noting that it was the tax collector, not the Pharisee, who **went home justified before God**.

To the parable Luke appends the saying found in v. 14b, a saying also appended to Jesus' advice on selecting one's seat at a banquet (14:7–11). The point that was made there is similar to the one being made here. The saying is a warning not to exalt one's self (before others, 14:11; or before God, 18:14b), lest one be humbled. Whereas the saying (and the parable preceding it) was originally addressed to Pharisees as a criticism of their self-righteousness, Luke intends it to be a warning to Christians to be careful how they view themselves, lest they become guilty of the same hypocrisy frequently associated with Pharisees.

Additional Notes   §45

18:1 / **Then Jesus told his disciples . . . that they should always pray**: The idea is not that Christians pray at every moment (though cf. 1 Thess. 5:17), but that their lives should be characterized by prayer (Fitzmyer, p. 1178; Marshall, p. 671). Of course, the major item for which the disciples are to pray is the Lord's return (Ellis, p. 213).

18:2 / **a judge**: What sort of official this "judge" is supposed to be in the context of first-century Palestine is not clear (nor does the parable require that the reader know). Marshall (p. 672) notes that "there does not appear to have been a uniform, organised system." Most matters of dispute were brought before the elders of the local synagogue, but a dishonest judge who had no respect for God hardly fits this picture. Thus, it is likely that a Gentile judge is in view, which would heighten the contrast made in v. 7 between the judge and God.

who neither feared God nor cared about men: Fitzmyer (p. 1178) and Tiede (p. 305) cite Josephus' description of King Jehoiakim as "unjust and wicked by nature, neither reverent toward God nor kind to people" (*Antiquities* 10.83).

18:3 / **a widow**: Once again a widow figures prominently in Luke (see 2:37; 4:25–26; 7:12; 20:47; 21:2–3). Widows, along with other unfortunates and outcasts of respectable Jewish society, are among those to whom Jesus regularly ministers and extends God's grace and favor. The judge's callousness toward the widow is clearly in violation of biblical injunctions (Deut. 10:18; Mal. 3:5; Sir 35:12–15).

18:4 / **For some time he refused**: Marshall (p. 672) suggests that the judge refused to act because of laziness. The description of the judge, however, suggests rather that he refused to act out of callous indifference.

18:5 / **eventually wear me out**: Lit. "finally hit me under the eye." The verb that means "to hit under the eye" (see 1 Cor. 9:27) is often used in a figurative sense ("to blacken the face" [i.e., besmirch one's character] or "to wear out completely"; Fitzmyer, p. 1179). Jesus could intend humor (as there is in many of his sayings, see Matt. 7:3–5) and so the literal rendering may be the most appropriate: "lest she come and give me a black eye." The humor is seen in the fact that this uncaring judge, who fears neither God nor man, finally relents, lest he suffer violence at the hands of a widow.

18:6 / **the Lord**: See commentary and note on 2:11 above.

the unjust judge: Lit. "the judge of unrighteousness." He is called unrighteous or unjust because he had not wanted to give the widow justice. The fact that he is described in v. 2 as having no regard for people also implies that the judge had little care for justice. In biblical literature there is a close relationship between justice and righteousness.

18:7 / **his chosen ones**: The expression heightens the difference between the widow, a person of insignificance for whom the corrupt judge had no regard, and God's children whom he loves dearly.
Will he keep putting them off?: Lit. "will he be slow for them?" Compare 2 Pet. 3:9 ("The Lord is not slow").

18:8 / **he will see that they get justice**: God will vindicate his children and make things right.
faith: Compare 7:9.
when the Son of Man comes: The saying harks back to 17:20–37. On "Son of Man" see note on 5:24 above.

18:9 / **some who were confident of their own righteousness and looked down on everybody else**: Although not stated, it is quite likely that Luke has the Pharisees in view (see 16:14–15). The role of the Pharisee in the parable itself (v. 10) also supports this supposition. The application, however, is much broader. Anyone, including Jesus' disciples, could easily fall into the way of the thinking of this parable's Pharisee. (Remember, not all of the Pharisees of Jesus' day were self-righteous hypocrites. The Christian himself should guard against a self-righteous attitude of contempt for the Pharisees.)

18:10 / **went up to the temple to pray**: People could enter the temple (in the area called the "Court of Israel") at any time to pray, although mornings (9 a.m.) and afternoons (3 p.m.) were reserved for public prayer (Fitzmyer, p. 1186).
Pharisee: See note on 5:17 above.
tax collector: See note on 3:12 and 19:2.

18:11 / **The Pharisee stood up**: Fitzmyer (p. 1186) suggests that the Pharisee stood up to pray in a prominent location, perhaps toward the front, of the temple's "Court of Israel." This may be the idea, since a contrast with the place where the tax collector stands (v. 13) seems to be intended.
God, I thank you that I am not like other men—robbers, evildoers, adulterers—or even like this tax collector: "Robbers" might also be translated "thieves" (the word can have a variety of meanings; NASB, "swindlers"; RSV, "extortioners"). The main idea is in taking what is not one's own, which would violate the eighth commandment ("You shall not steal," Exod. 20:15, RSV). The word translated "evildoers" may also be translated "unjust" (RSV, NASB; as in reference to the unjust judge of v. 6 above) or "unrighteous." The word has a general reference, and so it could refer to any of the commandments (although closest may be Exod. 20:16: "You shall not bear false witness against your neighbor," RSV). "Adulterers" are guilty of violating the seventh commandment ("You shall not commit adultery," Exod. 20:14, RSV). The expression, **like all other men**, makes it clear that the Pharisee does not include himself among sinners.

18:12 / **I fast twice a week**: See commentary on 5:33 above (Lev. 16:29, 31; Num. 29:7). Fasting was often done as an act of contrition, humility, or sorrow. By fasting twice a week, the Pharisee goes beyond the requirements of the law.

and give a tenth of all I get: See commentary on 11:42 above (Deut. 14:22–23).

18:13 / **But the tax collector stood at a distance**: The implication is that the tax collector, unlike the Pharisee (see v. 11), stood toward the back of the "Court of Israel" (Fitzmyer, p. 1188: "just within the confines"). Remember also that the ten lepers "stood at a distance" because of their uncleanness (Luke 17:12). The tax collector in Jesus' parable apparently viewed himself as unclean and unworthy.

He would not even look up to heaven: The tax collector's sense of sin is so great that he would not, as was customary, look toward heaven while he prayed. Tiede (p. 308) cites *1 Enoch* 13:5, which in reference to the fallen angels states: "they did not raise their eyes to heaven out of shame for their sins."

God, have mercy on me, a sinner: Unlike the Pharisee (vv. 11–12), the tax collector offers God no list of virtues (nor a list of excuses); he has done nothing to impress God, but can only admit his sinfulness and plead for God's mercy. In this we see the essence of grace, an idea that closely relates to the New Testament teaching of justification by faith (Ellis, p. 214).

§46 *Sayings on the Kingdom (Luke 18:15–34)*

This section has three parts: (1) Jesus' blessing of the children (vv. 15–17), (2) the rich leader and related sayings on possessions (vv. 18–30), and (3) Jesus' third passion prediction (vv. 31–34). To a greater or lesser degree the theme of the kingdom underlies all three of these parts. In the blessing of the children Jesus states that the "kingdom of God belongs to such as these" (v. 16). After his encounter with the rich ruler, Jesus declares, "How hard it is for the rich to enter the kingdom of God!" (v. 24). Finally, in Jesus' pronouncing for the third time his impending passion, the reader would likely see a kingdom connotation here as well, since the glorious return of the Son of Man, at which time the kingdom of God is established in its fulness, can take place only after he has first suffered and been rejected (vv. 31–32; see 17:25).

With 18:15 the evangelist Luke has resumed following his text of the Gospel of Mark. All three parts of this section are taken from Mark, and in the Marcan order (Mark 10:13–16, 17–31, 32–34).

18:15–17 / With respect to the **people** who **were also bringing babies to Jesus**, Marshall (p. 682) suggests that "the background to the story appears to be the practice of bringing children to the elders for a prayer of blessing upon them on the evening of the Day of Atonement." The **disciples**, however, **rebuked** the parents, no doubt because they viewed it as trivial and as a waste of Jesus' time. **But Jesus called the children to him.** (Here Luke omits Jesus' indignation directed at the disciples found in Mark 10:14.) Jesus' saying in v. 16 would indicate that the sincerity and eagerness characteristic of children are what make children a fitting example of what (as implied in v. 17) one who hopes to enter the **kingdom of God** should be like. Adults, by way of contrast to children, tend to be self-assured, independent, and proud—all characteristics that hinder people from entering the kingdom.

18:18–30 / Following Mark, Luke narrates an account of Jesus' encounter with a **certain ruler** (see note below) who inquires of Jesus what he must **do to inherit eternal life**. (For comments on the meaning of v. 19 see note below; according to Matt. 19:20, 22 this "ruler" is a young man.) **Jesus** reminds him of the **commandments** and cites five of the Ten Commandments concerning proper behavior toward fellow human beings. (The list comes from Deut. 5:16–20 [see also Exod. 20:12–16], but not in the Deuteronomistic order.) Not included in the list of the commandments are the first four concerned with a person's proper relationship to God (Exod. 20:3–11; Deut. 5:7–15). (Luke omits Mark's "do not defraud" [Mark 10:19], probably because the evangelist recognized that it was really not one of the Ten Commandments. Matthew also omits it.) The ruler is able to reply that **since** his youth he has **kept** all these commandments. Jesus, however, discerns that what this person lacks is an undivided loyalty to God, for his wealth occupies a central place in his life. Jesus asks him to give away his wealth, not because having it is bad (nor does Jesus require everyone to give everything away), but because in this case the individual is more concerned with his wealth than he is with following Jesus or with obtaining eternal life. Although it does not explicitly say so, the passage suggests that the wealthy ruler had failed to keep the tenth commandment, the commandment not to covet (Exod. 20:17; Deut. 5:21). Because of his covetous attitude toward wealth, he had become guilty of violating the first and foremost commandment as well: "You shall have no other gods before me" (Exod. 20:3; Deut. 5:7, RSV). This person could not give up his wealth and follow Jesus (hence his sadness in v. 23). His reaction well illustrates Jesus' pronouncement: "You cannot serve both God and Money" (Luke 16:13; see also Matt. 6:24).

Following this exchange Jesus utters three more pronouncements regarding the relation of wealth to the kingdom of God (vv. 24–25, 27, 29–30). The first saying in response to the inability of the rich ruler to comply with Jesus' demand is: **How hard it is for the rich to enter the kingdom of God! Indeed, it is easier for a camel to go through the eye of a needle than for a rich man to enter the kingdom of God**. Although Jesus does not actually state that it is *impossible* for a rich person to enter the kingdom of God, his likening the difficulty to a camel, the largest beast of Palestine, trying to pass through the eye of a needle, the smallest opening, suggests that it is impossible (see Luke 6:24). This understanding clearly lies behind the question of v. 26: **Who then can be saved?** This question must be understood against the popular view that rich people are those people who have been favored and blessed of God. If rich people do not qualify for entry into the kingdom, then what hope is there for the rest of us? Jesus' answer in v. 27 (his second pronouncement) makes it clear that whereas salvation is **impossible** for humans to achieve, it **is possible with God**. All people, whether rich or poor, are saved by God who is merciful, and not by themselves. Salvation is ultimately a matter of a gracious God who receives repentant sinners (see 18:9–14).

The third pronouncement of Jesus on wealth and salvation is in response to Peter's reminder in v. 28 of his and the other disciples' forsaking of their possessions to follow Jesus. Unlike the rich ruler, Jesus' disciples were willing to leave behind all that they had. Jesus reassures Peter and the others that whatever is left behind for the sake of the kingdom of God (Mark 10:29 reads: "for me and the gospel") will be paid back by a greater amount (Mark 10:30 reads: "a hundred times as much") **in this age and, in the age to come, eternal life**. God is a debtor to no human. Luke has modified Mark probably because he wishes to avoid the idea that the disciples are motivated to follow Jesus because they hope for a material reward in this life.

18:31–34 / The first two passion predictions were uttered in Luke 9 (vv. 21–22, 43b–45), the chapter in which the journey to Jerusalem began (v. 51). Now that the journey is almost completed, the third passion prediction is uttered (though there were other utterances of pending trouble in the journey itself, see 12:50; 13:32–33; 17:25). In the Lucan version there is found a significant addition: **everything that is written by the prophets about the Son of Man will be fulfilled**. This reference, taken together with the statement of incomprehension in v. 34, clearly anticipates Luke 24:25–27, 44–46, where the uncomprehending disciples have the Scriptures explained to them by the risen Christ. For now, however, the **disciples** do **not understand any of this**. And it is not because they are dull of understanding (which is the impression with which one is left in the Marcan version); it is because **its meaning was hidden from them**. This understanding would be imparted to them after the resurrection of Jesus. It is in his rejection that the Scriptures will be fulfilled. But it is in his resurrection that there can be a hope for a coming kingdom of God.

Additional Notes §46

18:15 / **babies**: For some strange reason Luke alters Mark's "children" (Mark 10:13) to "babies," although he retains "children" or "child" in vv. 16 and 17, respectively. Why he did so is hard to discern, though the word is a favorite (see 1:41, 44; 2:12, 16; Acts 7:19). Schweizer (p. 285) suggests that by saying "babies" Luke emphasizes their total dependency.

18:16 / **do not hinder them**: In Acts 8:36 (the baptism of the Ethiopian official) and 10:47 (the baptism of Cornelius and his household) the same expression is used in reference to baptism. For this reason and others it has been suggested that Jesus' words in Luke 18:16 mean that infants should not be prevented from baptism. The context of this passage, however, has nothing to do with baptism (as is acknowledged by Fitzmyer, p. 1194). The whole point of the saying is in the way children "receive the kingdom" (an action of which an infant is scarcely capable), as an example for adults (see v. 17).

18:18 / **A certain ruler**: Fitzmyer (p. 1198) translates "magistrate" and notes that it is not at all clear that this person was a "religious leader." It is most likely, however, that Luke has in mind either the leader of a synagogue or a member of the Sanhedrin (so Marshall, p. 684). Ellis's reference (p. 217) to this person as a "churchman" is confusing. (This curious and anachronistic epithet occurs frequently in his commentary.) Even if many of the episodes are applied to situations in the church, reference to Pharisees and other Jewish non-disciples of Jesus as "churchmen" is not only anachronistic, it is misleading.
Good teacher: See note on 7:40 above. On what is meant by "good" see note on v. 19.
inherit eternal life: The ruler's question probably encompasses both the hope of attaining to the resurrection of the righteous and inclusion in the kingdom of God.

18:19 / **Why do you call me good?**: This question has prompted numerous interpretations down through the centuries. Indeed, the earliest interpretation is Matthew's in 19:17: "Why do you ask me about what is good?" A favorite interpretation among early church fathers is that Jesus wanted the man to stop and realize that in recognizing Jesus as "good" he was really ascribing deity to Jesus (since only God is truly good).

Others have suggested that Jesus has rejected the compliment as cheap flattery. Another suggestion has been that Jesus actually acknowledged his sinfulness. To be preferred, however, is the approach that understands Jesus' question as "directing the man's attention to God and his will as the only prescription for pleasing him" (Fitzmyer, p. 1199; similarly Marshall, p. 684; Tiede, p. 311). Jesus' answer implies nothing about himself.

No one is good—except God alone: This statement reaffirms a major OT teaching (see Pss. 34:8; 106:1; 1 Chron. 16:34). Jesus is not implying that he himself is not good, nor is he subtly hinting that he is good only because he is himself God.

18:20 / **You know the commandments**: When asked the same question in 10:25 Jesus gives a different answer (see 10:26–28). How to account for the differing ordering of the commandments is not easy. Matthew follows Mark, but Luke reverses *murder* and *adultery*; while all three Synoptic Gospels differ from the order found in the OT.

18:21 / **since I was a boy**: The rich ruler claims to have observed the commandments faithfully since he had come of legal age (Fitzmyer, p. 1200). However, the real significance of the laws of the OT was not always grasped (see Matt. 5:21–48 for several examples).

18:22 / Matt. 19:21 begins Jesus' response by adding the qualifying clause, "If you want to be perfect" (see Gundry, p. 388), a statement that contributes to the Matthean concern to fulfill the true righteous standards of the law (see Matt. 5:20, 48).

treasure in heaven: In addition to eternal life, one who follows Jesus will lay up treasure in heaven through obedience, particularly in giving to others in need (see 12:33).

18:23–25 / Luke omits Mark's mention (10:22–23) of the young man's departure, thereby creating the impression that Jesus' comments about the difficulty of the **rich** entering the **kingdom of God** were heard by this person, as well as by his disciples.

18:24 / **to enter the kingdom of God**: This comment, coming where it does, suggests that receiving eternal life (v. 18) equals, or at least involves, entrance into the kingdom.

18:25 / Jesus' exaggerated comparison makes sense only if his reference to **camel** and **needle** is taken literally. The suggestion that camel should be translated "rope" (with great difficulty a rope threads a needle) is farfetched. Moreover, the popular view that Jesus made reference to a "Needle Gate" in the wall of Jerusalem through which a camel passes with difficulty (on its knees and only after unloading its burdens!) is utterly unfounded (but popular with tourists and locals in Jerusalem). Lachs (p. 331) cites a rabbinic saying about the difficulty of "an elephant passing through a needle's eye" (b. *Berakoth* 55b) a saying which Fitzmyer (p. 1204) suspects is based on the Gospels.

18:29 / Luke has added **or wife**. Leaney (p. 237) wonders if the evangelist has in mind the Apostle Paul, who apparently had no wife (1 Cor. 7:8; 9:5).

18:31 / **the Twelve**: See commentary and notes on 6:12–16 above. **Son of Man**: See note on 5:24 above.

This section includes the healing of the blind man at Jericho (18:35–43) and Jesus' encounter with Zacchaeus (19:1–10). In both passages we see individual men responding to Jesus in faith.

18:35–43 / Luke's account of the healing of the **blind man** at **Jericho** is taken from Mark 10:46–52. In the Marcan account the blind man is named "Bartimaeus" (10:46; Bartimaeus=son of Timaeus). In the Matthean version of the story, however, reference is made to two blind men (Matt. 20:29–34; cf. also Matt. 9:27–31). (Matthew's interest in pairs probably accounts for mentioning the two men; see Gundry, p. 405; see also Matt. 8:28–34; 21:1–7.) Another interesting difference is that in Mark 10:46 Jesus is apparently leaving Jericho (so also Matt. 20:29), but in Luke 18:35 Jesus is approaching Jericho. The reason that Luke wants to leave the impression that Jesus is not leaving Jericho when he heals the blind man is to accommodate the Zacchaeus episode that follows (19:1–10), which also takes place in Jericho. Jesus could hardly be in the process of leaving Jericho when he heals the blind man and then be back in Jericho again when he meets Zacchaeus.

Luke elects to omit the blind man's name, although he does describe him as a beggar. (That he is Bartimaeus of the Marcan story is beyond all doubt.) In v. 36 Luke tells us that the blind man heard the **crowd going by** and so asked what was happening. (Mark 10:47 says only that Bartimaeus heard that Jesus was present.) It is then that the crowd informs him that **Jesus of Nazareth is passing by**. The blind man cries out to **Jesus** calling him the **Son of David**, a title which is surely messianic (see note below). Almost certainly the blind man has heard of Jesus' fame and knows that in him there is hope. Hence he cries out, **have mercy on me**. The crowd, however, viewed this outburst as an impertinence (or perhaps as dangerous) and so they **rebuked him and told him to be quiet**. Nevertheless, he continued to cry out. Here again is an instance of the familiar prejudice against some—like the blind man—who would have been viewed as disabled be-

cause of some sin (see John 9:2). Jesus has important things to
do and cannot be bothered by such a person of no account, or
so many in the crowd may have reasoned.

But **Jesus stopped and ordered the man to be brought to
him**. Jesus did not share this prejudice but rather taught otherwise (see Luke 14:15–24; 18:9–14). He asks the blind man what
he desires and he replies: **Lord** (probably meaning no more than
"Sir," but for Luke the word in this context should be "Lord," since
the blind man will be commended for his faith, faith that Luke
probably understands as at least incipiently Christian), **I want to
see**. Jesus then responds with the command: **Receive your sight**,
adding by way of comment, **your faith has healed you** (see note
below). The blind man was immediately healed, and Luke notes,
as is his custom (see 2:13, 20; 5:26; 7:16; 9:43), that **all the people
. . . praised God**.

19:1–10 / In the preceding episode we saw the healing
touch of Jesus restoring the sight and faith of a religious outcast
of Israel. In the episode at hand we have another example of the
restoration of one who was an outcast, not because of physical
problems thought to be caused by sin, but because of his occupation. While passing through **Jericho**, Jesus encounters a **chief
tax collector** (see note below) named **Zacchaeus**, a man who was
wealthy. His desire to see **Jesus** was such he climbed a nearby
sycamore-fig tree (which surely would have been viewed as un-
dignified for a man of means). To the astonishment of all, Jesus
picked Zacchaeus out of the crowd as his host for the day. In response to this selection all the **people** begin to **mutter**, for in their
eyes Jesus has chosen **to be the guest of a sinner**. It is usually
assumed that at that very moment, or perhaps after dinner and
conversation with Jesus, **Zacchaeus stood up** and spoke what is
stated in v. 8: **Here and now I give half of my possessions to the
poor, and if I have cheated anybody out of anything, I will pay
back four times the amount**. The NIV gives the impression that
Zacchaeus has had a change of heart: no longer will he cheat
people, no longer will he ignore the poor. This translation certainly reflects the traditional interpretation of this episode (which
is followed by Marshall, pp. 694–99; Ellis, pp. 220–21; Tannehill,
pp. 123–25). Seen in this light, the story of Zacchaeus is a story
of conversion. The wealthy tax collector has seen the error of his
ways (materialism, dishonesty, greed) and now has repented; and

as evidence of his repentance he promises to give half of his wealth to the poor and much of what is left to those whom he has previously cheated.

The traditional interpretation, however, may not be correct. In the NIV the verb **give** is modified with **here and now**, words which are not found in the Greek text. This gives the impression that Zacchaeus' statement will go into effect from the moment he spoke it. It is now understood as a present-tense statement of what has been Zacchaeus' habit. Not only have extraneous words been added to the translation, the verb **will pay back** is not really a future at all; it is present tense. A more literal rendering of the verse is: "Behold, Lord, half of my wealth I give to the poor, and if I have ever cheated anyone I pay back fourfold." Translated literally one is not necessarily left with the impression that Zacchaeus' statement represents new behavior. Furthermore, there is no indication that Zacchaeus' statement is to be understood as uttered after dinner and conversation with Jesus (Ellis, p. 221), during which time a conversion could have taken place. Moreover, there is no hint of Zacchaeus making a confession of sin (as in the case of fellow tax collector in 18:9–14). The more probable interpretation of v. 8 understands the statement of Zacchaeus as an immediate protest against the muttering crowd which disapproved of Jesus' intention to dine with him and which had referred to the tax collector as a "sinner" (v. 7). In other words, Zacchaeus has responded to the sting of being called a sinner for no other reason than the mere fact of his occupation. He has protested, in effect, that whereas other tax collectors may cheat and gouge their fellow citizens he, Zacchaeus, regularly contributes to the poor and whenever he (accidentally) collects too much (not necessarily "cheated"), he always makes fourfold restitution. This interpretation seems to make the best sense of what is actually found in the Greek text (so Fitzmyer, pp. 1220–22).

In v. 9 Jesus pronounces that Zacchaeus is a true **son of Abraham**. The reason that he is such is because his actions of fairness (recall the Baptist's advice to tax collectors in 3:12–13) point to a sincere heart, one that is ready to respond to the invitation to enter the kingdom of God. Because he is a son of Abraham, as is evidenced by his welcoming of Jesus, **salvation has come to** his **house** (even though it is the house of a despised tax collector). Here again we see Jesus in the role of champion of the outcast and of those who are maligned because of unwarranted assumptions and religious hypocrisy.

Jesus' saying in v. 10 does not merely summarize the Zacchaeus episode but should be understood as a thematic statement that climaxes and concludes the journey narrative. (Fitzmyer [p. 1218] notes that Luke 19:10 recapitulates the whole of chap. 15.) Unlike many of his religious critics, Jesus does not condemn the **lost**, nor does he judge people according to outward appearances. Jesus calls all to repentance, religious and irreligious, healthy and sick, rich and poor.

Additional Notes §47

18:35 / **Jericho**: See note on 10:30 above.

blind man: Mark 10:46 gives his name as "Bartimaeus" (i.e., the son of Timaeus). Some scholars have suggested that the name was inserted into Mark long after Luke (and Matthew) had used Mark as their source. That is unlikely, however. In view of the scribal tendency to harmonize the Synoptic Gospels, one may wonder why the name was not added to the Matthean and Lucan versions as well. It is more likely that, not seeing any relevance in the man's name, both Luke and Matthew (who mentions two blind men instead of one) elected to drop it. Later in Mark's account of the crucifixion, the evangelist notes parenthetically that Simon of Cyrene was the "father of Alexander and Rufus" (15:21). Again, Luke and Matthew see no significance in these personal names and so choose to omit them (Luke 23:26; Matt. 27:32). It is quite possible, if not probable, that these names were important in the evangelist Mark's tradition (and in the case of the sons of Simon of Cyrene possibly known to him) and so were retained. When the evangelists Matthew and Luke later utilized Mark, these names were unknown to them and were of no importance and so were not retained.

18:37 / **Jesus of Nazareth**: Lit. "Jesus the Nazorean." Mark 10:47 reads: "Jesus the Nazarene" (NIV: "Jesus of Nazareth"). The name of the city itself is found in the New Testament spelled either *Nazaret* or *Nazara*. Fitzmyer (pp. 1215–16) has suggested that the curious spelling in Luke may have arisen from an early attempt to relate Jesus' place of origin (Nazareth) either to the OT idea of the Nazirite (from *nāzîr*, "consecrated one"; see Num. 6:2–3; Judg. 13:4–5), an idea with which Luke is familiar (see note on 1:15 above), or to the OT idea of the "Branch of David" (from *nēṣer*, "sprout," "scion"; see Isa. 11:1), an idea with which Matthew (2:23) was apparently familiar.

18:38 / **Son of David**: That Jesus is a physical descendant of David has already been made clear to Luke's readers in the genealogy (3:31), though I doubt if the evangelist thought that the characters in his story knew of it. The blind man's knowledge of Jesus' Davidic connection would stem from rumors of Jesus' messianic status. That the designation "Son of David" is to be understood messianically is also apparent in 1:27, 31–33 (and see 2:4, 11). It is not necessary to conclude that the blind man supposed that Jesus was literally a descendant of David.

18:41 / **Lord**: Mark 10:51 reads instead, *rabbouni*, "My Master." Luke's substitution is due to his desire to avoid Semitic expressions which would not be easily understood by his predominantly Gentile readership.

18:42 / **receive your sight**: Tiede (p. 318) notes that in giving sight to the blind Jesus is performing his messianic task, as seen in Isa. 61:1 (Luke 4:18) and Isa. 35:5 (Luke 7:22).

your faith has healed you: Lit. "Your faith has saved you." It is a common expression (see 5:20; 7:50; 8:48; 17:19).

18:43 / **and followed Jesus**: Luke has left out Mark's "along the road" (10:52). The expression would have lent itself well to Luke's travel theme that has run throughout the Central Section (9:51–19:10 [or 27]), but it is omitted because Luke wishes Jesus to remain in Jericho in order to meet Zacchaeus in 19:1–10.

19:1 / **Jesus . . . was passing through**: The reader is reminded that Jesus' journey to Jerusalem is still under way. Jericho is only seventeen miles or so east of Jerusalem (see note on 10:30 above).

19:2 / **chief tax collector**: Fitzmyer (p. 469) prefers to use the title "toll collector," since these people collect "indirect taxes (tolls, tariffs, imposts, and customs)." But for our purposes the traditional designation will serve. The chief tax collector was one who collected these tolls and tariffs and had several agents under his authority. "Since the [chief tax collector] usually had to pay the expected revenue to the Romans in advance and then seek to recoup the amount, plus expenses and profits, by assessing and collecting the tolls [or taxes], the system of toll-collecting was obviously open to abuse and dishonesty" (Fitzmyer, p. 470). Especially because of their relation to Gentile authorities, these tax collectors were despised by their fellow Jews. This is seen in their frequent association with all types of undesirable people: "tax collectors and sinners" (Matt. 9:10; 11:19; Luke 7:34); "pagan or a tax collector" (Matt. 18:17); "tax collectors and the prostitutes" (Matt. 21:31, 32); "robbers, evildoers, adulterers—even like this tax collector" (Luke 18:11). See also note on 3:12 above.

Zacchaeus: In later church tradition that can hardly be trusted, Zacchaeus becomes the bishop of Caesarea.

wealthy: That is, wealthy from his occupation; hence, all the more reason that his neighbors despised and resented him.

19:5 / Because Jesus addresses **Zacchaeus** by name, we may wonder if Jesus' knowledge is supposed to be supernatural. As the story stands, however, we cannot be sure.

19:6 / **welcomed him gladly**: Note the contrast between Zacchaeus and the rich young man in 18:23. Zacchaeus is an example of a rich man whose wealth does not prevent him from entering the kingdom. See Tiede, pp. 320–21.

19:7 / **mutter**: The same word describes the Pharisees' reaction in 15:2.
sinner: See note on 5:30 above.

19:8 / **Lord**: For Zacchaeus "lord" probably meant no more than "sir," but for Luke and his community it may have been understood as "Lord" (see 5:12).
four times the amount: Zacchaeus apparently applied the law of restitution for theft (see Exod. 22:1: " . . . four sheep for the sheep").

19:9 / **son of Abraham**: I.e., a true child of God. Although this was a common designation for a Jew (m. *Aboth* 5.19), Paul uses the expression of Christians (Gal. 3:29).

19:10 / **Son of Man**: See note on 5:24 above.
to seek and to save what was lost: Note Ezek. 34:16: "I will seek the lost, and I will bring back the strayed . . . " (RSV); the prophet likens Israel to sheep (cf. 34:2, 11; Luke 15:3–7).

§48   The Parable of the Ten Minas (Luke 19:11–27)

The Parable of the Ten Minas (or "Pounds") provides a transition from the visit with Zacchaeus (19:1–10), in which the proper use of wealth was thematic, to the Triumphal Entry (19:28–48), in which Jesus enters Jerusalem as its king. Both aspects of stewardship and kingship are seen in the Parable of the Ten Minas.

The Parable of the Ten Minas bears an uncertain relationship to the similar parable found in Matt. 25:14–30 (cf. also Matt. 25:14 and Mark 13:34 with Luke 19:12–13). In the Matthean version a man gives his slaves (25:14) five, two, and one "talents" (of either silver or gold; 25:15). The slaves entrusted with the five and two talents double their monies (25:16–17), but the slave with the single talent hid it in the ground (25:18). The Master returns, commends the first two slaves, placing them in charge over "many things" (25:19–23), but he condemns the "wicked, lazy slave" (25:26) for squandering his opportunity, takes away his talent (25:28) and consigns him to "outer darkness" (25:30). In the Lucan version a man of **noble birth** leaves in anticipation of being **appointed king**. Before leaving, he entrusted **ten of his servants** with **ten minas**. While he is gone some of his subjects send a **delegation** trying to prevent the nobleman from ruling as **king**. Having returned as **king** he summoned his **servants** to determine **what they had gained**. The **first one** reported that he had **earned ten more** minas. The servant is commended and placed in **charge of ten cities**. The **second** reported that he had **earned five** minas. He too is commended and placed in **charge of five cities**. A third **servant** reported that he had hidden the **mina** in a **piece of cloth**, probably because of his fear of what his master would do to him if he lost it. In anger the newly crowned king takes **his mina away from him** and gives **it to the one who has ten minas**. He then orders that his enemies, those who had opposed his kingship, be slain.

As this summary shows, despite their differences ("talents" vs. "minas"; "many things" vs. "cities"), the Matthean and Lucan parables are quite similar. In both versions the faithful servants earn ten times and five times as much as had been entrusted to them. In both versions the wicked servant earns nothing, is condemned for not at least banking his coin, and has his coin taken away and given to the faithful servant who had earned the most.

The major difference between the versions is the Lucan idea of the slaves' master going away to be made king. The king goes away and is absent for some time, and while he is absent his citizens oppose his sovereignty. When he returns he has his enemies executed. These elements are not echoed in the Matthean version of the parable.

Fitzmyer (pp. 1230–31) thinks that underlying both Gospels is a common parable, with the Matthean form closer to the original form, as it was found in the sayings source. Gundry (pp. 502–3), however, reasons that Luke's more complicated version is closer to the original. Since it is more likely that Luke would have added the part about the man going away to become king, rather than that Matthew would have dropped it (why should Matthew omit this component?), Fitzmyer's reconstruction is to be preferred. The distinctive features found in the Lucan version fit the evangelist's theology. The part about the **man of noble birth** who is to **have himself appointed king** but has to go to a **distant country** (v. 12), and while he is absent is **hated** by his **subjects** who do not want him to be their **king** (v. 14), is intended to explain the delay of Jesus' expected return and the inauguration of the **kingdom of God** (v. 11). The kingdom has not yet appeared, for the king (i.e., Jesus) is yet in a distant place. In the meantime his rightful rule as king is being rejected by his own subjects (i.e., unbelieving Jews and, perhaps, other opponents of early Christianity). When the king finally does return, he will not only call his servants to account, he will also condemn those who have rejected his kingship. This Lucan feature was probably derived from another parable about a king whose sovereignty was rejected by some of his subjects (so Ellis, pp. 221–22; Tiede, p. 323). Thus, Luke united the two parables around the theme of judgment and assessment when King Jesus returns to assume his rightful position over Israel. His faithful servants will be rewarded and given positions of authority in the kingdom (see Luke 22:28–30), while his enemies will be destroyed (see Fitzmyer, p. 1233).

Additional Notes §48

According to J. T. Sanders (pp. 208–9; idem, "The Parable of the Pounds and Lucan Anti-Semitism," *TS* 42 [1981], pp. 660–68) the Parable of the Ten Minas, the "climax and conclusion" of the Central Section, is meant to justify the slaying of the Jews. He thinks that it represents the clearest expression of anti-Semitism, in that Luke is advancing the idea that *all* Jews will be destroyed (pp. 61–62, 317; "Pounds," 667). Although it must be acknowledged that Luke's version of the parable strongly condemns those who oppose Jesus, we may well wonder if Luke intends his reference to be applied as widely as Sanders has taken it. Are all Jews condemned? Or, are only those who opposed the "king"? The parable says that only those who have opposed the king will be slain (v. 27; cf. Deut. 18:19, quoted in Acts 3:23). And, in light of Acts, the Jews of Jerusalem are given many opportunities to repent (see Tannehill, p. 161; idem, "Israel in Luke–Acts: A Tragic Story," *JBL* 104 [1985], pp. 69–85, esp. pp. 81–85). Moreover, to argue that the parable teaches that the king will slay all of his subjects is nonsensical. Who are the good servants (vv. 13, 15b–19)? They are just as Jewish as the subjects who opposed the king. Consequently, there is no justification to distinguish Jews from Gentiles (or Christians). The question of race has nothing to do with the parable.

19:11 / **parable**: See note on 5:36 above.

near Jerusalem: Jesus is in the vicinity of Jericho (see 19:1 and note on 10:30 above). Jesus still has a long walk ahead of him.

kingdom of God: Luke could be suggesting that those who followed Jesus expected the kingdom of God to appear when Jesus arrived in Jerusalem. If not, then Luke is echoing the popular view that expected the kingdom to appear at any time.

19:12 / **a man of noble birth**: That is, an aristocrat, one who would have claim to royalty.

went to a distant country: This statement suggests a delay in the nobleman's return and so corrects the popular belief that the kingdom would appear soon.

to have himself appointed king: This detail in the parable may have been suggested by the experience of Herod the Great, who was successful in his effort to obtain his status from the Romans as "king." After Herod's death (4 B.C.) his oldest son Archelaus traveled to Rome in an unsuccessful bid to obtain the title (Josephus, *Antiquities* 17.206–223; Fitzmyer, p. 1235). Like the "king" in the parable, many of Archelaus' subjects opposed his bid for the title king (*Antiquities* 17.299–314).

19:13 / **minas**: A mina is worth only one sixtieth of a talent. The small amount (twenty to twenty-five dollars according to Fitzmyer, p.

1235), perhaps reflects Luke's view that although many of those in the church are poor, they are, nevertheless, expected to be good stewards with what they do have.

19:14 / **sent a delegation after him**: Fitzmyer (p. 1235) notes that this is the very word used by Josephus (*Antiquities* 17.299–302) in reference to the delegation sent to Rome to oppose Archelaus' bid to be made king (see note on 19:12 above).

19:17, 19 / The **trustworthy** servants are placed in **charge of ten** and **five cities**, which are part of the nobleman's new kingdom.

19:21 / **a hard man**: It would be better to translate "severe" or "strict." Matthew (25:24) uses the word "hard" (or "merciless"). Since the nobleman is probably meant to represent Jesus, Luke may have chosen a less harsh word.

You take out what you did not put in and reap what you did not sow: This is the reason given for the servant's fear. The saying has a proverbial ring to it (see Marshall, p. 707; Fitzmyer, p. 1237). Perhaps the servant's fear lay in his belief that if he made a profit, his master would take it all (since he takes what is not his) and not give him his commission. It is more likely, however, that the servant feared severe punishment should he make a poor investment and lose his mina. The harshness and thievery of the master (or king) should not be allegorized in an attempt to find an application to Jesus.

19:22–23 / Since the **wicked servant** knew what kind of man his **master** was, he should have known that he would be very dissatisfied with the return of the mina without any profit. Therefore, the servant's **own words** can be used to **judge** him. According to Deut. 23:19–20, money could be lent at interest to Gentiles but not to fellow Israelites.

19:27 / The king's **enemies** (his "subjects" in v. 14) are probably understood by Luke and his readers as the Jews who reject Jesus. Fitzmyer (p. 1238) states: "[Luke] may be hinting at some form of secular destruction of enemies, possibly at the destruction of Jerusalem by the Romans and the slaughter of many of its inhabitants."

This section comprises four parts: (1) the Triumphal Entry
(vv. 28–40), (2) the lament over Jerusalem (vv. 41–44), (3) the
Cleansing of the Temple (vv. 45–46), and (4) a summary of
Jerusalem's reaction to Jesus' teaching in the temple area (vv. 47–
48). The journey to Jerusalem is finally concluded. Now we see
Jesus presenting himself to the Jerusalem religious establishment
as the first phase of passion week. But before Jesus will be arrested (22:47–53), he will have a brief teaching ministry in Jerusalem (19:47–22:46).

19:28–40 / Because Jesus is hailed king in v. 38, Fitzmyer
(p. 1241) refers to this part of Luke's Gospel as Jesus' "Royal Entry"
(Tiede, p. 327: "royal procession"). The observation is an important one, for among the Synoptics only Luke adds, **the king**, to
the quotation of Ps. 118:26 (see John 12:15). The cry of "king" links
the Triumphal (or Royal) Entry to the preceding Parable of the
Ten Minas (19:11–27), where the man of noble birth is "appointed
king" (19:12). Jesus is that "man of noble birth" (as seen in the
Infancy Narrative, 1:26–38; 2:1–38) who is to be absent for a time,
but who will receive a kingdom.

As Jesus and his followers **approached Bethphage and Bethany** (see note below) **he sent two of his disciples** ahead to fetch
a **colt** (either a young horse or donkey; see Matt. 21:2). Some commentators have argued that Jesus' instructions in vv. 30–31 imply
that Jesus has made a special prior arrangement with the colt's
owner (so Marshall, p. 713), but this is not likely, for the sense
of the passage suggests that Jesus, as **Lord**, is in control. At the
very least it would suggest divine foreknowledge (so Fitzmyer,
p. 1249).

The disciples follow Jesus' instructions and so bring the
animal **to Jesus.** By placing **their cloaks on the colt** and **on the
road**, his followers demonstrate their enthusiastic support for
Jesus, whom they hail as their **king.** (Fitzmyer [p. 1250] notes that

the spreading of the garments upon the ground may allude "to
the homage paid to the newly anointed Jehu in 2 Kings 9:13.")
As Jesus approaches **Jerusalem** his followers, described as a **crowd
of disciples** (see note below), **began joyfully to praise God in
loud voices for all the miracles they had seen**. The first part of
their praise in v. 38 comes from Ps. 118:26, a greeting customarily
extended to pilgrims who have come to Jerusalem to celebrate the
Passover (Fitzmyer, p. 1246).

Luke adds **the king** to this quotation, thus underscoring
that Jesus' disciples do not regard Jesus as just another pilgrim.
Rather, Jesus is *the king*. Equally significant is Luke's omission of
the second part of the greeting as it occurs in Mark 11:10: "Blessed
is the coming kingdom of our father David!" By omitting this exclamation, Luke is careful to convey the idea that what has arrived is not the "kingdom," but the "king." Saying that the
kingdom is coming could leave the impression that the kingdom
of God should have been inaugurated with Jesus' arrival at Jerusalem (or shortly thereafter). This idea Luke is careful to avoid.
This may explain why Luke omits mention of the palm branches
(see Mark 11:8), which signify political ideas (see 2 Macc. 10:7;
Talbert, p. 179). As the man of noble birth in the parable above
(19:11–27), Jesus arrives in Jerusalem to be made king, but soon
he will depart and remain absent for a period of time. Only when
he returns will the kingdom be established.

Jesus' arrival at Jerusalem begins the "fulfillment" of what
awaits him in the city of destiny (9:51). Although the kingdom
of God is not to be inaugurated at this time (nor at the time immediately following Easter; see Acts 1:6–7), it is the beginning of
peace in heaven and glory in the highest. Because of what will
be accomplished in Jerusalem, Jesus' atoning death on the cross,
there will be "peace in heaven" and, in fulfillment of the angelic
announcement in 2:14, "peace on earth."

In stark contrast to the shouts of joyful exclamation, **some
of the Pharisees**, who have apparently accompanied Jesus since
13:31, tell **Jesus** to **rebuke** his **disciples**. This exchange is found only
in Luke and provides the transition to the rejection that Jesus will
soon experience in the city. Jesus' reply (. . . **the stones will cry
out**) indicates that his kingship is a reality whether it is recognized
by people or not. The inhabitants of Jerusalem may not accept
their true king, but the very stones of which the city is built do.

19:41–44 / The rejection by the Pharisees in v. 39 also prepares for Jesus' lament over the city of Jerusalem, a passage also
found only in Luke's Gospel. Jesus weeps not for himself, though
his own death is only days away, but he weeps for the city, knowing what grim fate awaits it.

When Jesus says, **If you, even you, had only known on this
day what would bring you peace**, he means if only the city had
known that it must receive Jesus as its king, if it was to find true,
lasting peace. Fitzmyer (pp. 1256–57) has noted that the reference
to "peace" may play on the popular understanding that the name
Jerusalem meant "peace" (from an association between Salem
[Gen. 14:18] and *šālôm*, the Hebrew word for "peace"; see note
below). Therefore, Jesus laments ironically that the city of peace
does not know what to do in order to secure peace.

In vv. 43–44 Jesus describes the coming destruction with
descriptive phrases derived from prophetic passages, for the most
part having to do with the first destruction of Jerusalem and the
first temple (see notes below). Jerusalem, the city of peace, will
be besieged by **enemies** who **will dash** it **to the ground**, not leaving **one stone on another**. The reason for this catastrophe, for this
inability to know **what would bring peace**, is because, Jesus says,
Jerusalem **did not recognize the time of God's coming**. The last
part of this sentence reads literally: "the day of your visitation."
The idea of the Lord "visiting" his people is found frequently in
the OT. In Exod. 3:16 God tells Moses that he has "visited" his
people in Egypt and knows of their suffering. This visitation is
not just a fact-finding visit; it is itself an act of deliverance. God
visited his people in Egypt in order to lead them out of slavery
to freedom. In Ruth 1:6 Naomi learns that God has visited his
people in Judah by giving them a good harvest. Finally, in 1 Sam.
1:19–21 the Lord visits Hannah, enabling her to conceive and give
birth to Samuel. The same idea is seen in Luke's Gospel as well.
After the birth of John the Baptist, his father Zechariah prophesies:
"Praise be to the Lord, the God of Israel, because he has come
and has redeemed his people" (1:68; see also 1:78). Later, when
Jesus raises up the son of the widow from Nain (7:11–17), the
amazed crowd proclaims: "A great prophet has appeared among
us . . . God has come to help [lit. "visited"] his people" (7:16).
Clearly, then, Luke understands the appearance of Jesus as one
of these "visitations" of God through which an act of redemp-

tion will be accomplished. Because the people do not recognize this visitation, however, but reject Jesus, disaster and destruction await them. Realizing their blindness, Jesus weeps over the city.

19:45–46 / Luke's account of the cleansing of the temple is briefest of the Gospel accounts (see note below). Luke's account is briefest because he has omitted the various details regarding those who were selling and changing money (see Matt. 21:12; Mark 11:15; John 2:14–16). Also omitted in Luke is the cursing of the fig tree (see Mark 11:12–14), as well as a few other less noteworthy details.

The point of Jesus' action is twofold: (1) Positively, Jesus purges the temple in order to prepare it as a place where he can teach the crowds (as indicated in v. 47); (2) negatively, Jesus purges the temple because of his objection to the buying and selling. It should be remembered that wealth, property, and money are items of major concern in Luke. The mercantile activities of those within the temple precincts amounted to a violation of the purpose of the temple. Instead of being a place where God is worshipped, it has become a place where profits are made (recall Luke 16:13, "You cannot serve both God and Money"). While **driving out those who were selling,** Jesus quotes Isa. 56:7: **My house will be a house of prayer.** This is the temple's true purpose; it is a place where people commune with God. **But,** Jesus says alluding to Jer. 7:11, **you have made it "a den of robbers."** Both OT passages utilized in this saying are noteworthy.

The text from Isaiah 56 is part of a passage that anticipates the day when salvation will come and when the Lord's deliverance will be revealed (56:1); it will be a time when forgiveness will be offered (56:3, 6) and eunuchs will be welcomed into God's house (56:4). Because of the acceptance of foreign peoples, God's "house [or temple] will be called a house of prayer for all nations" (56:7). Ironically, at the Passover Jews and proselytes from many nations come to the temple in Jerusalem, but instead of entering a house of prayer, as the Isaianic passage describes, they enter a place of business.

The second part of Jesus' statement is taken from Jer. 7:1–15, a passage where the sixth-century prophet condemned those who had desecrated the first temple with their idolatry and crimes (among which is stealing; Jer. 7:9). Passover celebrants were almost surely being overcharged for sacrificial birds and animals (see note below), and were perhaps even being cheated when money was exchanged for the shekels needed to buy these animals.

Jesus' expulsion of those who were selling (and exchanging) would have been viewed by the temple leaders as contempt for their authority and possibly as contempt for the religion itself. It is sometimes wondered how Jesus could have gotten away with this action, for temple police were always present to prevent just such an occurrence. (Fitzmyer [p. 1264] raises the question but offers no answer.) Although far from certain, a plausible answer has been put forth that the year in which Jesus cleansed the temple was the first year that sellers of animals were permitted into the temple precincts (see notes below). If this is the case, then Caiaphas would hold the dubious distinction of being the first high priest to authorize this business activity in the temple. (The custom of exchanging money within the temple's precincts had apparently been established earlier.) Opinion over the appropriateness of such a new policy would have been sharply divided. It may be (and here we are only guessing) that many priests, Levites, and temple guards were looking on sheepishly when Jesus strode boldly into the temple and began driving out the sellers and money changers. Indeed, quite possibly Jesus' action not only did not provoke antagonism from most of the religious figures (although his action surely was upsetting to the merchants), but it may have actually been looked upon with secret approval. Seen in this light, it becomes understandable how Jesus could assault the temple and then not only escape arrest but continue teaching in the temple precincts.

19:47–48 / Following his dramatic entry, Jesus began to teach **every day** in the **temple** precincts. The **chief** (or ruling) **priests, the teachers of the law, and the leaders among the people were trying to kill him**. We have been told from time to time in Luke that a plot against Jesus was afoot (6:11; 11:53–54). This statement comes immediately after the incident of the temple cleansing (vv. 45–46) and is probably to be understood as in part a result of Jesus' action. They have plotted against Jesus for some time, but since he has directly challenged the religious authorities, steps must be taken to do away with him. Thus, the summary is a transition connecting Jesus' public ministry, climaxed by the temple cleansing, and his arrest, trial, and crucifixion.

The authorities, however, **could not find any way to do** away with Jesus, **because** he was surrounded by too many **people**. Therefore Jesus is able to continue his ministry within Jerusalem, at least for a few days.

Additional Notes §49

19:28 / **he went on ahead, going up to Jerusalem**: The city of Jesus' destiny. On Jerusalem see *HBD*, pp. 463–73. See also the note on v. 42 below.

19:29 / **Bethphage and Bethany at the hill called the Mount of Olives**: These small villages were situated "on the hill overlooking Jerusalem from the east (above the Kidron Valley)" (Fitzmyer, p. 1247). On Bethphage see Fitzmyer, p. 1247; on Bethany see *HBD*, p. 105; Fitzmyer, p. 1248. On the Mount of Olives see Luke 22:39 and note there; *HBD*, pp. 728–29; Fitzmyer, p. 1248.

19:30 / Whereas Mark (11:2, 4, 5, 7) and Luke (19:30, 33) know of only one animal, a **colt** (see also John 12:14–15), upon which Jesus rode as he entered Jerusalem, Matthew (21:2, 7) mentions a "donkey" *and* her "colt." According to Matt. 21:7, Jesus rides upon both animals (surely successively, not simultaneously!). What has apparently prompted Matthew's mention of the second animal is the quotation from Zech. 9:9 (which is prefaced by a phrase from Isa. 62:11): "See, your king comes to you, righteous and having salvation, gentle and riding on a donkey, on a colt, the foal of a donkey." The normal understanding of Zech. 9:9 is that only one animal is in view, that is, the king is mounted upon a donkey, *even* (or "that is") upon its colt. Matthew has taken what usually is translated "even" in the sense of "and" and so includes a second animal. Has the Matthean evangelist misunderstood the grammar of Zech. 9:9? Gundry (p. 409) believes that it is unlikely that Matthew has misunderstood Zechariah's synonymous parallelism. (The grammatical construction that is involved, after all, is commonplace.) The second animal has been introduced because of Mark's reference in 11:3 to the colt as one that had never been ridden, and since unridden colts are still with their mothers, Matthew has made no more than a logical inference.

19:35 / **put Jesus on it**: The same word is used in reference to Solomon in 1 Kings 1:33 (Schweizer, p. 298). Jesus' royal procession also echoes that of Jehu (2 Kings 9:13; Tiede, p. 329).

19:37 / Unlike Mark (11:8), Luke states that Jesus was hailed by **the whole crowd of disciples**. This distinction anticipates the hostile reception of the Pharisees in v. 39 below and, perhaps, also clarifies why a crowd that so joyfully welcomes Jesus would in a few days' time cry out for his blood (23:18, 23). Thus, Luke solves this problem by showing that it was Jesus' disciples who welcomed Jesus, but it was another crowd, among whom no doubt were Pharisees and religious leaders, that called for his crucifixion. On **Mount of Olives** see note on 22:39 below.

19:41–44 / In a fascinating study C. H. Dodd ("The Fall of Jerusalem and the 'Abomination of Desolation'," *JRS* 37 [1947], pp. 47–54) tried to show that Luke's passages predicting Jerusalem's destruction (19:42–44; 21:20–24) derive from an early oracle, pre-dating the destruction itself in A.D. 70, and are not written after the destruction, as is often supposed. Dodd pointed out that the language describing the destruction is borrowed from the Greek translation of the OT (LXX). There are five distinct descriptions of hostile action taken against Jerusalem that reflect this OT language (Fitzmyer, pp. 1258–59): (1) *your enemies will build an embankment against you:* Fitzmyer suggests that the phrase may have been borrowed from Isa. 29:3: "I will encircle you Ariel [a name for Jerusalem], throw up an embankment, and set towers about you" (see also Isa. 37:33; Jer. 6:6–21; Ezek. 4:1–3). (2) *and encircle you:* This may echo Isa. 29:3: "I will encircle you" (see also 2 Kgs 6:14). (3) *and hem you in on every side:* This phrase may echo parts of the following passages: "put siege works against it, and build a siege wall against it" (Ezek. 4:2; 21:22); "Nebuchadrezzar king of Babylon came with all his army against Jerusalem, and they laid siege to it" (Jer. 52:4). (4) *They will dash you to the ground, you and the children within your walls:* In reference to the hope of judgment against Babylon, Ps. 137:9 proclaims: "Happy shall he be who takes your little ones and dashes them against the rock!" (RSV). See also Hos. 10:14 (". . . mothers were dashed in pieces with their children . . ."). In reference to the fall of Nineveh, Nahum 3:10 states that "her little ones were dashed in pieces" (see also 2 Kgs 8:12). (5) *They will not leave one stone on another:* Fitzmyer (pp. 1258–59) suggests that 2 Sam. 17:13 may be echoed here: "so that not even a stone will be left there" (see also Ezek. 26:12 where the prophet predicts that the stones and timbers of Tyre will be picked up and thrown into the sea). Jesus' oracle concludes with a reference to Jerusalem's failure to "recognize the time of God's coming to you" (lit. "recognize the time of your visitation"), which is probably an allusion to Jer. 6:15 in the LXX: "in the time of their visitation they will perish" (see also Jer. 10:15; Fitzmyer, p. 1259). Dodd (p. 52) states: "It appears, then, that not only are the two Lucan oracles composed entirely from the language of the Old Testament, but the conception of the coming disaster which the author has in mind is a generalized picture of the fall of Jerusalem as imaginatively presented by the prophets. So far as any historical event has coloured the picture, it is not Titus' capture of Jerusalem in A.D. 70, but Nebuchadrezzar's capture in 586 B.C. There is no single trait of the forecast which cannot be documented directly out of the Old Testament." Dodd, however, believes that the oracles were uttered and "circulated in Judaea before Titus' siege of Jerusalem, but at a time when a war with Rome was a menacing possibility" and that "in Christian circles they [the oracles] were believed to go back to Jesus" (p. 52). Because the actual language of the oracles is derived from the LXX, the Lucan form of the oracles almost certainly does not go back to Jesus. However, there is no compelling reason to conclude that Jesus did not predict Jerusalem's destruction. (It is highly probable that he did and that his prediction of the destruction of the city and its temple was a major factor in the religious establishment's turn against him.) Luke has apparently obtained a tradition of such a prediction that, in passing from Aramaic (the language of Jesus) to Greek (the language of the LXX), has been worded in terms of the vocabulary and imagery of the LXX.

What was hinted at in Luke 13:35 is now made explicit. Jerusalem has not known the "things that make for peace," and the city has not recognized "the time of [its] visitation" (v. 44). Now the city faces destruction, and for this reason Jesus weeps. How J. T. Sanders (p. 210) can say that there is present no element of sadness in this passage is curious, for it appears that this is the very element that Luke himself has added (i.e., v. 41). There is nothing hateful or anti-Semitic about this pericope. To interpret it in such a way is to miss the pathos entirely. Indeed, as Tiede (p. 332) has noted, Luke's attitude toward Jerusalem is much more sympathetic than that of the Jewish historian Josephus who, speaking of Jerusalem's catastrophic defeat, believed that God sided with the Romans (*War* 6.392–413) and that "God perverted [the Jews'] judgment so that they devised for their salvation a remedy that was more disastrous than destruction" (*War* 4.573). The perspective of the Third Evangelist is no more anti-Semitic than that of Josephus.

19:42 / **peace**: Jesus' statement reflects a popular etymology that finds *šālôm* (peace) in the name Jeru*salem*. According to *Genesis Rabbah* 56.10 (cited by Lachs, p. 346) Jerusalem means "I shall see peace."

19:45–46 / When one compares the Synoptic account of the cleansing of the temple with that found in the Gospel of John, it is noticed that, whereas the episode occurs near the *end* of Jesus' ministry in the Synoptics (Matt. 21:12–17; Mark 11:15–19; Luke 19:45–46), in John it occurs near the *beginning* (2:13–22). Because of this discrepancy some have suggested that the four Gospels are telling us of two separate temple cleansings, one at the beginning of Jesus' ministry, and the other at the end. Many, if not most scholars, however, tend to regard the Synoptic and Johannine accounts as two versions of the *same* episode, an episode that actually took place near the end of Jesus' ministry, as the Synoptic Gospels tell us (see additional notes). Brown suggests that since John wanted the Lazarus story (John 11) to be the climactic "sign" that provokes Jesus' enemies to plot his death, he brought the temple cleansing episode forward so that it would follow closely after the appearance of John the Baptist. The reason for this may be seen, says Brown, in Mal. 3:1 where in the first half of the verse the Lord promises to send his "messenger" (i.e., John the Baptist; John 1:6–8, 15, 19–36), while in the second half of the verse the Lord (i.e., Jesus) "will suddenly come to his temple" (John 2:13–22). If Jesus' cleansing of the temple was to be understood as a fulfillment of this verse from Malachi, then it would be better to have Jesus enter the temple immediately after John's preaching. If the Synoptic positioning of the episode near the end of Jesus' life is original, then Brown's explanation for the Fourth Evangelist's relocation of the episode is plausible and as good as any. Fitzmyer (p. 1265), however, suspects that the cleansing was one of Jesus' first acts in his public ministry, as possibly suggested by his portrayal by the Baptist as a fiery reformer (Luke 3:17). Because the Synoptic Gospels, unlike John, have Jesus make only one trip to Jerusalem, his final trip, it was necessary to have Jesus cleanse the temple at that time, that is, at the end of his ministry. Both arguments are plausible and it not easy to decide between them. In view of the fact that such an assault upon the religious establishment would have undoubtedly incurred the wrath of the religious authorities, as the Synoptics actually depict, it is hard to imagine how Jesus could have survived for very long. Also in view of the fact that the Gospel of John from a literary point of view appears not to follow a strict chronological sequence of events, it seems best to this commentator to view the Synoptic sequence as more original.

Victor Eppstein ("The Historicity of the Gospel Account of the Cleansing of the Temple," *ZNW* 55 [1964], pp. 42–58) has suggested that Caiaphas was the first high priest to authorize the sale of sacrificial animals in the temple precincts (probably within the Court of the Gentiles). Caiaphas did this, Eppstein conjectures, out of greed and because of a personal dispute with the Sanhedrin. He thinks that when Jesus became aware of these factors he took action in the temple. Eppstein further argues that because Caiaphas' impure motives were probably well known, Jesus' action would have been viewed sympathetically by most of the onlookers. Hence Jesus was not arrested on the spot by the Levitical temple police. Eppstein's hypothesis is plausible, but it rests on much speculation.

19:45, 47 / On the Synoptic and Johannine accounts as two versions of the *same* episode, see Raymond E. Brown, *The Gospel according to John I–XII*, AB 29 [Garden City: Doubleday, 1966], p. 118. The area of the **temple** which Jesus entered when he cleansed it and later when he began to teach is the outer court area. Jesus did not enter the temple sanctuary (which in the Greek would be a different word) where the "holy of holies" is located. See *HBD*, pp. 1021–29.

19:47 / **the chief priests** have been mentioned only twice before (3:2; 9:22), but from now on they will appear more frequently as Jesus' enemies (20:1, 19; 22:2, 4, 50, 52, 54, 66; 23:4, 10, 13; 24:20). Many of the chief priests were wealthy and exercised considerable political power in Jerusalem. Their power and influence vanished with the destruction of the temple in A.D. 70. See *HBD*, pp. 821–23.

the teachers of the law: See note on 5:21 above.

the leaders among the people: The reference to the leaders of the people is a general designation which would include the religious leaders already mentioned in v. 47, as well as non-clergy members of the Sanhedrin (22:66).

§50 Disputes with Religious Authorities (Luke 20:1-47)

Luke 20 is a chapter in which we see Jesus teaching in the temple (19:47-48), having cleansed it so that he may reside in its precincts (19:45-46). The atmosphere is tense. The many questions put to Jesus are hostile and are designed to trap him into making an incriminating response (see esp. vv. 20-26). The chapter may be divided into the following six parts: (1) the question about Jesus' authority (vv. 1-8); (2) the Parable of the Wicked Vineyard Tenants (vv. 9-19); (3) the question about paying taxes (vv. 20-26); (4) the question about the resurrection (vv. 27-40); (5) the question about the Son of David (vv. 41-44); and (6) Jesus' warning about the teachers of the law (vv. 45-47). Virtually all of this material has been derived from Mark 11:27-12:40.

20:1-8 / In 19:47 we were told that the chief priests and the teachers of the law desired to do away with Jesus. Now these same persons approach Jesus, questioning his authority to do the things that he has done. The second question in v. 2 is more specific: **Who gave you this authority?** The question is a trap. Had Jesus answered that his authority to act the way in which he has acted (cleanse and teach within the temple) had been given him by God himself, the religious authorities could have accused Jesus of blasphemy and so could have strengthened their case against him. Although Jesus does not provide a direct answer to their questions, his reply is much more than a dodge.

By asking if **John's baptism** was **from heaven, or from men,** Jesus has forced his opponents either to deny John's heavenly authority altogether, which would fly in the face of popular opinion (even Pharisees had gone out to John), or to acknowledge John's authority, which would undermine their challenge to Jesus, since he had himself been baptized by John, who had declared Jesus to be superior (3:16). Of course, had they acknowledged John's heavenly authority, their indifference to John's ministry would then be difficult to explain or excuse. Their dilemma is acute. To answer that John's authority was "from men" might provoke the crowd to violence, while to answer that his authority was "from God" would leave themselves open to the criticism that they had failed to heed God's summons to repentance and, worse yet, had opposed John's mightier successor. Consequently, the religious authorities "feign ignorance" (Fitzmyer, p. 1273). Jesus, however, recognizes that in reality they have refused to answer, and so he too refuses to answer the question put to him.

20:9–19 / The Parable of the Wicked Vineyard Tenants follows the preceding exchange between Jesus and the Jerusalem authorities (20:1–8) and makes exceedingly clear Jesus' indictment of the religious establishment (see v. 19). This parable in effect summarizes the whole of the biblical history, including the gospel story. **Servant** after **servant** is sent, but the **tenants** refuse to hand over the **fruit of the vineyard**. Finally, the **son** of the **owner of the vineyard** is sent, but he is murdered. This outrage necessitates the punishment of the **tenants** and the transfer of the **vineyard to others**.

In the Marcan version of the Parable of the Wicked Tenants (12:1–12) there are approximately one dozen words borrowed from Isa. 5:1–7, Isaiah's Song of the Vineyard. Although Luke has retained only a few of these words in an effort to streamline the Marcan parable, the parable's essential indebtedness to Isaiah should not be overlooked. In his Song of the Vineyard the eighth-century prophet sings a parable describing God's loving care for his "vineyard" (his people Israel). He has denied his vineyard nothing. But when it is harvest time the vineyard does not yield good grapes, only sour grapes. What will God do? He will abandon his vineyard, allowing it to be drought-stricken, choked with weeds, and trampled under foot.

Later Jewish interpretation came to understand Isaiah's Song of the Vineyard as a prophecy of the destruction of the temple, a prophecy fulfilled when in 586 B.C. Nebuchadrezzar conquered Jerusalem. When Jesus utilizes the language of this Isaianic parable in order to tell his own parable, his audience cannot help but sense the judgmental tone of the parable. Whereas in Isaiah's version the vineyard itself (the people) is guilty, in Jesus' parable it is not the vineyard, but the tenants (=the religious authorities). They are the reason that God does not receive the fruit that is due. The people's leaders are selfish and disobedient. They will have to be replaced with new leaders who are obedient and responsive to God. This leadership consists, of course, of those whom Jesus has taught. His disciples will replace the old Jerusalem establishment and will serve God and his people more faithfully (see note below). In the context of Jesus' ministry this has reference only to new leadership *within Israel*. Of course, by the time of Luke, this new leadership was undoubtedly identified with the church (see note below).

Before his shocked audience can recover, Jesus asks them what Ps. 118:22 means. Quite possibly, especially in Luke's time, this OT passage was understood as implying the laying of a new foundation upon which a new faith would be built (cf. 1 Cor. 3:10–11; Eph. 2:20). Jesus is the **capstone** (or "cornerstone") that **the builders rejected** (as they had rejected the "son" in the parable in vv. 14–15), which will become the foundation. There is an additional touch of irony here when it is noted that the religious leaders called themselves the "Builders of Israel" (Fitzmyer, p. 1282). Israel's religious leaders, the "Builders," rejected the very one who would become the capstone for God's work to come (see note below).

Luke adds a unique saying (v. 18) that adds further interpretation to the **stone** of v. 17. This stone will become a stumbling block, that is, belief in the rejected and crucified Jesus as Messiah will not be easy. The gospel proclamation will cause offense. The stone will also fall in judgment upon those who reject the gospel. This is the significance of the second part of the saying. In v. 19 Luke makes it clear that the **teachers of the law and the chief priests**, the persons who had questioned Jesus' authority in vv. 1–2 above and who had begun planning to murder Jesus (see 19:47–48), realize that Jesus **had spoken this parable against them**. Although they desired to **arrest him immediately**, they had to wait for a more convenient time.

20:20–26 / The religious authorities try to trap Jesus by drawing from him a statement that could be construed as treasonous. Since the question about his authority had failed to trap Jesus, because the real motive underlying the question had been readily apparent, the religious authorities this time **sent spies, who pretended to be honest** (or sincere). Their question is prefaced in v. 21 in such a way as to coax a frank, but dangerous, response from Jesus. It is as though they have told Jesus: "We know that you always tell the truth, no matter whose toes get stepped on." Having said this, they ask Jesus if it is lawful (according to the law of Moses) **to pay taxes to Caesar or not?** Popular Jewish sentiment was strongly opposed to Roman taxation. Revolts from time to time had broken out. No doubt Jesus' opponents hoped that Jesus would answer their question by declaring that God's people were not to pay taxes to the Roman Empire. (In 23:2 he would, in fact, be accused of taking this very position.) Since, according to 20:20, his opponents were trying to build a case against him for the **governor**, such a popular answer would have provided them the very grounds that they sought for accusing and arresting Jesus. However, Jesus **saw through their duplicity** and requested to be shown a **denarius**. Ironically, the very ones hoping to lure Jesus into making an answer that would have been popular among his fellow Jews, but seditious to the civil authorities, have in their possession money that symbolized the very presence of the Roman Empire that they so detested. *They* have and produce the coin; *Jesus* does not, for he has none. **Whose portrait** is on the coin? **Caesar's.** Since the coin bears the image of the Roman Emperor, it belongs to him, but what bears God's image (humankind itself, Gen. 1:26–27) is **God's** (see note below). Once again, Jesus' answer proves to be too much for his opponents.

20:27–40 / The third question put to Jesus concerns the teaching of the resurrection. The **Sadducees** (see note below), who do not believe in the resurrection, ask Jesus a rather ridiculous question, one designed to show the incompatability of the law of Moses and belief in the resurrection. The Sadducees allude to Deut. 25:5 and Gen. 38:8, where the laws of what would eventually be called "levirate marriage" are laid down. **If a man's brother dies and leaves a wife but no children, the man must marry the widow and have children for his brother.** The question of the Sadducees supposes that **seven** brothers successively **married** one **woman**. In the event of the resurrection, **whose wife will she be, since the seven were married to her?** What the Sadducees entertain is that the resurrection could leave many men and women who kept Moses' laws of levirate marriage in what would amount to adulterous relationships. Undoubtedly to the Sadducees the whole question was amusing, and they no doubt often teased their Pharisaic rivals with it. Jesus answers by noting that the question was based upon the false premise that the institution of marriage would continue into the next life. Human existence in the **age** to come may be compared to that of the **angels**, who are immortal and who do not **marry**. Therefore, the idea of resurrection, which pertains to the next life, is not at all incompatible with the levirate laws of Moses, which pertain to this life.

In the next phase of his answer Jesus shows from the law of **Moses** itself (which the Sadducees respected) that **the dead rise**. When **God** spoke to Moses from the burning **bush** (Exod. 3:2–6) he identified himself as the **God** of the patriarchs **Abraham, Isaac,** and **Jacob**. Such a statement implies that there is yet hope of life (resurrection life) for them, even though it had been centuries since their deaths. The last phrase of v. 38, **for to him all are alive**, is found only in Luke and may be the evangelist's attempt to clarify the idea of life after death to his predominantly Gentile audience. The point of Jesus' answer, at least as it should be understood in the context of the whole passage, is that at death the righteous are in some sense alive to God and yet await the **resurrection**. Fitzmyer (pp. 1301–2) has shown that there is evidence that first-century Palestinian Jews believed that the soul was immortal and so at death would enter the presence of God, and that at some future time there would be a resurrection which would bring about the reunion of soul and body. (Perhaps this is how Paul's statements in 2 Cor. 5:8 and 1 Thess. 4:13–17 are to be harmonized.) The effect of his answer is seen in the approving response of **some of the teachers of the law**, who no doubt were pleased that the Sadducees had been answered so well.

20:41–44 / Having silenced his critics, Jesus takes the initiative and asks his own question, one that raises an interesting question about the **Christ**. Jesus' first question, **How is it? . . .** does not imply that he thinks that the Christ is not supposed to be a descendant **of David**, but it asks how he can be in light of Ps. 110:1, a psalm attributed to David and therefore cited by Jesus as potentially having messianic significance: "**The Lord** [God] **said to my Lord** [the Christ] . . . " That is, Jesus asks, "How can the Messiah [or Christ] be both David's Son [as held in popular opinion and suggested in certain prophetic passages] and lord [as

David himself states in Ps. 110:1]?" (Marshall, p. 745). Jesus' question in v. 44 is based on the assumption that to be a descendant of someone is to be lesser. For example, the descendants of Abraham are lesser than the great patriarch. Jesus' question would be puzzling to his original hearers, but not to the believing community; they would understand it in the light of the Easter event. How can any descendant of David, even if he *is* the Messiah, be David's Lord? He can be his Lord through the resurrection (see Acts 2:36).

20:45–47 / The section ends with Jesus' warning **to his disciples** to **beware the teachers of the law** who love to parade their religion but have no compassion for the poor and the defenseless. His warning is not intended to protect the disciples *from* these teachers, it is intended to warn them to take heed lest they become *like* them. Because of their (the teachers of the law) position of authority, which they abuse, they **will be punished most severely**. This passage probably should be linked, at least thematically, with the one that follows (21:1–4). The poverty of the widow, who gave her last pennies to the temple, illustrates what Jesus meant when he said that the teachers **devour widows' houses**. The poor are robbed, and the oppressive deeds are covered up with a show of prayer and religiosity.

Additional Notes §50

20:1 / **temple**: See note on 19:45, 47 above.

20:6 / **they are persuaded that John was a prophet**: See 1:76; 3:2–20; 7:26–30; 16:16.

20:9–16 / In the Marcan version (12:1–9) of this parable the vineyard has, among other things, a watchtower and a winepress. All of these details come from Isaiah's Song of the Vineyard (Isa. 5:1–7). Later Jewish interpretation equated the watchtower with the temple, while the winepress was understood as referring to the altar (see, for example, t. *Sukkah* 3.15). Thus, the destruction of the watchtower and the winepress was understood as a veiled prophecy of the coming destruction of the temple and its altar. The form and function of Jesus' parable and Isaiah's song are essentially the same. Both invited the hearers to pass judgment upon themselves. (For further details see Craig A. Evans, "On the Vineyard Parables of Isaiah 5 and Mark 12," *BZ* 28 [1984], pp. 82–86.)

20:16 / **to others**: J. T. Sanders (p. 212) thinks that the parable may teach that the kingdom will be taken from the Jews and will be given to the Gentiles. This is not likely. It is only "an attack on the religious bureaucracy" (Talbert, p. 189) that warns that the new religious authorities will be the Twelve (see Luke 22:28-30; Acts 1:15-26).

20:17 / Some have suggested that Ps. 118:22 was related to the Parable of the Wicked Tenants because of a word play involving "son" and "stone." In Hebrew the expression "the son" and "the stone" sound quite similar. This is probably the reason that the Aramaic version (the Targum) of Ps. 118:22 actually reads: "the son which the builders rejected." Thus, the parable and the Psalm quotation are linked together by the related theme of the rejected son. For this reason, and others, Klyne R. Snodgrass (*The Parable of the Wicked Tenants: An Inquiry into Parable Interpretation*, WUNT 27 [Tübingen: Mohr (Siebeck), 1983]) has argued that the citation of Psalm 118 was an original component of the parable and not, as most critics have either argued or assumed, a later Christian addition.

20:18 / This saying is reminiscent of the "stumbling-stone" passages found in the NT. In Rom. 9:32-33 Paul alludes to and quotes parts of Isa. 8:14 and 28:16. The idea is that Jesus is both a precious foundation stone (for him who has faith, Isa. 28:16) and a stone of stumbling (to the one who has no faith, Isa. 8:14) and crushing (see Dan. 2:34). See also 1 Pet. 2:6-8 where Ps. 118:22 is quoted along with and between the two passages from Isaiah. In one rabbinic text, which is apparently messianic (so Lachs, p. 355) Ps. 118:22 is cited along with a saying that parallels Luke's unique saying about the stone that crushes: "[The Israelites] are compared to stones, as it says, 'From thence the shepherd of the stone [i.e., Messiah] of Israel' (Gen. 49:24); 'The stone which the builders rejected' (Ps. 118:22). But the other nations are likened to potsherds, as it says, 'And he shall break it as a potter's vessel is broken' (Isa. 30:14). If a stone falls on a pot, woe to the pot! If a pot falls on a stone, woe to the pot! In either case, woe to the pot! So whoever ventures to attack [the Israelites] receives his desserts on their account" (*Esther Rabbah* 7.10); translation based on Maurice Simon, *Midrash Rabbah: Esther* (London and New York: Soncino, 1983), p. 85. This midrash also cites Dan. 2:34.

20:19 / **parable**: See note on 5:36 above. Because Jesus has been speaking to the "people" (v. 9), who respond to the Parable of the Wicked Vineyard Tenants with "May this never be!" (v. 16), J. T. Sanders (pp. 211-13) believes that Luke really intends the parable to apply to the entire nation, and not just to the religious leaders (as, contrary to Sanders, is made explicit here in v. 19). The response of the people means no more than that they hope that what Jesus has described in his parable will not befall their religious leaders and institutions (see Marshall, pp. 731-32; Fitzmyer, p. 1285; Tiede, p. 343).

20:20–26 / For additional NT teaching on the Christian's relationship to civil government see Rom. 13:1-7 and 1 Pet. 2:13-17. These passages acknowledge civil authority as established by God, and therefore **taxes** are to be paid.

20:22 / **Caesar**: That is, Tiberius Julius Caesar Augustus (see 3:1). Since the reign of Julius Caesar (assassinated in 44 B.C.) the Roman emperors called themselves "Caesar."

20:24 / **a denarius**: See the note on 7:41 above. Coins bearing the **portrait and inscription** of the Roman emperor were understood as belonging to the emperor (Fitzmyer, p. 1296). For a discussion of Jewish responses to Roman taxes and coinage see Lachs, pp. 358–59.

20:27 / **Sadducees**: The name is apparently derived from Zadok (2 Sam. 8:17). "They were priestly and lay aristocrats" (Fitzmyer, p. 1303). See *HBD*, pp. 891–92. They did not believe in the idea of resurrection. The idea of the resurrection was defended by Pharisees who often appealed to Exod. 6:4; 15:1; Num. 15:31; 18:28; Deut. 31:16. Fitzmyer (p. 1303) notes that "the rabbis also referred at times to non-pentateuchal parts of the OT: Job 19:26; Ps. 16:9, 11; Isa. 26:19."

20:28 / **Teacher**: See note on 7:40 above.

20:29 / **seven**: There is no theological meaning behind this number, although seven was "a favorite number among the Jews" (Fitzmyer, p. 1304).

20:36 / **like the angels**: The Sadducees, of course, did not believe in angels either! See *1 Enoch* 104:4, 6; *2 Bar.* 51:10.

20:38 / Fitzmyer (pp. 1301, 1307) has pointed out that this saying, especially as seen in the last phrase, is very similar to 4 Macc. 7:19: " . . . they believe that they, like our patriarchs Abraham and Isaac and Jacob did not die to God, but live to God."

20:43 / **footstool**: In great antiquity vanquished enemies were often depicted as bowed before the conqueror, whose feet would rest upon them.

20:44 / Fitzmyer (p. 1315) notes that "order in patriarchal society would demand that a son call the father lord, not vice versa, for whereas 'son' would connote subordination, 'lord' connotes the opposite."

20:46 / **teachers of the law**: Lit., "scribes." See note on 5:17.
flowing robes: Possibly robes similar to those worn by the priests (cf. Josephus, *Antiquities*, 3.151).
important seats in the synagogues: See 11:43.
places of honor at banquets: See 14:7.

20:47 / In what ways did the scribes **devour widows' houses**? Fitzmyer (p. 1318) lists six suggestions that have been made: (1) Scribes accepted fees for legal aid, though it was not permitted. (2) Acting as legal trustees, scribes cheated widows out of their estates. (3) Exploiting their religious and social prestige, scribes freeloaded upon widows. (4) Scribes may have mismanaged the property of widows who had dedicated themselves to temple service. (5) Scribes accepted payments for prayers. (6) Scribes foreclosed on houses that had been pledged against loans that were impossible to repay. Which of these abuses Jesus may have had in mind is impossible to say.

In the previous chapter we saw Jesus teaching in the temple precincts. There Jesus was asked hostile questions with the view to trap him into saying something for which he could be arrested. In the present chapter we shall see Jesus still teaching in the temple (from v. 1 to v. 38), only this time the teaching is about the temple itself. Most of the teaching concerns the coming destruction of the temple and the appearance of the Son of Man. The chapter may be divided as follows: (1) the Widow's Offering (vv. 1–4); (2) the Prediction of the Temple's Destruction (vv. 5–7); (3) Troubles and Persecutions (vv. 8–19); (4) the Destruction of Jerusalem (vv. 20–24); (5) the Coming of the Son of Man (vv. 25–28); (6) the Parable of the Fig Tree (vv. 29–33); and (7) the Admonition to Watch (vv. 34–38). With the exception of the last part, which is found only in Luke, the evangelist has derived his materials from Mark 12:41–13:31.

21:1–4 / The episode of the **poor widow** who gave to the **temple treasury** only **two very small copper coins** (see note below) stands in contrast to the nature of the religious piety and practice of the teachers of the law described above in 20:46–47, who "devour widows' houses." While these very religious-appearing persons swindle the poor and defenseless, this particular widow drops into the treasury what little she has **to live on**. Although tiny in comparison to the much larger gifts of the **rich**, her gift, declares Jesus, is **more than all the others**. For while it was no inconvenience for the wealthy to give greater amounts, it was with significant personal hardship that the poor widow made her contribution.

In view of Jesus' condemnation of Pharisaic oral tradition that was more concerned with ritual than with human needs (see Mark 7:9–13), one may wonder if Jesus was praising the widow's action (as is often assumed; see Marshall, pp. 750–52), or if he saw in the episode an illustration of what he had said earlier in 20:46–47. In other words, because of the teaching of the religious authorities of her day, the poor widow gives up her last penny and so is victimized for the sake of an oppressive religious system. Her wealth, or what little wealth there was, was "devoured" (see v. 47). Jesus' statement in 21:4, therefore, is not one of praise, but one of lament (so Fitzmyer, p. 1321; Tiede, pp. 354–55). It may be because of this great economic injustice that Luke is satisfied to have this episode immediately precede Jesus' prediction of the temple's destruction.

21:5–7 / The Lucan eschatological discourse differs from its Marcan source in one major way: The "end" (see v. 9) refers not to the return of the Son of Man, but to the destruction of the **temple**. This can be seen most clearly when one compares the question of the disciples in Mark 13:4 with the Lucan version of the question in 21:7. In Mark the disciples want to know *two* things: When the temple will be destroyed, and when the end will come. (In Matt. 24:3 it is even more explicit: when will the temple be destroyed, and what is the sign of Jesus' return and the end of the age?) In Luke, however, the question concerns only the destruction of the temple: **when will these things happen? And what will be the sign that they are about to take place?** Although the questions are put in the plural, there is only one event that is in mind, and that event is the destruction of the temple. A second observation that further demonstrates that Luke has only the end of the temple in view is that, unlike Mark 13:1–3, where Jesus speaks his discourse on the Mount of Olives overlooking the temple, according to Luke 21:37–38, Jesus remains in the temple, thus underscoring that his teaching concerns the temple.

Whereas in Mark 13:1 Jesus' prediction is prompted by the disciples' exclamation concerning the beauty of the "stones and buildings," in Luke 21:5 we are told only that the **disciples were remarking about how the temple was adorned with beautiful stones and with gifts dedicated to God.** This conversation prompts Jesus to predict that every **stone** will be **thrown down.** With this prediction the eschatological discourse begins, but one should remember that the "end" that is predicted has to do with the destruction of the temple. The coming of the Son of Man is carefully separated from this destruction (whereas in Mark 13, as well as in Matthew 24, one is given the impression that the destruction inaugurates the "end" which culminates in the return of the Son of Man). Jesus' startling prediction elicits further questions from his disciples. They want to know when the destruction will take place and what signs will portend this destruction. This exchange—the prediction and the questions—sets up the subsequent eschatological discourse.

21:8–19 / The signs that precede the destruction of the temple are characterized by deceptive claims to be the Messiah (**"I am he"**) and to know the time (**"The time is near"**). The disciples are to ignore them. In Luke's church these statements may very well have been applied to the messianic claimants who arose just prior to the war with Rome (e.g., Menachem) or to various frauds and false prophets who during the war with Rome promised miraculous deliverance and claimed that God's kingdom was about to appear. Jesus further instructs his followers not to be **frightened** when they **hear of wars and revolutions** (which Luke's church would surely have related to the Jewish war with Rome in A.D. 66–70). **These things must happen first**, "but the end will not follow at once" (Fitzmyer's literal translation, p. 1336). The **end** is not the end of the age or the time when the Son of Man returns (as is understood by Marshall, p. 764), but it is the end of the temple. What Jesus is saying here in Luke's version of this discourse is that there will be many dangers and difficulties for his followers before this final catastrophic event occurs. These dangers will include **earthquakes** (see Acts 16:26), **famines** (see Acts 11:28), and **fearful events and great signs from heaven** (as in the case when Antiochus IV invaded Jerusalem in 169 B.C.; see 2 Macc. 5:2–3 and Fitzmyer, p. 1337).

But before all this (i.e., the events attending the temple's destruction), Jesus warns his followers, their opponents **will lay hands on** them **and persecute** them. Much of what Jesus describes appears in the Book of Acts (see 4:16–18; 8:1–3; 12:1–5). The Apostle Paul would later **be brought before kings and governors** before whom he would bear witness to the truth of the gospel (see Acts 22:30–23:9 where Paul speaks to the Sanhedrin; 24:10–23 where Paul is before Governor Felix; 25:1–12 where Paul speaks to Governor Festus; 26:1–32 where Paul speaks to King Agrippa and Bernice; 27:1 where Paul is handed over to the "Imperial Regiment," having appealed to Caesar). Jesus promises to give his followers such **words and wisdom that none of** their **adversaries will be able to resist or contradict** them (see Acts 4:13, hostile Sanhedrin members are amazed at the learning of Peter and John;

Acts 7:2-53, Stephen gives eloquent testimony to his accusers) yet he warns them that **some** of them will be put to **death** (see Acts 7:54-60, Stephen is stoned; 12:1-2, James the brother of John is executed). Finally, Jesus encourages his followers to stand **firm** and so **save** themselves. (Luke has omitted the last part of Mark 13:13, which is noted in italics: "but he who stands firm *to the end* will be saved," because the Lucan evangelist has not been talking about the end of the age.)

21:20-24 / The discourse now advances to Jesus' description of Jerusalem's fate. During the interval between Jesus' departure and the "end" of the temple and Jerusalem, the disciples may expect troubles and persecutions. **When** they **see Jerusalem surrounded by armies** (lit. "camps"), then they **will know that its desolation is near**. This will be the sign indicating when the temple will be destroyed (21:7). Now the disciples will know that the "end" has indeed come (21:9). The "camps" that will surround Jerusalem are the camps of Titus, commander of the Roman legions sent to subdue the Jewish rebellion. This catastrophic war ends with the overthrow of the city and the temple's complete destruction in A.D. 70. Therefore, when these things begin to happen, Jesus' followers are to flee from **Judea** and **not enter the city**. (There is some evidence that some Christians actually did flee the city when the Roman army approached; see Fitzmyer, p. 1345.) The reason that the danger is so great and that every step should be taken to avoid it is because this period of time is designated prophetically as the **time of punishment** (alluding to Hos. 9:7) in **fulfillment of all that has been written**. Because Jerusalem did not recognize the day of God's visitation (see 19:44 and commentary), the days of punishment (lit. "vengeance") are coming. Although Jesus came to proclaim the acceptable year of the Lord (4:18-21), because of his people's obduracy he sadly announces impending judgment (see also 2:34). When Jerusalem is surrounded and besieged it will be a dreadful time, especially so for **pregnant women and nursing mothers**. (Josephus [*War* 6.204-205] tells us of one mother who cooked and ate her infant because of the famine brought on by the siege; Fitzmyer, p. 1343.) Some **will fall by the sword** (see Sir. 28:18) **and will be taken as prisoners to all the nations** (see Deut. 28:64), and **Jerusalem will be trampled on by the Gentiles** (see Zech. 12:1-3). These scriptural allusions are examples of all that the scriptures say concerning Jerusalem's fate.

21:25–28 / Jesus now leaves behind his prophecy concerning the end of the city of Jerusalem and foretells what is coming upon the whole earth. By omitting Mark's "in those days" (13:24) Luke distinguishes between the coming of the Son of Man and the days of Jerusalem's destruction. The coming of the Son of Man will be preceded by various cosmic signs (see Isa. 34:4; they are elaborated upon at great length in Revelation 6–20). These signs will cause great fear among unbelievers (and rightly so from what is described in Revelation), but for Jesus' followers these signs should be an occasion for joy, for they indicate that Jesus' return as **Son of Man** (see Dan. 7:13) and his followers' **redemption** are **drawing near**. (That Jesus identifies himself as the Son of Man seems clear enough from Luke 12:8–9 and esp. 22:22, 48; see note below.)

21:29–33 / This part of Jesus' eschatological discourse is made up of the Parable of the Fig Tree and has appended to it two brief, more or less related sayings (vv. 32–33). The lesson of the **fig tree and all the trees** is clear enough. **When they sprout leaves** one knows that **summer is near**. Likewise, when the events described in vv. 25–28 occur one should realize that the **kingdom of God is near** (through the agency of the Son of Man).

Verse 32 presents a problem for interpreters. To what does **all these things** refer? And, what is meant by the comment, **this generation will certainly not pass away**? If "this generation" refers to Jesus' contemporaries then "all these things" must refer to the destruction of the temple and Jerusalem (21:6–24). If this is the case, then why has Luke placed v. 32 here, after passages concerning the coming of the Son of Man (21:25–28) and the coming of the kingdom of God (21:29–31)? But if "this generation" refers to those who observe the signs described in vv. 25–31, then "all these things" may refer to the coming of the Son of Man and the appearance of the kingdom of God. Fitzmyer (p. 1352) suggests that v. 32 was an independent saying about something that "this generation" would live to see. Since Luke places this saying into the present context by adding a word of certainty to the lesson of the fig tree, he probably does understand it as referring to those events that will take place immediately before the appearance of the kingdom (v. 31). Therefore, the evangelist is saying that when the signs of the fig tree are observed, the eschatological drama will most certainly come to completion before its generation passes away.

Verse 33 is also an independent saying (cf. Matt. 5:18; Luke
16:17), probably modeled after similar sayings found in the OT
(see Isa. 40:8; 55:10–11; Ps. 119:89). The saying reassures the
people of God not to lose faith, even though the return of Jesus
has been delayed.

21:34–38 / This part consists of a final warning to **be careful** (vv. 34–36) and a summarizing statement of Jesus **teaching
at the temple** (vv. 37–38). In vv. 34–35 Jesus warns his followers
not to become too involved with the routine of life so as to become distracted and unprepared for **that day** (see note below) that
will come suddenly **like a trap . . . upon all those who live on
the face of the whole earth** (see Isa. 24:17; cf. Rev. 3:10). (Here
Matthew [24:37–51] adds related materials from the sayings
source, which Luke had inserted into his account earlier in 12:39–
40, 42–46; 13:28a; 17:26–27, 34–35; 19:12–13.) Jesus admonishes his
followers to **be always on the watch** and to **pray** that they **may
be able to stand before the Son of Man.**

Luke reminds his readers in vv. 37–38 that Jesus is still
teaching at the temple, although **each evening he went out to
spend the night on the hill called the Mount of Olives** (perhaps
in Bethany; see John 12:1, 9; Luke 19:29). Even though his lodg-
ings were outside the city, Jesus would spend his days teaching
in the temple. Thus, the discourse ends where it began (21:5)—
"at the temple."

Additional Notes §51

21:1 / **temple treasury**: The phrase could also be translated
"money box." See Neh. 12:44; 1 Macc. 14:49. According to m. *Shekalim*
6.15 "there are thirteen shofar-chests in the temple" which were used
for the collection of contributions and dues.

21:2 / **small copper coins**: The *lepton* was worth only a fraction
of a denarius, itself worth a day's wage. What the widow cast into the
temple treasury was scarcely enough to buy a meager meal.

21:5–7 / There is some tension in the eschatological discourse
since, in Mark 13:3–13, Jesus does not actually answer the disciples' question. Both Matthew and Luke attempt to rectify this problem. G. B. Caird
(*The Gospel of St. Luke,* Pelican Gospel Commentary [Baltimore: Penguin,

1963], p. 230) has described the Synoptic version as follows: "Jesus' prediction of the destruction of the temple calls forth from the disciples a question which, in all three Synoptic Gospels, leads to a long prophetic discourse. Mark's discourse, however, is no answer to the question; it relates to the end of the present age and the signs that will foreshadow it, and one of those signs is, not the destruction, but the desecration of the temple. Matthew has removed the inconsistency by making the question fit the answer, Luke by making the answer fit the question" (cited by Fitzmyer, p. 1324). As seen in the commentary above, Luke relates the discourse primarily to the disciples' question regarding the prediction of the temple's destruction (whereas in Mark the destruction of the temple is the "beginning of the birth pains" that will culminate in the end of the age).

21:5 / The **temple** was magnificent, built with white **stones**, and overlaid with gold. According to Josephus (*War* 5.222) the reflection of the sun upon the temple was more than the eyes could bear. Fitzmyer (p. 1330) notes that the temple was completed in A.D. 63, a mere seven years before it would be destroyed. Because it was still under construction when Jesus was in Jerusalem, it is possible that the reference to the **beautiful stones** was to the stones that were not yet lifted into place.

21:6 / Jesus' saying, **not one stone will be left on another**, may have been prompted by his observation of the stones lying about and not yet mounted upon one another. Like the stones yet lying about, all of the stones will be thrown down upon the ground.

21:7 / **Teacher**: See note on 7:40 above.

21:17 / **All men will hate you because of me**: Leaney (pp. 260–61) wonders if this saying "might refer to the calumny fastened by Nero upon Christians, which gave great impetus to hatred of them throughout the empire."

21:20–24 / This prediction of the destruction of Jerusalem brings to a conclusion Jesus' previous related statements about coming troubles and disaster uttered during his ministry (12:35–48; 13:34–35; 17:20–37; 19:41–44). While being led away to crucifixion, of course, he will utter yet one last woe upon the inhabitants of Jerusalem (23:28–31). Although this section (21:20–24) is significantly different from Mark 13:14–19 (as well as from the entire discourse), I must agree with Fitzmyer (p. 1326) that it is best to understand the Lucan version as an edited version of Mark 13, into which Luke has inserted a few distinctive sayings from material unique to him. What was in Mark an apocalyptic oracle describing the desecration of the temple has become in Luke a prophecy of Jerusalem's destruction (see Tiede, pp. 362–63). In the case of Luke 21:20–24 it is possible that its distinctive wording derives from an early oracle that has been colored by the language of the LXX, concerned with Jerusalem's first destruction (see note on 19:41–44 above). (Others, such as *2 Bar.*, 4 Ezra, and Josephus, described the destruction of Jerusalem in A.D. 70 with the words of the biblical accounts concerned with Jerusalem's first destruction.) Luke may have omitted Mark 13:18 ("pray that this will not take place in winter") because the evangelist is writing after Jerusalem was destroyed and knew that it had been destroyed in the summer (the siege was from April to August) and not in the winter.

The closest parallels with the LXX include the following:

desolation (21:20): Dan. 12:11 (cf. also 9:27; 11:31).

those in the city (21:21): Lit. "those in the center of her." See Ezek. 9:4.

the time of punishment (21:22): Lit. "the days of vengeance." See Hos. 9:7 (cf. also Deut. 32:35; Jer. 46:10; 50:31 [LXX, 26:10; 27:31]; Ezek. 9:1). Remember that the similar line in Isa. 61:2 had been omitted in Jesus' Nazareth sermon (see Luke 4:18–19). The implication may be that the divine vengeance that many Israelites had hoped would fall upon the Gentiles will tragically fall upon Jerusalem.

distress . . . and wrath (21:23): See Zeph. 1:15 (cf. also 2 Kings 3:27).

fall by the sword (21:24): See Sir. 28:18.

to all the nations (21:24): See Deut. 28:64 (cf. also Josephus, *War* 6.420–427).

Jerusalem . . . trampled by the Gentiles (21:24): See Zech. 12:3 (cf. also Isa. 63:18; Dan. 8:13; Rev. 11:2).

21:24 / until the times of the Gentiles are fulfilled: J. T. Sanders (p. 218) does not believe that this phrase implies the restoration of Jerusalem. He believes that this Lucan oracle (21:20–24) is one more passage that betrays the evangelist's anti-Semitic perspective. Sanders is, however, once again incorrect. By itself the phrase probably hints at Jerusalem's restoration in that it clearly implies a limit to Gentile domination (see Dan. 2:44; 8:13–14; 12:5–13; 1QS 4.18–19: "God . . . has appointed a time for . . . wrongdoing, but at the time of visitation he will destroy it forever"; from a positive perspective—Rom. 11:25–27: "Israel has experienced a hardening in part until the full number of the Gentiles has come in. And so all Israel will be saved . . . "). Robert L. Brawley (*Luke–Acts and the Jews: Conflict, Apology, and Conciliation*, SBLMS 33 [Atlanta: Scholars, 1987], p. 125) finds "uncanny verbal resemblances" between Luke 21:24 and Ezek. 39:23 and Zech. 12:3, passages that go on to foretell national restoration (see Ezek. 39:24–29; Zech. 12:4–9). Tiede (p. 365) rightly finds the phrase implying that "God is not done with Israel." The wider Lucan context also points to an expectation of Israel's restoration. When certain cosmological signs take place (21:25–27) Jesus enjoins his audience to "stand up and lift up [their] heads, because [their] redemption is drawing near" (21:28; cf. 1:38; 24:21). After the Parable of the Fig Tree (21:29–30) Jesus concludes: "when you see these things happening, you know that the kingdom of God is near" (21:31). In view of the question that the disciples put to Jesus in Acts 1:6 ("Lord, are you at this time going to restore the kingdom to Israel?"), the saying certainly does leave open the possibility of Israel's restoration. Moreover, Luke has all of this material (i.e., Luke 21) uttered in public; he has not limited it to the disciples alone, as it is found in Mark 13. The plural "you," therefore, addresses all Jews who heard Jesus, not just Jesus' disciples. (Throughout chaps. 20–21 Jesus is addressing the people in and about the temple.) The point of all of this is that when Jesus says, "your redemption is drawing near" and the "kingdom of God is near," he is speaking to the Jewish people. Such prophecies and promises belie an anti-Semitic interpretation of the Lucan oracle.

21:25–26 / These signs reflect apocalyptic imagery from several passages: Deut. 28:28; Ps. 65:7 [LXX, 64:8]; Isa. 13:10; 17:12; 24:18–20; 34:4; Joel 2:10; 2 Esdras 5:4; *1 Enoch* 80:4–7; *T. Levi* 4:1; *T. Moses* 10:5; 2 Pet. 3:12; Rev. 6:12–14; *2 Bar.* 70:2.

21:27 / **the Son of Man**: See note on 5:24 above. **Coming in a cloud with power and great glory** is an unmistakable allusion to Dan. 7:13. This apocalyptic image symbolizes the handing over of the kingdom to God's anointed one. Daniel 7:13–14 was interpreted in a messianic sense widely in Jewish circles (*1 Enoch* 69:29; *Numbers Rabbah* 13.14; *Midrash Psalms* 21.5; b. *Sanhedrin* 96b–97a).

21:28 / **lift up your heads**: See Isa. 8:21.

21:32 / **this generation**: This expression is often used in reference to the generation that will experience the "Day of the Lord" (see following note).

21:33 / **Heaven and earth will pass away, but my words will never pass away**: This saying implies that Jesus' very words are equivalent in authority and permanence to the Word of God. Lachs (p. 88) cites the following rabbinic parallel: "Everything has its end, the heavens and earth have their end; only one thing is excepted which has no end, and that is the Law" (*Genesis Rabbah* 10.1; see also Philo, *Life of Moses* 2.3).

21:34 / **that day**: The "day" came to be a technical term in the NT; it is usually an abbreviation for "the day of the Lord," an idea ultimately derived from the OT (see Amos 5:18–20; Joel 1:15; 2:30–32; Zeph. 1:14–18). Compare 1 Thess. 5:2; Rom. 2:5; 1 Cor. 1:8; Phil. 1:6, 10; Rev. 6:17; 16:14.

21:37 / **Mount of Olives**: See note on 22:39 below. According to Mark 11:11 Jesus lodged in Bethany, a town near Jerusalem.

§52 The Last Supper (Luke 22:1–38)

With Luke 22 the Passion Narrative begins. In the first 38 verses the reader is told of Jesus' betrayal, Passover meal, and final instructions to his disciples before his arrest. Most of Luke's materials are derived from Mark 14:1–31 and may be divided into the following parts: (1) the Conspiracy of the Religious Leaders (vv. 1–2); (2) Judas' Betrayal of Jesus (vv. 3–6); (3) the Preparation for the Passover Meal (vv. 7–14); (4) the Lord's Supper (vv. 15–23); (5) Teaching on Greatness in the Kingdom (vv. 24–30); (6) Peter's Denial Foretold (vv. 31–34); and (7) the Saying on the Two Swords (vv. 35–38).

22:1–2 / One of the reasons that the **chief priests and the teachers of the law** would have renewed their efforts to do away with **Jesus** at the time of the **Passover** (see note below) was because Jesus, like many other Jews, would be present in Jerusalem for the feast and so would afford the religious authorities their best opportunity to lay their hands upon him. Had they delayed in taking action, Jesus might have left Jerusalem and could have slipped through their fingers. Another reason probably had to do with the feast itself. During Passover political feelings ran high, as the locals and the pilgrims reflected upon God's saving act that had brought forth their ancestors from Egyptian slavery. Such reflection often stirred messianic hopes of a deliverance from the oppressive yoke of Imperial Rome. As his Triumphal Entry revealed (19:28–40), Jesus had acquired messianic status (rightly or wrongly understood) in the minds of at least some. This would scarcely have gone unnoticed by the religious authorities, particularly the Sadducees, the aristocratic priestly class, who feared the social and economic consequences of an insurrection.

To arrest Jesus openly, however, would likely touch off the very insurrection that they feared. Therefore, it was necessary for them to find a way to remove Jesus quietly. This is why the betrayal of Judas was so important to the authorities.

22:3–6 / Luke omits Mark's account of Jesus' anointing in Bethany (Mark 14:3–9), probably because the evangelist has already included a similar episode (see Luke 7:36–38) and has shown a marked tendency to avoid repetition. Luke moves immediately from the notice that the religious authorities were trying to find a way to do away with Jesus secretly to his account of Judas' betrayal. Of the Synoptic evangelists only Luke reports that **Satan entered Judas** (cf. John 13:2, 27). Fitzmyer (p. 1374) describes the Third Evangelist as "baffled as to how he should explain the sinister betrayal of Jesus by one of his own" and can find no explanation other than that of Satanic influence. This may be so, but the fact that the same idea appears also in the Fourth Gospel suggests that the idea of Satan entering Judas was part of the passion tradition which Luke felt best explained Judas' otherwise inexplicable behavior.

Judas offered the religious authorities the very opportunity that they sought. Because he was **one of the Twelve**, he would know where the group met in the evening and when they might be alone. After striking his evil bargain he **watched for an opportunity to hand Jesus over to them when no crowd was present**.

22:7–14 / With the sinister conspiracy between Judas and the religious authorities in the background, **Jesus** and his disciples begin making preparations for the **Passover** meal. Luke notes that Jesus sent **Peter and John** (Mark 14:13 says only "two of his disciples") into Jerusalem to meet **a man carrying a jar of water** (which was a task women usually performed), to whom they will convey the word of the **Teacher**. The **owner of the house**, the disciples are told, **will show** them **a large upper room, all furnished**. There the disciples are to **make preparations**. Luke probably does not intend his readers to understand any of this as miraculous, but only that in yet another situation Jesus is firmly in control. Jesus deliberately works out the final details of his ministry.

22:15–23 / Jesus' solemn declaration in v. 15 reveals how much he has looked forward to that final **Passover** meal. He has anticipated it eagerly, not because he looks forward to his death (see v. 42), but because he will be able to establish a **new covenant in his blood**. In v. 16 Jesus vows not to **eat the Passover again until it finds fulfillment in the kingdom of God**. The exact meaning of this statement is uncertain, but it probably parallels Jesus' vow in v. 18: He will neither eat the Passover nor drink wine **until the kingdom of God comes**. (The **cup** that is drunk in v. 20 is not a violation of this vow, for the vow is meant to go into effect after the Passover meal itself.)

Luke's account is unusual because of its mention of a **cup** first (v. 17), followed by the traditional **bread/cup** sequence of vv. 19–20. A few Greek manuscripts omit half of v. 19 and all of v. 20. Some commentators believe that this shorter form is original, with vv. 19b–20 added in order to restore the traditional bread/cup sequence. Equally tenable, however, is the theory that a few early Christian scribes chose to omit vv. 19b–20 in order to eliminate the second cup (or such an omission was unintentional). There is nothing unusual in the reference to a second cup, for there were *four* cups drunk at a Passover meal (see m. *Pesahim* 10.1–7). The cup mentioned in v. 17 may have been the first cup in which God is blessed for his gift of wine or the second cup in which the question about the significance of Passover is raised, thereby eliciting a response from the father or, in the Gospel context, from Jesus. What Jesus states in vv. 17b–18 may very well be a summary of his explanation of the significance of the Passover meal as far as he himself is concerned. Rather than looking back to the Exodus, Jesus is looking forward to the kingdom of God.

In vv. 19–20 the "institution" of the Lord's Supper is established for all Christians. The **bread** is broken and described by Jesus as his **body given for** his followers. All Christians are to observe this ritual **in remembrance of** Jesus. Likewise Jesus distributed a **cup** (the third cup, the "Cup of Blessing") which he describes as the **new covenant in** his **blood, which is poured out for** his followers (Mark 14:24: "This is my blood . . . which is poured out for many"). Jesus will shed his blood (perhaps an allusion to Isa. 53:12) in order to establish a new covenant. This new covenant undoubtedly is to be understood in terms of the "new covenant" of Jer. 31:31, a covenant that will be written not upon stone tablets, but upon hearts (cf. 2 Cor. 3:3, 6).

The meal ends with Jesus' declaration that the hand of the betrayer is **with** his **on the table**. But that is the way it must be, for the **Son of Man will go as it has been decreed**. Jesus thus declares that his fate is unavoidable, and part of that unavoidable fate is betrayal. It will still be terrible, however, for **that man**

who betrays him. Even though Jesus' fate is part of God's plan, it does not excuse the betrayer. Shocked, the disciples **began to question among themselves which of them it might be who would do this**. Such disloyalty was beyond comprehension for them.

22:24–30 / The conversation turns abruptly to the question of who is the **greatest** among the disciples. Coming where it does, this passage is unique to Luke, for Mark tells of no further conversation at the table. Luke's material seems to be a reworking of the similar discussion in Mark 10:42–45, a part of Mark omitted in an earlier part of Luke (cf. Mark 10:32–52 with Luke 18:31–43; one will notice that Luke has omitted Mark 10:35–45). From time to time Luke brings in some of the details of this omitted material (see Luke 12:50) into new contexts. This passage would seem to be a case in point. One may question the logic of having this conversation appear immediately after Jesus' declaration of betrayal in vv. 21–22. Fitzmyer (p. 1412) is probably correct in suggesting that if the worst disciple is he who betrays his Lord, who is the greatest?

The passage is actually comprised of two parts: the discussion of greatness (vv. 24–27) and Jesus' pronouncement that his disciples will someday rule with him (vv. 28–30), with the second part originally a distinct unit (probably from the sayings source; cf. Matt. 19:28). Most people seek power over other people; that is what they think makes them great. But for the followers of Jesus this is not the way. The **greatest among** Christians is the one who sees himself as the **youngest** (or "least significant"). The Christian **who rules** should be **like the one who serves**. In v. 27 Jesus asks a question about social conventions; its answer is obvious: the **one who is at the table** is greater than the **one who serves**. The one who sits is the master, while the one who waits on him is the servant. But this is not the way it is to be among Jesus' followers, as Jesus himself gave example (see John 13:4–17).

Jesus explains in vv. 28–30 that a time of vindication and exaltation will come for his faithful followers. Since they have remained loyal throughout all of Jesus' **trials**, they may anticipate sharing in his **kingdom** rule as well (see note below). This statement may seem strange in light of the disciples' desertion at the time of Jesus' arrest. That detail, however, is omitted by Luke, and although he retains the tradition of Peter's denials (22:54–62) in the prediction of his denials that follows, Peter's repentance and restoration are also predicted (v. 32).

22:31–34 / Verses 31–32 are unique to Luke, while vv. 33–34 appear to be a modification of Mark 14:29–31. Although what he has to say applies to all of his disciples, Jesus speaks to **Simon** (Peter) as their spokesman. In the part that is unique to Luke (vv. 31–32) Peter is warned that **Satan has asked to sift** them all **as wheat**. That is, Satan desires to test the disciples severely for the purpose of destroying their faith. The danger here is not to be taken lightly. It is so grave that Jesus assures Peter that he has **prayed for** him, in order that his **faith may not fail**. In light of Peter's impending denials, this failure of faith concerns more than this temporary lapse. The idea is probably that in the wake of the denials Peter may be tempted to abandon his faith in Jesus altogether. This, however, will not happen because of Jesus' intercessory prayer. Peter will suffer a momentary lapse, but he will recover and return to Jesus and then will be able to **strengthen** his **brothers** (as is seen dramatically in Acts 1–5 where Peter is the bold spokesman and leader of the infant church).

Peter, however, wishes to affirm his loyalty to his Master (v. 33). He is **ready**, he declares, **to go with** Jesus **to prison and to death**. There is irony in this well-intentioned declaration, for Peter will indeed suffer imprisonment (Acts 5:18; 12:3) and martyrdom (according to early church tradition); but during this dark hour his courage will fail him. Jesus then prophesies that **before the rooster crows** that day, Peter **will deny three times** that he knows Jesus.

22:35–38 / These verses find no parallel outside of Luke and so are usually thought to have been derived from the evangelist's special source. Verses 35–36a presuppose the sending of the Twelve in 9:1–6 and the Seventy(-two) in 10:1–12. Whereas the apostles on those occasions traveled lightly (taking no wallet, bag, or sandals), this time they will need provisions, for the ministry that lies ahead of them will be long and difficult. Indeed, it will be so difficult that they had better arm themselves with a **sword**. The sword is a symbol of the violence and opposition that his followers will face. It is an especially appropriate symbol for Jesus, according to v. 37, because he will share the fate of criminals (alluding to Isa. 53:12). This is seen most vividly in his crucifixion

between two criminals in 23:33 and perhaps in Peter's unfortunate, literal employment of the sword in 22:49–50. There may also
be the idea of Jesus and his followers being classified by opponents of the faith as outlaws (as seen in Acts). Tannehill (p. 267)
has suggested that Jesus knows that the disciples will temporarily
depart from the path of true discipleship and will act as criminals:
"Jesus' command does not cause something to happen but reveals what the disciples have already done out of fear." This is
probably correct.

The import of Jesus' remarks is completely misunderstood
by his disciples, who produce **two swords**. In a spirit of popular
messianic enthusiasm his men are ready to take up arms. As Peter
had said only moments before, they are ready to go to prison,
even to death. Jesus, however, is no doubt disappointed (unless
he took the comment of the disciples in a figurative sense) in their
lack of perception and ends the discussion with the words,
"Enough of this" (which is clearer than the NIV's **That is enough**;
see Fitzmyer, p. 1434; cf. 22:51) or "They are enough" (i.e., enough
for the fulfillment of Isa. 53:12). This conversation confirms that
the disciples are scarcely prepared for what lies ahead. Their inability to cope with the coming trials is dramatically portrayed
in the very next episode.

Additional Notes §52

22:1 / The **Feast of Unleavened Bread** and the **Passover** were actually two holidays. Whereas the Passover was observed on the 14th day
of Nisan (approximately April 1), the Feast of Unleavened Bread was celebrated the following week, Nisan 15–21. Unleavened Bread originally celebrated the beginning of harvest, but later was combined with Passover,
a holiday where only unleavened (yeastless) bread could be eaten. In
Hebrew the Passover is called *Pesaḥ*, while in the Greek it is called *Pascha*.
Because the Greek verb meaning "to suffer" is *paschein*, the early church
came to see a connection between the Passover and Jesus' suffering (see
1 Cor. 5:7). On Passover see *HBD*, pp. 753–55.

22:2 / On **chief priests** see note on 19:47 above; on **teachers of
the law** see note on 5:21 above.

22:3 / Recall the devil's departure "for an opportune time" (4:13).
Unable to stop Jesus at the beginning of his ministry, **Satan** now hopes

to ruin the end of his ministry by subverting his followers. Satan is Hebrew for "Adversary"; see note on 10:15 above and *HBD*, pp. 908–9. On
Judas, called Iscariot see note on 6:16 above.

22:4 / **temple guard**: According to Fitzmyer (p. 1375), these persons may have handled the temple funds and so may have conferred
with Judas not only in order to know when and where to arrest Jesus,
but to pay the betrayer as well.

22:5 / **money**: According to Matt. 26:15, Judas is paid thirty pieces
of silver, which later are cast into the temple (Matt. 27:5). Compare the
accounts of Judas' death (Matt. 27:3–10; Acts 1:18–19).

22:7–13 / Whereas the Synoptic Gospels agree that the "Last Supper" is a **Passover** meal, in the Gospel of John the "Last Supper" takes
place "before the Passover feast" (13:1–2). John certainly means this as
the day before Passover, because the next day, when Jesus stands before
Pilate, the religious authorities refuse to enter Pilate's headquarters lest
they be defiled and so disqualified from eating the Passover (John 18:2–
3, 12–13, 28). Attempts to explain this discrepancy in terms of two different calendars (which would put Passover on different days) create more
difficulties than they solve. How the Johannine and Synoptic accounts
can be harmonized, or if they can, is unknown (see Fitzmyer's thorough
and fair discussion, pp. 1378–83).

22:14–38 / Luke has combined his traditions in such a way as
to produce a farewell discourse. See William S. Kurz ("Luke 22:14–38 and
Greco-Roman and Biblical Farewell Addresses," *JBL* 104 [1985], pp. 251–
68) who has compared Luke 22:14–38 to Greco-Roman (e.g., Plato, *Phaedo*;
Diogenes Laertius, *Epicurus* 10:16–18) and biblical (e.g., 1 Kings 2:1–10;
1 Macc. 2:49–70) farewell addresses. Kurz rightly maintains (p. 253, n.
7) that Luke is familiar primarily with the biblical examples.

22:19 / **This is my body**: That Jesus is speaking figuratively
should be clear. The **bread** *symbolizes* his body, just as Jesus speaks
figuratively of being a gate, a shepherd, or a vine (see John 10:7, 11;
15:1).

22:20 / **the new covenant in my blood**: See also Exod. 24:8; Lev.
17:11; Fitzmyer, p. 1402.

22:22 / That Jesus is himself the **Son of Man** is obvious from
this verse (see also v. 48). See note on 5:24 above.
woe to that man who betrays him: Omitted is the grim statement
in Mark: "It would be better for him if he had not been born" (14:21b).

22:25 / **Benefactors**: This title was bestowed upon various gods
and rulers in antiquity. Luke wishes to portray Jesus as humankind's true
Benefactor, one who is serving, not self-serving.

22:28–29 / Compare Rom. 8:17; 2 Tim. 2:11–13.

22:30 / Matthew 19:28 states that the apostles will sit upon "twelve thrones." Luke only has **thrones** because in placing this saying immediately after the reference to Judas' betrayal there are no longer twelve genuine apostles (though Judas will later be replaced; Acts 1:12–26). Whereas Jesus will sit upon the throne of his father David (recall 1:32), his apostles will serve as his vice-regents, **judging the twelve tribes of Israel**. Fitzmyer (p. 1419) suggests that Ps. 122:4–5 may be in view. Gundry (p. 393) suggests that the saying may in part be inspired by Daniel 7. Marshall (p. 818) cites both. Since both OT passages in fact do appear together in Jewish exegesis and in the context of discussion concerned with the "great ones of Israel" and the thrones that they will be given (see *Midrash Tanhuma* B, tractate *Qedoshim* 1.1), it seems that these are indeed the passages that ultimately lie behind Luke 22:30 and context. See also Rev. 21:12, 14. I agree with Tiede (p. 386) that the emphasis on the twelve in Luke 22:28–30 "is an explicit signal that God is not done with Israel." For more on this, see David L. Tiede, " 'Glory to Thy People Israel': Luke–Acts and the Jews," in Joseph B. Tyson, ed., *Luke–Acts and the Jewish People* (Minneapolis: Augsburg, 1988), pp. 21–34. Luke 22:28–30 is not fulfilled in what takes place in the Book of Acts. The promise is eschatological. Tannehill (p. 270) agrees, and correctly goes on to say that "mention of the twelve tribes also suggests Israel in its restored wholeness."

22:32 / **But I have prayed for you**: In Rom. 8:34 Paul declares that Jesus intercedes for his disciples (cf. 8:26–27 where the idea has something to do with praying).

22:36 / **sword**: Compare the more elaborate metaphors of weaponry as spiritual armament in Eph. 6:11–17.

22:38 / The NIV translation, **That is enough**, is misleading in that it could convey the sense that Jesus felt that the **two swords** showed to him by the **disciples** were examples of what he had actually been talking about. Had Jesus actually advocated armed combat two swords could scarcely have been "enough" (although one will be enough in 22:49–50!). Moreover, had Jesus' remark been one of approval, then we might have expected his reply to be in the plural, "They are enough." On the contrary, Jesus' answer must be seen as a word of frustration whereby he cut the conversation short. Jesus may have intended his comment to be tinged with a bit of sarcasm.

§53 The Betrayal and Arrest (Luke 22:39–62)

The Passover meal is now over. In this section we see Jesus' ministry come to an end with his betrayal and arrest. The moment of testing for Jesus and for his disciples is now at hand. The section under consideration consists of three parts: (1) Jesus' Prayers on the Mount of Olives (vv. 39–46); (2) Jesus' Betrayal and Arrest (vv. 47–53); and (3) Peter's Denials of Jesus (vv. 54–62). Luke has derived his material from Mark 14:32–50, 53–54, 66–72.

22:39–46 / As has been his practice (see 21:37) **Jesus went . . . to the Mount of Olives** (see note below) with **his disciples**. In keeping with Lucan interest, the emphasis of the passage falls on prayer. In v. 40 Jesus admonishes his disciples, **Pray that you will not fall into temptation,** and in v. 46 he states this again to his drowsy companions. Prayer is necessary at this moment because the hour of sorest testing will shortly come upon them. The test is to be so severe that Jesus prays to God the **Father** that **if** willing would he **take this cup** of suffering away (see note below). Jesus knows what is coming and he does not like it. If it were possible to accomplish God's purposes some other way, he would only be too happy to do it. We see in Jesus' request genuine sorrow and dread. "Nowhere else in the gospel tradition is the humanity of Jesus so evident as here" (Fitzmyer, p. 1442). Nevertheless, Jesus is willing to do his Father's **will.** Throughout his ministry Jesus insisted that following him was no easy task (9:57–62). Now he himself faces a difficult task that calls for the utmost commitment to God's will. Some manuscripts insert vv. 43–44 here, which surely reflects an early Christian scribe's desire to show an immediate and dramatic answer to Jesus' prayer. Fitzmyer (p. 1444) gives several reasons why he thinks that these verses should not be regarded as part of the original Gospel of Luke (Marshall [p. 832] accepts the verses as original, "but with very considerable hesitation"; Ellis [p. 258] thinks that they are part of a "genuine extra-canonical tradition," but are not Lucan).

In stark contrast to the agonized Jesus, the **disciples** are **asleep**, although Luke excuses them to some extent by adding that they were **exhausted from sorrow** (a detail not found in the other Gospel accounts, see note below). Instead of remaining alert, sober, and prayerful, the disciples sleep. Once again Jesus urges them to **pray so that** they **will not fall into temptation**. Now more than ever they need to be praying (cf. 1 Thess. 5:4–8).

22:47–53 / Luke tells us that **while Jesus was still speaking a crowd came up** (which, according to v. 52, included **chief priests, the officers of the temple guard, and the elders**) led by **Judas, one of the Twelve**. Judas **approached Jesus to kiss him** (according to Mark 14:44–45 he does kiss him, for it was the sign by which Jesus would be identified to his enemies). Jesus' question in v. 48 (found only in Luke and possibly inspired by Mark 14:44, which Luke otherwise does not have) underscores the treachery of Judas' act. With a kiss, a sign of great affection and loyalty, Judas betrays his Master, the Son of Man. The disciples who possess the "two swords" (22:38) react, thinking that this is the time to use force. (Verse 49 also has no counterpart in Matthew or Mark and is inserted here by Luke to link vv. 35–38 to the act of striking the slave.) One of them (John 18:10 tells us that it was Simon Peter) struck the servant of the high priest (or chief priest), cutting off his right ear. Only Luke notes that it was the right ear and only Luke tells us that Jesus healed the man's wound. (Do we have here a hint of Luke's medical interest?) Here we see Jesus' last act of healing, and it is ironic that the one healed was one of those about to arrest him.

In vv. 52–53 Jesus scolds those who would arrest him for approaching him **with swords and clubs**, as though he were **leading a rebellion**. Since at least two of Jesus' disciples were armed, and since one of them actually attacked a member of the arresting party, Jesus' rebuke initially seems odd and unjustified. However, Mark 14:43 states that the approaching crowd was, so to speak, "armed to the teeth" (a point that has gone unmentioned in Luke), so it is likely that this menacing crowd provoked and frightened the disciples into a rash act. Accordingly, Jesus scolds those who have approached (in Matt. 26:53 Jesus scolds his disciples as well). Violence will not be necessary, for Jesus has never preached inaugurating God's kingdom through violence. Jesus reminds his captors that **every day** he had been **with** them **in the temple courts** (21:37), but then, in broad daylight, they had **not** laid a **hand on** him. **But this is** their **hour—when darkness reigns**. The darkness of night symbolizes the moral and spiritual darkness of the moment. When Jesus taught in the temple during the daylight hours the religious authorities were afraid to act, but now, under the cover of darkness, and away from the purified temple, they act.

22:54–62 / Significantly Luke omits Mark's reference to the disciples' flight (14:50), but he does go on to narrate Peter's three denials. Perhaps nowhere else in the gospel tradition does the careful reader encounter more discrepancies in matters of detail and chronology than in the account of Peter's denials and Jesus' trial. (For a discussion of the problems pertaining to Jesus' trial see the commentary on 22:63–23:25 below.) Peter's denials present the greatest difficulties, as illustrated by the following points: (1) Whereas Matthew (26:57), and presumably Mark (14:53) and Luke (22:54), has Peter deny Jesus all three times at the house of Caiaphas the high priest, John (18:13, 17, 24) has Peter first deny Jesus at the house of Annas, a former high priest and father-in-law of Caiaphas, and then deny Jesus the other two times at the house of Caiaphas (18:25–27). This discrepancy is not serious, for it reads as though the evangelist John has digressed after mentioning Caiaphas in 18:14. In all likelihood the fire by which Peter stood warming himself in 18:25–27, where he denied Jesus a second and third time, is the same fire mentioned earlier in 18:18, at which time Peter had denied Jesus the first time (18:17). John's narrative is clumsy, but it is not at real variance with the Synoptic tradition at this point. (2) Of greater difficulty is the identity of the various persons who either question or accuse Peter. Similarly, (3) there are significant divergences in Peter's various denials themselves. The questions and responses may be viewed synoptically as follows:

Denial One

Matt. 26:69–70

. . . a servant girl came to him. "You also were with Jesus of Galilee," she said. But he denied it before them all. "I don't know what you're talking about," he said.

Mark 14:66–68

. . . one of the servant girls of the high priest came by. When she saw Peter. . . . "You also were with that Nazarene, Jesus," she said. But he denied it. "I don't know or understand what you're talking about," he said.

Luke 22:56–57

A servant girl saw him . . . and said, "This man was with him." But he denied it. "Woman, I don't know him," he said.

John 18:17

"Surely you are not another of this man's disciples?" the girl at the door asked Peter. He replied, "I am not."

Denial Two

Matt. 26:71–72

. . . another girl saw him and said to the people there, "This fellow was with Jesus of Nazareth." He denied it again, with an oath: "I don't know the man!"

Mark 14:69–70

When the servant girl saw him there, she said again to those standing around, "This fellow is one of them." Again he denied it.

Luke 22:58

. . . someone [masc. gender] else saw him and said, "You also are one of them." "Man, I am not!" Peter replied.

John 18:25

. . . Simon Peter . . . was asked, "Surely you are not another of his disciples?" He denied it, saying, "I am not."

Denial Three

Matt. 26:73–74

After a little while, those standing there went up to Peter and said, "Surely you are one of them, for your accent gives you away." Then he began to call down curses on himself and he swore to them, "I don't know the man!"

Mark 14:70–71

After a little while, those standing near said to Peter, "Surely you are one of them, for you are a Galilean." He began to call down curses on himself, and he swore to them, "I don't know this man you're talking about."

Luke 22:59–60

About an hour later another [masc. gender] asserted, "Certainly this fellow was with him, for he is a Galilean." Peter replied, "Man, I don't know what you're talking about!"

John 18:26–27

One of the high priest's servants [masc. gender], a relative of the man whose ear Peter had cut off, challenged him, "Didn't I see you with him in the olive grove?" Again Peter denied it.

As can be readily seen from the above synopsis, the discrepancies are numerous. But before examining them, several points of agreement should be noted: (1) All four evangelists agree in having three accusations and denials; (2) all four agree that Peter denied Jesus at the house of the high priest; and (3) all agree that the first to put the question to Peter was a female servant. Beyond these agreements the accounts vary widely: (1) Whereas in the second denial Mark claims that it was the same female servant who spoke to Peter, Matthew says that it was "another" (female servant), while Luke says that it was a man. John has the second question framed by a group. (2) Matthew's account of the third denial follows Mark's "those standing near," while Luke and John select individual men as Peter's questioners. (3) The differences in the actual wording of the questions put to Peter and his replies are too numerous to examine exhaustively for our purposes, but a few examples should suffice. In the first question Matthew refers to Jesus "of Galilee," while Mark has Jesus "that Nazarene." Matthew brings "Nazareth" into the second question (probably from Mark's first question), while the other three evangelists have their respective questions refer to the disciples, not to Jesus. In the third question Peter is recognized as a Galilean (Mark and Luke), which is also the idea presupposed by Matthew, who explains how the questioners knew Peter to be a Galilean (i.e., by his speech). In John, however, Peter is recognized as one of Jesus' disciples, not because anyone thinks he is from Galilee, but because he was seen in the garden where Jesus was arrested and where Peter cut off the ear of one of the high priest's slaves. Peter's answers also vary. Matthew, following Mark's lead, has Peter "curse and swear" the third time; but John and Luke say nothing of this. In the first denial Mark and Matthew have Peter say that he does not know what his accuser is talking about, but in Luke, Peter denies Jesus. Of all the evangelists, the Johannine Peter's replies are the briefest; in the third denial no utterance is even provided.

How are all of these discrepancies to be understood and accounted for? There are at least two factors that must be taken into consideration. First, the four evangelists may have had (and probably did have) access to various sources, whether oral or written, of which we today know little or nothing. The sources underlying the Marcan and Johannine accounts are literarily independent and yet are similar. (Only a few scholars have ever argued that John utilized one or more of the Synoptic Gospels as a source, and even if the evangelist did, it would not preclude the possibility of the use of a non-Synoptic source.) Whereas Matthew has followed Mark fairly closely, there is enough variation in the Lucan account to lead some scholars to suspect that Luke may have had access to passion traditions other than those before him in Mark (see Marshall, pp. 839–40). Those various sources may account for the presence of some of the discrepancies now readily apparent when the four Gospels are read synoptically. Second, some discrepancies are probably due to the respective evangelists' (and here I am thinking primarily of Matthew and Luke) desire to tell the passion story differently from the way it was told in their source(s) (such as in Mark and whatever else they may have had). In the case of Luke, reference to Peter's cursing and swearing (Matt. 26:74; Mark 14:71) was perhaps omitted (Luke 22:60) out of respect for the apostle and out of a desire to present him in a better light, especially in view of his coming role of prominence in Acts. Also, Luke's shift from a "female servant" to a "man" in the second denial (cf. Luke 22:58 with Matt. 26:71 and Mark 14:69) allows the evangelist to confirm the accuracy of the report of the denials by showing that men, who alone would be regarded as trustworthy witnesses, were involved in at least *two* of the denials (see Fitzmyer [p. 1460] who cites Deut. 19:15).

It should be readily acknowledged that all four accounts of Peter's denials (as well as the respective accounts of the passion) cannot be harmonized on the basis of the materials that we have. A complete, thorough harmonization that omits no detail is impossible, unless one wishes to entertain naive proposals in which, for example, it is claimed that Jesus warned Peter of his impending denials *twice* (once in the upper room and once later in the garden) and that Peter denied Jesus *six* times, in two sets of three each, with a rooster crowing *once* after each set of three. (For an attempt to harmonize the four Gospels along such lines see Johnston Cheney and Stanley Ellisen, *The Life of Christ in Stereo* [Portland: Multnomah, 1984].) The results of this approach are unrealistic, even comical, and frequently lead to a distortion of the Gospel portraits themselves.

Additional Notes §53

22:39 / **Mount of Olives**: sometimes called "Olivet." Mark (14:32) and Matthew (26:36) call the place "Gethsemane" (Fitzmyer, pp. 1436–37: "probably a grecized form of Hebrew/Aramaic [word meaning] 'oil-press' "). The Mount of Olives is one of three mountains east of Jerusalem, whose summit is 2660 feet above sea level, some 230 feet above the temple mount. See *HBD*, pp. 728–29.

22:41 / **a stone's throw beyond**: Jesus is still within sight but is far enough away that he cannot be heard (Fitzmyer, p. 1441).

22:42 / **this cup**: The cup metaphor carries the OT idea of destiny (see Isa. 51:17, 22; Jer. 25:15; Ps. 16:5). We are given an important glimpse of Jesus' humanity in this utterance.

22:43–44 / As suggested in the commentary on 22:39–46, vv. 43–44 were not part of the original Lucan Gospel. (Talbert [p. 214], however, accepts the verses as original because they fit Luke's presentation of Jesus as a martyr.) The appearance of the **angel from heaven** is probably meant to be understood as an answer to Jesus' prayer in vv. 41–42. The descriptive sentence, **his sweat was like drops of blood falling to the ground**, should be understood as describing the size and quantity of the drops of perspiration (*like* drops of blood) and not as a statement that Jesus' perspiration was actually bloody.

22:45 / **exhausted from sorrow**: Luke may not intend this addition to excuse the disciples' failure to watch and pray. Tannehill (pp.

263–64, 271) suggests that their lack of prayer made the disciples vulnerable to Satan's attack (see 22:31, 53). Their grief is a sign of spiritual weakness.

22:48 / **Son of Man**: See note on 5:24 above.

22:52 / **Am I leading a rebellion**: The NIV here is quite paraphrastic. The Greek literally reads: "robber." The word may mean "insurrectionist" or "revolutionary" (hence the reading found in the NIV), a meaning that would be entirely in keeping with the original political and religious setting of the time.

22:54 / Tannehill (p. 272) suggests that Luke omitted the flight of the disciples not to lessen their failure but to avoid creating the impression that they were not witnesses to all that happened in Jerusalem (see Luke 24:48; Acts 1:8, 21–22).

22:61 / The sentence, **The Lord turned and looked straight at Peter**, occurs only in Luke and helps to heighten the drama. Peter has denied his Lord and has been exposed.

§54 The Trial of Jesus (Luke 22:63–23:25)

Most of Luke's account of the trial of Jesus derives from Mark 14:55–15:15, with the exception of 23:4–16, which appears only in Luke. Luke has introduced a few noteworthy changes that will be commented upon below. The section may be divided as follows: (1) Jesus is mocked and beaten (22:63–65); (2) Jesus is brought before the Sanhedrin (22:66–71); (3) Jesus is brought before Pilate (23:1–5); (4) Jesus is brought before Herod (23:6–12); and (5) Jesus is sentenced to death (23:13–25).

22:63–65 / Luke's account of Jesus' mistreatment at the hands of the guards parallels Mark 14:65, but, unlike the Marcan order, *precedes* Jesus' appearance before the Jewish Sanhedrin (cf. Mark 14:55–65). Luke says nothing about an evening interrogation (see Mark 14:53–55), but only describes the daytime proceedings (vv. 66–71; cf. Mark 15:1), thus simplifying the whole account. The Lucan order reflects consummate irony. As soon as Jesus' prophecy that Peter will deny him is fulfilled (v. 61), the guards blindfold Jesus, strike him, and ask him to **prophesy** to determine **who** has **hit** him. A dramatic contrast also exists between the cowardly Peter, who although suffering no violence, denied Jesus, and Jesus, who suffers violence, but does not suffer a moral collapse.

22:66–71 / Unlike Mark 14:55–64, the Lucan version of Jesus' trial before the **council** (or "Sanhedrin") says nothing of the accusation brought by the two false witnesses who claimed that Jesus had threatened to destroy the temple (but see Acts 6:13–14). According to the Lucan account, Jesus is asked directly if he is the **Christ** (see 2:11; 3:15). He responds by saying that as **Son of Man** (see note on 5:24) he **will be seated at the right hand of the mighty God** (see note below). From this answer members of the Sanhedrin then ask Jesus whether he is the **Son of God**. Whether Jesus' implicit claim of messiahship, his self-designation as Son of Man, or both prompt this question is uncertain. Since

the latter title is related to Ps. 110:1, which was probably understood as a messianic Psalm (see note below), the title Son of Man
would also have been understood in a messianic sense. From this
his accusers infer that Jesus has claimed to be the Son of God
and so ask him if this is so. Jesus avoids self-incrimination by
answering (lit.), "You say that I am" (NIV: **You are right in saying
I am**). Jesus has not disagreed with the question (so the NIV's
paraphrase is not incorrect); he has avoided the trap (which is
obscured by the NIV). In fact, Jesus' statement implies that his
accusers themselves have confessed his true identity (remember
Herod's question in 9:9). Nevertheless, because Jesus has not denied his messianic identity his accusers **have heard** enough.

23:1–5 / When Jesus is brought before **Pilate**, the religious
charge against him is transformed into a political one. Before the
Sanhedrin Jesus was asked if he claimed to be the Messiah. Now
Pilate is told that Jesus has challenged the political sovereignty
of **Caesar**. Jesus is accused before Pilate of three things: (1) **subverting** the Jewish **nation**, (2) opposing **payment of taxes to Caesar**, and (3) claiming **to be Christ, a king**. The second accusation
probably stems from a misunderstanding of what Jesus said about
giving what belongs to Caesar and to God (20:25). The third accusation probably reflects the joyful shouts of the Passover pilgrims in 19:38: "Blessed is the king who comes in the name of
the Lord!" The Sanhedrin members want Pilate to believe that
Jesus is a political rival and threat to Caesar.

Although Jesus does not deny Pilate's question (**Are you
the king of the Jews?**), the Roman governor finds **no basis for
a charge against** him. The Sanhedrin, however, presses Pilate
further. Jesus **stirs up the people all over Judea by his teaching**,
just as other messianic claimants have done, often in response
to Roman taxation (see Acts 5:35–37). This seditious activity, Pilate
is told, **started in Galilee and has come all the way** to Jerusalem.
Galilee had often experienced unrest (Acts 5:37).

23:6–12 / The reference to Galilee gives **Pilate** the opportunity to be rid of a problem (see Fitzmyer, p. 1480) by sending
Jesus to **Herod**, the ruler of Galilee, who happened to be **in Jerusalem at that time**. This **pleased** Herod greatly, not only because **he had heard about** Jesus and had **hoped to see him
perform some miracle**, but also because Pilate's action was a po-

litical courtesy which would likely have been the real reason for
Herod's and Pilate's new-found friendship (v. 12). Herod had been
wanting to see Jesus since the days of his Galilean ministry (9:9).
Now he hopes that Jesus will perform a miracle. Herod's questions were probably requests to perform miracles, as well as questions about Jesus' identity and mission. **But Jesus,** however, **gave
him no answer.** This refusal to cooperate no doubt frustrated and
angered Herod. **The chief priests and the teachers of the law** seize
the opportunity to accuse Jesus before the Galilean ruler. Pilate
had not found him guilty, perhaps Herod would. But Herod pronounces no verdict of guilt, but joins in with his **soldiers** in their
mockery and mistreatment of Jesus. In light of Luke's theme of
two witnesses (Deut. 19:15; cf. Matt. 18:16), it is significant that
Herod also finds no guilt in Jesus. Thus, both Palestinian rulers,
Pilate of Judea and Herod of Galilee, although by no means sympathetic, find Jesus innocent.

23:13–25 / This idea of innocence is conveyed clearly in
Pilate's speech to **the chief priests, the rulers and the people** in
vv. 14–16. Jesus has been examined by the two supreme secular
authorities of the land and has not been found deserving of
death. Pilate offers to **punish him** (by whipping), probably as
a warning to avoid getting into trouble in the future, before re-
leasing him. But the chief priests, rulers, and people will have
none of this, crying out, instead, for Jesus' death (a fact of which
Peter will remind the inhabitants of Jerusalem in Acts 2:23, 36;
3:13–15) and the release of **Barabbas.** Although v. 17 is probably a later scribal addition based on Mark 15:6 (**Now he was
obliged to release one man to them at the feast;** see footnote
in NIV), Luke knew this verse from his Marcan source and so
presupposed it in writing his account. The people are not interested in Jesus, the man of peace. They want the release of Barabbas, a man of violence, one who fits more closely the cruder
aspects of popular messianic expectation. Although Jesus has
done nothing deserving of death, the crowd shouts for his crucifixion; while for Barabbas, a man who has committed **murder,**
they shout for clemency.

Despite finding Jesus innocent, Pilate, nonetheless, bows
to the pressure of the crowd. His was a harsh and unpopular rule
in Judea, and the last thing that this governor needed was more

trouble. Thus, Pilate's authority yields to the demands of the people, thereby enabling Luke to place the blame for Jesus' execution more squarely on the shoulders of the Jewish religious leaders. Not only does this serve Luke's broader theological program in which he consistently portrays Jewish religious leadership as stubborn and as always resisting the Spirit of God (see Acts 7:51–53), but it also serves as an apologetic with regard to early Christianity's relationship to the Roman state. Luke bears bold testimony: Whereas it may be true that Jesus was executed by Roman authority, he had been, nevertheless, pronounced innocent three times by this authority (23:4, 14–16, 22). Jesus was executed because of a failure of nerve on the part of Pilate, the Roman governor. Had he had the courage to do his job properly, Jesus would never have been handed over to be crucified.

Additional Notes §54

22:65 / **insulting things**: Lit. "blaspheming." Luke is suggesting that the guards were speaking things contrary to God's truth in their abuse and ridicule of Jesus.

22:66 / The **elders of the people** probably refers to the **chief priests** (see note on 19:47 above) and the **teachers of the law** (see note on 5:21 above). The **council** (lit. "Sanhedrin") was made up of approximately seventy members, some of whom were priests and Sadducees, while others were Pharisees (see Acts 23:1–9). Many, whether favoring the Sadducees or the Pharisees, were professional scribes and teachers of the law. This body represented the highest Jewish political and religious authority of the time. One of the tractates of the Mishnah named *Sanhedrin* describes this council's function. See *HBD*, pp. 905–6.

22:68 / What Jesus (or Luke) means by this statement has baffled commentators (Marshall [pp. 849–50] is uncertain; so is Fitzmyer, p. 1467; Ellis [p. 262] says nothing). Marshall, as have others before him, hesitatingly suggests that this verse may be understood in light of 20:1–8, where "the chief priests and the teachers of the law" refuse to answer Jesus' question regarding the source of John's authority to baptize. Since there is no other plausible explanation, this may very well point to the truth of the matter.

22:69 / Jesus' reference to sitting **at the right hand of the mighty God** is an allusion to Ps. 110:1, a psalm describing the enthronement of God's anointed king. This text was understood by early Christians as messianic, as seen in Luke 20:42–43 (and parallels in Matthew and Mark); Acts 2:34–35; Rom. 8:34; Heb. 1:3, 13; 8:1; 10:12; 12:2 (see further David M. Hay, *Glory at the Right Hand: Psalm 110 in Early Christianity*, SBLMS 18 [Nashville: Abingdon, 1973]). Since the **Son of Man** title can have a "judicial connotation" in 11:30 (Fitzmyer, p. 1467), Jesus' statement may very well mean that the next time the members of the Sanhedrin see him, they will see *him* as *their* judge.

22:70 / Tiede (pp. 401–2) notes the irony in the Sanhedrin's question, "You are the Son of God, right?" and in Jesus' reply, "You are correct." Israel's religious leaders have made a proper confession, but they are blind to the significance of it, a point that Paul will later make (see Acts 13:27–28).

23:1 / Talbert (p. 214) suggests that Luke is portraying Jesus as the righteous martyr. He points to the martyrdom of Eleazar in 4 Maccabees 6–7.

23:2 / **Christ, a king**: Or, "an anointed king." See note on 2:11 above. The accusation against Jesus rings hollow when later the crowd cries out for the release of Barabbas (v. 18), a man who truly does represent a threat to the peace.

23:4 / **Chief priests** equals the council or Sanhedrin. See note on 22:66 above.

23:5 / **started in Galilee**: Jesus' Galilean ministry began in 4:14 and continued through 9:50. In 9:51 Jesus started his journey to Jerusalem, arriving in 19:28.

23:7–9 / **Herod**: See commentary and notes on 3:1 and 9:7–9 above.

23:17 / The oldest Greek manuscripts do not contain this verse. An early Christian scribe could have added the verse to harmonize the account with Mark 15:6.

23:18, 25 / Outside of the Gospel narrative nothing is known of Pilate's "Passover pardon," as it usually called, whereby the governor apparently set free any one prisoner the people wanted released (see Mark 15:6). "Presumably Pilate was trying to appease the Jews" (Marshall, p. 860). Fitzmyer (p. 1489) notes the irony in the crowd's request for the release of Barabbas, whose name means "son of the father." The crowd demands the release of a criminal "son of the father" and the death of the Father's true Son. According to some manuscripts this man's given name was Jesus. In this case, Pilate may have been asking the crowd which Jesus they would like to have released.

23:21 / **Crucify him!**: Crucifixion was a form of execution whereby the victim was hanged, usually by nailing, upon a large wooden stake, often with a cross beam (see note on 23:33 below).

23:23-25 / Outside of the NT that are a few brief reports of Jesus' crucifixion. In a letter to his son, one Mara bar Serapion writes (ca. A.D. 73): "For what advantage did . . . the Jews [gain] by the death of their wise king, because from that same time their kingdom was taken away?" (See Robert Dunkerley, *Beyond the Gospels* [Baltimore: Penguin, 1957], p. 27.) From Josephus (ca. A.D. 90) we have: " . . . Pilate, upon hearing him accused by men of the highest standing among us, had condemned him to be crucified . . . " (*Antiquities* 18.63-64; this passage is suspected by many to have been tampered with by later Christians). Elsewhere this same passage from Josephus is quoted in the following manner: "Pilate condemned him to be crucified and to die" (Agapius, *Book of the Title*). Note that here there is no mention of the involvement of the Jewish religious leaders. According to Slavonic Josephus (an Old Russian version whose references to NT personages are largely regarded as later Christian interpolations, although not all its interpolations have a bearing on the NT and its origins), Pilate initially released Jesus, since he had healed the procurator's wife. Nevertheless, after being bribed with thirty talents, Pilate eventually permitted the teachers of the law to crucify Jesus (*War* 2.9.3 [2.172-174, LCL]; see also 5.5.4 [5.207-214, LCL]). The Roman historian Tacitus (ca. A.D. 110-120) reports: "This name [i.e., "Christian"] originates from 'Christus' who was sentenced death by the procurator, Pontius Pilate, during the reign of Tiberius" (*Annals* 15.44). According to the Babylonian Talmud: "On the eve of Passover they hanged Jesus the Nazarene. And a herald went out, in front of him, for forty days saying: 'He is going to be stoned, because he practiced sorcery and enticed and led Israel astray. Anyone who knows anything in his favor, let him come and plead in his behalf.' But not having found anything in his favor, they hanged him on the eve of Passover" (b. *Sanhedrin* 43a).

§55 The Crucifixion (Luke 23:26–43)

The crucifixion account consists of three parts: (1) the journey to the place of crucifixion (vv. 26–31), (2) the crucifixion (vv. 32–38), and (3) the story of the two crucified criminals (vv. 39–43). Although most of this material comes from Mark 15:21–32, much of it appears only in Luke (vv. 27–32, 33b, 39b–43); consequently, many commentators think that the evangelist had access to another account of the crucifixion story.

23:26–31 / Verse 26 describes how **Simon from Cyrene** is **made** to **carry** Jesus' **cross**. This detail is derived from Mark's account, but the rest of Luke's paragraph consists of yet one other unique Lucan oracle of doom pronounced against **Jerusalem** (see 13:31–35; 19:41–44; 21:20–24). Jesus describes part of the horror that will come upon the inhabitants of Jerusalem. The days will be so bad that childless **women**, usually viewed as quite unfortunate, will consider themselves **blessed**. They will have no other mouths to feed during the famine that will grip the besieged city, and they will be spared the grief of seeing their **children** die in the overthrow of the city. The experience will be so dreadful that the people will wish for death and burial (the meaning of the allusion to Hos. 10:8) to put an end to the horrors. Jesus' final saying (v. 31) is proverbial and probably means (although it is disputed) if God is willing to permit such a disaster as the death of the innocent Jesus, how much more severe will guilty Jerusalem's coming disaster be. The fact that Jesus' cross is made of wood probably has nothing to do with the saying (against Fitzmyer, pp. 1498–99).

23:32–38 / **Jesus** and **two** other **criminals** were brought to **the place called the Skull**, where they were **crucified** (see note below). Many of Mark's details are omitted: the Aramaic name Golgotha, the wine mixed with myrrh, the time of day, the people who wag their heads, and the taunt about Jesus and the destruction and rebuilding of the temple. The main thrust of the narrative, however, remains essentially the same. There are at least three allusions to lament Psalms in vv. 34–36 (**divided up his clothes . . . casting lots**, Ps. 22:18; **watching . . . sneered**, Ps. 22:7; **wine vinegar**, Ps. 69:22). These allusions would indicate that Jesus' experience parallels the experience of the righteous sufferer of the Psalms. Moreover, since these Psalms were attributed to David (see their superscriptions) allusion to them would only underscore Jesus' relationship to King David, the prototype of the coming Messiah.

In v. 35 the **people** are to be understood as the Jews. Their **rulers** jeer at Jesus; if he were truly the Messiah then he could save himself as he supposedly had saved others. Likewise in v. 36, the Roman **soldiers also came up and mocked him**. They too command Jesus to **save** himself (v. 37). At long last his murderous opposition has succeeded in putting an end to him (19:47–48). The inscription, THIS IS THE KING OF THE JEWS, was placed over his cross as a final insult. There is irony in this, however, for although Jesus was no king in terms of popular expectation, he was Israel's King nevertheless. It is also ironic in that this written statement was the first thing about Jesus committed to writing and probably the only thing concerning Jesus actually written during Jesus' lifetime (see note below).

23:39–43 / According to Mark 15:32, the **criminals** who were crucified with Jesus also ridiculed him. Luke's version, however, is unique in that it presents us with a conversation between Jesus and one of the criminals. In this scene we are told that one of the criminals (who were probably political zealots) rebukes the other for joining in the taunts (vv. 40–41). The repentant criminal tells his companion that whereas their sentence is just, Jesus' is not. Thus, the reader is again told of Jesus' innocence. Furthermore, by his request (v. 42) the criminal implicitly recognizes Jesus' kingship (**when you come into your kingdom**; recall 22:30). Jesus will not only **remember** this man, but he promises him that he will be **with** him that very day **in paradise** (see note below).

Additional Notes §55

23:26 / Because Luke omits Mark 15:16–20a, the passage that describes the Roman soldiers' mistreatment of Jesus, it could be that the evangelist intends to leave the impression that the Jews themselves crucified Jesus. J. T. Sanders (p. 226) thinks so. This could be, but Luke does mention the centurion later in v. 47. Surely this is supposed to be a *Roman* centurion (and not a Jewish one). Sanders (p. 228) agrees. Because Luke leaves this Roman at the site of the crucifixion, one could argue that Luke has all along understood that the Romans crucified Jesus, and he no doubt assumed that his readers would know this. Who else had the authority to crucify people in the Roman Empire? I think that Luke has omitted the part about the abuse of Jesus not to implicate the Jews, but to mitigate Roman cruelty. Luke retains the centurion's confession (modifying it, of course, to that of a pronouncement of Jesus' innocence), just as he will in the Book of Acts provide other Roman pronouncements that favor Christianity.

23:26–31 / With the exception of the opening verse (v. 26, cf. Mark 15:20b–21), this passage is unique to Luke. J. T. Sanders (p. 226) comments that this episode "dramatically brings [Jewish] guilt into view." True, Jerusalem's guilt in executing Jesus is implied, but the main point of the passage consists of Jesus' warning, not in finding yet more reason to condemn the Jews. The women should weep for themselves, for catastrophe will befall the city. The pathos of this scene belies an anti-Semitic orientation (see also 23:48). Tiede (p. 414) catches the import of the passage when he says that "the meaning of the oracle is its profound declaration that Jesus' death is more a tragedy for Israel than for the Messiah himself."

23:29 / The *Gospel of Thomas* 79b (see note on 11:27–28 above) has apparently picked up this otherwise unique Lucan saying: "For there will be days when you will say, 'Blessed are the womb which has not conceived and the breasts which have not given milk.' " This saying has been combined with the similar saying found in Luke 11:27–28.

23:30 / The citation of Hosea is appropriate to the Lucan context. In Hos. 10:7–8 the prophet predicts the destruction of Israel's high places and altars (i.e., Israel's places of idol worship).

23:33 / **The Skull:** As to why the place of Jesus' execution was called the Skull opinions vary. Fitzmyer (p. 1503) states that the "place was probably so called because of the physical shape of a hill, not because it was a place of skulls." The exact opposite opinion is expressed in *HBD*, p. 150. Following a Jewish legend, a few early church fathers entertained the notion that Golgotha was the place where Adam was buried, and it was his skull that gave the place its name.

they crucified him: *HBD* (p. 194) provides this description of Roman crucifixion: "With a placard proclaiming the crime hung around the neck, the condemned prisoner carried the crossbar, not the whole cross, to the place of execution where the upright stake was already in place. There the offender was stripped and flogged. The prisoner's arms were affixed to the crossbar with ropes or nails, and the crossbar was then raised and attached to the upright stake. A small wooden block attached to the stake beneath the buttocks supported the weight of the suspended body, which was bound to the stake with ropes. Often the feet were also affixed to the stake with ropes or nails. Because deterrence was a primary objective, the cross was always erected in a public place. Death came slowly, often only after several days, and resulted from the cumulative impact of thirst, hunger, exhaustion, exposure, and the traumatic effects of the scourging. After death the body was usually left hanging on the cross. Because of the protracted suffering and the extreme ignominy of this manner of execution, it was viewed by the Romans as the supreme penalty, the 'most wretched of deaths' (Josephus), and generally reserved for the lowest classes and the most heinous crimes" (see *HBD*, pp. 194–95 for further discussion). For further discussion of important archaeological data pertinent to Roman crucifixion see James H. Charlesworth, "Jesus and Jehohana: An Archaeological Note on Crucifixion," *ExpTim* 84 (1973), pp. 147–50. When the victims were nailed to the cross, the iron spikes transfixed the wrists (not palms). For further discussion see J. A. Fitzmyer, "Crucifixion in Ancient Palestine, Qumran Literature, and the New Testament," *CBQ* 40 (1978), pp. 493–513.

23:34a / The earliest manuscripts do not contain the first part of v. 34 ("Jesus said, 'Father forgive them, for they do not know what they are doing.' "). The saying may have been inserted as a parallel to Acts 7:60b where Stephen offers a similar prayer of forgiveness (see Fitzmyer, pp. 1503–4). If original (so Ellis, pp. 267–68; Marshall, p. 868; Schweizer, pp. 359–60; J. T. Sanders, p. 227), it presents Jesus as willing to forgive those who have committed an inexcusable crime against him. Jesus asks that they be forgiven on the grounds that they did not know what they were doing. According to Lev. 4:2 and Num. 15:25–29, atonement is possible for one who has sinned unwittingly. Perhaps this underlies Jesus' prayer. Sanders (p. 63) thinks that the purpose of this prayer is only to make possible the initial offer of repentance to the Jewish people (as seen in the early chapters of Acts), an offer that is withdrawn after the martyrdom of Stephen. This line of interpretation is surely faulty. Since Stephen's prayer (Acts 7:60) closely parallels the prayer of Jesus, should not the same function be assigned to it as well? Why would Jesus' prayer of forgiveness make possible the offer of repentance to Jews, while Stephen's similar prayer would not? The Lucan prayers of forgiveness are not clever devices that are designed, as part of an anti-Semitic agenda, to advance the plot of the Lucan narrative (as J. T. Sanders maintains). These prayers represent a genuine desire for reconciliation. It is hard to believe that if the evangelist were truly anti-Semitic, as Sanders supposes, he would go out of his way to supply two prayers of forgiveness in behalf of persons who have been presented as wrongly putting to death Jesus and one of his followers. Had Luke truly hated the Jews, and believed that there could be no forgiveness for them, he could have adopted a much harsher biblical precedent. Consider the words of an angry Isaiah: "Forgive them not!" (Isa. 2:6, 9). Compare also the unforgiving words of the martyred sons of the Maccabean revolt: "For you [i.e., Antiochus IV] there will be no resurrection to life!" (2 Macc. 7:14); "Keep on, and see how [God's] mighty power will torture you and your descendants!"

(2 Macc. 7:17); "Do not think that you will go unpunished for having tried to fight against God!" (2 Macc. 7:19; cf. the parallel versions in 4 Macc. 9:9, 32; 10:11, 21; 12:12, 14, 18; 5 Macc. 5:17, 23, 46–51). Nothing is more out of step with these embittered expressions than the prayers of forgiveness we find on the lips of two significant protagonists in the narrative of Luke–Acts.

23:35 / **rulers**: By this expression we are probably to understand members of the Sanhedrin, ruling priests, and other persons of influence.

23:38 / The inscription on Jesus' cross presents some difficulties, for it appears in a variety of forms in the Gospels:

Mark 15:26	THE KING OF THE JEWS
Luke 23:38	THIS IS THE KING OF THE JEWS
Matt. 27:37	THIS IS JESUS, THE KING OF THE JEWS
John 19:19-20	JESUS OF NAZARETH, THE KING OF THE JEWS
	(written in Aramaic, Latin, and Greek)
Slavonic Josephus	[. . . at one of the gates leading into the temple] with inscriptions hung a . . . tablet with inscription in these [Greek, Roman, and Jewish] characters, to the effect: Jesus has not reigned as king; he has been crucified by the Jews because he proclaimed the destruction of the city and the laying waste of the temple (from the Slavonic version of *War* 5.5.2 [5.190–200, LCL]).

23:43 / **in paradise**: The word ultimately comes from the LXX translation of "garden" in Gen. 2:8 and 13:10. Eventually it came to refer to the abode of the righteous dead (see 2 Cor. 12:4 and Rev. 2:7). See *HBD*, pp. 749–50.

§56 Death and Burial (Luke 23:44–56)

This section may be divided into two parts: (1) the death of Jesus (vv. 44–49) and (2) the burial of Jesus (vv. 50–56). As in the previous section (vv. 26–43) the Lucan account basically follows Mark (15:33–47), but not without various omissions, additions, and modifications.

23:44–49 / There are four noteworthy differences between the Lucan and Marcan accounts: (1) Whereas in Mark 15:38 the temple veil tears *after* Jesus' death, in Luke 23:45 it *tears* before his death (see note below). (2) Luke omits Jesus' cry of dereliction found in Mark 15:34 ("My God, my God, why have you forsaken me?"; see Ps. 22:1). (3) Luke 23:46 alludes to Ps. 31:5, which Mark does not. (4) Finally, the Roman soldier's exclamation following Jesus' death is different. Instead of recognizing Jesus as the "Son of God" (see Mark 15:39) the Lucan soldier declares, **Surely this was a righteous** [or innocent] **man** (v. 47).

With his death, his "ascent," begun in 9:51, has taken a major step forward. Having been placed into the hands of men (see 9:44), Jesus now places his spirit into the hands of his Father. Even in his last moment of life Jesus is able to quote Ps. 31:5 as a demonstration of his faith in his heavenly Father (see note below). Luke probably omitted the Marcan cry of dereliction because he felt that it was inappropriate. He presents Jesus as in control of his destiny, in such control that even while hanging on the cross he could forgive a man his sins and offer his assurances of entry into Paradise (see vv. 39–43 above). By changing the exclamation of the Roman soldier, Luke is able yet one more time to declare Jesus' innocence, an innocence recognized by a second Roman (Pilate being the first, see vv. 4, 13–16, 22). Such recognition of innocence by Roman officials would serve Luke's larger purpose of portraying Jesus and his followers as law-abiding citizens who are not guilty of treason, insurrection, or misconduct.

In v. 48, a verse found only in Luke, the evangelist tells us that **when all the people who had gathered to witness this sight saw what took place, they beat their breasts and went away**. Already, the turning point has been reached. Now that the terrible deed has been done, the perpetrators are having second thoughts. This clearly anticipates the sorrow and repentance displayed following Peter's Pentecost sermon in Acts 2:14–39 (esp. v. 37). Jesus' followers (v. 49), rather than running away as they do in Mark 14:50, **stood at a distance, watching these things**. The evangelist keeps the disciples on hand, as witnesses, ready to resume the ministry as soon as the Good News of Easter is learned.

23:50–56 / Luke's account of Jesus' burial follows, but in abbreviated form. **Joseph . . . from the Judean town of Arimathea** is described as a **good and upright** (same word used of Jesus in v. 47 above) **man**. This man, like the righteous Simeon (2:25), **was waiting for the kingdom of God**. By describing him thus, the evangelist is implying that Joseph was in sympathy with John the Baptist's earlier call to repentance (3:3) and Jesus' later proclamation of the kingdom (4:43). This man was a **member of the Council** (see 22:66 above), **who had not consented to their decision and action**. Having obtained the permission of **Pilate** to take **Jesus' body**, he gave it a proper burial. Unlike most who were crucified and then thrown into a common grave, Jesus was laid **in a tomb cut in the rock, one in which no one had yet been laid**. Although he had suffered an ignominious death, at least his burial was more befitting a king. The loyal **women** from **Galilee**, who in v. 49 had "stood at a distance, watching" the crucifixion, observed the place of Jesus' burial so that they might return after the **Sabbath** (a day on which such labors were strictly forbidden) to anoint Jesus' body with **spices and perfumes**.

Additional Notes §56

23:44 / At the brightest time of day, from noon till 3 p.m., **darkness came over the whole land**. This darkness is probably a vivid illustration of Jesus' reference to his arrest as an "hour—when darkness reigns" (22:53). It may also be a portent that foreshadows the strange phenomena that accompany Jesus' return as "Son of Man" (21:25). In reference to the darkness at the time of Jesus' crucifixion, Julius Africanus (d. after A.D. 240) reports (according to fragment 18 of Africanus' five-volume *Chronography,* preserved in Georgius Syncellus, *Chronology*) that "this darkness Thallus [the Samaritan Chronicler], in the third book of his *History,* calls, as appears to me without reason, an eclipse of the sun." See A. Roberts and J. Donaldson, eds., *The Ante-Nicene Fathers* (Grand Rapids: Eerdmans, 1951), vol. 6, p. 136.

23:45 / The **curtain of the temple** probably refers to the curtain, or veil, separating the "Holy of Holies" from the rest of the inner temple area. Marshall (p. 875) thinks that the tearing of the curtain "is a forewarning of the destruction of the temple." Such a conclusion, however, carries more conviction in the Marcan context where there is developed an anti-temple motif. Tiede (p. 423), however, suggests that the tearing of the curtain may have been understood as a sign of divine displeasure. Fitzmyer (p. 1519) thinks that the tearing of the curtain is a sign of the reign of evil during the time of Jesus' passion (Luke 22:53). I suspect that there is some truth in both of the latter views. Slavonic Josephus (*War* 5.5.4 [5.207–214, LCL]) repeats the tradition of the torn curtain: "[The temple curtain] had, you should know, been suddenly rent from the top to the ground, when they delivered over to death through bribery the doer of good, the man—yea, him who through his doing was no man. And many other signs they tell which came to pass at that time." The "other signs" would include the darkness and the earthquake (see Matt. 27:51; Amos 8:9). Lachs (p. 434) notes that there are rabbinic stories claiming that in some cases strange events attended the death of notable rabbis.

23:46 / **spirit**: "The whole of the living person" (Fitzmyer, p. 1519). Jesus' utterance is taken from Psalm 31, a psalm attributed to David that is a prayer of lamentation and thanksgiving. The psalmist has been ill (vv. 9–10), has been the object of lies and traps (vv. 4, 18, 20), has been scorned by enemies and abandoned by friends (v. 11), and has sought refuge in God in the face of death (vv. 5, 13). The suitability of this psalm for Jesus' passion is obvious: Jesus, the son of David (Luke 1:32; 18:38), has been falsely accused, entrapped, scorned, betrayed, and now, hanging on the cross, faces death. Rabbinic interpretation of this psalm, emphasizing messianic and eschatological themes (*Midrash Psalms* 31.2–3, 5–7, 8), further clarifies why such a psalm would be utilized in the passion tradition. The specific verse that the Lucan Jesus has quoted was employed as a prayer before going to sleep (*Numbers Rabbah* 20.20; *Midrash Psalms* 25.2). It was a prayer that God protect one's spirit until one awakens. "Sleep" could mean either literally sleep or figuratively death (note Acts 7:59–60, where the dying Stephen prays, "Lord Jesus, receive my spirit" [alluding to Luke 23:46 and Ps. 31:5], and then "falls asleep"). Thus understood, Ps. 31:5 is particularly suitable for the dying Jesus. Implicit is that Jesus, like David, faced opposition from his own people, and, like David, entrusts his spirit to God (see Fitzmyer, p. 1519).

23:47 / **praised** [or "glorified"] **God**: Luke has added this idea, which is in keeping with his wider concern to portray his characters as praising and glorifying God (see 2:20; 5:26; 13:13; 17:15–16; 18:43; Acts 4:21; 11:18; 21:20).

righteous: Tiede (p. 425) suggests that the centurion's confession that Jesus was "righteous" may have had christological implications (see Acts 3:14; 7:52; 22:14, where Jesus is called the "Righteous One").

23:48 / J. T. Sanders (pp. 228–29) wonders if the people **beat their breasts** because they are worried about their future. This is not likely. Tiede (p. 425) notes that the people "returned"/"repented" (*hypostrephein*)— the NIV reads **went away**—much as Jesus predicted that Peter would "return"/"repent" (*epistrephein*) after denying his Lord (see 22:32). Luke's description anticipates the remorse and repentance that will be expressed at the Pentecost sermon (Acts 2:37–38). Leaney (p. 287) suggests that in this verse, Luke may have in mind Zech. 12:10–14.

23:49 / **Galilee**: See note on 17:11 above. These **women** are probably those mentioned in 8:1–3.

23:51 / **Arimathea**: Where this city was in the time of Jesus is not easily determined. It may have been one of two cities situated five and ten miles north of Jerusalem. See Fitzmyer, p. 1526; *HBD*, p. 63. Lachs (p. 436) thinks that it is Haramatiam, ten miles east of Lydda and about ten miles southeast of Antipatris.

23:52 / **Pilate**: See note on 3:1 above. Pilate, of course, was the Roman governor who ordered Jesus' execution (see 23:24).

23:53 / **tomb**: "Tombs hewn out of rock, dating from the first century, are found in abundance in the area around Jerusalem" (Fitzmyer, p. 1529).

23:55 / **The women who had come with Jesus from Galilee**: See note on 23:49 above.

23:56 / **But they rested on the Sabbath**: The Sabbath is from sundown (6 p.m.) Friday until sundown Saturday. The command to rest (or cease from work) is found in Exod. 20:10; Deut. 5:12–15.

§57 The Empty Tomb (Luke 24:1–12)

Luke 24 consists of a series of resurrection appearances of Jesus to various of his followers and culminates in his ascension (v. 51). Unlike the passion narrative, where there is fairly close agreement, the resurrection narratives of the Gospels diverge widely. Where the Gospels come the closest is in the telling of the discovery of the empty tomb (Luke 24:1–12). The reason for this is that this is the part of the narrative that Mark preserves (16:1–8). Since Mark breaks off rather abruptly with the frightened women at the tomb speaking to no one, the other evangelists have no common guide; hence they diverge. (Matthean and Lucan divergence in their respective infancy narratives is analogous.) Unlike the account of Jesus' arrest, trial, and crucifixion where apologetic concerns made it necessary to give a more detailed and chronological account to explain why it was that Jesus the Messiah was rejected and put to death by his own people, there is no need for such a presentation in the case of the resurrection narratives. The resurrection narratives reveal fully distinctive emphases of the evangelists (see Grant R. Osborne, *The Resurrection Narratives: A Redactional Study* [Grand Rapids: Baker, 1984]). All that is needed is a convincing account or two of Jesus' appearances. Such accounts the evangelists Matthew, Luke, and John provide (with a later scribe adding a similar account to Mark's ending, i.e., Mark 16:9–20). Luke's account is perhaps the most eloquent of all and consists of the following four components: (1) the Discovery of the Empty Tomb (vv. 1–12); (2) the Walk to Emmaus (vv. 13–35); (3) the Appearance to the Disciples (vv. 36–43); and (4) the Farewell and Ascension (vv. 44–53). This section will consider the discovery of the empty tomb.

24:1–12 / The major points of difference between the Marcan and Lucan accounts involve the appearance of **two men** (24:4), instead of Mark's "young man" (Mark 16:5), Luke's reference to Jesus' earlier passion predictions (Luke 24:7), and Peter's inspection of the tomb (24:12).

Having prepared "spices and perfumes" and having rested on the Sabbath "in obedience to the commandment" (23:56), the **women** now come **to the tomb** early **on the first day of the week** (i.e., Sunday). They find the tomb open and empty; the **body of the Lord Jesus** was not present. While the women are **wondering about this, suddenly two men in clothes that gleamed like lightning stood beside them**. Luke's preference for two, instead of one, is probably again due to his concern to have two witnesses to the resurrection. This twofold witness idea continues throughout Luke 24 (two men on the road to Emmaus, two appearances of the risen Jesus, two times the witness of Scripture is appealed to). The two men, whose apparel shines (cf. 9:29), are undoubtedly to be understood as angels (as is so stated in Matt. 28:2, 5 and later in Luke 24:23). They announce to the women that Jesus has been raised and remind them of what Jesus himself had predicted, namely, his crucifixion and resurrection (see 9:22). His prediction has now been fulfilled. The women **remembered his words** and so **came back from the tomb and told all these things to the Eleven** disciples. Luke identifies these women as **Mary Magdalene, Joanna, Mary the mother of James** (see note below). They **and the others with them** reported what they had discovered **to the apostles**. The response of the apostles, however, was one of disbelief. Such a report **seemed to them like nonsense. Peter, however,** his curiosity aroused, **got up and ran to the tomb.** When he peered into the tomb **he saw the strips of linen** grave clothes **lying by themselves** (cf. John 20:3–6). Even this sight, however, did not produce faith. He was only puzzled and left **wondering,** so **he went** home (cf. John 20:10).

In telling his story this way the evangelist Luke has placed his readers ahead of the apostles themselves. The reader knows that Jesus has been raised, but the apostles do not. It will take "many convincing proofs" (Acts 1:3) before they will be persuaded. Some of these proofs Luke will provide in the remaining paragraphs of chap. 24.

Additional Notes §57

24:1 / **the women . . . went to the tomb:** Luke omits Mark's report of the women wondering how the stone will be rolled aside for them. Luke may have sensed a difficulty in this, but since the stone will be found rolled aside anyway (v. 2), he elected to abbreviate his account at this point.

24:2 / **found the stone rolled away**: A rock tomb was sealed by a large wheel-shaped stone that rolled in a carved rut or track running across the floor of the opening of the tomb.

24:4 / **two men in clothes that gleamed like lightning**: Appealing to the similar language in Luke 9:30–31, Leaney (p. 71) thinks that Luke believes that these two men are Moses and Elijah. Perhaps; but the two are explicitly referred to as "angels" (or "messengers") in v. 23. According to the apocryphal *Gospel of Peter* (see 9:35–10:42), two men descend from heaven and assist the resurrected Jesus to exit the tomb.

24:6 / **he has risen**: Luke means that Jesus has been raised by God (see Acts 3:15; 4:10) and not by his own power. This resurrection, as we shall see, is to be understood in physical terms. A phantom has not been raised, or else why would the tomb be empty?

On **Galilee** see note on 17:11 above.

24:7 / **Son of Man**: See note on 5:24 above. On the allusion to the passion prediction see commentary and note on 9:22 above.

24:9 / **the Eleven**: Although he will not tell of Judas' death until Acts 1:16–19, the evangelist clearly means the Twelve Apostles minus Judas Iscariot. According to Matt. 27:3–10, Judas commits suicide *before* the resurrection. The chronology of the Lucan version is vague. Moreover, the mode of Judas' death according to Acts is not easily harmonized with the Matthean account.

24:10 / **Mary Magdalene**: See note on 8:2 above.
Joanna: See note on 8:3 above.
Mary the mother of James: Lit. "Mary the one of James." She might be the wife, mother, or even sister of James. Mother is preferred since she may be the same Mary mentioned in Mark 15:40 where there is mentioned a "Mary the mother of James the younger and of Joses" who is with Mary Magdalene. Although not previously mentioned, she is probably one of the women who had followed Jesus from Galilee (8:2–3; 23:49, 55).

The account of the appearance of the risen Christ to the two persons on the road to Emmaus (see note below) is unique to Luke. Several features in this account reflect Lucan themes: (1) The appearance takes place while the two persons were going along a road (24:13–15). This detail recalls the Central Section (9:51–19:27) in which Jesus taught while traveling along the road to Jerusalem. The idea of teaching and traveling might anticipate the traveling ministries of the apostles in the Book of Acts. (2) The risen Christ explains to his followers how Scripture was fulfilled in what has happened to him during the past few days (24:25–27, 32). This has been a characteristic mark of Jesus' ministry as presented in Luke. Beginning with his Nazareth sermon (4:16–30) Jesus announced that Scripture was fulfilled (see 4:17–21 where Isa. 61:1–2 is quoted as fulfilled). Later, in answer to the question of the messengers of the imprisoned Baptist, Jesus refers to his ministry as fulfilling Scripture (7:18–23, esp. v. 22). Moreover, in his third prediction of his coming passion (18:31–33) Jesus says that "everything that is written by the prophets about the Son of Man will be fulfilled." Twice in Luke 24 this theme is repeated. In the passage presently under consideration Jesus tells his confused followers that "all that the prophets have spoken" has been fulfilled and that "all the Scriptures" pertain to him (vv. 25–27). Later, he will tell his disciples that "everything must be fulfilled that is written about me" (v. 44). (3) There is also a eucharistic theme present in the walk to Emmaus (see v. 30): Jesus "took bread," "gave thanks," "broke it," and "g[a]ve it" to his followers, enabling them finally to see him. These words recall the similar words used when Jesus fed the five thousand (9:10–17, esp. v. 16) and the words of the Last Supper (22:14–23, esp. v. 19). They also anticipate the "breaking of bread" by Christians in Acts (2:42, 46; 20:7, 11; 27:35).

24:13–27 / The first important fact to be observed is the dejection of the **two** followers. They **had hoped that** Jesus **was**

the one who was going to redeem Israel. After all, in view of
Jesus' popularity and apparent power and authority from God,
his followers fully expected him to triumph over the religious establishment in Jerusalem and even to subjugate the Romans. Israel
at last would be free. But now that Jesus had been crucified and
buried, it was obvious to them that these glorious things were
not destined to be. They did not realize that an even greater victory had been won.

They related these events to this stranger, **only a visitor to
Jerusalem** and one who did **not know the things that have happened** recently. Because of this setback they are not only discouraged, they are confused as well. Their confusion is only
compounded by the strange report of **some of** the **women** who
claim that they found Jesus' **tomb** empty and that **they had seen
a vision of angels, who said he was alive**. Others (one of whom
was Peter, see v. 12) **went to the tomb and found it** empty, **but
they did not see** Jesus. The report of the women had failed to
convince. (Women of first-century Palestine had little credibility.
Had it been Peter and other disciples who had seen the angels,
then the report probably would have been more readily believed.
But the prominence Luke gives to the role played by the women
in the discovery of the empty tomb, a role based squarely on early
tradition, is yet one more example of the high view accorded
women in the Lucan Gospel.) But the report of the women had
only added to their perplexity. But this should not have been so,
for the angels (or "two men in clothes that gleamed like lightning" according to v. 4) had reminded the women of what Jesus
himself had predicted (v. 7 referring to the prediction of 9:22).
Had they remembered and believed the words of Jesus, they
would have understood and believed the report of the women
now. This is why the still-unrecognized risen Jesus rebuked them.
His followers were **slow** in believing **all that the prophets have
spoken** (v. 25) and in remembering his teaching about the necessity of his suffering (v. 26). Jesus, **beginning with Moses and
all the Prophets**, then **explained to them what was said in all
the Scriptures concerning himself** (v. 27).

This conversation, and the similar one in vv. 44–49, allows
Luke to show that Jesus' rejection and death, though not in keeping with popular expectation, were in fulfillment of Scripture. The

idea of scriptural fulfillment, then, is reflected in the birth narratives in Luke 1–2 and now again in the resurrection narratives of Luke 24.

24:28–32 / Although Jesus has explained the Scriptures to his two followers, they still have not discovered the identity of this "visitor." By delaying their discovery Luke heightens the suspense of the story for his readers. The reader wonders, when will they finally realize that it is Jesus who accompanies them? **Jesus** pretends to go on **farther**, thus giving the two followers the opportunity to urge him to **stay with** them. This Jesus does, and **when he was at the table with them, he took bread, gave thanks, broke it and began to give it to them**. This act is surely meant to recall the Lord's Supper (22:14–23), and possibly the feeding of the five thousand (9:10–17), and so would make Jesus' identification more readily apparent. But their recognition is not simply natural; it is divinely given. The expression, **their eyes were opened**, should be understood as *God opened their eyes*. With this recognition, and the previous Scriptural instruction, the purpose of the appearance is now accomplished, and so Jesus **disappeared from their sight**. This "disappearance" is not disappearance in a natural sense, that is, as if Jesus simply got up and walked outside; rather, it is a supernatural act of departure. Jesus disappears from one place and reappears in another. His mode of existence is no longer as it was before his death and resurrection. The two recognized that Jesus' presence and interpretation of the **Scriptures** had been like fire **burning within** their **hearts**. This fiery enthusiasm would soon be unleashed with the Pentecost proclamation.

24:33–35 / After this astounding experience, the two **got up and returned at once to Jerusalem** in order to report the experience to **the Eleven and those with them**. But the Eleven have already become convinced of the resurrection because Jesus (**the Lord**) **has appeared to Simon** (Peter). Luke has not narrated this appearance (see 1 Cor. 15:5), but he has reported it in order to protect Peter's place of priority among the apostles and eyewitnesses of the resurrection. It would have seemed odd if the first men to see the risen Christ were not the Eleven, Jesus' closest associates. The report of the two from Emmaus also confirms the report of the appearance of the Lord to Peter: **It is true! The Lord has risen. Then the two told what had happened on the way, and how Jesus was recognized by them when he broke the bread.** It was in the act of remembering the Lord's death that the full import of the Easter event could be grasped.

Additional Notes   §58

24:13 / **Emmaus**: There is considerable uncertainty about the original location of this city. Luke tells us that it was **about seven miles** (lit. "sixty stadia" or about 6.8 miles) **from Jerusalem**. If Luke means sixty stadia *one way* (instead of a round-trip), then the two disciples indeed made a long journey for one day and evening. Fitzmyer (p. 1562) queries if the "sixty stadia" may mean a round-trip (from Jerusalem to Emmaus and back again). If this is so, then such a journey in a single day and evening is much more plausible. Moreover, there is a city called "Emmaus" by Josephus (*War* 7.217; see also 1 Macc. 9:50), which, he tells us, is about "thirty stadia" from Jerusalem. If Luke meant round-trip, then this "Emmaus" may very well be our city. For further discussion of the alternatives see Fitzmyer, pp. 1561–62; *HBD*, pp. 261–62; Marshall, pp. 892–93.

24:16 / **they were kept from recognizing him**: Lit. "their eyes were held in order not to know him." A supernatural cause was behind their inability to recognize Jesus, just as there later would be a supernatural enabling (see v. 31). The expression is reminiscent of the experience of Elisha's servant in 2 Kings 6:15–17 (Leaney, p. 293).

24:18 / **Cleopas**: A shortened form of the Greek name *Cleopatros*, not to be confused with *Clopas* (a Semitic name) found in John 19:25. Who this Cleopas was is unknown. Also unknown is his unnamed companion. The suggestion that the unnamed companion is Simon Peter (see Origen, *Against Celsus* 2.62.68) rests on sheer speculation and runs into difficulty in vv. 33–34.

24:19 / **He was a prophet, powerful in word and deed before God and all the people**: Cleopas' description of Jesus may intentionally allude to the promise of the great prophet who would be like Moses (see Acts 3:22; 7:35–37; Tannehill, p. 280).

24:21 / **the one who was going to redeem Israel**: That is, that Jesus would liberate Israel from Roman domination. The disciples' hope probably paralleled the hope of fellow Israelites. Various OT passages express the same sentiment: Isa. 41:14; 43:14; 44:22–24; 1 Macc. 4:11; cf. also Acts 1:6.

24:27 / **Moses and all the Prophets . . . all the Scriptures**: These parts of the Bible comprise the first two (major) parts of the Hebrew Bible (i.e., the OT). See also Luke 16:16, 31; Acts 26:22; 28:23. In v. 44 below the "Psalms" will be mentioned (see note there). See "Canon" in *HBD*, pp. 153–54.

§59   An Appearance to All the Disciples
(Luke 24:36–43)

The appearance to the disciples in Jerusalem constitutes Jesus' third resurrection appearance. Of the first two only one is actually narrated (the appearance to the two on the road to Emmaus, vv. 13–28), while the other is merely reported (the appearance to Simon Peter, v. 34). The appearance to the Eleven disciples will be Luke's second narrated appearance of the risen Christ and it, like the first one, will culminate in an explanation of the relevance of Scripture for understanding the person and ministry of Jesus. These two appearances are also similar in that both times Jesus eats and both times the unbelief and incomprehension on the part of the disciples give way to belief and understanding.

24:36–43 / The second narrated appearance follows right on the heels of the first. While the two **were still talking about** their experience, **Jesus himself stood among them and said to them, "Peace be with you."** Although a few manuscripts omit the last part, the earliest ones have it and so it should probably be regarded as original (cf. John 20:19). This sudden, dramatic appearance terrifies the disciples, who think that Jesus is a **ghost** (or "spirit"; cf. Mark 6:49 where the disciples suppose that the water-treading Jesus is a phantom). The disciples' fear, of course, gives Jesus the opportunity to stress that he is real, corporeal (made of **flesh and bones**). His request that they **look at** his **hands and** his **feet** ensures he is who he claims to be. The marks of the nails used in crucifying him would verify that the one before them was none other than the crucified Jesus of Nazareth. The whole incident, like the incident involving "doubting" Thomas in John 20:24–29, has an apologetic purpose. The purpose is to counter arguments that the disciples perhaps saw nothing more than a vision, but had not actually seen a real, living Jesus. This Jesus is indeed real and recognizable. His hands and feet are recognizable because of the nail prints. His physical reality is evident because they can *feel* him. Not only that, Jesus eats a **piece of broiled fish** as a final proof (see Acts 1:3), since angels and spirits do not eat (Tob. 12:19; Philo, *On Abraham* 118; Judg. 13:16; Talbert, p. 228). Their doubts are now dispelled; the disciples are ready for their final instructions before the Lord departs from them for the last time.

Additional Notes   §59

24:36 / **Peace be with you:** The Greek wording is identical to that found in John 20:19, 20. Because of this some commentators have argued for a direct literary dependence of one Gospel upon the other. Although Luke shares a few similarities with John elsewhere, their common traditions probably come from a pre-literary stage. This is less the case with the other Synoptic Gospels. Jesus' greeting is quite common, moreover, being the Jewish greeting "shalom."

24:37 / **a ghost:** Lit. "a spirit," the immaterial essence of a person's being that survives physical death. Of uncertain relation is the suggestion that the excited Rhoda in Acts 12:15 had seen Peter's "angel." In Mark 6:49 the terrified disciples believe that Jesus is a phantom. The main point in refuting the "ghost" idea has to do with the concern to establish the idea of **resurrection.** Christian resurrection involves far more than the limited idea of a disembodied spirit surviving physical death. The resurrection involves physical reconstitution and an undoing of the physical, as well as spiritual, negative effects of sin. Resurrection involves the rehabilitation of the physical order, both for human beings and for the cosmos itself (see 1 Corinthians 15). See *HBD*, pp. 864–65.

24:40 / **his hands and feet:** Although not stated, it is quite probable that the showing of his hands and his feet was meant to reveal the marks of the nails as evidence of identity and as an evidence of being more than a ghost. (Compare the wording in John 20:20, another point of similarity between Luke and John.)

24:41 / The idea here is that the news of Jesus' resurrection was almost "too good to be true." Sensing this, Jesus asks for some food to eat in order to provide final proof.

24:42 / **a piece of broiled fish:** Compare John 21:9–13 where Jesus and the disciples eat broiled fish on the shore of the Lake Gennesaret. Fitzmyer (p. 1577) notes the question that may be raised about the eating of a piece of broiled fish in Jerusalem (since Jerusalem is some distance from the lake). Is this detail evidence that the episode originally took place in Galilee and that it has been transported to the Lucan

setting in Jerusalem? The mention of fish alone, however, is scarcely sufficient warrant for such speculation, for there is adequate evidence that
fish was in good supply in Jerusalem (see Marshall, p. 903; Neh. 13:16).

24:43 / **ate it in their presence**: By describing Jesus' eating in the
presence of the disciples, Luke drives home the point of Jesus' reality.
Nothing is left to chance. Jesus really did eat the fish; he ate it right before
their very eyes.

§60 Farewell and Ascension (Luke 24:44–53)

This final section consists of two parts: (1) Jesus' commission to his disciples (vv. 44–49) and (2) Jesus' ascension (vv. 50–53). Although giving no evidence of any literary relationship, this section does bear some resemblance to Matt. 28:16–20 and John 20:19–23. It will later be recapitulated in Acts 1:6–11. (Cf. also Mark 16:9–20.)

24:44–49 / The main point that Jesus makes in v. 44 is that there really is nothing new or unexpected in his resurrection on the third day. This is so for two reasons: (1) **While** he **was still with** them he had **told** them of these things. This is especially seen in the passion predictions (9:22, 44; 18:31–33), particularly that of 9:22 and 18:33 where he predicted the resurrection *on the third day*. (2) The disciples should understand the events of Jesus' passion and resurrection because they are foretold in Scripture (i.e., the OT). This time all three parts of the OT are referred to (not just two parts, as in v. 27 above): **the Law of Moses, the Prophets and the Psalms**. The Psalms should be understood as referring to the third division of the Hebrew Bible usually known as the "Writings." Here this third division is referred to simply as the Psalms, probably because of all the Writings, the Psalms yielded the greatest relevance for a christological interpretation of the OT. This is evident in the allusions to the lament Psalms (Psalms 22, 31, and 69) in the Lucan passion account (see 23:26–43).

Verse 45 demonstrates that Jesus had to enable his disciples to interpret Scripture and thus to be able to see in it the things relevant to Christ. In Pauline terms, the disciples have been given "the mind of Christ" (1 Cor. 2:16). This new understanding will make it possible for the disciples to glean christological truths from Scripture. A dramatic illustration of this new hermeneutical insight is mirrored in Peter's Pentecost sermon in Acts 2:14–39, where Peter cites a variety of Scriptures and applies them to the experience of Christ and the earliest Christians.

But what are the apostles of Christ to know? The Risen One goes on to explain in v. 46 that the following **is written: The Christ will suffer and rise from the dead on the third day**. But where in the OT are such things written? Fitzmyer (p. 1581) remarks: "It is impossible to find any of these elements precisely in the OT, either that the Messiah shall suffer, or that he is to arise, or that it will happen on the third day." Fitzmyer is correct in noting that nowhere in the OT are such things stated *precisely*. But if they were, then the disciples would scarcely have been in need of having their minds opened to a new and deeper understanding of the Scriptures. Judging by the preaching in the Book of Acts, the OT's relationship to these aspects of Jesus the Messiah's experience is anything but obvious.

Also judging by which texts of Scripture are actually cited in the Lucan writings, we may infer which passages are in mind in v. 46. With reference to the need of the Messiah to suffer, the Lucan Jesus probably has in mind Isaiah 53, a portion of which is cited by the Ethiopian Eunuch in Acts 8:26–39 and applied to Jesus by Philip the Evangelist. When approached by Philip, the Ethiopian was reading Isa. 53:7–8: "As a sheep led to the slaughter or a lamb before its shearer is dumb, so he opens not his mouth. In his humiliation justice was denied him. Who can describe his generation? For his life is taken up from the earth" (as cited in Acts 8:32–33, RSV). Since this OT text is actually cited in one of the Lucan writings and explicitly applied to Jesus of Nazareth (see Acts 8:35), it is quite reasonable to suppose that this is at least one of the OT passages understood as indicating that **the Christ will suffer** and die.

Also found in Acts is the quotation of an OT passage which was understood as a promise that **the Christ will . . . rise from the dead**. In his Pentecost sermon Peter cites Ps. 16:8–11, in which the Psalmist, understood as David, the father of the Messiah (or Christ), declares: "For thou wilt not abandon my soul to Hades, nor let thy Holy One see corruption" (Ps. 16:10, as cited in Acts 2:27, RSV). The Lucan Paul also would later quote this OT text (Acts 13:35). According to the Lucan Peter's interpretation, this text has come to fulfillment in Jesus' physical death and resurrection. Since David's body is yet in its grave, this passage could not refer to him. Because Jesus has left his grave, the passage must refer to him instead (see Acts 2:29–32).

Finally, there are allusions to OT writings in Luke's Gospel that may explain the necessity of **the Christ** to **rise from the dead on the third day**. One text that immediately comes to mind is the Jonah typology in Luke 11:29–32, where Jesus promises the evil people of his day no "miracle" (or sign) except the "sign of Jonah" (11:29). In his parallel passage, Matthew (12:39–41) states: "For as Jonah was three days and three nights in the belly of a huge fish, so the Son of Man will be three days and three nights in the heart of the earth." It might be objected that it is only in the Matthean version that reference to "three days" is found. This is true, but the possibility does remain that Luke had seen the fuller version of the saying, since in all likelihood the saying was part of the sayings source common to the Gospels of Matthew and Luke. It is also quite possible, however, that Luke 24:46 is actually alluding to Hos. 6:2: "After two days he will revive us; on the third day he will raise us up, that we may live before him" (RSV). This may be the very Scripture that Paul has in mind when he states: " . . . he was raised on the third day in accordance with the scriptures" (1 Cor. 15:4, RSV). That this similar formulation occurs in Paul indicates that the "third day" tradition was known prior to the time of Luke's writing.

But Jesus goes on to say in v. 47 that **repentance and forgiveness of sins will be preached in his name to all nations, beginning at Jerusalem**. This verse is part of the thought that had begun in v. 46, and so it likewise is part of what is "written" in Scripture. Again we may ask where in Scripture is there the command to preach repentance and forgiveness of sins . . . to all nations, beginning in Jerusalem? At least two OT passages are quoted in Acts that may have made up part of the scriptural testimony presupposed in Luke 24:47. In Acts 2:21 Peter quotes Joel 2:32: "And everyone who calls on the name of the Lord will be saved." Although the verse seems to be making a universal appeal, in the context of the Pentecost sermon, however, only Jews are addressed (both those of Palestine and those of the Diaspora). However, when Paul cites this same text in Rom. 10:13 his context indicates a universal meaning: both Jew and Gentile can freely call upon the name of the Lord. Another OT passage quoted in Acts applies to Gentiles as well. In Acts 13:47 the Lucan Paul quotes Isa. 49:6: "I have made you a light for the Gentiles, that you may bring salvation to the ends of the earth." The Greek word "ends" is the same as that in Acts 1:8 and 13:47. The idea of this proclamation "beginning at Jerusalem" could come from an OT text such as Isa. 2:2–3, where it is prophesied that "It shall come to pass in the latter days that . . . all the nations . . . and many peoples shall come. . . . For out of Zion shall go forth the law, and the word of the Lord from Jerusalem" (RSV; cf. also Mic. 4:1–2). Other OT texts used in early Christian circles that suggest that the Gentiles will have a part among God's people include Hos. 1:10 and 2:23, both of which are cited by Paul in Rom. 9:24–26. See also Paul's use of Isa. 65:1 in Rom. 10:20 and his use of Ps. 18:49; Deut. 32:43; Ps. 117:1; and Isa. 11:10 in Rom. 15:9–12.

Verses 48–49 are brief summaries of what will be more fully treated in Acts 1:6–2:4. In v. 48 Jesus tells his disciples that they are witnesses of these things (see Acts 1:8). They are witnesses of his entire public ministry, his passion, and now, most importantly, his resurrection. But the idea of being witnesses is not a passive one. They are to become proclaimers of repentance and forgiveness of sins. Theirs will be an active ministry of outreach to all nations. This active ministry, however, can only be accomplished through the power from on high with which, Jesus instructs his disciples, they will be clothed. This power, as we discover in Acts 1:8 and 2:2–4, is the Holy Spirit.

24:50–53 / Having given them his final commission, which will be repeated in Acts 1:4–8, Jesus led his disciples **out to the vicinity of Bethany** (about a mile and a half from Jerusalem) and **lifted up his hands and blessed them. While he was blessing them, he left them and was taken up to heaven**. Although this last phrase is omitted in two manuscripts, many other old manuscripts, among them the very oldest, do include it, and so it is probably best to regard it as an original part of the account. Even without it the meaning is scarcely changed, for the account of the ascension in Acts 1:9–11 confirms that Luke had a departure via ascension in mind, an idea which was probably in mind since the beginning of the journey to Jerusalem in 9:51 (see note there).

Now at last the disciples fully understand Jesus. Gone are their fear and unbelief. **Then they worshiped** Jesus **and returned to Jerusalem with great joy**. Jesus now is truly understood as "Lord." While awaiting the promise of the Father (v. 49) **they stayed continually at the temple, praising God**. This setting not only resumes where Jesus left off (see 19:47), but it anticipates Peter's temple sermon in Acts 3. Here is an important Lucan idea. The Good News of the kingdom was preached in the temple of Jerusalem, the seat of Jewish religious authority, both by Jesus and by his apostles. (However, when the Spirit descends upon the disciples, they are not at the temple, but in an "upper room" [Acts 1:13] in Jerusalem.)

The way Luke's Gospel concludes makes it evident that a sequel volume is planned. The disciples are left waiting in Jerusalem and are not engaged in their apostolic ministry of evangelism. This ministry does not begin in earnest until the sending of the Spirit, at which time the activities of the risen, glorified Christ will resume in the lives of his followers.

Additional Notes §60

24:44 / **in the Law of Moses**: Where in the Pentateuch does one find anything about the Messiah? The only references to "anointed" (messiah) ones refer to anointed high priests (Lev. 4:3, 5, 16; 6:15). It was argued in the commentary on the Lucan version of the Transfiguration (9:28–36; see commentary and notes) that the evangelist has compared Jesus with Moses and with various aspects of the Pentateuch. Also it was suggested that by arranging his material in the Central Section (10:1–18:14) to follow the sequence of Deuteronomy 1–26, Luke hoped to portray Jesus as the prophet like Moses (see commentary on 10:1–24). In Acts 3:22–23; 7:37, however, there is an explicit quotation of Deut. 18:15–16, 19, in which Jesus is indeed identified as that prophet whom God would raise up after Moses. This would surely count as one of the texts of the Pentateuch in which something about the Messiah is revealed. Furthermore, Deut. 21:22–23 (quoted in part by Paul in Gal. 3:13) could easily have been understood as relating to Jesus' crucifixion.

Paul Schubert ("The Structure and Significance of Luke 24," in *Neutestamentliche Studien für Rudolf Bultmann*, BZNW 21, W. Eltester, ed. [Berlin: Töpelmann, 1954], pp. 165–86) explores the "double-witness" theme in Luke 24, particularly with reference to vv. 27 and 44–47, where twice the risen Christ explains the Scriptures to his disciples. Schubert concludes that "Luke's proof-from-prophecy theology," an important aspect of Lucan theology, stands at the heart of this chapter. For a recent and thorough examination of Luke's use of the OT see Darrell L. Bock, *Proclamation from Prophecy and Pattern: Lucan Old Testament Christology* JSNTSup 12 (Sheffield: JSOT, 1987).

24:46 / **Christ**: See note on 2:11 above.

24:47 / **repentance and forgiveness of sins**: The earliest manuscripts actually read "repentance for the forgiveness of sins" (cf. Luke 3:3, though the other reading is supported by Acts 5:31) and is to be preferred. Another aspect of apostolic preaching is faith in Jesus the Christ. The formula in Luke 24:47 says little about the christological content of this preaching. The phrase, **in his name**, provides the only christological content. The context (esp. v. 46), however, would indicate that faith in Jesus as the Messiah who suffered and whom God raised up from death is a necessary component. Tannehill (p. 295) notes that the references to preaching and forgiveness recall Jesus' opening sermon at Nazareth (Luke 4:18–19).

It was believed that national repentance was necessary before there could be national deliverance. Rabbi Eliezer (ca. A.D. 90) said: "If Israel repent, they will be redeemed; if not, they will not be redeemed" (b. *Sanhedrin* 97b; trans. from H. Freedman, *The Babylonian Talmud: Sanhedrin* [London: Soncino, 1935], p. 660). See also *T. Judah* 23:15; *Pirqe Rabbi Eliezer* 43. This is obviously the view of the Lucan Peter in Acts 3:19–21. It was further believed that when Israel repented, messianic blessings would first be felt in Jerusalem (Lachs, p. 444; see *Pesiqta Rabbati* 41.1 where Isa. 2:3 is interpreted). This is likely what lies behind Jesus' words, **beginning at Jerusalem**. The blessings of the gospel would first be felt in Jerusalem and then would eventually be felt throughout the world.

24:49 / **what my father has promised**: According to Tiede (p. 443), the Father's promise constitutes "the fulfillment of the hopes for 'the consolation of Israel' (2:25), the 'redemption of Jerusalem' (2:38), 'the kingdom of God' (23:51), and the 'redeeming of Israel' (24:21). This will not be accomplished for these disciples until Jesus has been exalted and the Holy Spirit has been sent to authorize the renewal of Israel's vocation. The 'promise of my Father' or 'the promise of the Father' (Acts 1:4) is a scriptural promise of the pouring out of the Spirit on Israel (see Joel 2:28–29; Isa. 32:15; 44:3; Ezek. 39:29). It will be fulfilled quite specifically at Pentecost (see Acts 2:16)."

24:51 / **he was blessing them**: Before leaving his disciples, Jesus puts them under God's care, much as a priest might (see Sir. 50:19–20; Talbert, pp. 232–33).

he left them and was taken up into heaven: Here "taken up" recalls 9:51 ("to be taken up"). Jesus' mission, which was to be accomplished in Jerusalem, is now completed. It is only appropriate that the disciples return to Jerusalem (v. 52) and continually praise God in the temple (v. 53). Talbert (p. 233) provides references to other ancient sources that describe the departures of remarkable figures. For further discussion see M. C. Parsons, *The Departure of Jesus in Luke–Acts: The Ascension Narratives in Context*, JSNTSup 21 (Sheffield: JSOT, 1988).

For Further Reading

Balmforth, H. *The Gospel according to St. Luke in the Revised Version with Introduction and Commentary*. Oxford: Clarendon, 1930. Reprinted, 1958.

Barrett, C. K. *Luke the Historian in Recent Study*. London: Epworth, 1961.

Bock, D. L. *Proclamation from Prophecy and Pattern: Lucan Old Testament Christology*. Journal for the Study of the New Testament, Supplement 12. Sheffield: JSOT, 1987.

Brawley, R. L. *Luke–Acts and the Jews: Conflict, Apology, and Conciliation*. Society of Biblical Literature Monograph Series 33. Atlanta: Scholars, 1987.

Brown, S. *Apostasy and Perseverance in the Theology of Luke*. Analecta Biblica 36. Rome: Biblical Institute, 1969.

Browning, W. R. F., *The Gospel according to Saint Luke: Introduction and Commentary*. London: SCM, 1972.

Cadbury, H. J. *The Making of Luke–Acts*. Second edition. London: SPCK, 1958.

_____ . *The Style and Literary Method of Luke*. 2 volumes. Harvard Theological Studies 6. Cambridge: Harvard University, 1919 and 1920.

Caird, G. B. *The Gospel of St. Luke*. Pelican New Testament Commentaries. Baltimore: Penguin, 1963.

Carroll, J. T. *Response to the End of History: Eschatology and Situation in Luke–Acts*. Society of Biblical Literature Dissertation Series 92. Atlanta: Scholars, 1988.

Cassidy, R. J. *Jesus, Politics, and Society: A Study of Luke's Gospel*. Maryknoll: Orbis, 1978.

Clark, K. S. L., *The Gospel According to Saint Luke*. London: Darton, Longman & Todd, 1972.

Conzelmann, H. *The Theology of St. Luke*. New York: Harper & Brothers, 1960.

Creed, J. M. *The Gospel according to St. Luke*. London: Macmillan, 1930.

Danker, F. W. *Jesus and the New Age according to St. Luke: A Commentary on the Third Gospel*. St. Louis: Clayton, 1972.

_____ . *Luke*. Proclamation Commentaries. Philadelphia: Fortress, 1976.

Dillersberger, J. *The Gospel of Saint Luke*. Westminster: Newman, 1958.

Drury, J. *Luke*. J. B. Philips' Commentaries. New York: Macmillan, 1973.

_____ . *Tradition and Design in Luke's Gospel: A Study in Early Christian Historiography*. London: Darton, Longman & Todd, 1976.

Easton, B. S. *The Gospel according to St. Luke: A Critical and Exegetical Commentary*. New York: Scribner's, 1926.

Edwards, O. C. *Luke's Story of Jesus*. Philadelphia: Fortress, 1981.

Ellis, E. E. *Eschatology in Luke*. Facet Books. Philadelphia: Fortress, 1972.

_____ . *The Gospel of Luke*. Revised edition. New Century Bible. Grand Rapids: Eerdmans, 1981.

Erdman, C. R. *The Gospel of Luke*. Philadelphia: Westminster, 1942.

Esler, P. S. *Community and Gospel in Luke–Acts: The Social and Political Motivations of Lucan Theology*. Society for New Testament Studies Monograph Series 57. Cambridge: Cambridge University, 1987.

Fitzmyer, J. A. *The Gospel According to Luke*. 2 volumes. Anchor Bible 28 and 28a. Garden City: Doubleday, 1981 and 1985.

Flender, H. *St. Luke: Theologian of Redemptive History*. Philadelphia: Fortress, 1967.

Ford, J. M. *My Enemy is My Guest: Jesus and Violence in Luke*. Maryknoll: Orbis, 1984.

Franklin, E. *Christ the Lord: A Study in the Purpose and Theology of Luke–Acts*. London: SPCK, 1975.

Geldenhuys, N. *Commentary on the Gospel of Luke*. New International Commentary. Grand Rapids: Eerdmans, 1951. Reprinted, 1972.

Giblin, C. H. *The Destruction of Jerusalem according to Luke's Gospel*. Analecta Biblica 105. Rome: Biblical Institute, 1985.

Godet, F. *A Commentary on the Gospel of St. Luke*. 2 vols. Edinburgh: T. & T. Clark, 1888–89.

Green-Armytage, A. H. N. *A Portrait of St. Luke*. London: Burns and Oates, 1955.

Hannam, W. L. *Luke the Evangelist: A Study of His Purpose*. New York: Abingdon, 1935.

Harnack, A. *New Testament Studies I: Luke the Physician: The Author of the Third Gospel and the Acts of the Apostles*. London: Williams and Norgate, 1908.

Harrington, W. *The Gospel according to St. Luke: A Commentary.* Westminster: Newman, 1967.

Hastings, A. *Prophet and Witness in Jerusalem: A Study of the Teaching of Saint Luke.* Baltimore: Helicon, 1958.

Hobart, W. K. *The Medical Language of St. Luke.* London: Longmans, Green, 1882.

Jervell, J. *Luke and the People of God: A New Look at Luke–Acts.* Minneapolis: Augsburg, 1972.

_____ . *The Unknown Paul: Essays on Luke–Acts and Early Christian History.* Minneapolis: Augsburg, 1984.

Johnson, L. T. *The Literary Function of Possessions in Luke–Acts.* Society of Biblical Literature Dissertation Series 39. Missoula: Scholars, 1977.

Juel, D. *Luke–Acts: The Promise of History.* Atlanta: John Knox, 1983.

Karris, R. J. *Luke: Artist and Theologian. Luke's Passion Account as Literature.* Theological Inquiries. New York: Paulist, 1985.

_____ . *Invitation to Luke: A Commentary on the Gospel of Luke with the Complete Text from the Jerusalem Bible.* Image Books. Garden City: Doubleday, 1977.

_____ . *What Are They Saying about Luke and Acts? A Theology of the Faithful God.* New York: Paulist, 1979.

Keck, L. E. and Martyn, J. L. Editors. *Studies in Luke–Acts: Essays Presented in Honor of Paul Schubert.* Nashville: Abingdon, 1966.

LaVerdiere, E. *Luke.* New Testament Message 5. Wilmington: Michael Glazier, 1982.

Leaney, A. R. C. *A Commentary on the Gospel according to St. Luke.* Harper's New Testament Commentary. New York: Harper & Row, 1958. Reprinted Peabody, Mass.: Hendrickson, 1988.

Luce, H. K. *The Gospel according to St. Luke: With Introduction and Notes.* Cambridge: Cambridge University, 1936.

Maddox, R. L. *The Purpose of Luke–Acts.* Forschungen zur Religion und Literatur des Alten und Neuen Testaments 126. Göttingen: Vandenhoeck & Ruprecht, 1982.

Manson, W. *The Gospel of Luke.* Moffatt New Testament Commentaries. London: Hodder & Stoughton, 1930. Reprinted New York: R. R. Smith, 1963.

Marshall, I. H. *Commentary on Luke.* New International Greek Testament Commentary. Grand Rapids: Eerdmans, 1978.

_____ . *Luke: Historian and Theologian.* Grand Rapids: Eerdmans, 1970.

Martindale, C. C. *The Gospel according to Saint Luke: With an Introduction and Commentary.* Westminster: Newman, 1957.

McLachlan, H. *St. Luke, the Man and His Work.* Publications of the University of Manchester, Theology Series 3. New York: Longmans, Greem, 1920.

Melinsky, H. *Luke.* The Modern Reader's Guide to the Gospels. London: Darton, Longman & Todd, 1966.

Minear, P. S. *To Heal and to Reveal: The Prophetic Vocation according to Luke.* New York: Seabury, 1976.

Moorman, J. R. H. *The Path to Glory: Studies in the Gospel according to Saint Luke.* London: SPCK, 1960.

Morris, L. *The Gospel according to St. Luke.* Tyndale New Testament Commentary. Grand Rapids: Eerdmans, 1974.

Morton, A. Q., and Macgregor, G. H. C. *The Structure of Luke and Acts.* London: Hodder & Stoughton, 1964.

Moxnes, Halvor. *The Economy of the Kingdom: Social Conflict and Economic Relations in Luke's Gospel.* Overtures to Biblical Theology 23. Philadelphia: Fortress, 1988.

Navone, J. *Themes of St. Luke.* Rome: Gregorian University, 1970.

Neyrey, J. *The Passion according to Luke: A Redaction Study of Luke's Soteriology.* Theological Inquiries. New York: Paulist, 1985.

Nuttall, G. F. *The Moment of Recognition: Luke as Story-Teller.* London: Athlone, 1978.

O'Toole, R. F. *The Unity of Luke's Theology: An Analysis of Luke–Acts.* Good News Studies 9. Wilmington: Michael Glazier, 1984.

Pallis, A. *Notes on St. Luke and the Acts.* London: Oxford University, 1928.

Parsons, M. C. *The Departure of Jesus in Luke–Acts: The Ascension Narratives in Context.* Journal for the Study of the New Testament, Supplement 21. Sheffield: JSOT, 1988.

Pilgrim, W. E. *Good News to the Poor: Wealth and Poverty in Luke–Acts.* Minneapolis: Augsburg, 1981.

Plummer, A. *A Critical and Exegetical Commentary on the Gospel according to S. Luke.* International Critical Commentary. Edinburgh: T. & T. Clark, 1896.

Ragg, L. *St. Luke with Introduction and Notes.* Westminster Commentaries. London: Methuen, 1922.

Ramsay, W. M. *Was Christ Born at Bethlehem? A Study on the Credibility of St. Luke.* Third edition. London: Hodder & Stoughton, 1905.

Reicke, B. *The Gospel of Luke.* Richmond: John Knox, 1964.

Reiling, J., and Swellengrebel, J. L. *A Translator's Handbook on the Gospel of Luke.* Helps for Translators 10. Leiden: Brill, 1971.

Ringe, S. H. *Jesus, Liberation, and the Biblical Jubilee.* Overtures to Biblical Theology 19. Philadelphia: Fortress, 1985.

Robertson, A. T. *A Translation of Luke's Gospel with Grammatical Notes.* New York: Doran, 1923.

Schweizer, E. *The Good News according to Luke.* Atlanta: John Knox, 1984.

_____ . *Luke: A Challenge to Present Theology.* Atlanta: John Knox, 1982.

Seccombe, D. *Possessions and the Poor in Luke–Acts.* Studien zum Neuen Testament und seiner Umwelt. Freistadt: Plöchl, 1982.

Stoll, R. F. *The Gospel according to St. Luke: A Study of the Third Gospel with a Translation and Commentary.* New York: Pustet, 1931.

Stonehouse, N. B. *The Witness of Luke to Christ.* London: Tyndale, 1951.

Stronstad, R. *The Charismatic Theology of St. Luke.* Peabody, Mass.: Hendrickson, 1984.

Summers, R. *Commentary on Luke: Jesus, the Universal Savior.* Waco: Word, 1972.

Talbert, C. H. *The Certainty of the Gospel: The Perspective of Luke–Acts.* DeLand: Stetson, 1980.

_____ . *Literary Patterns, Theological Themes, and the Genre of Luke–Acts.* Society of Biblical Literature Monograph Series 20. Missoula: Scholars, 1974.

_____ . Editor. *Luke–Acts: New Perspectives from the Society of Biblical Literature Seminar.* New York: Crossroad, 1984.

_____ . *Luke and the Gnostics: An Examination of the Lucan Purpose.* Nashville: Abingdon, 1966.

_____ . Editor. *Perspectives on Luke–Acts.* Special Studies Series 5. Edinburgh: T. & T. Clark, 1978.

_____ . *Reading Luke: A Literary and Theological Commentary on the Third Gospel.* New York: Crossroad, 1982.

Tannehill, R. C. *The Narrative Unity of Luke–Acts: A Literary Interpretation.* Volume 1: The Gospel according to Luke. Philadelphia: Fortress, 1986.

Taylor, V. *Behind the Third Gospel: A Study of the Proto-Luke Hypothesis.* Oxford: Clarendon, 1926.

_____ . *The Passion Narrative of St. Luke: A Critical and Historical Investigation*. Edited by O. E. Evans. Society for New Testament Studies Monograph Series 19. Cambridge: Cambridge University, 1972.

Thompson, G. H. P. *The Gospel according to Luke in the Revised Standard Version*. New Clarendon Bible. Oxford: Clarendon, 1972.

Tiede, D. L. *Luke*. Augsburg Commentary on the New Testament. Minneapolis: Augsburg, 1988.

_____ . *Prophecy and History in Luke–Acts*. Philadelphia: Fortress, 1980.

Tolbert, M. O. *Luke*. Broadman Bible Commentary. Nashville: Broadman, 1970. Pages 1–187.

Tyson, J. B. *The Death of Jesus in Luke–Acts*. Columbia: University of South Carolina, 1986.

_____ . Editor. *Luke–Acts and the Jewish People*. Minneapolis: Augsburg, 1988.

Van Linden, P. *The Gospel of Luke and Acts*. Wilmington: Michael Glazier, 1986.

Walaskay, P. W. *'And So We Came to Rome!' The Political Perspective of St. Luke*. Society for New Testament Studies Monograph Series 49. Cambridge: Cambridge University, 1983.

Wilson, S. G. *The Gentiles and the Gentile Mission in Luke–Acts*. Society for New Testament Studies Monograph Series 23. Cambridge: Cambridge University, 1973.

_____ . *Luke and the Law*. Society for New Testament Studies Monograph Series 50. Cambridge: Cambridge University, 1983.

Subject Index

Aaron, 75

Abiathar, 101

Abijah, 27

Abila, 51

Abilene, 51

Abraham. *See also* Abram; bosom, 251; father of Israel, 12, 58, 62, 251, 255; in the genealogy, 17, 57–58, 62; meaning of the name, 62; promises to, 27, 32, 34, 39.

Abraham, son of, 280, 283

Abrahamic covenant, 62

Abram. *See also* Abraham; meaning of the name, 62.

Abyss, the, 135, 137. *See also* Gehenna; Hades; Hell; Sheol.

Acts, book of: authorship, 1–2; relation to the Gospel of Luke, 1, 3, 6–9, 15, 17–20, 256, 361

Adam, 178; burial place, 339; in the genealogy, 57–58, 64, 67; temptation of, 58, 67

Admin, 62

Adoptianism, 60

Agapius, 336

Agrippa, 308

Ahimelech, 101

Alexander, 281

Almsgiving, basis of uprightness, 243, 246

Alphaeus, 97, 110; meaning of the name, 111

Amminadab, 62

Amos: in the genealogy, 61; martyrdom, 75

Ancient of Days, God as, 92

Andrew, 103–4

Andronicus, 105

Angel of the Lord, 27

Angelic anthem, 38, 289

Angels, 301, 304, 348

Anna, 23, 40–41, 46

Annas, 325; term in office, 52

Annius of Viterbo, 57

Anointed One. *See* Messiah.

Antiochus IV, 132, 308, 340

Apollos, 105

Apostles, the. *See also* Disciples of Jesus; calling of, 83, 85, 94–95, 103–7, 109; dispute about greatness, 318; incomprehension, 145, 157–58, 320, 347, 354; mission of, 140–42, 155; number, 103, 105–7, 109; sharing in kingdom rule, 318, 322.

Apostleship, qualifications, 20, 122

Aram, 62

Aramaic, 73

Archelaus, tetrarch of Judea, 43, 51, 286–87

Ariel, 294

Arimathea, 345

Arni, 62

Arpachshad, 63

Arphaxad, 62–63

Assyria, 258

Baal-Zebub, 186

Baal-zebul, 186

Babylon, 173, 294

Babylonian exile, 73

Balaam, 161

Balak, 161

Baptism, 49, 52, 178; with fire, 49; with the Holy Spirit, 49, 56; of infants, 275

Barabbas, 333; meaning of the name, 335

Barnabas, 105, 109, 142

Bartholomew, 103–5; meaning of the name, 110

Bartimaeus, 278, 281

Baruch Adonai, 146

Beatitudes, 112

Beelzebub, 184–85. *See also* Belial; Beliar; Devil, the; Lucifer; Satan; Serpent, the; meaning of the name, 186.

Beelzebul, 186

Belial, 186. *See also* Beelzebub; Beliar; Devil, the; Lucifer; Satan; Serpent, the.

Beliar, 174, 186. *See also* Beelzebub;

Scripture Index

62; **2:11**, 62; **3:5**, 61; **3:17**, 61 [LXX];
3:19, 61; **11–29**, 61; **15:24**, 27; **16:34**,
276; **16:36**, 33; **23:6**, 27; **24:7–18**,
27

2 Chronicles, 191; **9:4**, 202; **9:13–22**,
201; **9:20**, 202; **24**, 191; **24:20**, 216;
24:20–21, 190–91, 216; **28:8–15**, 178;
28:15, 178; **35:8**, 27; **36:11–16**, 14;
36:15–16, 75; **36:22–23**, 35

Ezra **1:1–4**, 35; **2:2**, 61

Nehemiah **8:1–8**, 73; **8:14–17**, 154;
10:28, 97; **11:12**, 27; **12:1–7**, 27;
12:44, 311; **13:16**, 356

Esther **4:3**, 173

Job **2:8**, 173; **8:12**, 202; **12:19**, 30;
19:26, 304; **22:9**, 30; **25:6**, 92; **31:24–
28**, 201; **35:8**, 92; **35:11**, 201

Psalms, 26, 357; **1**, 235; **1:1**, 112; **2**,
60; **2:7**, 56, 60, 74; **2:12**, 112; **3:6**, 28;
6:8, 213; **16:5**, 329; **16:8–11**, 358;
16:9, 304; **16:10**, 358; **16:11**, 304;
17:8, 217; **18:2**, 33; **18:17**, 33; **18:49**,
360; **22**, 357; **22:1**, 342; **22:8**, 338;
22:17, 338; **23:1**, 36; **25:5**, 29 [LXX];
28:9, 36; **31**, 344, 357; **31:4**, 344;
31:5, 342, 344; **31:9–10**, 344; **31:11**,
344; **31:13**, 344; **31:18**, 344; **31:20**,
344; **34:3**, 29; **34:8**, 112, 276; **35:9**,
29; **36:7**, 217; **37:2**, 202; **37:11**, 173;
41:1, 112; **41:14**, 33; **49:16–17**, 201;
54:1, 159; **57:1**, 217; **59:5**, 119; **61:4**,
217; **64:8**, 314 [LXX]; **65:7**, 132, 314;
69, 357; **69:22**, 338; **69:30**, 29; **72:18**,
33; **78**, 75; **78:19–20**, 145; **80:14**, 32
[LXX], 33, 119; **80:17**, 92; **84:4**, 112;
85:8, 173; **89:2**, 30; **89:9**, 29 [LXX],
132; **89:10**, 30; **89:24**, 33; **89:32**, 119;
89:48, 173; **90:5–6**, 202; **94:12**, 112;
97:10, 34; **98:3**, 30; **100:3**, 36; **102:11**,
202; **103:13**, 30; **103:15–16**, 202;
103:17, 30; **104:6–7**, 132; **105**, 75;
105:8, 34; **106**, 68, 75; **106:1**, 276;
106:4, 32 [LXX], 33; **106:10**, 33;
106:45, 34; **106:48**, 33; **107:2–3**, 213;
107:9, 30; **107:10**, 34; **107:23–30**, 132;
110:1, 301–2, 332, 334; **111:9**, 33;

113:5–6, 29; **117:1**, 360; **118:22**, 299,
303, 303 [Targum]; **118:26**, 216, 288–
89; **119:2**, 112; **119:9**, 29; **119:89**,
311; **122:4–5**, 322; **124:8**, 159; **132:17**,
33; **137:9**, 294 [LXX]; **144:3**, 92; **147:9**,
201; **148:2**, 38

Proverbs **1:15**, 235; **1:20–33**, 191; **2:11–
15**, 235; **8:32**, 120; **8:34**, 112; **15:25**,
222; **16:5**, 243; **21:2**, 243; **25:6–7**,
221, 226; **31:22**, 250

Ecclesiastes **12:13**, 200 [Targum]

Isaiah **1:6**, 179; **2:2–3**, 360; **2:3**, 362;
2:6, 14, 340; **2:9**, 14, 340; **4:1**, 25;
5:1–7, 298, 302; **5:2**, 230; **6:1**, 52;
6:1–5, 24; **6:9**, 126, 129–30, 130
[LXX]; **6:9–10**, 129, 129 [Targum],
130, 130 [LXX]; **6:10**, 126, 129–30,
130 [LXX]; **6:11–13b**, 129; **6:13**, 48;
6:13c, 129; **7:14**, 21; **8:6**, 206; **8:14**,
303; **8:21**, 314; **9:1–2**, 32; **9:1–7**, 25;
9:2, 34; **9:6**, 28, 38; **9:6–7**, 61, 173;
10:33–34, 48; **11:1**, 34, 101, 281;
11:1–2, 61; **11:1–3**, 25; **11:10**, 101,
360; **13:10**, 314; **13:11**, 222; **13:26**,
314; **14:4**, 173; **14:12**, 173; **14:13**, 173;
14:15, 173; **17:12**, 314; **23:1–18**, 173;
23:17, 119; **24:17**, 311; **24:18–20**, 314;
26:19, 304; **28:2**, 133; **28:16**, 303;
28:17, 133; **29:3**, 294 [LXX]; **29:18–
19**, 116; **30:14**, 303; **32:15**, 362; **34:4**,
310, 314; **34:13**, 314; **35:5**, 116, 282;
37:27, 202; **37:33**, 294 [LXX]; **38:4**,
47; **38:20**, 34; **40:1**, 45; **40:3**, 17, 34,
47, 52; **40:3–5**, 52–53; **40:4–5**, 47;
40:5, 45 [LXX]; **40:6–8**, 202; **40:8**,
311; **40:11**, 235; **41:8–9**, 30; **41:14**,
352; **42:1**, 56, 74–75, 151; **42:6**, 39,
45; **42:7**, 34; **43:14**, 352; **44:3**, 362;
44:22–24, 352; **44:28–45:1**, 34; **45:15**,
37 [LXX]; **45:16**, 209; **45:21**, 37 [LXX];
46:13, 39, 45 [LXX]; **49:6**, 9, 39, 45,
359; **49:18**, 98; **51:8a**, 202; **51:17**,
329; **51:22**, 329; **52:7**, 44, 74; **52:7–
53:12**, 74; **52:10**, 39, 45; **52:11**, 235;
52:13, 74 [Targum], 152 [Targum];
52:13–53:12, 75, 152; **52:15**, 172; **53**,
152, 358; **53:3–8**, 152; **53:5**, 152
[Targum]; **53:7–8**, 358; **53:10**, 74
[Targum]; **53:11**, 152; **53:12**, 317,

John **1:1–18**, 17; **1:6–8**, 295; **1:10–11**, 71; **1:14–18**, 151; **1:15**, 295; **1:19–36**, 295; **1:29–34**, 56, 59; **1:35–40**, 104; **1:38**, 123; **1:40**, 104; **1:42**, 104, 109; **1:43**, 104; **1:43–45**, 110; **1:44**, 146; **1:45**, 105; **1:45–46**, 110; **2:1–11**, 78; **2:13**, 215; **2:13–22**, 295; **2:14–16**, 291; **3:29**, 97; **3:35**, 171; **4:9**, 161; **4:35**, 169; **4:42**, 36; **4:46–53**, 114; **5:23**, 170; **6**, 145; **6:1–15**, 143; **6:4**, 215; **6:9**, 143, 146; **6:16–21**, 78; **6:30–58**, 144; **6:71**, 111; **8:41**, 44; **9:1–2**, 205; **9:1–3**, 78; **9:2**, 279; **9:7**, 206; **9:39**, 129; **10:7**, 321; **10:11**, 321; **10:15**, 171; **11**, 250–51, 295; **11:11–14**, 136; **11:16**, 104, 110; **11:21**, 136; **11:23–24**, 136; **11:43–44**, 77; **11:55**, 215; **12:1**, 311; **12:1–8**, 121; **12:6**, 105; **12:9**, 311; **12:14–15**, 293; **12:15**, 288; **12:21**, 146; **12:21–22**, 110; **12:28**, 59; **12:36**, 241; **12:40**, 129; **13:1–2**, 321; **13:2**, 316; **13:4–17**, 318; **13:20**, 170; **13:21–27**, 110; **13:23**, 110; **13:26**, 111; **13:27**, 316; **14:7**, 171; **14:9**, 110, 171; **14:22**, 104–5, 111; **14:27**, 173; **15:1**, 321; **15:1–6**, 48; **15:13–15**, 200; **16:33**, 173; **17:1**, 163; **18:2–3**, 321; **18:10**, 324; **18:12–13**, 321; **18:13**, 52, 325; **18:14**, 325; **18:17**, 325–26; **18:18**, 325; **18:19**, 52; **18:24**, 325; **18:25–27**, 325; **18:26–27**, 327; **18:28**, 321; **19:19–20**, 341; **19:25**, 123, 352; **19:25–27**, 40; **19:26**, 110; **20:1**, 123; **20:2**, 110; **20:3–6**, 347; **20:10**, 347; **20:11**, 123; **20:16**, 123; **20:18**, 123; **20:19**, 173, 354–55; **20:19–23**, 357; **20:20**, 355; **20:21**, 173; **20:24**, 110; **20:24–29**, 354; **20:26**, 173; **21:1–11**, 83; **21:2**, 110; **21:7**, 110; **21:9–13**, 355; **21:20**, 110; **21:21–23**, 153

Acts **1–5**, 45, 319; **1–9**, 5; **1–11**, 83; **1:1–2**, 17; **1:2**, 154; **1:2–11**, 154; **1:3**, 154, 347, 355; **1:3–28:31**, 8; **1:4**, 362; **1:4–8**, 360; **1:5**, 50; **1:6**, 154, 313, 352; **1:6-7**, 261, 289; **1:6–8**, 244; **1:6–11**, 357; **1:6–2:4**, 360; **1:8**, 8, 141, 152, 195, 244, 330, 360; **1:9**, 154, 160, 164; **1:9–11**, 154, 360; **1:11**, 164, 261; **1:12–26**, 322; **1:13**, 103–5, 138, 361; **1:14**, 59, 123, 127; **1:15–26**, 303; **1:16**, 105; **1:16–19**, 348; **1:18–19**, 321; **1:21–22**, 20, 122, 330; **1:22**, 50, 154; **1:26**, 105; **2**, 70, 149; **2–3**, 12, 195; **2:1–4**, 59; **2:2–4**, 9, 360; **2:3**, 49, 199; **2:4–18**, 195; **2:4**, 26, 174; **2:5–7:60**, 8; **2:14–39**, 343, 357; **2:16**, 362; **2:16–36**, 73; **2:16–39**, 244; **2:17**, 19; **2:21**, 359; **2:22–23**, 195; **2:23**, 333; **2:27**, 358; **2:29–32**, 358; **2:34–35**, 335; **2:36**, 152, 195, 302, 333; **2:37**, 343; **2:37–38**, 345; **2:40**, 252; **2:42**, 349; **2:44–45**, 203; **2:46**, 349; **3**, 361; **3:6**, 79; **3:8**, 207; **3:13**, 152; **3:13–15**, 333; **3:14**, 345; **3:15**, 348; **3:17**, 195; **3:19–21**, 362; **3:22**, 352; **3:22–23**, 361; **3:23**, 286; **3:25**, 12; **4:1–22**, 9; **4:6**, 52; **4:8**, 26, 196; **4:10**, 79, 348; **4:13**, 308; **4:16–18**, 308; **4:18**, 40; **4:21**, 345; **4:27**, 75; **4:29**, 257; **4:31**, 85; **4:32**, 124; **5:15**, 90; **5:15–16**, 107; **5:17–18**, 40; **5:17–42**, 9; **5:18**, 319; **5:19**, 27; **5:31**, 36, 362; **5:33–39**, 74; **5:35–37**, 332; **5:36**, 43, 74; **5:36–37**, 7, 43, 247; **5:37**, 43–44, 53, 74, 332; **6–28**, 45; **6:1**, 230; **6:1–6**, 203; **6:2**, 85, 230; **6:6**, 82; **6:7**, 85, 230; **6:13–14**, 40, 331; **7:2–53**, 309; **7:19**, 275; **7:27**, 201; **7:35–37**, 352; **7:37**, 361; **7:48**, 217; **7:51**, 195; **7:51–53**, 14, 75, 334; **7:52**, 345; **7:54–60**, 309; **7:58**, 75; **7:59–60**, 344; **7:60**, 14, 216, 340; **7:60b**, 340; **8:1**, 40; **8:1–3**, 308; **8:2–24**, 8; **8:12**, 123; **8:14**, 85; **8:14–17**, 9; **8:18**, 82; **8:26**, 27; **8:26–39**, 358; **8:32–33**, 152, 358; **8:35**, 358; **8:36**, 275; **9:1**, 230; **9:2**, 52, 163; **9:10**, 230; **9:12**, 82; **9:17**, 82; **9:19**, 230; **9:26**, 230; **9:34**, 79; **9:38**, 230; **10**, 114; **10:1–11:18**, 8; **10:30**, 68; **10:35**, 74; **10:38**, 55, 75; **10:44–47**, 9; **10:47**, 275; **11**, 234; **11:1**, 85; **11:15–18**, 9; **11:16**, 50; **11:18**, 345; **11:28**, 7, 308; **12:1–2**, 110, 309; **12:1–5**, 308; **12:3**, 319; **12:7**, 27; **12:12**, 109; **12:13–16**, 6; **12:15**, 355; **12:18**, 6; **12:23**, 27; **13:2–3**, 96; **13:2–28:31**, 8; **13:3–4**, 82; **13:5**, 85; **13:7**, 85; **13:9**, 26; **13:16–41**, 8, 73; **13:16–47**, 9; **13:23**, 36; **13:24–25**, 50; **13:27–28**, 335; **13:33**, 56; **13:35**, 358; **13:40–41**, 40; **13:41**, 9, 19; **13:42–43**, 9; **13:44**, 85; **13:45**, 9, 40; **13:46**, 9, 85; **13:47**, 9, 45, 359–60; **13:48**, 9, 38, 85;